A LIVING HISTORY
of the OZARKS

D1557810

(Courtesy of Bittersweet, Inc.)

A LIVING HISTORY of the OZARKS

PHYLLIS ROSSITER

PELICAN PUBLISHING COMPANY
Gretna 1992

The word "Pelican" and the depiction of a pelican are
trademarks of Pelican Publishing Company, Inc., and are
registered in the U.S. Patent and Trademark Office.

Library of Congress Cataloging-in-Publication Data

Rossiter, Phyllis.
    A living history of the Ozarks / Phyllis Rossiter.
       p. cm.
    Includes index.
    ISBN 0-88289-935-X. -- ISBN 0-88289-801-9 (pbk.)
      1. Ozark Mountains--Guidebooks. 2. Ozark Mountains--History.
Local. I. Title.
F417.O9R67   1992
917.67´10453--dc20   92-5309
                                                          CIP

Manufactured in the United States of America

Published by Pelican Publishing Company, Inc.
1101 Monroe Street, Gretna, Louisiana 70053

To the settlers of the Ozarks, including my grandparents, whose unwavering faith in the powers of these rocky hills and their stumpy fields, and whose heartbreaking labors have enabled us, their posterity, to live comfortably and securely where they toiled endlessly—to them this book is respectfully and affectionately dedicated.

And to Ellen Gray Massey, who has done so much to preserve their history and culture.

Contents

Maps

Acknowledgments

The author gratefully acknowledges the assistance and cooperation of the following: Darvin Taylor, Gainesville, Mo.; David G. Massey, Lebanon, Mo.; Gene GeRue, Zanoni, Mo.; Gordon McCann, Springfield, Mo.; *OzarksWatch* (SMSU), Springfield, Mo.; Robert K. Gilmore, Springfield, Mo.; W. K. McNeil, Mountain View, Ark.; Jimmy Peacock, Sapulpa, Okla.; Arline Chandler, Heber Springs, Ark.; Carthage Historic Preservation, Inc., Carthage, Mo.; Jim Reed, Cotter, Ark.; Fae Sothman and Missouri State Historical Society, Columbia, Mo.; Old Stagecoach Stop Foundation, Waynesville, Mo.; College of the Ozarks, Point Lookout, Mo.; Edith McCall, Hollister, Mo.; Townsend Godsey, Branson, Mo.; Silver Dollar City; The Shepherd of the Hills Homestead; Missouri Department of Tourism; Arkansas Department of Parks and Tourism; and many chambers of commerce and historical societies throughout the Ozarks.

And that of all the inspirational and informational Ozarks historians and writers who blazed the trail.

Very Special Thanks to Ellen Gray Massey and Bittersweet, Inc., Lebanon, Mo., for their generosity in lending photographs from their archives and for their other assistance with this book.

And to the magazine—and its people—who started it all, *The Ozarks Mountaineer*, Branson, Mo.

Except as otherwise noted, all photographs are by Phyllis Rossiter.
The cover scene is of Dawt Mill from the North Fork River in Ozark County, Missouri, as photographed by David G. Massey.
Maps © Copyright 1991 by Gene GeRue, Zanoni, Mo.

Still seen occasionally are the remains of a storm cellar, or " 'fraidy hole," often the only clue to the location of a former homesite. Many families in the Ozarks built such cellars following the great Marshfield (Missouri) tornado of 1880, in which more than a hundred people reportedly were killed. (Courtesy of Bittersweet, Inc.)

Guideposts to Living History

In the Ozarks, things have a way of skewing into the fourth dimension. Time seems somehow out of synch: A high-speed highway slices through a farmer's hard-cleared field and deflects the hot rays of the sun into a tumbledown log house. The soaring flight of a turkey buzzard, with but one lazy wingflap, overlooks the tangle of primeval life in a secluded hollow—and that of the multitrafficked craft fair on the ridgetop. From the corner of your eye you can almost glimpse a riderless horse hitched to the rail in front of an old mill, or a barefoot lad shooting marbles in the dusty road while Paw's corn is ground inside.

Even the landscape fosters the feeling that you can simply glance over your shoulder into the past. The so-ancient hills that are "nobody knows how old" seem to wait with a timeless expectancy for the next act in the eons-old drama we call the Ozarks while we, the players, try to straddle the barriers between past and present—struggling to keep one foot firmly in the Ozarkian past and one in the easier-living present. Betwixt and between, modern Ozarkers are, living on the ragged fringes of our time frame.

And the Ozarks is bewitched. Not even modern highways and bridges and manmade lakes can change that. If you were born here and went away, you feel the pull of the hills. If you have visited, you know that someday you must return. And even if you have never seen these hills save in your mind's eye, you too feel their magic calling in your soul.

Analyzing the Ozarks Mystique

So prevalent throughout the region is the acceptance of this mystique of the Ozarks that it is commonplace to hear people speak of it. "Natives" (those who were born here and whose parents and grandparents, at least, were born here) appear to take the phenomenon for granted. But "newcomers" (those who came here from somewhere else, even if fifty years ago) find lingering fascination in trying to analyze the *what* and *why* of its secret.

There is the *landscape*, of course. Although it lacks the dazzle and youthful vigor of the Rockies, or the excitement of the pounding sea, the quiet, ever-changing drama of the hills is often mesmerizing—and always mysteriously calming. Though picturesque hilly landscape is scarcely unique, here in the Ozarks you *feel* the country, experience it, rather than just admire it. For those who seek it, a sweet serenity dwells here, a restful tranquility.

And there is the closeness of nature: Sun-dappled paths, woods twilighty at noon, the dusky hoot of owl and howl of coyote—all serve to establish the mood for the unfolding scene. Away from the scattered urban centers, there are few people. In some remote areas the population is less now than it was in 1900. But there is a pervading sense of *family*, a clannish emphasis on kith and kin that time—and distance—cannot diminish.

While it is possibly more effect than cause, there is among Ozarkers, both native and newcomer, an uncommon sense of place—an awareness of regional identity perhaps unsurpassed elsewhere. The words *Ozark* and *Ozarks* appear everywhere as place names.

But the prime contributor to the mystique of the Ozarks is that well-recognized sense of *timelessness*—the incalculable age of the hills themselves and their brooding patience, their very endurance in spite of all they have suffered at the hands of man.

Indeed, *history* is very close to the surface in the Ozarks. This sense of history presses even on newcomers, many of whom appear more interested in its preservation and study than the natives—who seem to have absorbed it through the soles of their feet and take it as much for granted as good fishing and lasting air quality.

The Visible Past

Because the Ozarks is so resistant to rapid change—and because custom and tradition are still so important here—there is among many rural Ozarkers a marked distrust of technology. And a tenacity of the old ways. Intermingled with out-of-state license plates are the ubiquitous "Ozarks convertible," old pickup trucks. Party lines, heritage crafts, country music, and an extraordinarily laid-back attitude, a total lack of urgency seem to epitomize the popular philosophy of the region: "Go ahead—but not too far, not too fast."

"Several decades of tourism, miles of paved highways and mega-lakes created by mega-dams have not obscured the fact that the Ozarks is a very special historic place, a region where America as it once was can still be seen, sensed and even experienced," believes Dr. Robert K. Gilmore, Director of Travel and Tourism at Southwest Missouri State University.

Remainders of the past are everywhere. Off the beaten path, and sometimes not far off it, the Ozarks of old still slumbers. Concrete roads and satellite dishes notwithstanding, to visitors from super-cosmopolitan areas, it is still Sleepy Hollow time in the Ozarks.

In the fall, hullers still buy and hull black walnuts by the pound at crossroads stores; black powder muzzleloaders and archers still stalk white-tailed deer. Hounds and hunting survive, as does "mule hunting," or hunting from muleback, fishing, canoeing, and anything to do with horses. Wild turkeys still gobble, there are still yellow suckers to gig from silent, stable johnboats. An occasional black bear still robs forest-neighborhood bee hives. Crystal streams, dense woods, sparsely populated mountaintops are still commonplace. Ozarkers can still see the stars that are elsewhere obscured by pollution's haze.

Just as importantly, there are relics from a more humane time: a neighborly attitude only a memory in more "modern" places, the help and love and concern for each other that seems to survive only in predominantly rural areas. Churches are numerous and well attended, evangelical revivals frequent.

Folk musicians, virtuosos who can play any tune they have ever heard and can coax a baby's cry from a fiddle, yet not read a note of music, still come out of the hills regularly to perform at neighborhood jam sessions, music parties, square dances, and, in a few cases, for the tourists. Fiddles, banjos, acoustical (nonamplified) guitars, basses, and mandolins, all turn up regularly at get-togethers. And youngsters of all ages still jig, a sort of foot-stomping celebration of the music's infectious rhythm.

More echoes of the past are heard, farther out of the mainstream, in the speech of the natives. Some of the old-timers' speech, like their rich heritage of ballads, superstitions, and folklore, descends from seventeenth-century England, either more or less directly or by way of the King James Version of the Bible, in either case preserved by the region's isolation and the inhabitants' conservatism. "Among the most striking features of the hillman's speech," wrote folklorist Vance Randolph several decades ago, "is his habitual use of picturesque comparisons, outlandish metaphors and similes, old sayings and proverbs, cryptic allusions to esoteric mountain lore, and bucolic wisecracks

Old-timers of the neighborhood say this log structure—built about the turn of the century—was a corn crib on this creek bottom farm that is now a cattle ranch. Native Ozarkers rarely demolish an old building, and this one will probably stand until it sags to ruin—unless it is felled by a spring windstorm.

Contrary to the "lazy hillbilly" image, the hardworking and frugal Ozarker made good use of the rocks in his fields: he built fences and corner posts of them. Some can still be seen on the back roads of the region, though they are becoming increasingly rare.

generally. Some of these expressions are very old, used in their old form. Others are changed to fit the current situation, while many are brand new spontaneous creations." Though one must listen carefully these days to hear such hill speech, especially near the larger towns, it still surfaces in the backwoods among the older generations. And even a blind hog finds an acorn now and then.

The Ozarks, however, is a very big place. Just as variances in the native speech are encountered in fringe locales and in more metropolitan areas, so Ozarks reality is determined by what particular veneer one examines of the multilayered Ozarks society.

The Real Ozarks

The real Ozarks is not "a state of mind," and it is not a neon-lighted four-lane highway jammed with motels and music shows. It is a land of more-than-hills-but-less-than-mountains that has been hauled, more or less reluctantly, into the present by the technology of manmade lakes, good roads, and satellite television. The region is distinctive, set apart by four major geological features: rugged topography, rocks that are generally much older than those in surrounding areas—and of types that produce thinner and less fertile soils—and an abundance of caves, springs, and clear streams.

No single characteristic is necessarily peculiar to the Ozarks, but the combination of distinguishing features makes the Ozarks a unique area—and a distinctive cultural region. Its culture is distinctive because it is a combination of elements from diverse origins—and because it has preserved much of its past. Traditional lifestyles persist here amid the slowness to accept change.

Geographically, the Ozarks is shaped roughly like a parallelogram covering fifty thousand square miles. Southern Missouri has the lion's share, more than thirty thousand square miles, eastern Oklahoma about one thousand square miles, and the rest is northwest and north-central Arkansas. Together with the Ouachitas, the region is the only major highland between the Rocky Mountains and the Appalachians and comprises the oldest exposed land in North America. On its surface are oak- and hickory-forested hills, scattered high prairies, and glades—parklike benches or hillsides where the bedrock is exposed and the soil very thin and poor. Beneath the lavishly abundant springs, rivers, and lakes lies a Swiss-cheese arrangement of caves, porous rocks, sinkholes, and other characteristics of karst topography.

The boundaries of the Ozarks correspond generally with major rivers and their tributaries: On the north, the Missouri; on the east, the Mississippi; the Arkansas River on the south; on the west the Grand River of northeast Oklahoma; and in southwest Missouri, the

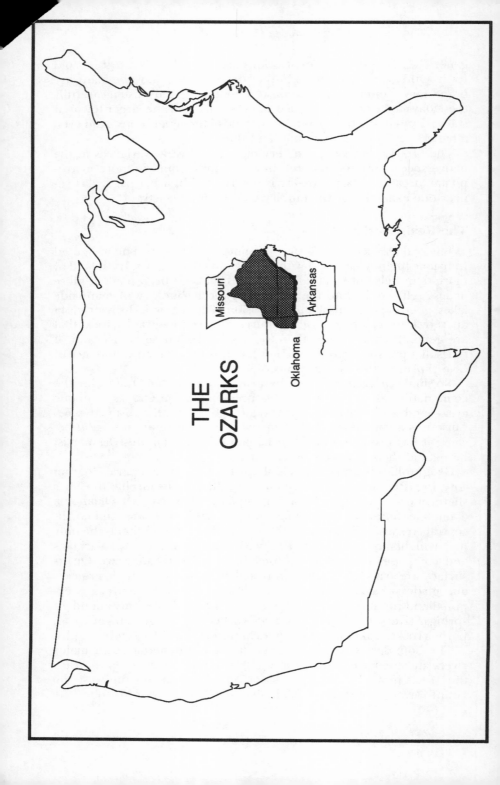

THE
OZARKS

Missouri

Arkansas

Oklahoma

Sac and Osage Rivers serve as boundary. On the southeast, a line from Cape Girardeau, Missouri, to near Conway, Arkansas, follows the Ozark Escarpment and is probably the most distinct boundary. There the lowlands of the Mississippi Valley abut against the Ozarks highland.

Once part of a vast inland sea, during which time the sedimentary rocks of the Ozarks were laid down, the region was slowly and repeatedly uplifted. The uplifting ultimately formed a large flat dome. Over its surface meandered numerous rivers and streams. As the dome was uplifted ever higher and tilted slightly from northeast to southwest, the waterways began to run faster and cut deeper. But they retained their meandering ways, creating the unique Ozarks terrain.

North of the Ozarks' own "great divide" along the axis of the dome—roughly paralleling Interstate 44—waters generally drain into tributaries of the Missouri; south of it, ultimately to the Arkansas. The clarity of rivers and streams in the Ozarks is due in part to their

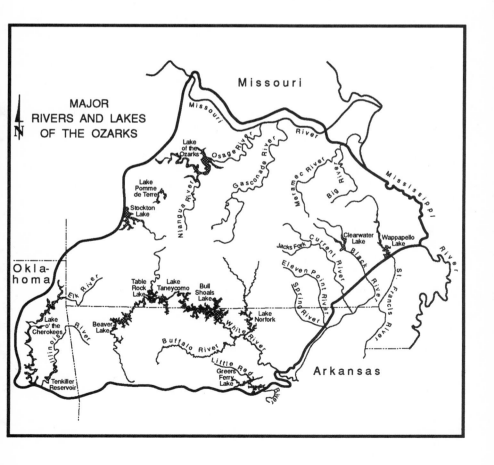

rock-lined beds and the fact that few flow far through cultivated lands—and because much of the water has come from underground sources and is not yet dirtied by flowing on the surface.

For 250 million years or more, the Ozarks highland has stood high and dry while the surrounding landscape was repeatedly scoured by glaciers, seas, or floods. The dome, over time, took on the character of a refuge for plants and animals from the more beleaguered areas. These migrants were able to find a toehold on survival in the natural refuge of the Ozarks thanks to what scientists call "microclimates"— pockets of highly individualized weather conditions resulting from varying terrain, exposure, and elevation. The diversity of rock types, soils, and topography created habitats for a great many species of animals and plants.

In addition to the numerous Ozarks species that are found nowhere else on Earth (plants, fish, and amphibians), having adapted to their own unique and localized environment, there are a great many "relict" species (mostly plants) still with us that really do not belong here: a moss from the Arctic tundra, prickly pear cactus and scorpions from the desert Southwest, ferns from the North Woods, to name but a few. (The process appears to be continuing in our own age: armadillos and roadrunners are found here in increasing numbers.)

The climate of the Ozarks is as varied as the topography. While the northern part of the region shares a more typically "Northern" winter, the southern half frequently enjoys generally mild weather. Extremes are likely at sometime during the season, but snow rarely lingers long. A foglike drizzle or a glaze of ice is more common.

But an Ozarks spring comes early and lingers long—a delightful season of "sarvissberry" and wild cherry blossoms, redbud profusion, and dogwood drama. Although summer can—and often does—tend to hot and humid, it compensates by cool, often misty nights and calm, wispy mornings perfect for outdoors activities.

Autumn in the Ozarks ushers in the most perfect weather of the year, a time when Ozarkers congratulate each other for living in the region and glory in the spectacularly colorful foliage and intensely blue skies. While summertime vistas may be partially obscured by the enchantment of blue haze, the long-range viewing is much better in the fall. As an added bonus at this time of the year, the "blue highways" (secondary roads) are almost empty.

Although all areas of the vast Ozarks have in common the distinguishing traits already described, there are considerable differences obvious as one travels throughout the region. (Another aspect of the region's overall sense of place is its habit of naming parts of itself, "vernacular regions," Southwest Missouri State University professor Milton Rafferty calls them. These small subregions—most with no defined boundaries—are recognized and named. Examples are the White River Hills sprawling across the Missouri-Arkansas border; the Shepherd of the Hills Country in Taney County, Missouri; the Irish Wilderness of southeastern Missouri; the Boston Mountains of Arkansas; the Cookson Hills in Oklahoma. Geographers have also named these subregions for their own ease of identification, but one does not ordinarily hear Ozarkers referring to these labels, except in the occasional cases where they echo the "vernacular.")

Curiously, and in spite of the strong sense of regional identity obvious throughout the region, each of the subregions is as different from its neighbors as the region as a whole is from the land around it. Not only does the landscape vary, but so does the architecture, the presence or absence of the Ozarks "dialect," and other vestiges of the past. Some locales have better documented their history than others. In some of the less-isolated areas, particularly along the northern and eastern borders, the past has already been largely obliterated.

Indeed, traveling "the Ozarks" is very much like the seven blind men who gave seven varying reports on the characteristics of an elephant: it depends on your location and your point of view. Such factors as population centers, proximity of major highways and railroads, the presence or lack of local industrialization, tourist attractions, and new immigrants, all play a part in determining what is "Ozark."

Visitors from elsewhere often scoff at the Ozarks' use of the "mountain" label, for although the region is generally higher than its surrounding neighbors, no where does the elevation top about twenty-five hundred feet. While the youthful vigor of the Rockies or the Tetons is undeniably magnificent, it also sometimes makes them as hard to cozy up to as a teenager with a boom box. The Ozark hills, on the other hand, are as comfortable and as homey as trusted lifelong friends, the kind that only get better with age. Their presence is like a loving embrace, an enfolding, solacing comfort. And their grandeur is every bit as awe-inspiring, simply on a more comprehensible scale.

But because of the ruggedness of much of the terrain—extremes of elevation complicated by narrow and twisting ridges, steep-sided valleys, and mighty limestone bluffs—traveling is still difficult except on the most modern highways. The region must have seemed mountainous indeed to the settlers dependent on wagons. Even travelers on horseback have to make sweeping detours on this landscape.

Reportedly the Boston Mountain region, on the southern edge of the Ozarks, earned the reputation among passengers on the Butterfield Stagecoach in the mid-1800s as the "most rugged terrain between St. Louis and San Francisco."

"It ain't that the hills are so high," Ozarkers admit, "but that the valleys are so deep."

The Ozarks Aquifer

Water is everywhere in the Ozarks—underground as well as on the surface. Scientists sometimes refer to the huge underground water supplies as aquifers; that is, water-bearing rocks or rock formations. Some even consider the Ozarks as a whole to be one gigantic "super-aquifer."

And it is water that has literally created the Ozarks. Rain and melted snow seeping through decaying vegetation gradually becomes slightly acidic and slowly eats away at the alkaline bedrock. The water also dissolves carbon dioxide, forming weak carbonic acid to aid in its corrosive shaping. Joints, fractures, and other minute cracks through which the mildly acidic water seeps slowly enlarge; the bedrock is virtually hollowed out.

In the meantime, on the vast geologic time scale, pressures from deep within the planet have slowly pushed the Ozarks upward. As the ground level rose, the erosive power of streams was constantly rejuvenated. The rivers and streams have literally carved the rugged hills and hollows by cutting ever deeper into their valleys.

In fact, the rugged Ozarks landscape clearly demonstrates the erosive action of this abundance of water: rivers and gorges, towering bluffs, frequent springs, and their abandoned tubes that we call caves. Underground evidence of the water is even more graphic, but seldom seen by most of us. Just as small tributaries converge to feed big rivers above ground, small cracks and caverns converge to feed big cave streams underground. Often surface streams "leak" underground into crevices in their beds; we call them *sinking creeks*. The water thus "pirated" reappears at the surface downstream, usually as a spring.

Basic to the Ozarks system of internal plumbing is the *sinkhole*. Usually a collapsed cave, a sinkhole is literally a funnel-shaped hole in the earth, functioning in the manner of the drain on your bathtub. Sinkholes form a natural, efficient system of surface drainage, but since this method of draining the surface is rapid and direct—without the benefit of filtering through deep topsoil—the system carries with it whatever pollutants are on the surface directly into the groundwater.

A term often heard in explanation of the Ozarks waterworks is *karst topography*. *Karst* is defined as "an area of irregular limestone in which erosion has produced fissures, sinkholes, underground streams, and caverns." But in fact, it helps to visualize the Ozarks underground as a water-filled sponge. Water moves through the subterranean regions in much the same way. And at the same time that the rivers flowing on the surface are wearing down into the spongeworks, much of the water inside the sponge is working its way to the surface by way of

Sinkholes such as this one function much like funnels to channel pollution directly into the groundwater. Visible evidence of the "spongeworks" underlying the Ozarks, most sinkholes result from the collapse of a cave roof. (Courtesy of Bittersweet, Inc.)

cave-and-spring conduits. In the process, much of the water-soluble rock is being carried away in solution every day. Quite literally, the Ozarks is in the process of wearing itself away.

The Karst Environment
and Rural Poverty

Conversely, the rates of soil formation in karst areas are among the slowest on earth. The rock that is dissolved in the copious water leaves the area; it is unavailable for the formation of soil. Says hydrologist Tom Aley, "Weather away a thickness of 100 feet of typical Ozark karstland rock and you derive perhaps 10 'feet worth' of mineral material for soil. . . . There are three types of soils found in karst areas. These are the shallow soils, the rocky soils, and the imported soils."

And, as Aley points out, good agricultural soils are neither shallow nor rocky. What little "imported" soil there is in the Ozarks—the alluvial soils found on terraces along the major streams of the region —are now to a large extent submerged beneath the manmade mega-lakes.

What's more, many of the nutrients critically needed for good plant growth are carried away with the precipitation that moves directly into and through the karst area's groundwater system. Says Aley, "Nutrient impoverishment of karst soils is the norm." What this means, simply, is that the karst environment is a poor one. Few crops can be raised. In most areas the soil is too thin and rocky to support even sparse grazing lands for cattle. With little agriculture and even less industry to offer jobs, the scattered residents of the rural Ozarks—unless they have independent incomes—are often poor.

"History is but geography in motion."

The Misunderstood Ozarks

Most visitors are surprised to learn that so many different ethnic groups have always shared the region. From the Indians who claimed it first and the earliest newcomers, the French and Spanish, it has been home—in addition to the predominant "Americans" who continually pushed the frontier westward from earliest times—to immigrants from Germany, Scotland, Sweden, Italy, Switzerland, Poland, Belgium, Austria, Africa, Denmark, Holland, Greece, Hungary, Ireland, Portugal, Russia, Wales, and Yugoslavia, as well as to the Amish and Mennonites. While most of these groups came in relatively small numbers and were assimilated rather quickly, their presence can still be detected from their telltale place names: Bonne Terre, New Madrid, Freistatt, Rosati, Swedeborg.

In the eastern Ozarks, the French influence still faintly lingers, and a creole French was still spoken in a neighborhood there until about two decades ago. Although their influence in the Ozarks remained essentially localized near the Mississippi River, by 1700 the French had explored much of the interior of the region, mapped and named many of its rivers and geological features, and lived peaceably with the Indians.

In the 1830s and 1840s more than a dozen organized German settlement societies established colonies in the northern and eastern Ozarks. Many have clung tenaciously to their language, architecture, and lifestyle in the Ozarks—so much so that some, notably Hermann, have remained more like nineteenth-century Germany than Germany itself. A visit to Hermann today affords the traveler a glimpse—and taste—of the Europe of nearly two centuries ago.

But the Scotch-Irish, or Ulster Scots, were the group who influenced the history of the Ozarks most strongly and whose culture of self-sufficiency is more generally associated with the region. It is their music, their cabin crafts, their dance, their folktales that attract most visitors to the Ozarks and that most expect to find throughout the region.

The total population of the Ozarks region has ballooned since about 1965. Most new residents, however, are concentrated along the corridors of Interstate 44 (east-west) and U.S. Highway 71 (north-south) and their related urban centers. Secondary areas of growth are clustered around the huge manmade lakes that have attracted retirees and opportunity seekers.

Perhaps as more evidence of the extraordinarily strong sense of place throughout the region, Ozarkers more often identify with each other, even across state lines, than they do with the rest of their states at large—who have historically treated their Ozarks neighbors as "poor relations" or orphaned children. While there are a few references to "the Missouri Ozarks" or "the Arkansas Ozarks," and even, rarely, the "Oklahoma Ozarks," usually by the respective states' tourism departments, more often one hears simply, "the Ozarks."

Occasionally, especially in old literature of the region, there are references to *Lapland*, defined as that area of Missouri that "laps over" into Arkansas—or vice versa. In *The History of Baxter County* (Arkansas), Mary Ann Messick infers that the term dates to the Civil War: ". . . here the north lapped down on the south and the grey lapped up on the blue." Today the Lapland concept seems particularly apt because of still another kind of "lapping." Since the past so thoroughly engages the present and, perhaps, the future of the Ozarks, a curious overlapping of time is apparent here, the blending of past with present.

The strong regional identity, coupled with the fact that Ozarkers

The limestone and dolomite of the Ozarks dissolve readily in groundwater, which flows through the rocks in much the same way it does a sponge. The manifest results are caves and springs. (Courtesy of Bittersweet, Inc.)

Just as he found a purpose for the rocks everywhere on his land, the Ozarker also made use of discarded objects. Here a rusted milk can serves as a support for a rural mailbox. Other popular mailbox holders are wagonwheels, tractor seats, walking plows, welded chain, and the like.

have more in common with each other than they do with other Missourians or Arkansans, has led some to suggest, more or less tongue-in-cheek, that there should be a separate state of Ozarkia. One favorite Ozarks writer, the late Dan Saults, said of his imagined state, ". . . a gentle peace seeps out of the rocky soil at twilight, like mist rising from a float stream." And, said Clay Anderson, publisher of *The Ozarks Mountaineer* and a recognized spokesman for the region, ". . . there are many of us who—if there were only a peaceful and practical way—would fervently work for statehood for the Ozarks."

But, perhaps because Ozarkers have traditionally been regarded as backward at best and ignorant at worst, many inhabitants of some of the subregions of the Ozarks deny any affiliation with the region. Particularly on the northern and eastern fringes, the traveler finds few who admit to being part of the Ozarks—whatever and wherever that may be.

And not many Ozarkers—even those who readily admit to the label—can say how the region got its name. A traveler once exclaimed to me that for two weeks he had been asking people in the region about the origin of the name before finally getting an answer to his question. There are so many theories that he might well have received many different replies.

But most modern scholars agree that the name Ozarks originated as an English-speaking corruption of the French prepositional phrase, *aux arcs* (pronounced *ohs ark*), a shortened form meaning "toward or to Arkansas" or "to Arkansas Post," a fur-trading post. Arkansas was also the name of an Indian tribe in the lower Mississippi region, and *aux arcs* could also refer to those Indians and by extension to the mountains northwest of where they lived. An English traveler by the name of John Bradbury first used the name *Ozark* in print in 1809. The term *Ozark Mountains* first appeared on a map by government explorer S. H. Long in 1815, and historians generally agree that Major Long officialized the distinctive name.

In response to the question, "Is the Ozarks is, or are the Ozarks are?" the director of the Center for Ozarks Studies at Southwest Missouri State University, Dr. Robert Flanders, concludes "that 'Ozarks,' like 'Great Plains,' is a singular noun ending in 's' (can one Ozark be found, anymore than one Great Plain?)." Native speakers, however, seem not to share Dr. Flanders' opinion; they consistently use "Ozark" as an adjective.

Because of the mystical, almost palpable sense of place, the overlapping of past and present, and the region's comparative remoteness—real and imagined—from the rest of the country, outsiders see the Ozarks as intriguing, quaint, and mysterious. But at the same time, the region is often regarded as old-fashioned and ignorant.

And outlanders fail to understand that the mountaineer's fierce independence and his deliberately easygoing resourcefulness stem from his reluctance to be "beholden" to anyone. He still will not be forced into an unnatural relationship with time and money, those symbols of the city which have never held much meaning in the Ozarks. His caution is often mistaken for unfriendliness.

Even the hill man's "poverty" has been misinterpreted. In the 1930s, when the New Deal agencies brought in "relief commodities," Ozarkers discovered such new foods as grapefruit and oranges. But, for the first time for many, they learned that they were poor. Townsend Godsey, a noted long-time historian and photographer of the vanishing Ozarks, has written, "Perhaps a minimum concern about money and material things is why life is good in the hills. . . ."

Others would argue that the condition known as a depression in urban America had become a way of life for the Ozarkers. Often the poverty perceived by urbanites and newcomers is, to a large degree, the manifestation of inborn determination to be as nearly self-sufficient as possible and, therefore, independent of the prevailing economic winds. Luxuries—beyond the most basic food, clothing, and shelter— are often seen as self-indulgent, and a make-do attitude is frequently found in those who could do "better" but see no reason to. As a result, the natural order of things is disturbed less in the Ozarks by depression and recession, when the lack of excess cash is nothing new.

Although grossly exaggerated and arguably chauvinistic, the popular image of hillbilly isolationists did have *some* basis in fact. While the people were neither ignorant nor backward, they did face the hardships of living in a remote area where rugged terrain made education, socialization, and travel difficult and "civilization" relatively late in coming. As recently as the early 1950s, many of the more isolated hilly regions were still awaiting electricity. Telephones and paved highways came only thirty years ago to others. Most county roads are still unpaved, for there is scarcely any need for pavement when one drives directly on the bedrock.

Another common misconception of the Ozarks is that—at the very least—its residents have always been pitiful prisoners of their geography, the victims of terrible *enforced* isolation. The truth is, not all subregions of the Ozarks are isolated and they never were. Three of the world's largest and most navigable rivers, the Mississippi, the Missouri, and the Arkansas, border the Ozarks. Highways of travel and commerce since the earliest exploration of this continent, the rivers brought a steady flow of social exchange as well.

Further, the plateau areas of the Ozarks have, since prehistoric times, served as avenues of travel into and across the region. Present-day Interstate 44, which bisects the Ozarks, was first an Indian trace,

Ozarkers contended with many rivers and large streams; they crossed either at shallow places called fords, or on a ferry. This is the Powder Mill Ferry on Current River at Owl's Bend in 1946; it ferried as many as 150 cars a day, one or two at a time, until a bridge replaced it in the 1960s. (Courtesy of Bittersweet, Inc.)

After a ferry, the next best way to get across one of the frequent rivers or streams was on a paved ford such as this—still common on the back roads of much of the Ozarks. Because the water is so clear, it often looks shallower than it is. In times of heavy rain, such fords are subject to dangerous flash flooding.

then an early wagon road for freighters, then the Wire Road, so called because it was paralleled by the first telegraph wires, then the Military Road because it served as highway for troops of both sides during the Civil War, and, most recently, Route 66, one of the major arteries traversing almost the entire continent.

And, while many of the interior regions, particularly the most rugged terrain, were certainly isolated, they were not impossibly so. While it might have taken considerable effort to enter and leave, the main reason that most Ozarkers did not do so is, simply, they did not choose to. They *chose* to live in isolation, deliberately preferring privacy and self-sufficiency, in the company of a very few others who shared their outlook, to an interchange with the world at large.

Ozarkers have always taken what they consider best and most worthwhile from the "outside" world and then retreated into their own. They have traditionally selected the best of both worlds, deliberately shunning the perceived negative aspects of modernity. To a great extent, this is still true, even for newcomers. In fact, Ozarkers move between both worlds, putting on or taking off the language of the hills as easily as they change their clothes to go to town or to "the city." Today's teenagers think nothing of making a hundred-mile drive to ultraprogressive shopping malls, where they fit right in with others their age, then returning home to a more conservative way of life. And, importantly, more and more of them are finding ways to remain in the hills, though many are forced to leave to find work or to pursue careers for which there is no demand at home.

But among those who have left the Ozarks, even a half-century or more ago, there appears to be a universal longing for "home." Many who abandoned the area during the Depression still subscribe to regional publications and newspapers from their old communities. Their letters, full of yearning and homesickness, are published frequently on editorial pages.

Among "newcomers," those people who have chosen to live in the Ozarks, there are a great many intelligent, talented, creative, people —artisans and artists, writers, weavers, sculptors, musicians, educators—most of whom could live anywhere they choose and came here from the "advantaged" cities they were glad to leave behind. Those who were born here and have had the good sense to stay—even if they take the Ozarks for granted—love it nonetheless. They look out on the rest of the world with a sort of bemused amazement, serenely confident that their so-called hillbilly lifestyle is the only sane way to live.

Far from a disadvantage, the modern perception of the Ozarks as a refuge from the present, as a place where the old-time values and advantages of rural living are nurtured, has created a new awareness of—and interest in—the region. Private developments such as Silver Dollar City, a theme park near Branson, Missouri, and governmental entities like the Ozark Folk Center, a cultural time capsule where history lives and works near Mountain View, Arkansas, capitalize on the public's yearning for the slower olden days forever vanished except from the Ozarks and a few other "backward" folk regions.

Today the mythical comic-strip image is promoted by tourist-baiters and indulged by tongue-in-cheek "hillbillies" who are "stupid" enough to set up a stand by the side of the road and sell rocks to the tourists. Though they may laugh all the way to the bank, such good-natured acceptance—for profit or otherwise—is not likely to be duplicated by any other ethnic group anywhere in the world.

The Twenty-First Century Ozarks

There are still a very few unpaved highways and—in some rough, mountainous areas—a few homes are being built beyond the electric and telephone lines and out of reach of any vehicle save a four-wheel drive. Nowadays, of course, these residents accept such conditions by choice. Far from being hillbillies, they are often highly educated dropouts from polluted metroplexes, refugees seeking a more tranquil lifestyle.

If not hillbillies, who are the modern Ozarkers? They fall into two general categories: natives and newcomers. The terms are used descriptively in conversation, in writing, and everyone knows who is included in each. Within those two broad groups, there are further breakdowns.

The term *natives* is generally understood to mean those who were born here, but is usually meant to include those whose parents—and even grandparents—were born here. Of the natives, "remainees" are those who, born here, have remained. "Returnees," or "come backs," are natives who went away, perhaps to make a living in the city, but have come back upon retirement. A relatively new group of younger returnees comprises those who left but ultimately discovered that the economic advantages elsewhere did not outweigh the quality of life at home.

Most of the *newcomers*, or "come heres," are retirees. Drawn by the region's spectacular scenery, milder winters, lower cost of living, and a multitude of recreational opportunities, their generally assured incomes are a boon to economically depressed areas in the Ozarks. Many of the newcomers adopt the perceived Ozarks lifestyle, but not the Ozarks way of life. They may be pursuing a dream of a frontier now vanished and cling desperately to the remnants of mountain greenery wildness. Often they pretend that they have left behind the plastic tawdriness of late-twentieth-century America. Here in the boondocks, they want to believe, is not only the pure heart of America, but a country of the heart, and the means to go back to the simpler, safer past.

Yet the larger Ozarks towns are like those anywhere in the country. Computerlands, Pizza Huts, and McDonald's thrive beside body shops and beauty parlors. Symphony orchestras, museums, libraries, video stores, luxury cars, colleges—all the accoutrements of modern America—are as obvious in the Ozarks as elsewhere. Even beyond the city limits, the signs of the times are not easily ignored. Satellite dishes sprout along country roads like mutated mushrooms. Hot-rodders and drug runners share the highways with retirees and vacationers.

The old ways and the old ideas are slipping away. Forests are being bulldozed, hills leveled to facilitate better bridge approaches, roads straightened and widened to accommodate motor homes and boat trailers. Once known only by local names and left unmarked, unpaved country roads are now numbered and signed to ease the jobs of the latter-day paramedics and firemen.

But native talent that has too frequently been lost to the larger job market of the cities is more often staying home to help run the region's booming tourist industry. Built to furnish jobs and hydroelectric power, a number of large manmade reservoirs have also brought recreation, development, and outlanders. Now visitors flock to the Ozarks by the millions, and more come every year.

It is often the highly publicized and artificial "tourist attractions," representing big-money developers from the outside, that lure most tourists for their initial visits. But once here, visitors also discover the less-disturbed natural world, as well as the sense of traveling back in time, still to be enjoyed in the Ozarks. They return often for another tour of the past along canoeable wild and scenic rivers, ranging from placid streams to experts-only whitewater rapids, through miles of pristine scenery; national forests and official wilderness areas in which to backpack, hunt, hike; and many other back-to-nature and back-to-the-past opportunities.

Despite this influx of new population and new development, however, the Ozarks on the eve of the twenty-first century determinedly remains a folk region, stubbornly resisting change. "Ozarkers, whether natives or newcomers, tend to want the best of both worlds; so they work at achieving a synthesis," says Dr. Robert Flanders. "It is that synthesis which does much to define the Ozarks as a distinctive place in our generation—a place both modern and traditional, isolated and connected."

The Allure of the Ozarks

Historians and geographers sometimes refer to the Ozarks as an "arrested—or perpetuated—frontier." They believe it has been deliberately arrested, that the perceived negative aspects of modernity have been intentionally ignored. Religion, politics, value system—all have remained essentially conservative. The net result is that the past is very recent here.

Says Dr. Flanders, "The Ozarks remained more raw than cooked." It was not until after World War I, despite the coming of the railroads, the telephone, the timber and mining industries, the automobile, and the radio, that the winds of change found a crack in the self-perpetuating wall around the Ozarks. When the veterans came home after the war with their new awareness of the outside world, the chink began to widen.

Ozarkers found it even harder to ignore tourists, paved highways, Roosevelt's New Deal agencies, World War II, and all the wars since then, the Corps of Engineers, television—especially via satellite—Wal-Martization, videos, newcomers, and commuters. But still they resist.

And as a result, the bewitchment remains. At the riverfront of an old steamboat town, the river eddies around the dock as though just closing around the passing of a sternwheeler. On the back roads, the Ozarks-that-used-to-be and the Ozarks-of-right-now flow into and around each other like the vapors swirling in the hollows at dawn.

Inevitably, the rest of the harried world has discovered the peace that still reigns in the hills.

But analyzing that "peace," describing the allure of the Ozarks on paper, remains difficult. It is one thing to delimit the region's boundaries, to describe its physical characteristics, and quite another to explain the peace one feels in the presence of these remarkably aged, patient hills.

It is simple enough to speak of clear, unpolluted skies, of easy-on-the-lungs atmosphere and the crisp aroma of pine needles rather than urban sprawl. But how does one explain the serenity inherent in a wisp of wood smoke? Or the deep satisfaction of damp humus in the awakening woods of spring?

Even the regional aspects of the Ozarks that might be considered disadvantages—such as the ever-present rocks and sheer cliffs—are part of the feast for the senses that helps to explain the allure. The bluffs are dramatic in the wintertime: cascades of ice draperies that glisten like sequins. From earliest spring to latest autumn, a vast rock garden thrives among the stony outcrops and the counterpointing green of cedars and pines—wildflowers of every hue and height, a

One step up from a paved ford is the low-water bridge, so called because it is only usable in times of low water. If the river is "up," or in flood, the bridge is awash—and dangerous. This one is across the North Fork River in Ozark County, Missouri.

The suspension, or "swinging," bridge came into use with the arrival of the automobile—which was much less capable of wading a river than the faithful team of horses or mules. Most of these bridges have yielded to the forces of floods and time, but some are still used cautiously on the back roads. (Courtesy of Bittersweet, Inc.)

carpet of tiny violets, knee-deep orange Butterfly Weed, Brown-eyed Daisies, purple Asters, waist-high Queen Anne's Lace, sky-blue Chicory, and wild Yucca and Wild Roses.

From the first cloudlike blossoms in the woods to the last hurrah of scarlet sumac and maple, the crimson-and-gold-of-setting-sun hickory and oak, the Ozarks are alive with intensity. Even when draped with the gauze of mist or fog, color is omnipresent and demanding—as in winter, when the sunlight finds a prism in every crystal of "ice fog," an almost snowlike freezing of the fog on every twig, every cedar needle, every seared leaf, every blade of grass.

Although the calm of nature is difficult to explain to "outsiders," Ozarkers find it impossible to be uptight for long. It is hard to frown when exchanging glances with a raccoon peering down from leafy branches reaching over the road; you can not long dwell on sleep-robbing problems after listening to the coyotes communicate with the night. And surely there is a lesson in the headlong flight of a swallow apparently about to dash to its death against the sheer face of a bluff, only to fold its wings at the last possible moment and slip to rest in a well-sheltered nest hidden there.

Most of us, having learned to forego the dehumanizing "convenience" of the city, unstressed by crowded, competitive conditions, find our souls renewed by sunsets behind the cedars rather than by afternoons on the psychiatrist's couch, or drugs, or drink. The midnight intruder on the porch is a 'possum; the thief in the woodpile is a pack rat; the high-rise on our horizon, a white oak older than this nation.

And the past is part of the present everywhere in the Ozarks, and much of it is still visible—and visitable. "The Ozarks is one of the few remaining places where one can not only view but also can participate in selected fragments of America's past," says Dr. Milton Rafferty of Southwest Missouri State University. "It is the persistence of fragments of departed lifestyles that holds intrinsic fascination for visitors."

The pervading suffocation of the city, the lack of nature's refreshing greenery, the backlash of the high-technology workplace, are filling many urbanites with a hunger for the natural places, for food for the senses, a need to return—if only for a few days—to wilderness. Coupled with the drive to return to physical fitness, the Ozarks' bountiful opportunities to hunt, fish, canoe, hike, camp, and for many other outdoor pursuits, makes it all the more attractive. The Ozarks' regional distinction, its one-of-a-kind atmosphere, especially as a pocket of the past, is seen as a retreat from the homogenized sameness of most urban areas where travelers can change their locations by thousands of miles without really changing their environment.

But today's traveler often wants more than a change of scene and a chance to exercise. As part of their rebellion against the cold detachment of the mass production of most everyday things, many come in search of the personal touch, so often overlooked in their cities. They want a sense of involvement with the creators of one-of-a-kind crafts, improvisational musicians, proprietors who recognize them and call them by name, perhaps even remembering their personal likes and dislikes (which may be why so many return again and again to the same places). And above all, most of us are nostalgic for the past even as we enthusiastically embrace the easier life of the future.

The Ozarks offers all this and much more—to both tourists and travelers. "Tourists" are defined as those who desire to be entertained with little or no effort on their own part, to be lulled and pampered. Ozarkers, of course, welcome visitors of this type, but they often speak in wonder and disappointment of those who visit only the famous attractions and then go home thinking they have "seen the Ozarks." It makes no more sense than going to Coney Island and thinking you have seen New York.

"Travelers" want to be challenged and stimulated, to *experience* a different culture and to learn its history. Here they will find a chance to reconnect with our country's history, both natural and social. They realize that to understand the present, they must comprehend the past. As a last outpost of a time when people at least appeared to be able to make sense of the world, the Ozarks offers many of those tantalizing "fragments of departed lifestyles."

But where is the visitor or newcomer, unfamiliar with even one corner of the vast area we call the Ozarks, to find these fragments?

Guideposts to Living History:
How to Use This Book

This book will be your guide to the living history of the Ozarks. Of course, one book cannot pretend to illuminate more than ten thousand years of successive layers of human history over a fifty-thousand-square-mile area. Nor can one book be a comprehensive travel guide to such an enormous region.

But this book will provide a familiarizing overview of the Ozarks and direct the way to the many places and the many ways you can visit the region's past and, to a large extent, the past of America. The book will introduce you, in particular, to the author's favorite sections, those that seem to be most representative of the whole, some of the most celebrated and, often, the most overlooked.

The chapters are arranged to lead the way on self-guided driving tours while furnishing a "popular" history of the most significant sites in each. While you can pick and choose among the individual chapters (tours) if you wish, the overview chapters are almost entirely history— and are all essential to your understanding of any of the parts. Taken together, they offer a fairly comprehensive "overview" of Ozarks history.

Following each chapter, or group of related chapters, a chart of "practical matters" offers concrete suggestions for places to stay, to eat, and to play, both indoors and out.

The "Practical Matters Charts" also provide the addresses of places to write or call for more detailed information. Many chambers of commerce, especially in the more developed areas, have invested in lavish, illustrated brochures to give you the information you need. Another good reason for sending for their data is so that you can be sure the attractions you wish to visit will be open when you arrive. Many are seasonal; that is, open only during the tourist season—

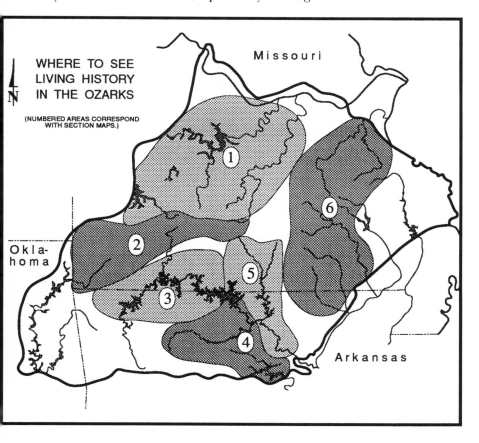

roughly May through September. It may vary locally, of course, or with individual businesses.

Do be aware that many of the most rewarding historical sites and museums are staffed by volunteers, which means they may be open only on weekends and not at all on holidays. A few minutes invested in advance planning will pay great dividends on your trip. On the other hand, such sites very often stay open—on a limited schedule—all year. Many private museums, as well as those operated by historical societies, will open on appointment for visitors who express a genuine interest in their collections or site; the Practical Matters Charts list telephone numbers.

Another important reason to send for brochures is to acquaint yourself with the endless number and variety of fairs, festivals, crafts shows, historic celebrations, re-enactments, pageants, etc., that are staged throughout the region in the spring, summer, and fall. The best of them are noncommercial and offer excellent historical background, authentic musical performances, crafts demonstrations, and the like.

During the past few years some attractions have begun reopening for the Christmas holiday season and investing in elaborate decorative lighting and seasonal displays to attract visitors, but so far this is limited to the most heavily trafficked areas. A little advance planning can prevent disappointment upon arrival.

A few caveats: Remember that the lack of many superhighways is one reason why the region has so much remaining past. Back roads afford wonderful vistas but require careful driving. This is dawdling country.

To enjoy it best, come with an open mind. Cultivate the *seeing eye*—the ability to see the forest in spite of the trees, unshadowed by preconceived notions of beauty, habit, or conditioning and unrealistic expectations.

The concept of beauty and its perception are apparently uniquely human, but even our definitions of beauty differ. If, for example, one's values are pinned to manicured lawns and artificiality, he will find little beauty in meadows of wildflowers. If another needs concrete sidewalks and curbstones, she will fail to see green mosses in the snow or orange lichens nearly fluorescent under a gray sky.

So view the Ozarks with your mind's eye, and mix a little philosophy with the color and contour. Be open to new concepts of beauty. Look for the fullness of everything, and you will not be disappointed.

The best way to learn to see the Ozarks is to spend time outside. Not just fishing and hunting or sightseeing, but time spent in walking, listening, and feeling, in stopping, touching, and smelling. While a great deal of the wonder of the Ozarks is in its diversified wildlife, the profusion of wildflowers and trees, there is so much more to experience.

Gaze at the sky, marvelously visible and unpolluted, with its kaleidoscope of clouds and spectacular sunrises and sunsets. Even so-called bad weather is enjoyable if you are open to beauty. Look for ice flowers, icicle-draped bluffs, dewdrops on spider webs, snow in the cedars, fog in the woods. When it is hot and humid, seek beauty in the morning mists on the river, moonlight on the lake, the cool green shade of deep woods.

You will need no coaching to enjoy spring and fall in the Ozarks. Those seasons are a bewilderment of beauty, and no one who has ever been under their spell will ever forget it.

But sometimes our visitors, even if they appreciate the natural beauty, see it in only negative terms—the absence of city things: no traffic, no noise, no fumes, no bright lights, no fast food. People who perceive the Ozarks negatively, in what they are missing from the city, usually cannot adjust to the absence of the negatives and the presence of the positives. They never learn to look beyond the ticks and chiggers, never feel more than rocky roads and steep hills.

Mysteriously, the Ozarks often rewards those who *seek* it with a peculiar serendipity that will lead them to many discoveries of their own. "There is something strange about the Ozarks, a feeling almost fey in the Auld Sod sense," wrote the late Dan Saults, and "the region attracts those marching to a different drummer, who do not fit social patterns or cultural stereotypes."

Some of the visitors, Saults said, might be looking for the myth of "pioneers who were happier, wiser, better than we are today, who above all were spiritually pure." He thought perhaps that "is why tourists come among us and want to see 'real hillbillies' who are barefoot, illiterate, bearded, talk funny, know little, but are 'real' people, unlike filling station proprietors, motel operators and mistresses of souvenir stands."

This is certain: If you look for ugliness, that is what you will see; if you look for beauty, you will discover it everywhere. But whatever you are searching for, the chances are good you will find it—and a soothing homeyness, comforted by the wrinkled, peaceful brow of the aged hills in these magical, mystical Ozarks.

A LIVING HISTORY
of the OZARKS

SECTION 1

Lake of the Ozarks Region

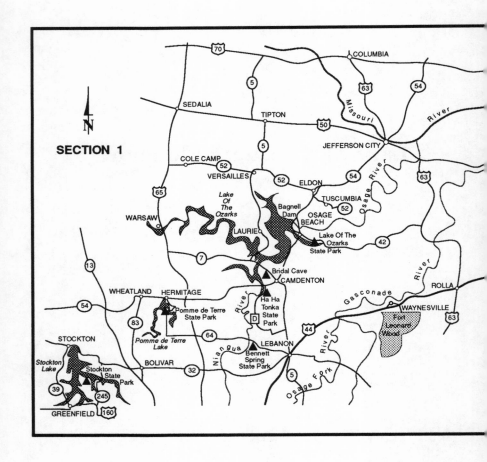

CHAPTER 1

Overview: Indian Traces, Stagecoaches, and River Roads

Extraordinarily tall and powerful—the undisputed masters of the Ozarks region—the Osage Indians were skilled hunters who ranged widely over their domain. Audubon considered them "well formed, athletic and robust men of noble aspect." It is said that the braves commonly walked sixty miles in a day. Strangely, though they could mimic the sounds of many animals and birds, they were astonished and disconcerted by the white man's habit of whistling. Cleanshaven to the point of plucking their eyebrows, Osage warriors were disgusted by the bearded, unkempt Europeans they encountered in the early 1700s.

Although archaeologists believe that several ancient Indian civilizations once lived in the Ozarks, the Osage dominated the region when the first Europeans arrived. They lived in permanent villages on the perimeter of the Ozarks plateau and several times a year traveled into the interior to hunt. They took mainly buffalo, beaver, and deer—and used every scrap of their kill. The women raised corn, beans, and gourds and gathered nuts, berries, and persimmons.

Those who were more fortunate in the hunt provided for the destitute, and it was customary to send provisions to the lodges of the poor, the widows, and the fatherless. Conspicuous among the various Indian tribes for their general sobriety, the Osage remained for more than a century but little changed by their association with white traders and visitors.

45

Indian "thong trees" pointed the way to water, a secure cave, or other necessity of life. Thong, in this case, does not mean a leather strap, but the forked sticks used to train the trees. Positive identification of a thong tree depends on the presence of well-defined thong scars in the bark under the first bend and on top of the second bend. (Courtesy of Bittersweet, Inc.)

Thong Trees

Very little remains of the Osage—arrowheads and a few other artifacts, descriptions of their towns and hunting villages recorded by explorers. But still dotting the landscape, notably in the Lake of the Ozarks area, are *thong trees*, deliberately bent as saplings by the Indians to train their growth. Used to mark trails, the deformed trees also pointed the way to water, medicinal herbs, salt licks, and shelter caves.

Because the existence of the trees was a sacred tribal secret—as was the word for *thong*—the earliest white settlers did not understand their significance. But eventually the newcomers realized their connection with the availability of water and sometimes referred to them as "water trees." They also called them "buffalo trees" because squaws aired buffalo hides over the bent trees and sometimes pulled cured hides back and forth across the rough bark until the hides were soft enough for moccasins and clothing.

Since natural calamities may cause a tree to be similarly misshapen, close examination is necessary. Several authentic trees have been identified in the central Ozarks region and are protected by garden clubs and other interested parties.

Indian Reservations in the Ozarks

Following the Louisiana Purchase, which encouraged American settlers to pour into the region west of the Mississippi—where formerly they had trickled—the United States took advantage of the added territory as a place to get rid of the eastern Indians. Four reservations were established in southwest Missouri. The Kickapoo reservation lay south of the Osage River and included what is now Greene County and the city of Springfield. South of that, the Delaware reservation extended to the Arkansas border and east to a line running north and south across Beaver Creek about halfway between Ava and Forsyth. From that line to the North Fork River at Tecumseh in Ozark County lay the Shawnee reservation. Small clans from other displaced tribes drifted into the area and lived among these groups. Those who lived in the Upper White River valley were referred to collectively as the White River Indians. But they clashed frequently with the mighty Osage, who still claimed hunting privileges on the land even though they had "ceded" it not long after the Louisiana Purchase.

But the reservations in the Ozarks were short-lived. Hardy pioneers moved into the region in greater numbers, demanding that the Indians be pushed farther west. Eventually all the tribes were shunted into Kansas and Oklahoma along with the Osage and the Cherokees who survived the march on the "Trail of Tears" across the rugged Ozarks.

Many of Indian blood intermarried with white settlers, however, and were assimilated into Ozarks society. Particularly the Cherokees, who had long mingled with whites east of the Mississippi, found it easy to "pass" into white society. A great many Ozarks natives today count among their ancestors—often on both sides—a Cherokee maiden or brave.

Butterfield Overland Mail

Long before the white settlers arrived, the Indians had found the easiest routes across the land. Their trails, or "traces," in many cases were the foundations of our routes of discovery, our network of trade roads, and, finally, our system of modern highways.

Over one such Indian "highway," along the western edge of the Ozarks where the rolling hills flatten into prairie, the stagecoaches of the Butterfield Overland Mail once raced the clock westward. Today it is possible to retrace their trail through the Ozarks.

In March 1857, responding to the popular demand for improved mail service between the coasts, Congress passed a bill providing for the establishment of an East-West mail-and-passenger service. Due in part to the pressures leading up to the Civil War, the route of the new service was controversial and hotly contested. To avoid the political fallout, Congress left the decision up to the postmaster general, stipulating only that the new service should take no longer than twenty-five days one way and that it must begin within twelve months after the contract was awarded.

They Said It Couldn't Be Done

The successful bidder for the contract was John Butterfield. An experienced mail contractor, Butterfield chose a southern route to California—across the Missouri and Arkansas Ozarks into Indian Territory (now Oklahoma), then Texas and points west. Although the citizens of the East and North resented his choice, he justified his route by citing its superiority in terms of climate, topography, and roads.

But Butterfield faced a tough year of preparation. While the country watched and waited and counted down the stipulated year after the awarding of the contract—and detractors said it could not be done—Butterfield's crews established 141 stations between Tipton, Missouri (the western terminus of the railroad), and San Francisco. The number eventually swelled to nearly two hundred as entrepreneurs established hotels and saloons near the route.

The Butterfield Overland Mail Company made its maiden run beginning on September 16, 1858. John Butterfield himself left St. Louis with the mail bags on the train for Tipton, where his son, John Jr., was waiting to drive the first stagecoach over the new route through the Ozarks: the world's then-longest passenger-and-mail service line. Local newspapers ignored the event. Only a special correspondent for the *New York Herald*, one Waterman Ormsby, was sent to cover the first trip. Ormsby, in fact, was the only passenger on that maiden run to remain with the stage all the way to San Francisco.

After the stage left Tipton, it bore southwestward through Cole Camp, an old town settled between 1840 and the Civil War by more than four hundred families of immigrants from the low country of northern Germany. (From Cole Camp the stage passed through Warsaw, now the site of a Corps of Engineers visitor center jutting from the face of Kaysinger Bluff above Truman Lake. Outstanding historical exhibits, including some Harry Truman memorabilia, and interesting dioramas depicting the area's natural history make it an enjoyable stop if time permits. On the grounds is a house built in the 1800s by Molly and John Hooper and reconstructed in 1984 by the Corps of Engineers. Be sure to include a stop at the riverfront wharf where steamboats once docked. On the lawn of the courthouse in Warsaw, amid towering old maple trees and a fish pond, is a plaque marking the Butterfield Stage stop. From Warsaw, the stage passed through the town of Quincy, where a placard marks the spot of the station, and Wheatland, just west of Hermitage on Hwy. 54.)

As roads permitted and where the demand existed, stage lines had crisscrossed the Ozarks for several years before the advent of the Overland Mail. Today the stops along those lines are often confused with those of Butterfield's line. But it was his Overland Mail Company that had the most impact upon the Ozarks, connecting its people with those in other parts of the vast new country.

Unfortunately, Butterfield's southern route was abandoned in favor of a more northerly route during the hazardous early days of the Civil War. But tales of the colorful Butterfield stagecoach days have passed into our folklore. Mark Twain told of a driver for the Overland Mail who finally quit his job because "he came as near as anything to starving to death in the midst of abundance, because they kept him so leaky with bullet holes that he couldn't hold his vittles."

The Osage River

Zebulon M. Pike explored the Osage River in 1806. The Osage, like the other large rivers in the Ozarks, served until well into the twentieth century as a "highway" for settlers into the roadless interior—and was their most important link with the rest of the country. It brought new immigrants in, supplied them, then hauled their products out.

Since the shoals on the Gasconade River presented a serious problem to navigation, steamboats were built with an extremely shallow draft. Because they could not, as a result, carry much cargo, they pushed barges that drew only a few inches of water when "light." Here the Royal *transfers her cargo to the railroad. (Courtesy of State Historical Society of Missouri)*

Many an Ozarker fed his family during the Depression by hacking railroad ties. The job lasted from the advent of the railroads into the region until the mid- to late 1930s. A skilled tie hacker, on a good day, might hack from ten to twenty ties. (He had to be careful of his toes!) But then he still had to get the ties to market, either by loading them onto a mule-drawn wagon for carting over long distances on poor roads, or by floating them down an accessible river to the railhead. (Courtesy of Bittersweet, Inc.)

Beginning in the mid-1800s, steamboats that drew only about a foot of water were built especially for the shallower Ozarks rivers. And because the rivers meandered in looping bends, the boats were also shorter than steamboats elsewhere. River pilots are said to have claimed that at night, owls would twist their heads off trying to follow the lights of a steamboat winding its way up the Osage. For small towns along the Osage, the Gasconade, the White, the Black, and the St. Francis rivers, the steamboats played just as important a role as did their more glamorous sisters on the Mississippi and the Missouri. On the Osage, paddlewheelers traveled regularly as far upriver as Warsaw, which could dock seven boats at a time.

But the rivers required continuous work to clear them of shoals, rocks, trees, and submerged logs. Traffic depended on the season and the weather. And because of their smaller size, the steamers' cargo space was limited. To compensate, the Osage River steamboats pushed barges that could move two or three train car loads of merchandise.

Tie Hacking and Rafting

Lumbering came early to the Ozarks' great forests. As early as 1818, camps were already in place in the pinery along the headwaters of the Gasconade River—the nearest source of good lumber for the burgeoning St. Louis metropolis. And, as the most northwesterly extension of native Southern-pine forests, the Ozarks offered lumbermen geographical advantages to tap the markets of Nebraska, Kansas, and Indian Territory. Much of this timber was hauled by ox-team to Springfield or to the Osage River ports for shipping. The Gasconade Valley was still an important source of pine as late as 1852, although the Arkansas border was then beginning to be exploited. By 1880 the best timber in the Gasconade region had been cut.

One regionwide aspect of the logging business in the Ozarks was tie hacking, or whacking. During the rapid expansion of the railroads, as many as three thousand crossties were required per mile of new track, with replacement ties in constant demand. Many of them came from the Ozarks, hacked one at a time by one man using a broadax according to the railroads' strict specifications: the tie must be of white oak cut six inches by eight inches by eight feet. Those of good quality brought about twenty-five cents at the railhead; those not to specification were rejected.

Always desperate for cash, tie hackers cut timber wherever they could. Some of them cut on their own land; some paid a fee to landowners to cut their trees, and occasionally they cut on absentee-owners' lands without permission. Men who made tie cutting their business would sometimes acquire timberland very cheaply by pur-

The finished ties were formed into "snake rafts"—so called because they were joined with green saplings to allow them to "snake" around the tight bends of an Ozarks river—and floated downstream to the railhead. Sometimes great distances were covered, and the rafting crew had to walk home. Note the reflection of the barrel in the clear water. (Courtesy of Bittersweet, Inc.)

After being floated down the river to the railhead, the railroad ties were stacked beside the track to await shipment. Although the ties might weigh four hundred pounds each, crews of blacks were hired to load them—by hand—onto flatcars for shipment. Note the man with a tie on his shoulder, behind the men in the foreground beside the train. (Courtesy of State Historical Society of Missouri)

chasing land being sold for taxes and cutting off the timber before reselling the property.

Along the Niangua River, contractors leased large tracts of land and set up tie camps. When the timber was all cut in an area, they moved the camp to a new location. Contractors usually built stores to supply food and clothing near large tie bankings. If the banking was at a railhead, the ties could be loaded directly onto flatcars. Such camps hired as many as two to three hundred men. The ties they hacked were hauled to "bankings" on the Niangua, where they were branded. The buyer's mark—a circle, a cross, an initial, or an odd-shaped figure—was carved into the hammer's face. When the hammer was struck against the end of a tie, it left the inspector's symbol in the wood. Identification was important since several companies might drive ties at the same time.

In rough or isolated areas where there were no railroad lines, ties were banked above the high-water mark of a river. When they had dried for six months to a year, they were light enough to float down the river to the railhead. At first the ties were floated loose in the water. In the early summer when the risk of flash floods was low, the ties were slid off tall bluffs or down steep slopes called chutes, crashing and roaring into the river below. Caught by the swift current, the timbers were free to float downstream. The size of the drive increased as additional ties were added from other bankings. Some of the tie drives accumulated as many as 500,000 ties before reaching their take-out point at the railhead.

Experience taught that it was safer and easier to form the ties into rafts. About twenty ties were collected into a section one tie wide and about sixteen feet long. A pliable white oak sapling was split into strips; the strips were used to join several blocks of ties into a hinged "snake raft" that could negotiate the sharp bends in the river.

For two generations, from 1880 to 1920, railroad ties were floated down Ozarks streams to railheads to be loaded onto flatcars. In 1912 alone, fifteen million hand-hewn ties were sold in Missouri. Begun in some places before the Civil War, tie rafting on Ozarks rivers was eventually halted by improved roads and bridges and the advent of trucks to haul the ties to railroad centers.

But Ozarkers continued to cut and hew ties by hand as late as 1935. During the early Depression, selling ties kept many families from starving and provided needed cash income for many more. But when the market for stave bolts opened in the region, about 1933, men found that they could make more money with less labor cutting and selling stave bolts. And about 1935 the railroads switched to machine-made ties (earlier they had thought the hand-hewn ties lasted longer).

Most of the timber was gone, and so, in many cases, were the rivers. Almost overnight, a way of life was gone.

In less than a decade the then-largest manmade lake in the country and one of the largest in the world had drowned the Osage and the Niangua rivers and modernity had come to the Ozarks. Bagnell (named for the railroad contractor who completed the railroad to this point) changed overnight from a quiet ferryboat landing on the Osage River and the terminus of the Missouri Pacific branch line from Jefferson City, to a boom town.

CHAPTER 2

The "Inland Coast"

Of all the names applied to the "subregions" of the Ozarks, one of the most intriguing is the *Inland Coast*—appropriate because of the numbers of lakes in the area—and the miles of "coastline." It is one of the most highly developed areas in the region in terms of tourist facilities and attractions.

In August 1929, construction began on Bagnell Dam, which formed the Lake of the Ozarks. For most of the area farmers, still using real horsepower, the trucks, steam shovels, and other equipment employed in building the dam were marvels of technology. Said a lifelong area resident: "The building of Bagnell Dam literally pulled this part of the state, sometimes kicking and screaming, into the twentieth century."

For the first time ever, aerial photography was used to survey transmission power lines, to record construction progress, and to survey the reservoir. Using Union Electric's Ford Tri-Motor aircraft, the pioneering photographic team mounted the camera through a hole cut in the cabin floor.

Bagnell Dam was the largest and the last major dam financed solely by private capital to be built in the United States; it cost thirty million dollars. During the two years required to build it, work continued around the clock, and men worked nine-to-twelve-hour shifts. The pay scale ranged from 35 cents to about $1.25 per hour. Most of the local men were hired as laborers at the lower figure; they were happy to get it. The Crash of '29 came just two months after the project began. The building of Bagnell Dam was the largest construction project going on anywhere in the country. Thousands of men came to the area seeking jobs. Acres of tents and rented shacks sprang up, and people even slept in cars.

Jammed into crowded schools, the local children became aware of places they had never heard of and of sights and sounds they had never dreamed possible. Bagnell boomed like a mining camp and with all the bawdiness of one.

And many were unhappy about it. The citizens of Linn Creek, in particular, fought the project. Camden County and Linn Creek pleaded in vain for a federal injunction against the project. Prominent citizens and lawyers, including the county's prosecuting attorney, "fought the project from every possible angle and endeavored in every way to handicap the progress of the work." They failed; the entire town was demolished and the five hundred residents were forced to move elsewhere. Many left farms that had been in the family for generations. Thirty-two cemeteries and seventy-four scattered graves were moved to higher ground. Thirty thousand acres of timber were cleared from the bed of the reservoir, along with nine hundred miles of fences and numerous buildings. On February 2, 1931, the lake began to fill; by May 30, lake traffic had begun.

The lake covers eighty-six square miles in four Missouri counties, and the serpentine shoreline runs for some thirteen hundred miles. The main channel is 129 miles long, and at one point the lake is more than three miles wide. Nowadays the main channel is often choked with boat traffic, but there are an additional sixty miles of tributary waters.

Stalled by World War II, development of the area was slow at first. But because of its location almost equi-distant from the metropolises of Kansas City and St. Louis, the lake soon became a popular getaway, particularly for fishermen. Gradually they began to bring their families, and within a few decades the lake's accessibility made it popular throughout the Midwest.

Now the lakeshore is crowded by private homes, ranging from rough cabins to plush palaces, and by resorts of all stripes, from world-class to fishing camps. Union Electric sprays the shoreline to control mosquitoes. The lake is stocked every year with game fish from the hatchery operated by the power company in cooperation with the Missouri Department of Conservation.

The interesting free tour of Bagnell Dam is almost nostalgic, for much of the equipment originally installed in 1931 is still in use today. Although bypassed now by a new multilane highway, Business Route 54 still carries traffic across the dam. Excursion boats offer sightseeing trips on the lake itself, and there are three public launch ramps for your own boat. (Two are located in the Lake of the Ozarks State Park, and the other is on Hwy. 5 in Gravois Mills.)

(For tips on where to stay and what to see and do around the giant, dragon-shaped lake, be sure to write to the addresses given in the Practical Matters Chart following the chapter.)

Two Missouri state parks at Lake of the Ozarks offer an excellent introduction to the northern Ozarks—both above ground and underground.

Lake of the Ozarks State Park

Originally established by the National Park Service in the mid-1930s following the creation of the lake, the park was turned over to Missouri in 1946. The largest in the Missouri state park system, Lake of the Ozarks State Park sprawls over 17,087 acres and most of the Grand Glaize arm of the lake. Easiest access is from Hwy. 54 north of Camdenton. Prominent signs mark the entrance. The term "glaize," as used in this area, is a corrupted abbreviation of *au glaise*, a French phrase meaning "at/to the clay," an apt description of the red soil in the area.

So huge and varied is Lake of the Ozarks State Park that it offers something for everyone. Approximately 230 tent and trailer campsites, both basic and improved, are available to campers year-round. Some of the campsites are reserveable in advance, and a few are designed for the convenience of the handicapped. Facilities at the camping area include a dumping station, modern rest rooms, a laundry, and a store. An Indian thong tree is located near the amphitheater at the campgrounds in Area Three (inquire at the park office for assistance in finding the tree). The park also offers two free swimming beaches with bathhouses and shady picnic areas. Rental boats are available, as are paved boat-launching ramps.

For a look at geology and the delicate ecosystem that exists below ground, tour the park's Ozark Caverns. Missouri, the "Cave State," leads all other states in the number of known caves, with more than five thousand. Since caves are such common geological features in most parts of the Ozarks, visitors to the region should arrange to tour at least one of them.

Picnic sites are available on the cave grounds, as is the entrance to Coakley Hollow Trail, a one-mile self-guided interpretive trail on an easy-walking boardwalk that provides a glimpse into the varied habitats of the Ozarks—a glade, a fen, a spring branch, and a dam and mill site. Wildflowers are often there in profusion. (See the Practical Matters Chart for information on how to obtain brochures about both the trail and the cavern.)

Other hiking and horseback trails wind through the enormous park, ranging in length from one-half mile to six miles and lead

Many visitors are introduced to the Ozarks at the Lake of the Ozarks on the northern edge of the region. Because the shoreline is in private ownership, this lake is much more highly developed than most others in the Ozarks. (Courtesy of Missouri Division of Tourism)

At Lake of the Ozarks State Park, a log cabin built by the Civilian Conservation Corps (CCC) in the 1930s is still in use and in fine shape.

through rugged forests and ravines, along towering bluffs overlooking the lake, and through sunny glades. One trail, two miles long, bears the colorful name of Squaw's Revenge. Trail rides are offered for a nominal charge at the park stables. During the summer months, the park naturalist leads guided nature hikes and presents evening programs on topics such as wildflowers, caves, birds, astronomy, and history.

A special treat is the self-guiding aquatic trail for boaters. Marked by buoys, the trail offers glimpses of such historical sites as a logging chute, the remains of reefs from the ancient sea that once covered this area, and a geological curiosity called a "slice arch."

The park is also home to an official "wild area." Established in 1978, the Missouri Wild Area System was partially modeled after the National Wilderness Preservation system. Wild areas are protected for the benefits they provide for hiking and backpacking as well as outdoor classrooms for environmental education and as increasingly important reservoirs of scientific information.

Prominent in the Lake of the Ozarks State Park are monuments to the Great Depression—in the form of WPA-built structures and buildings. The Works Progress Administration spent almost 1.5 million dollars "improving" and landscaping this park. Strongly evoking a sense of the past, the surviving structures are cultural treasures recently placed on the National Historic Register. Watch for the rustic log and stone structures throughout the park and for the rock "check dams," built to control erosion in roadside ditches near the main entrance.

In the Neighborhood of "The Lake"

Although the development near the dam is locally intense, it does not extend far into the countryside. As is the case throughout the Ozarks, once the visitor is a mile from the congested area, he is once again in the old Ozarks. History can be seen and visited.

For example, there is the Camden County Museum at Linn Creek (the new town site) near the junction of Hwy. 54 and Road V. In its archives are the cemetery records of all the graves in Camden County, including those moved as a result of inundation by the Lake of the Ozarks. Six rooms of exhibits at the museum depict the history of the area. In the weaving room, visitors may watch rugs being woven on a handmade loom. In other rooms they may visit a turn-of-the-century schoolroom, a blacksmith's forge, an exhibit of the tools and vehicles used by pioneer families, an 1853 post office, and more.

Because of recent work to stabilize the ruins of Ha Ha Tonka Castle at Ha Ha Tonka State Park near Camdenton, Missouri, the remains of the castle now more nearly resemble a movie set than they do "ruins." The physical setting of the park, however, is still outstanding and no visitor to the Lake of the Ozarks region should miss it.

Castle in the Air

Rearing high into the air atop a towering Niangua River bluff known as Deer Leap Hill, the ruins of a "castle" form the centerpiece of Ha Ha Tonka State Park. About four miles southwest of Camdenton via Hwy. 54 to Road D, the park encompasses 2,507 acres on the Niangua arm of the Lake of the Ozarks. It is a rich mixture of natural beauty, geological oddity, romantic history, and abiding mystery. The most significant natural and manmade features are concentrated in a 750-acre area adjacent to the lake and its confluence with Ha Ha Tonka Spring, one of Missouri's largest. The spring issues approximately forty-eight million gallons of water a day.

Although experts view it as probable folklore, Ha Ha Tonka is said to be an old Osage Indian name for this area—Laughing Water. Several groups of Osages held tribal gatherings at the spring. French fur trappers floating the Osage and Niangua rivers also knew of Big Spring, as they called it. In the early 1800s Daniel and Nathan Boone trapped beaver on Ha Ha Tonka Lake. In 1806 President Thomas Jefferson dispatched a message to the Osage Indians assembled at "Big Spring on the Niangua River," informing them of the Louisiana Purchase. The first permanent white residence in the area was established in 1830 by a man named Garland, who constructed a gristmill.

But the mill was only a front. Garland was apparently a ringleader for a band of criminals responsible for many crimes, even robbery and murder, but their main activity was the counterfeiting of U.S., Canadian, and Mexican money. The counterfeiters used several local caves as workshops for their trade—and put so much phony money in circulation that the area was called "Bank Branch" and "Bank of Niangua." It is said that the widow of one of the "bank directors," enraged because her husband had been denied his share of the profits, aided local law enforcement in bringing about the downfall of the criminal element. Garland's mill was destroyed, but sometime later was rebuilt by an honest miller who did a thriving business.

Formed as a vigilante group to combat the counterfeiters, horse thieves, and cattle rustlers, the "Slickers," made up of townspeople and farmers, made it their business to "slick" with hickory switches all suspected lawbreakers. But thieves and counterfeiters reportedly managed to join the organization and gave it a bad name. The "Anti-Slickers" were organized to combat the desperadoes, and war broke out between the two factions. Terror reigned from 1841 to 1845: murders, shootings from ambush, public whippings, night rides, raids, indictments, and trials were common. Nine persons lost their lives, and much blood was shed before the trouble ended.

The first post office, known as Gunter's Big Spring and later just

Gunter, was established in 1872 and operated until 1937. The native-stone building also served as a general store; it still stands in the park. In 1895 the name was changed officially to Ha Ha Tonka (earlier records and historians spelled it Hahatonka).

Around the turn of the century, a prominent Kansas City business-man, Robert McClure Snyder, visited the area. Enthralled by the rugged grandeur of the area, he bought twenty-five hundred acres and dreamed of building a private retreat that would rival European-style castles. To ensure authentic construction techniques, he imported stonemasons from Scotland and a European supervisor. The mansion was to have sixty rooms grouped on three floors, all of which opened to a central hall rising three and a half stories to a skylight. Besides guest rooms with fireplaces, there were smoking rooms, bil-liard rooms, and banquet rooms.

Other buildings on the estate included a similar stone carriage house, an eighty-foot-high matching water tower (into which water was pumped from the spring five hundred feet below), and nine greenhouses. Construction began in 1905 with stone and timber taken from the immediate vicinity. Sandstone was quarried nearby and transported to the site by a mule-drawn wagon on a miniature railroad. Oak and walnut timber, cut on the property, went into the woodwork and polished floors.

But for Snyder, the castle remained only a dream. One of the first car owners in Kansas City, he was killed in an automobile accident in 1906 when his chauffeur attempted to miss a child who had run into the street. The mansion remained unfinished until 1922, when Snyder's sons completed the upper floors and entertained guests from Kansas City and Columbia.

There followed years of adversity while the Snyder family fought to keep the castlelike mansion in the family and waged a legal battle against Union Electric, the builders of Bagnell Dam, because the wa-ters of the Lake of the Ozarks were encroaching upon the natural spring-fed lake at the foot of Ha Ha Tonka cliff. In 1937 the family leased the castle for operation as a vacation lodge. For a time rental cottages stood along the spring branch. A restaurant served giant crayfish that had been raised in cages in the cold spring water. But in 1942 sparks from one of the mansion's many fireplaces ignited the roof. Within hours the castle was gutted by a spectacular windswept fire, as was the stable. All that remained were the stark devastated outside walls that still brood on the edge of the cliff.

In 1978 the State of Missouri purchased the estate and opened it to the public as a state park. In 1990 the stone ruins of the mansion were "stabilized" by stonemasons for safety's sake. Unfortunately, the work rendered them artificial-looking, almost like a movie set. At that time only the ruins of the carriage house and the water tower appeared "real." But because of the castle's romantic history and the magnificent natural setting, a visit to Ha Ha Tonka is almost mandatory for visitors to the Lake of the Ozarks.

And there are other ruins at Ha Ha Tonka State Park—natural ruins. Geologically, the area is a classic example of karst topography, characterized by sinkholes, caves, underground streams, large springs, and natural bridges. In the park are the remnants of one immense cavern system. A natural bridge served as the only road access to the castle until 1979. Eight caves have been discovered in the park so far, including Counterfeiter's Cave and Robber's Cave, which were used by the 1830s-era criminals. Another remarkable feature is the Colosseum, an expansive theaterlike pit at the southern mouth of the natural bridge. Local legend has it that the Indians used it for tribal meetings and that, later, church revivals were held there.

The park terrain also demonstrates the transition area between the prairie landscape farther west and the rugged forested hills to the east. Several hiking trails wind through the park; a map is available at the parking lot. The trail leading from the parking area to the castle is accessible to the handicapped and features a developed overlook from which most of the natural and cultural features of Ha Ha Tonka State Park can be viewed, including the chasm.

Ha Ha Tonka State Park is also accessible to boaters from the Lake of the Ozarks.

Heading north from Camdenton, Hwy. 5 traverses lake country, crossing the lake twice and offering excellent views along the way. A few miles out of Camdenton is the turnoff on Thunder Mountain to Bridal Cave.

Bridal Cave

Not only does Missouri lead the nation in the number of known wild caves, but it is also first in the number of show caves, with thirty-one open for tours. They are also common in the Arkansas portion of the region. In fact, caves are so numerous in the Ozarks that they form the rocky skeleton of the hills. Nowhere else are you more aware of the great age of the region than in the caves—some of which were formed before the plateau was uplifted and eroded. To fully appreciate the staggering age of the Ozarks, stand in a cave and realize that the spot was once solid rock.

Over the years, Ozarks caves have had a multitude of uses. They have been hiding places and dens for animals dating back to the Ice Ages—saber-toothed tigers, mastodons, sloths and many others. Native Americans used them long before the first European settlers

At Bridal Cave, the Pipe Organ formation in the Bridal Chapel is twenty-five feet tall and over sixty feet in circumference. It requires from thirty to a hundred years for one cubic inch of onyx to form. Visible in the right foreground is the Altar. The color of these onyx formations is breathtaking. (Photo Courtesy of Bridal Cave)

arrived on this continent. In more recent times, they have been hide-outs for outlaws, field hospitals during the Civil War, livestock pens, machine sheds, produce lockers, trash dumps, beer gardens, mush-room farms, ballrooms, warehouses, fallout shelters, meeting sites, and homes.

One of the most popular of the show caves is Bridal Cave, two miles north of Camdenton on Hwy. 5, then 1.5 miles on blacktopped Lake Road 5-88. The cave may also be reached by boat; free docking facili-ties are at the 10.5 mile marker on the Big Niangua arm of the Lake of the Ozarks.

New areas of the cave were opened to the public in 1990, including "Mystery Lake," doubling the length of the tour. The cave is open daily year around except for Christmas and Thanksgiving. Printed tour guides are available in French, German, Spanish, and Japanese. A nature trail is also accessible from Thunder Mountain, site of the cave.

There are several other developed caves in the Lake of the Ozarks area (see the Practical Matters Chart following this chapter).

Just beyond Bridal Cave, watch on your left for Lake Road 5-87. Three-tenths of a mile from Hwy. 5 is a large rustic sign marking the entrance to a trail that circles around four Indian thong trees. Smaller signs point the way from one thong tree to the next on the trail, which loops a short distance into the woods.

Back on Hwy. 5, be sure to notice the Hurricane Deck bridge across the Osage arm of the lake. Originally a toll bridge charging forty cents for a car and driver and a nickel each for passengers, the bridge was awarded first prize by the American Institute of Steel Construction in 1936 as the most beautiful medium-sized steel span erected that year. The unique moniker, *Hurricane Deck* derives from a great bluff above the Osage channel of the Lake of the Ozarks, and is suggestive of the strong wind that sometimes sweeps the edge of the bluff.

At the little town of Laurie is a prominent junction with Road O. Right on O for about a mile is the Shrine of St. Patrick, completed in 1863 by a group of Irish immigrants from County Farmaraugh and led by one Thomas Fitzpatrick, with some help from a non-Catholic neighbor. The native stone for the walls of the church came from a nearby quarry by oxen. The mortar used to set the stones was made on the grounds from area limestone. Trees from the surrounding forest provided the wood for the rafters, sheeting, shingles, window frames and sashes, the door and door frame, and the altar. The split-log pews rested originally on an earthen floor, and it was two decades before the interior was finished. The last mass at the church was in 1952, when a larger church became necessary. In 1980 St. Patrick's was placed on the National Register of Historic Places.

For a worthwhile side trip, follow Hwy. 5 farther north to the little town of Versailles (pronounced Ver-SAILS), established in 1835. In 1858 the Missouri Pacific Railroad reached the northern portion of the county, and after the Civil War large numbers of Swiss and German families, many of them Mennonites, opened farms in the prairie uplands. Versailles is home to two historic buildings on the National Historic Register—the striking, brick Morgan County Courthouse, located in the center of the square, and a turn-of-the-century hotel. The Morgan County Historical Museum, housed in the two hotel buildings, built in 1877 and 1884 to replace a log inn that the Martin family had operated as a hotel since 1853, consists of twenty-eight rooms filled with antiques. A large community of Amish and Mennonites still live in the Versailles area.

In addition to the Lake of the Ozarks, lakes Pomme de Terre, on the Pomme de Terre River, and Stockton, on the Sac, have added so much water—with so much potential for fun and scenery—that the area earns its title of the Inland Coast. With the three lakes' combined shorelines of *thousands* of miles, the first-time visitor is likely to be bewildered by so much to choose from.

"Potato Lake"

A Butterfield relay station was at Hermitage, about six miles west of Hwy. 65 on Hwy. 54. From Versailles, you can turn west on Hwy. 52 to Cole Camp, then south on Hwy. 65. From Camdenton, take Hwy. 54 west to Hermitage. There, on the lawn of Hickory County's 1896 courthouse of red brick with a white cupola, several big old trees shade a placard marking the spot.

Hickory County was named for "Old Hickory" himself, President Andrew Jackson. From 1819 to 1832 the Kickapoo Indian Reservation was west of the Pomme de Terre River in the county. An Indian quarry, mounds, and campsites have been found.

It is thought that the French named the river "apple of the earth" for the potatolike plant they saw the Indians eating, probably the potato bean (*Apios tuberosa*). Settlers from Tennessee and Kentucky came in the late 1820s. Hermitage, the centrally located county seat on the Pomme de Terre River, was laid out in 1846-47 and named for Andrew Jackson's home in Tennessee. At Bone Spring near Avery on Pomme de Terre River numerous mastodon bones were found in the late 1830s and early 1840s. Zinc was mined here in the 1890s.

On the courthouse lawn at Hermitage is a stone jail built in 1870-71. Prisoners were chained to iron rings fastened to the floor. The stone

This exhibit at Ha Ha Tonka solves the mystery of how the stone for the castle was brought up the steep hill from the quarry site on the property. The carts were drawn by mules.

The "stony lonesome" jail at Hermitage, Missouri, now near Lake Pomme de Terre on the western edge of the Ozarks. The interiors of such jails were abysmal places to spend time, but many have been replaced only in the past few years.

blocks are "cotton rock," three to seven feet long and twenty-two inches wide. Two steel balls were placed between stones to add strength to the walls. Twenty-one feet square, the building originally had a second story; steel cells were installed in 1899.

Just south of Hermitage via Hwy. 254 to Hwy. 64 is Lake Pomme de Terre, popular with anglers. If you are camping, there are ten Corps of Engineers campgrounds and a state park to choose from. The lake is surrounded by four thousand acres of public land for hunting and other outdoor uses including two hiking trails. Below the earth-and-rockfill embankment that forms the dam, the Pomme de Terre River is popular for both fishing and canoeing.

There are several excellent swimming beaches, boat launching ramps, hiking trails, picnic areas with playgrounds, and tennis courts, all available free of charge. There is a bowling alley, a nine-hole golf course, and a mini-golf course. Canoes may be rented to float the river. Four marinas serving the lake offer boats and motors for rent. Those holding Golden Age Passports receive a discount on camping fees in Corps of Engineers public use areas, and the Missouri State Parks offer a Senior Citizen Discount. There is a visitor's center at the east end of the dam.

The terrain at Lake Pomme de Terre is characteristic of the rolling Springfield Plateau. In presettlement times, much of the land was covered by savannas where the great tall-grass prairies of the west intermingled with the Ozarks forests of the east. Widely spaced groves of native post oak and eastern red cedar, with ground cover of luxuriant prairie grasses and wildflowers, created a parklike appearance. Natural fires and grazing by bison and elk helped maintain the savanna. Today, much of the state park is covered with thick oak-hickory forests, but some savanna remains. The area is very rural; Hickory County claims not to have a single traffic signal. It is still possible to rent a room at a motel or resort for as little as twenty-five dollars a night for two people.

From Hermitage, head south on Hwy. 83, which roughly traces the route of the Butterfield Stage south to Bolivar. There is a stage stop marker at Elkton. Hwy. 83 is also the scenic route between the Pomme de Terre area and Stockton—much more pleasant than "Bloody 13" (Hwy. 13), and its heavy, dangerous traffic. Be aware, however, that there are few gas stations or other tourist services on Hwy. 83.

The interesting thing about traveling in the area of Pomme de Terre and Stockton Lakes is that you never know what kind of view is going to greet you around the next curve or over the next hill or ridge. It may be an arm of one of the lakes or a typical prairie vista—or the encroaching Ozark hills.

A Stop on the Underground Railroad

At the junction of Hwys. 83 and 32, turn west on Hwy. 32, through Fair Play, to Stockton Lake, famous throughout Missouri for its excellent sailing, thanks to the prevailing southwest winds sweeping across the lake. Stockton is a "new" lake on the Sac River, first filled to normal operating pool level in December 1971. Considerably larger than Lake Pomme de Terre with 298 miles of shoreline and almost twenty-five thousand acres of water, Stockton is another Corps of Engineers impoundment.

South of Hwy. 32, via Hwys. 123 and 215, is Stockton State Park, site of a large, clean campground, a motel, a restaurant, and a marina filled with sailboats. Several Corps of Engineers campgrounds also dot the shoreline (see chart).

Platted in 1841, Greenfield, at the junction of Hwys. 39 and 160 (turn at the sign, "Business District," to reach the square), is a town of tree-lined avenues, stately old houses, and antique shops prominent in the business district. It is said to have one of the finest genealogical reference libraries in Missouri.

The museum on the square opened for business as the Washington Hotel in 1879, and has been the home of various social activities. Built by the Washington Lodge of the Masonic Order to fill the town's need for a good hotel, it is now furnished with items dating prior to the Civil War, relics of that war, antique tools, old musical instruments, a portrait of Belle Starr, and an authentic Ku Klux Klan robe and hood.

The area beneath the hotel, honeycombed with caves, was reportedly a station of the Underground Railroad during the time when slaves from the South were struggling to find freedom.

Down the street from the venerable hotel is an opera house (now the community theater) and an elderly variety store. The red brick courthouse shares its space with a bandstand, and both are flanked by several brick buildings with fancy facades.

West of Greenfield about twenty-five miles on Hwy. 160 is Lamar, the birthplace of President Harry Truman.

Ozarks Black Gold

Another interesting side trip from Stockton Lake is the town of Stockton, at the junction of Hwys. 32 and 39, seat of Cedar County. The first settlers in the area located two miles east of the present Stockton, where a big hollow sycamore afforded partial shelter. At the city park is a spring, which issues from a cave underlying the town.

Furnishing troops to both sides, Cedar County was torn by violence during the Civil War and little of Stockton remained intact. Confederate general Joseph Shelby routed a Federal garrison and burned the courthouse on October 5, 1863. The present courthouse was dedicated in 1940.

The access to the Stockton Lake dam is east of Stockton on Hwy. 32. The access road goes across the dam and offers a stunning view of the lake from one side of the road and the surrounding countryside on the other. At the dam are the bedrock cores that were drilled during construction of the dam. The rock is estimated to be about 450,000,000 years old.

Stockton is the home of Hammons Products Company, the world's largest processor of American black walnuts, founded in 1946 by Ralph Hammons. Hammons Products still furnishes hullers for placement at small country stores or gas stations where there is a good supply of nuts. It is not uncommon in the fall months to see lines of pickups loaded with nuts waiting to be hulled on the spot. The hulled nuts are later collected by trucks.

Gathering and selling black walnuts has a long tradition in the Ozarks—part of the cultural heritage, much like picking greens and gathering herbs. Early settlers in the Ozarks also valued the black walnut trees for the rich brown dye obtained from the green hulls of the nuts, and the wood is also extremely valuable. First gathered for home use, walnuts were once bartered for groceries by Ozarks farm wives. Eventually companies were formed that ran scheduled truck routes for the collection of walnut kernels from grocers and produce dealers.

In Depression days, rural people also filled the demand for hand-cracked, or "country run" walnuts: farm families often occupied the long fall and winter evenings by cracking walnuts gathered from their farms. Sometimes, the family could even earn enough money for Christmas presents or for the children's school supplies. But this practice was curtailed by the Federal Pure Food laws and minimum wage laws of the 1930s. Gradually the cottage industry was discontinued and hand-cracking operations were carried out in central cracking plants using farm women for the tedious task of separating the kernels from the shells.

The shell of the Eastern Black Walnut, after processing to one of various sizes and consistencies, has many industrial uses, including "sand" blasting. Unlike sand, the shells do not pit the surface being cleaned. During the renovation of the Statue of Liberty, six trailer truckloads of ground walnut shells from the Ozarks were sent to New York.

From Stockton, head east on Hwy. 32 to surprising Bolivar, home of a symphony, an art gallery, and a great deal of living history.

Practical Matters

Chapter 2 — The "Inland Coast"

Checking Out	A Sampling	Phone
Lodging	Rock Harbor Resort, Rt. 3 Box 350, Sunrise Beach MO 65079;	(314) 374-5586
	Bass Point Resort, Rt. 1 Box 127, Sunrise Beach MO 65079;	(314) 374-5205
	Inn at Grand Glaize, P.O. Box 969 (Hwy. 54, 1/4 mile west of the Grand Glaize Bridge) Osage Beach MO 65065;	(800) 348-4731
	Stockton State Park Inn, Stockton MO;	(417) 276-5329
	Russ T Lake Shore Resort, Rt. 1, Box 335, Wheatland MO 65779	(417) 282-6241
Bed & Breakfasts	Ozark Mountain Country Bed & Breakfast (Reservation Service for the area), Box 295, Branson MO 65616	(417) 334-4720 or (417) 334-5077 or (800) 321-8594
Campgrounds	Lake of the Ozarks State Park, P.O. Box C, Kaiser MO 65047;	(314) 348-2694
	Harwood's Fun Valley, Rt 1, Box 1525, Osage Beach MO 65065;	(314) 348-2410
	Der Vater's Edge RV Park, Rt 1, Box 42, Camdenton MO 65020;	(314) 346-5230
	Corps of Engineers Campgrounds at Lakes Stockton and Pomme de Terre (see Where to Write);	
	Pomme de Terre State Park, Hermitage MO;	(417) 745-6909
	Western Trails, Hwy 64B, Pittsburg MO;	(417) 852-4249
	Stockton State Park, Stockton MO	(417) 276-4259
Restaurants	Breakfast or Dinner Cruises on the Lake, Casino Pier, 100 yards west of Bagnell Dam;	(314) 365-2020
	Kenny's Kountry Pines, 245 W. Hwy. 54, Camdenton MO;	(314) 346-4618
	Quinns Restaurant, in the Holiday Inn, Lake Ozark MO;	(314) 365-2334 Ext. 591
	Stockton State Park Dining Lodge, Stockton	(417) 276-4600
Main Historical Attractions	Miller County Historical Society Museum, Hwys. 52 & 17, Tuscumbia MO;	(314) 369-2317
	Morgan County Historical Museum, 210 N. Monroe, Versailles MO;	(314) 378-5556
	Ha Ha Tonka State Park, Rt. 1 Box 658, Camdenton MO 65020;	(314) 346-2986
	Camden County Museum, Hwy. 54 and V, Linn Creek MO;	(314) 346-7191
	Kelsey's Antique Car Museum, Hwy. 54, 1 Mile East of Camdenton Square;	(314) 346-2506
	Stone Jail, Courthouse Lawn, Hermitage MO;	
	Greenfield Museum and Opera House, Greenfield MO	

Checking Out	A Sampling	Phone
Other Attractions	Lee Mace's Ozark Opry, 1/2 mile north Jct. Hwys. 54 and 42, Osage Beach MO;	(314) 348-2270
	Bridal Cave, Hwy. 5 North, Camdenton MO;	(314) 346-2676
	Fantasy World Caverns, Hwy. 54, 1/4 So. of Jct. Hwy. 52, Lake Ozark MO;	(314) 392-2115
	Indian Burial Cave, Osage Beach MO;	(314) 348-2207
	Jacob's Cave, Handicapped Accessible, Versailles MO;	(314) 378-4374
	Tour of Bagnell Dam;	
	Stockton Cheese, Hwy. 32, Stockton MO;	(417) 276-3618
	Missouri Dandy Pantry, 212 Hammons Drive East, Stockton MO 65785	
Outdoor Recreation	Indian Rock Golf Club, Laurie MO;	(314) 372-3023
	Casino Pier, Excursion Boats, Bus. Rt. 54, Lake Ozark MO. Handicapped Accessible;	(314) 365-2020
	Hiking: Ha Ha Tonka State Park and Lake of the Ozarks State Park (see above);	
	Fishing, Boating, Swimming: Lake of the Ozarks State Park as well as area resorts and marinas;	
	Pomme de Terre Golf Club, 4.5 mi. so. of Wheatland on Hwy. 83, then left on Road 270;	(417) 282-6544
	Nemo Landing, HC 77, Box 724, Pittsburg MO 65724; (Lake Pomme de Terre)	(417) 993-5160
	Oreans Trail Marina, Rt. 3, Stockton MO 65785 (Stockton Lake)	(417) 276-5161
Where to Write for More Details	Lake Area Chamber of Commerce, P.O. Box 193, Osage Beach MO 65065;	(314) 348-2730
	Camdenton Area Chamber of Commerce, P.O. Box 1375, Ryland Center, Camdenton MO 65020;	(314) 346-2227
	Greater Lake of the Ozarks Visitors Bureau, P.O. Box 98, Lake Ozark MO 65049;	(314) 365-3371 or (800) 325-0213
	Versailles Chamber of Commerce, Versailles MO 65084;	(314) 378-4634
	Wildlife Code & Fishing Regulations: Mo. Dept. of Conservation, P.O. Box 180, Jefferson City MO 65101;	
	Lake Pomme de Terre: Corps of Engineers, Hermitage MO 65668;	(417) 745-6411
	Pomme de Terre Lake League, P.O. Box 36, Hermitage MO 65668;	(417) 645-6432
	Stockton Lake: Corps of Engineers, P.O. Box 610, Stockton MO 65785;	(417) 276-3113
	Stockton Lake Association, P.O. Box 345, Stockton MO 65785;	
	Stockton Area Chamber of Commerce, P.O. Box 410, Stockton MO 65785	(417) 276-5213

CHAPTER 3

The Land of the Big Red Apple

Because the town of Bolivar (pronounced BALL-uh-vur) developed along the Overland stage route, its streets are "offset approximately 22 degrees to the west." The stage stopped for meals and fresh horses at the Franklin Hotel, the site now marked by a placard behind the library on the courthouse square. The town was occupied by troops of one side or the other during most of the Civil War. (The nearby town with the curious name of Humansville was settled by James Human in 1834.)

On July 5, 1948, a typical July day in Southwest Missouri when air-conditioning was still a longed-for rarity, President Harry Truman and Venezuela's president Romulo Gallegos and party came to Bolivar to dedicate the South American country's gift to the town. Venezuela had donated and erected a statue of Simon Bolivar to commemorate the name of the liberator of their country and to thank this Ozarks city for perpetuating his name.

Since air travel was still not too popular, the two presidents traveled from Washington, D.C., in a special Pullman car with an attached Fred Harvey diner. From St. Louis the Frisco railroad hooked their car to a fast passenger train. For the last thirty-five miles from Springfield to Bolivar, the Frisco furnished a new engine and a select crew. In Bolivar the streets from the Frisco Depot to the courthouse square were jammed by eager spectators.

For the ceremonial unveiling of the statue, President Truman gave the formal address. Venezuela's president replied in Spanish, then pulled a lanyard to drop the shroud covering the statue of Simon

Bolivar. Since there was no facility for turning the VIPs' steam locomotive around in Bolivar, their return trip to Springfield on the
branch line was made in reverse.

Actually Bolivar was named after a town in Tennessee. The pioneers who settled the original Bolivar in Tennessee were impressed
by the exploits of the Venezuelan patriot, who was much in the news
at the time, so they called their new home after him. Immigrants from
that Bolivar to the Ozarks brought the name with them. The statue—
and a time capsule—are located in a small park south through town
on Hwy. 83 and Business Rte. 13.

1841/1903 North Ward School/Museum

A few blocks north of the square, at Locust and Main (two blocks
north of the Polk County Bank on the square, which is visible from
Hwy. 83) is an unusually worthwhile museum, once a school. Built on
a shoestring in 1903, the North Ward school building salvaged and
incorporated the usable portions of a previous school erected on the
site in 1841—including old arch-type windows. But since there were
not enough of the old windows to do the whole job, "modern" sash
windows were used in about half of it; this has led some to believe that
the building was constructed in two different time periods.

The Polk County Historical Society raised the money to restore and
equip the building as a museum. Three floors of fascinating historical
artifacts now include a barber shop, a Model-T Ford, a fringed surrey,
and a veterans' room. The two-story log cabin next door was built in
1867; it was moved to this site and furnished with primitives as part of
the museum complex.

A few blocks south of the North Ward Museum, just off the square,
is another interesting museum in the old jail building.

1880 Jail Museum

At 214 South Main, two blocks south of the Polk County Bank on
the square, the Old Jail was built about 1880 and used for that purpose until 1978. Made of locally handmade bricks, the building now
contains a variety of donated historical items, including Indian artifacts and one of the last copies of a Southern newspaper printed on
wallpaper during the final days of the Civil War. (Paper became so
scarce in Arkansas during the war that some public records were used
to make Confederate ammunition.)

The two museums are open on alternate days.

Also in Bolivar is charming Dunnegan Memorial Park, north on
Main Street to West Forest and North Park Streets. Looking for all the
world like a photograph from a Victorian album, Dunnegan Park

boasts a rock bandstand beside a babbling brook. Strutting—and calling—peacocks roam the large park, while swans, ducks, and geese gossip and stroll near a large lagoon. Enormous shade trees cool the picnic grounds and several venerable shelterhouses. Nearby are playgrounds, winding paths that invite a walk into the deep shade and across footbridges over the stream. There is so *much* shade in this old park that moss grows on the roofs of several of the buildings, as though they were thatched with green velvet.

From Bolivar, head east on Hwy. 32 through formerly fruit-growing country to the home of the Big Red Apple.

"The Magnetic City"

Founded in 1849 as the seat of newly organized Laclede County, Lebanon was named for Lebanon, Tennessee. The streets are named for U.S. presidents in the same order in which they served. During the Civil War, Lebanon gained strategic importance through its location on the Military Road between St. Louis and Springfield, the line of march for both armies. Occupied alternately by the North and the South, the town's economy was badly disrupted. When the railroad came by in 1868, the town denied it free land for a depot, which it then located a mile from the village.

Lebanon picked itself up and moved to the new site; the original location became "Old Town." In *The Calling of Dan Matthews*, his novel set in and around the town, Harold Bell Wright said the residents "left the beautiful, well-drained site chosen by those who cleared the wilderness and stretched themselves along the sacred right of way." It was in Lebanon, as pastor of the First Christian Church there from 1905 to 1907, that Harold Bell Wright began his literary career. Also recognizable in *The Calling of Dan Matthews*, which tells the story of the son of the main characters of *The Shepherd of the Hills*, is Brice village and Bennett's Mill, both once in nearby Bennett Spring State Park.

Lebanon gained early fame as the "Magnetic City." The iron pipes inserted into a deep well drilled in 1887 became strongly magnetized. A pocket knife that had been rubbed against the well pipe would pick up a nail, and a compass in the vicinity of the well was powerfully deflected within a radius of three feet.

Of course the water was not magnetic; the rocks through which the pipes passed were. (Magnetic surveys conducted by the Missouri Geological Survey in the 1930s and the 1960s identified several magnetic highs in the Ozarks—including one in the vicinity of Lebanon.) Nevertheless, during the health spa craze around the turn of the century, a resort developed around the "magnetic water." One of the largest resort hotels in the Ozarks, the Gasconade Hotel, was erected.

Many smaller vestiges of the past can be seen in the Ozarks by the observant traveler. This treasure is on the lawn of the historic jail building, now a museum, at Lebanon, Missouri.

In 1903 the local newspaper declared, "Years of test and experience have furnished abundant proof that the Magnetic water will afford relief for various ills to which human flesh is heir."

In the 1880s Lebanon boasted a Shakespeare Club that presented the bard's plays—and was a highlight of the social season. There was also an opera house where traveling dramatic companies often stopped for a week's engagement. As in many other Ozarks towns, Lebanon's band was a source of civic pride and was supported in 1926 by a city tax. The band had its own park and gave concerts weekly throughout the summer months.

Land of the Big Red Apple

In 1897 thirty million Laclede County apples sold for eighteen million dollars. Ozarks apples won prizes at exhibits and fairs all over the world. At the St. Louis World's Fair in 1904, they claimed blue ribbons and won for their exhibitor the title, "Apple King of the Ozarks."

The apple king, Absalom Nelson of Lebanon, and many others like him—at first the representatives of land companies and railroads interested in encouraging settlement—established huge orchards in the Ozarks, predominantly on the upland plateau areas such as that around Lebanon.

But by the second decade of the 1900s, an increasing number of fruit diseases and parasites made growing and spraying the apples prohibitively labor-intensive and expensive. Some of the trees were sacrificed when the second generation of Nelsons in Lebanon donated land for the new highway, Route 66, which Lebanon celebrated as the "Main Street of America." Gradually the orchards disappeared. Nothing now remains of them but the name of a housing development, "Orchard Hills," built on the site of an orchard.

Another Old Jail

On the corners of Second and Third Streets on Adams are two of Lebanon's historic attractions, the Bland statue and the Old Jail Museum. On the National Register of Historic Places, the jail was built in 1876; the sheriff's quarters were added in 1922. The building, constructed of locally made brick, now houses a museum displaying items of local history.

Several interesting side trips are close to Lebanon. West on Hwy. 64 is Bennett Spring State Park, one of the oldest such parks and site of beloved Bennett Spring.

As with all Ozarks springs, there is an Indian legend attached to Bennett. The Osage Indians believed they had been sent down from

Erected in 1902, the statue of Richard Parks Bland, on the southwest corner of the courthouse lawn in Lebanon, Missouri, commemorates the town's most distinguished citizen. In 1872 Bland was elected to Congress. He so distinguished himself that he was returned to office twelve times. Bland was called "Silver Dick" for his fight for unrestricted coinage of silver.

the stars to care for the "Sacred One," the earth. The spring, they believed, is the eye of the Sacred One.

Bennett Spring

Giant-but-peaceful Bennett Spring pours forth one hundred million gallons of water a day into the Niangua River. Settlers were quick to take advantage of that power; by the early 1840s James Brice had built a mill on the spring branch.

There were several mills here at different times, but none more successful than Peter Bennett's. Bennett was known for his generous donations of hundreds of bushels of grain and flour to needy families during the Civil War.

In such pleasant surroundings, customers did not mind waiting for their turn at the mill, even when they had to camp overnight. To pass the time, the campers would fish, hunt, or visit the mill store. A few days of rest at Bennett Spring became traditional. Trout were first introduced into the stream in 1900; when they thrived, a private trout hatchery was established which later became the basis of the state hatchery.

The village of Brice grew up around the mill, but the church, built in 1917, is all that is left of the town. The first land was purchased for the state park in 1924, but it was not developed until the Great Depression and the availability of Civilian Conservation Corps (CCC) labor. The company of CCC men who lived and worked at Bennett Spring was composed essentially of World War I veterans.

"Veteran Company 1772" of the CCC was organized at Fort Leavenworth, Kansas, on June 27, 1933, "198 strong, with men from all walks of life: school teachers, preachers, laborers (skilled and unskilled), farmers, clerks, salesmen and derelicts. These latter were soon eliminated because they could not take it . . . . It was during these days that the faint of heart dropped by the wayside."

A yearbook for the CCC company records that its men built ". . . an $8,000 dam, a $13,000 bridge, a $14,000 dining lodge, and six beautiful cabins, a store and post office building, shelter houses, roads and trails. During their stay in the park the veterans have stopped several fires that threatened park property. In June 1935 when a flood threatened to destroy the dam and hatchery and leave the new bridge in a dry channel, the men of Company 1772 worked continuously in rain and flood waters to save the property."

The "CCC boys" also renovated the old mill and constructed a second set of hatchery rearing pools. The rustic dining lodge they built first opened in February, 1938, and is still in use—growing more precious and valued with each passing year. Even if you are not a fisherman, try to visit Bennett Spring just to enjoy the spring and a trout dinner at the historic dining lodge. Be sure to notice the hand-worked copper chandeliers and the great stone fireplaces. The stone-arch bridge across the spring branch is another aesthetically pleasing CCC structure.

A ferry operated across the Niangua River until 1932; the Niangua River bridge on Hwy. 64 was built in 1931. The last mill on the spring branch burned in March 1944; the scars on nearby sycamores still bear witness to that sad event. Part of the mill foundation and the large square stones that supported the turbine are visible along the hatchery pools.

An excellent interpretive center at the park offers displays of Indian history and artifacts, the area's early settlers, and the CCC. There is a dramatic model explaining the functioning of springs and caves, and several beautiful dioramas about marine life in the spring as well as the flora and fauna of the area. One fascinating exhibit shows artifacts found by divers at the bottom of the spring. Also on display is machinery from the old mill at Brice.

Thanks to the large trout hatchery and its stocking of the spring branch—in addition to the lovely natural surroundings—Bennett Spring State Park is very popular with Missourians and their visitors. A large campground is here, as well as numerous housekeeping cabins and motel rooms. Canoers also revere the Niangua River and Osage Fork (of the Gasconade); canoe liveries line the road between Lebanon and the park.

Downtown Trout

East of Lebanon on I-44 is Waynesville, where Business Route 44 through town is a portion of Missouri Historic Highway Route 66. Be sure to notice the two contrasting courthouses on the main street in town. The old courthouse, 1904, is dwarfed by the new one, 1989, right beside it. Its ultramodern lines offer striking contrast to the red brick bell tower of the old building.

Drive north of Waynesville for a few miles on Hwy. 17, where the Gasconade River Valley yields glimpses of unusual buff-colored bluffs, and Roubidoux Creek paralleling the highway is wide and pretty. Both waterways were named by the French. *Gasconade* derives from Gascony, a province of France, while *Roubidoux* was the name of a family of French traders prominent in the state during settlement.

Now stocked with trout by the state, spring-fed Roubidoux Creek was a watering place for Indians on the Kickapoo Trace, forerunner of Route 66 and I-44. French explorer du Tisne traveled the Indian trail in 1719, and Cherokee Indians camped at the spring on their 1837 Trail of Tears removal to Oklahoma.

The Roubidoux wanders through the small town of Waynesville, which has built parks along its course; you can fish for trout within the city limits. Because fishing quality depends on the water level of the creek, however, the Department of Conservation recommends that visitors check with it or the Waynesville Chamber of Commerce before driving far to fish (see Practical Matters Chart at the end of this chapter).

Roubidoux Creek is a classic example of a *sinking stream*; that is, its waters actually flow underground for much of its course, then resurface at Roubidoux Spring.

Another Stagecoach Stop

Waynesville was on the route of the Burden and Woodson Stage Line, which held the contract for mail and passenger service between St. James and Springfield. The line owned six Concord coaches and made the run three times a week. Their stagecoach stop and tavern still stands in Waynesville and has been preserved and protected by the Old Stagecoach Stop Foundation there. The white, two-story building is prominently visible a half block to your left when you pass the new courthouse.

A preservation architect dates the tavern to about 1860. The Old Stagecoach Stop Foundation places the construction a little earlier— between 1854 and 1860. Originally the building was a log cabin, the site of an early post office. It is not certain whether two cabins were joined at some point or whether the original structure was a dogtrot cabin (that is, two separate rooms joined by a breezewaylike corridor). The foundation is fairly certain that the Old Stagecoach Stop served as the hospital for a Union fort overlooking Waynesville during the Civil War. And excavations under the building have unearthed two Federal uniform buttons, an 1867 nickel, bullets, and other period artifacts.

After the war, the building was a hotel, probably known as the Waynesville House. At one time it housed people from European countries, believed to be construction workers on the postwar expansion of the railroad. In 1894 Lewis and Eliza Black purchased the building, joined the two cabins, and over the original logs added weatherboarding painted white. The dogtrot disappeared inside. The Blacks served three meals a day and rented rooms, especially to the many customers brought to town by county court week. Church

Part spectacle and part religious ceremony, river baptisms were always well attended. This one took place about 1940 at Bennett Spring, Missouri. (Photo by Townsend Godsey)

Once a dogtrot log cabin dating to the middle 1800s, the Old Stagecoach Stop in Waynesville, Missouri—following its service as a stop on the stage line—was remodeled and updated several times over the years to serve as a hotel and as a hospital for Civil War soldiers. It is being restored to its appearance in the 1890s. (Courtesy of Old Stagecoach Stop Foundation)

people ate their Sunday dinners there and lounged on the long veranda of the white house.

The structure fell into disuse by the mid-1950s; in 1982, the building was condemned as a hazard. Reluctant to let it be demolished, citizens formed a nonprofit foundation in early 1983 to save the structure and restored the outside with the aid of a small matching grant from the Missouri Department of Natural Resources.

Once again the old building is in sound condition thanks to the efforts of the Old Stagecoach Foundation. The foundation has decided to restore the structure to its appearance in an 1890s-era photograph, but the work is slow and dependent upon the availability of funds. Plans for the future include displays of artifacts unearthed there and other museum pieces. In the meantime, research into its history continues. Interpretive tours are available by arrangement (see the Practical Matters Chart).

Prisoners of War in the Ozarks

Just south of Waynesville is Fort Leonard Wood, where for the past two or three generations hundreds of thousands of young people have received their first introductions to the Ozarks. In Pulaski County's Mark Twain National Forest, the fort was founded in 1940 as a World War II training and replacement center. During the war period it also served as a camp for German prisoners of war. By 1960, the fort was the nation's largest center for training U.S. Army Engineers.

Open to the public is a military museum that specializes in the World War II era. Building No. 1321 houses a "model" barracks that will be an experience in déjà vu for ex-GIs, and an education for their families. In another building are weapons and uniforms from World War II; nearby are displays of artillery pieces and a Sherman tank. There are life-size dioramas and historic artifacts to tell the story of military engineering from the time of Alexander the Great to the space era.

Since Fort Leonard Wood is an "open post," it is not necessary to check in with a gate guard. Do stop at the information center on your right just inside the gate, however, to pick up a map and directions to the museum. Admission is free, and Business Loop 44 leads straight from Waynesville into the post.

Then return to Lebanon and turn south on Hwy. 5 to Hartville—site of a Civil War battle and a Victorian mansion—and from there to Mansfield, the "Little House in the Ozarks," where Laura Ingalls Wilder wrote her famous "Little House" books. On the way, just south of Lebanon watch on your right for White Oak Pond, an example of an unusual natural lake formed in a sinkhole.

Representative of the many derelict general store buildings still to be seen in the region, this one is near Lebanon, Missouri. Once of vital importance to the isolated community because it was a long walk—or trip in a wagon—to any town, the stores were no longer necessary with the advent of good, paved roads and dependable automobiles. (Courtesy of Bittersweet, Inc.)

Practical Matters

Chapter 3 — Land of the Big Red Apple

Checking Out	A Sampling	Phone
Lodging	Colony Inn Motel; Hwy. 13 & T, Bolivar MO; Bennett Spring State Park, Lebanon MO; Fort Niangua River Resort, Rt. 16, Box 1020, Lebanon MO 65536	(417) 326-8004 (417) 523-4307 or (800) 334-6946 (417) 532-4377
Bed & Breakfasts	Eden Bed & Breakfast, Rt. 1, Box 76, Brighton MO 65617; Apple Orchard Bed & Breakfast, 1105 So. Lillian St., Bolivar MO 65613; Boggs Bed & Breakfast, 216 N. Wilson, Bolivar MO 65613	(417) 467-2820 (417) 326-5490 (417) 326-8052
Campgrounds	Bennett Spring State Park, Lebanon MO	(417) 532-4338
Restaurants	Western Sizzlin, Hwy. 13 & T, Bolivar MO; Bennett Spring State Park Dining Lodge; Stonegate Station, Hwys. 5 & 32, Lebanon MO; Sand Spring Resort & Restaurant, Hwy. 64, Lebanon MO	(417) 326-4949 (417) 532-4307 (417) 588-1387 (417) 532-5857
Main Historical Attractions	Old Jail Museum, 214 S. Main, Bolivar MO; North Ward Museum, Main & Locust, Bolivar MO; Old Stage Coach Stop on the Square, Waynesville MO (see Where to Write); Old Jail Museum and Richard Bland Statue, 262 N. Adams, Lebanon MO; Onyx Mountain Caverns, Rt. 2, Box 549, Newburg MO 65550	(417) 326-6850 (417) 326-6850 (314) 762-3341
Other Attractions	Dunnegan Gallery of Art, 511 N. Pike, Bolivar MO; Dunnegan Park, West Forest & N. Park, Bolivar MO; Simon Bolivar Statue, Neuhart Park, So. Springfield and E. College, Bolivar MO; Antiques & Flea Markets: N. Jefferson and W. Second Streets, Lebanon MO; Bennett Spring, Nature Center, Trout Hatchery, Bennett Spring State Park, Lebanon MO	 (417) 532-3925

Checking Out	A Sampling	Phone
Outdoor Recreation	Nine Hole Golf Course, W. Hwy. 32, Bolivar MO	(417) 326-6600
Where to Write for More Details	Wildlife Code & Trout Info: Missouri Dept. of Conservation, P.O. Box 180, Jefferson City MO 65101; Waynesville Chamber of Commerce, P.O. Box 6, Waynesville MO 65583; Old Stage Coach Stop Foundation, P.O. Drawer W, Waynesville MO 65583; Lebanon Area Chamber of Commerce, 321 South Jefferson, Lebanon MO 65536; Bolivar Area Chamber of Commerce, 454 S. Springfield, Bolivar MO 65613	 (314) 336-5121 (314) 774-5864 or (314) 435-6766 (417) 588-3256 (417) 326-4118

SECTION 2

Springfield Plateau

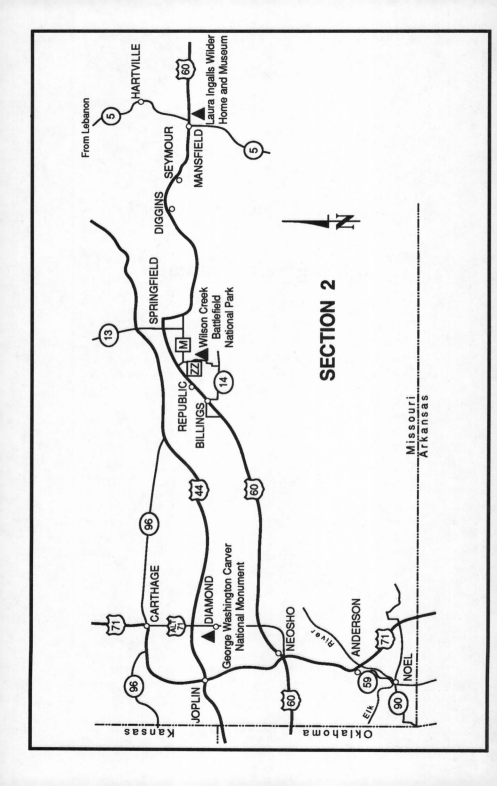

SECTION 2

CHAPTER 4

Overview: From Victorian Miners to the Amish

Almost from the beginning of white settlement in the Ozarks, a curious dichotomy has existed: a quiet conflict of new versus old. The region has always been remarkable for the persistence of long-held traditions in the face of change.

This is true even on the Springfield Plateau—the high ground between the watersheds of the Gasconade, which drains north into the Missouri River, and the White, which drains south and east into the Mississippi. Because of its more moderate terrain, the plateau area has always been more accessible and more trafficked and, therefore, on the leading edge of modernity in the Ozarks. But in spite of this— and the huge influx of newcomers to this area—it is still the Ozarks: rock-solid conservative, tenaciously clinging to the old values and concepts of morality. In a small town not far from Springfield, the third largest city in Missouri, the school board has consistently refused to allow dances to be held in the school building, a decision upheld by the courts.

Grass Roots Lead

Lead was discovered early in the Ozarks (see also Chapter 20). It is thought to be universally present throughout the region, albeit in varying amounts and qualities. The deposits range from the size of a garden pea or a walnut to veins several feet in thickness. They may be numerous or sparse in a given area.

Even early settlers made use of the lead, devising homemade smelters to make bullets and shot. As early as 1838 settlers discovered places where rain had eroded the surface, exposing lead at ground level or in the grass roots—lead that could be melted by wood-chip fires and molded into bullets. Even after fixed ammunition came into common use, settlers followed their old practice of digging the ore and smelting it in a seasoned hollow oak stump. In the days of muzzle-loading rifles, many of the pioneer hunters molded bullets from their own home supply of lead or from bars of lead purchased at the local trading centers.

Mining on a relatively large scale by companies formed for that purpose was done throughout the Ozarks, though with the exception of the Leadbelt in the eastern Ozarks (see Chapter 20), the Rush District in Marion County, Arkansas (see Chapter 12), and the Tri-State District in southwest Missouri, southeast Kansas, and northeast Oklahoma, it is likely that little profit was realized. The ore was difficult to obtain and prohibitively time-consuming, labor-intensive, and expensive to ship.

But where it was found to exist in great quantities, the age-old lure of instant riches brought prospectors and speculators. And when lead was in particular demand, as during the Civil War, or when the price of lead and zinc was high, as during the boom days of World War I, Ozarks mines were taken very seriously indeed.

The Tri-State District

The Ozarks' Tri-State Lead and Zinc Mining District extended over about 1,188 square miles: embracing Jasper and Newton counties in Missouri; Cherokee County, Kansas; and Ottawa County, Oklahoma. The terrain is rolling prairieland except along the rivers and creeks, where low hills attest to the power of water to change the landscape. The climate in winter is mild enough to permit mining throughout the year. The area is also sometimes called the Joplin District; almost from its beginning, Joplin, originally a mining camp, dominated the region. Its mushroom growth soon included wholesalers who supplied the other camps.

One of the earliest known explorers of the Ozarks, geologist Henry Rowe Schoolcraft, wrote of the lead in the area in 1819. He reported that he found good lead specimens in the creek banks of this "howling wilderness," as well as traces of shallow mining and crude log furnaces presumably used by Indians and hunters; lead was already a major product of trade in the Southwest. Schoolcraft himself mined some lead on the banks of local streams, smelted it in a shallow pit, its sides insulated with flat river stones, and molded bullets on the spot.

This scene was repeated many times over in the Tri-State Lead Mining District near Joplin, Missouri, in the late 1800s and early 1900s. (Courtesy of State Historical Society of Missouri)

This street scene in Carthage, Missouri, clearly shows the tracks of the trolley that linked the towns of the Tri-State District in the late 1800s. (Courtesy of State Historical Society of Missouri)

The mineral wealth of the Tri-State District was first tapped commercially around 1850. As the story is told, prospectors flooded into the area following the discovery—by a young slave digging for bait—of some heavy, cubed material his master identified as lead. Tales are told of how settlers digging for a well or a cellar also found quantities of lead and zinc.

Almost immediately professional miners immigrated into the area from other mining regions, especially the lead mines of the eastern Ozarks. And within a century, miners had extracted, processed, and sold a billion dollars worth of lead and zinc.

The zinc, however, was apparently at first an unknown entity: "a strange dark substance adhering to the lead ore." Under the unscientific refining methods of that period, this "blackjack" was thrown into the chat heaps. Lack of interest in the zinc may be partly attributed to its limited commercial use and consequent low price at that time. Tossed onto the waste piles, the accumulated zinc at Granby was used to construct a stockade for the protection of the women and children against the many local Civil War raids. Some of it was subsequently utilized by railroads for ballast and by counties for road building. It is estimated that ten thousand dollars worth of the material per mile was used on the chat-graveled roads around Joplin before it was realized that the foreign substance in the lead was zinc of a high quality.

A Poor Man's Camp

At first the lead ore, found from ten to seventy-five feet below the surface, was raised in buckets by windlass and crank, or by ox power. The shallowness of the deposits and the lack of mechanized competition enabled men with little or no capital to become mine operators. The region became known as "a poor man's camp." Sometimes wives and children assisted by washing dirt from the ore and sorting it by hand. Because there was no railroad, and transportation painstakingly slow and difficult, the mines developed slowly.

One method of transporting the lead to markets was to haul the smelted "pigs" in wagons to Spring River and Cowskin (Elk River), load them onto flatboats, float to the Grand River in Indian Territory, then to the Arkansas River, and on to New Orleans. Several operators shipped refined lead by horse- and ox-drawn wagons to Osceola, on the Osage River. From there it went by flatboat to St. Louis via the Osage and the Missouri.

Early Tri-State miners lighted their way underground with candles fastened to their caps with balls of clay. Small lard-oil lamps had replaced candles by 1900, and carbide mining lamps were in wide use ten years later. By 1940, electric cap lamps, powered by small batteries, had been universally adopted. The miners followed the veins—drilling, blasting with dynamite, picking and shoveling the ore into cars drawn by well-trained mules.

In recovering the lead and zinc from the rock, much chert and limestone was extracted, and this substance—called chat when crushed—was used widely as road surfacing material. (Piles of chat may still be seen throughout the Tri-State District.)

But when the Civil War erupted, the mining camps came under constant attack by both the Union and Confederate armies, eager to control the source of lead for munitions. Many mining camps were destroyed by war operations and guerrilla warfare. William Quantrill, the most famous of the guerrilla chieftains, cut a swath of ruin and destruction from Leadville Hollow in Missouri to Baxter Springs in Kansas.

When the war was over, the region was poised to expand and, despite the lack of efficient transportation for its products, rapidly resumed mining operations. Rail transportation first entered the district in 1870, and eventually spurs connected all the mining camps. Today, while the evidence of many camps has been otherwise obliterated, the weed-bound rail beds and tailings piles still testify to mining activity.

The Mining Camps

Eighty-one mining camps sprang up throughout the district. In his book, *Wilderness Bonanza,* historian Arrel Gibson points out, "Most of the villages and towns of southwest Missouri, southeast Kansas, and northeast Oklahoma owe their existence in the first place to the discovery of lead and zinc deposits in the vicinity of each." But where the deposits exhausted quickly, the camp soon vanished. Of the eighty-one camps, only thirty remained by 1950, and then only when they found other, more permanent means of survival, such as agriculture. Joplin alone developed into a small metropolitan center.

Promoters referred to Joplin, a boom town in every sense, as "the Klondike of Missouri." In 1870 there was not a single house in Joplin, but by 1874 it had become a city of three thousand people. In 1875, seventy-five saloons were open day and night. A local miner-poet pointed out that "Suez was still east of us and there were no Ten Commandments, for way down yonder in Southwest Missouri, where women drink and curse like fury; where the barkeepers sell the meanest liquor which makes a white man sick and sicker, where the tinhorns rob you a little quicker, that's where Joplin is." A sophisticated program was offered by the local opera house, however, for the more respectable citizens.

From 1889–1939 the Southwest Missouri Electric Railway Company, headquartered at Webb City, operated over a ninety-four-mile system, with streetcars leaving towns on the circuit every half hour from 6 A.M. until 10:30 P.M. Some miners lived under the better conditions in the surrounding towns and commuted to the mines. One could board a trolley at Carthage, travel through Carterville and Webb City into Joplin, then to Galena, Kansas, and into Oklahoma through the mining towns of Picher, Commerce, and Miami, a distance of fifty-five miles. Brick city streets in many area towns still show evidence of the railway track lines

The highlight of the week's activities for the miners and their families was Saturday night: "a sight worth going miles to see." The banks stayed open until 8 P.M. and paid out an estimated hundred thousand dollars in several counting rooms. From eight o'clock until midnight, the stores were crowded with people making purchases, paying the week's grocery bill, laying in supplies for next week, and swapping experiences.

Because zinc prices were low, the unappreciated metal continued to be thrown out with the tailings. (Some of these tailings piles reached a height of three hundred feet, covering thirteen acres with a volume of over seven million tons of gravel.) But by 1872 a process for treatment of zinc blende had been discovered and almost immediately zinc production became more important than lead. By 1926, fifteen thousand tons of lead and zinc were being shipped out of the district weekly. But even then horse-drawn vehicles were more numerous than trucks because the roads were so bad that motor vehicles bogged down.

Water was a perennial problem in the mines, and each was equipped with a sludge pond into which mine water was pumped. Considerable water was required to wash and mill the ore, and the sludge pond served as a reservoir for the waste. After the sludge pond had been filled, the mine water pumped from the shaft was channeled into nearby creeks. This practice polluted the waters, destroyed wildlife and vegetation, and produced much litigation.

Because of the power required by the mines, smelters, and mills, natural gas service and electric utilities were available early in Tri-State towns. In 1890 the Southwestern Power Company built a hydroelectric station at Grand Falls on Shoal Creek, the first power plant in the Tri-State District. Several others were soon established. In 1913 Powersite Dam at Taneycomo was built to produce additional electric power for the area. After 1931 Bagnell Dam supplied electricity to the Leadbelt and the St. Louis area. These neighborhoods benefitted from electricity much earlier than other locations in the Ozarks.

The Cost to Humans

"Joplin is at the present about the most prosperous mining district in the country," investors reported around the turn of the century. Joplin wages were lower and each worker's productivity was higher than anywhere else in the country. Although the wage level generally increased through the years, it was still below the national average for lead and zinc miners. In 1929 the local wage of $4.00 a day compared to the national average of $4.90.

Many laborers were recruited from farms of the district. A contemporary observer wrote that the "Ozark hills are rich in hungry hillbillies . . . all you have to do to get fresh miners is to go out in the woods and blow a cowhorn."

But the miners were vulnerable to hazards from many sources. There was always the danger of mine accidents: pieces of rock roof fell into the shaft, or tunnels collapsed, or explosives were used unwisely or inexpertly.

Some of the underground water was strongly charged with hydrogen sulfide gas; workmen who came in contact with this gas were blinded temporarily if they were exposed to it for more than a two-hour shift. Most of the mines were wet; the miners worked standing in water, their clothing soaked.

Despite the dampness, rock dust pervaded the tunnels and accounted for a high incidence of silicosis, a lung disease, in Tri-State mines. Weakened by "miner's consumption," the workers were then highly susceptible to tuberculosis, spread by contagion to their wives and children. And those who worked in smelters were doomed to lead poisoning.

All mine tragedies were said to be credited to "Blind Tom," a folklore character who worked on the "graveyard shift" (from midnight to morning) and weakened timbers and started cave-ins.

Many workers and their families lived in substandard housing, termed "mining slums" by one investigator, who found the water and sanitation facilities deplorable. Until 1940 the outside privy was a common sight in some portions of the district, while water for drinking and bathing was bought by the barrel and left to stand outside, vulnerable to pollution of every kind.

But because most of the labor force was recruited locally from the small farms of the Ozarks, they were better able to endure temporary shut-downs brought on by sagging ore prices or a surplus of concentrates. Until 1920 it was common for workers to have a small farm or garden plot and a cow, a pig or two, and chickens. The wives and children generally took care of the livestock. The women canned food, and the pigs were butchered and processed for the winter's use. The wooded sections around the camps furnished wildlife for food and fuel for cooking and heating. The many district streams—unless contaminated by mine water—supplied bass and catfish.

This was not possible, however, in camps like Picher, where the mines and piles of tailings extended literally to the workers' residences. In some places board or stone barricades were required to protect the highway from the encroaching manmade hills.

By 1930, most of the mining and smelting had been concentrated in the hands of the Eagle Picher Mining and Smelting Company. From then until 1955, mining was done mostly in the Kansas and Oklahoma fields, but Joplin continued to be the leading supply and financial center of the mining district. In 1951, because Picher, Oklahoma, was extensively undermined, a part of the business district was in danger of caving. The Eagle Picher Company granted financial assistance to businessmen to move buildings and improvements to a safe location. In 1967, when Eagle Picher closed its facilities, mining in the Tri-State District ceased.

Ozarks Marble

Next in importance to lead and zinc was limestone, of which several types are found in the Ozarks. Burlington limestone, important as a building material and for the manufacture of quicklime, is found around Carthage and Phenix, both in Missouri. Deposits near Beaver, Arkansas, also contain marble of exceptional quality. Both states have used the stone extensively in public buildings, especially county courthouses.

"Carthage White Marble" came to prominence in the 1880s and in time secured a national market. Marble from the area was used by architects in some of America's best-known buildings, including the Macy's department store building in New York, the Field and Rosenwald museums in Chicago, and the Rust Building, San Francisco. Victorian mansions, too, were built of Ozarks marble, particularly in the Tri-State District and on the Springfield plateau. Many survive today. Close inspection may reveal something of their origins. In Carthage, for example, is one with the pick-and-shovel motif of a mine owner in bold relief. Occasionally, in more rural areas, the country mansion of a mining or railroad baron often peers across the hollow at a log cabin, their proximity serving to emphasis the dichotomy that is the Ozarks.

Life in the Countryside

Despite the more cosmopolitan nature of the Springfield Plateau, life in the countryside was typically Ozarkian. People supplemented

A perfect example of the beauty of "Carthage marble" may be seen in the courthouse of Carthage, Missouri, built in 1894 and still one of the most beautiful courthouses in the Ozarks. (Courtesy of Carthage Historic Preservation, Inc.)

Children's Day at a neighborhood church in 1929 provided the perfect reason to get together for a dinner on the grounds. (Courtesy of Kirk Pearce)

their subsistence farming however they could: cutting cedar logs or railroad ties and floating them down the river to the railhead; raising tomatoes for a local cannery; working in the sweltering cannery— scalding, peeling, and canning tomatoes; picking fruit—apples, peaches, strawberries grown locally and needing a large amount of temporary labor to harvest; gathering and picking black walnuts; hunting and trapping; fishing, gigging, noodling—even dynamiting fish or paralyzing them with black walnut juice; hunting for pearls in the freshwater mussels found in the region's rivers; or working in area sawmills or mines. Often it was a combination of several of these pursuits—and by every able-bodied member—that helped to feed the family.

Ozarkers worked hard to survive. And because many lived in comparatively isolated, lonely locations, they seized every opportunity to socialize with their neighbors. Churches and schools, often sharing one small building, were the centers of community life and served as well for "entertainment."

By 1900 literary society meetings were being held regularly in almost every community throughout the Ozarks, nearly always on Friday nights at the schoolhouse. The Friday evening "literaries" also included debates, spelling bees, ciphering matches, and kangaroo courts. Attendance often meant a hazardous trip after dark by lumber wagon, buggy, horseback, or on foot. Stream crossings could be dangerous at night, and the roads themselves were treacherous. Box and pie suppers were attended for the entertainment as well as for the good food. Much of the enjoyment derived from the time-honored ritual of identifying the supposedly unmarked boxes or pies and of purchasing the desired one at the best possible price.

Picnics were always popular, especially when a large spring or popular river swimming hole was nearby. Large community celebrations on the Fourth of July and "Decoration Day" (Memorial Day) were common throughout the Ozarks. There would be sack races, baseball games, homemade ice cream, and watermelon. Attractions at the organized picnics often included balloon ascensions, orators, circle swings, lemonade stands, the shooting of firecrackers, recitations, songs, and instrumental music.

School programs offered another opportunity for entertainment and to indulge the competitive spirit. Proud parents crowded into the one-room building to enjoy Christmas programs and, most auspicious of all, the closing-of-school ceremonies. Students gave plays, dialogues, recitations, and speeches. Frequently the schoolhouse was decorated for the occasion with flowers, evergreens, and students' work. Preparation for the event occupied a large part of the last two months of school, and many teachers felt that their chances of being rehired for the following year depended upon their producing a program that not only would entertain their patrons but also would compare favorably with previous programs.

Ordinarily families did not have a Christmas tree at home, for the church could be counted on to have a special program, called "the Christmas Tree," complete with gifts for all. In fact, religious gatherings of all kinds were extremely important to Ozarkers. Church meetings provided the opportunity to have fellowship with their neighbors, to participate in group singing, to witness the emotional performances of others, and to be entertained by the preacher. (Ministers often gained reputations for their ability to preach an interesting and entertaining sermon. Their messages were emotional, lengthy, and fundamentalist, frequently dramatized by pantomimic action and humorous anecdotes.)

Knowing that these "entertainments" were part of a religious service, and therefore approved by the community, left one free to enjoy them without guilt.

Camp meetings added to the usual enjoyment the extra dimension of spectacle, of crowds of people, of camping out, and of an intensified emotional atmosphere. For the same reasons, brush arbors were well attended. The men of the neighborhood constructed a framework of poles or saplings over which the leafy branches of trees could be laid to form a shady bower. Benches of split logs or other seats were then arranged under the arbor and the congregation gathered to sing hymns or hear the sermon, sometimes offered by a visiting preacher.

"A good protracted meeting had all of the elements of good theatre," says Dr. Robert K. Gilmore, author of *Ozark Baptizings, Hangings, and Other Diversions.* And because of the church's attitude toward many recreational opportunities—dancing, card playing, theater going, and even music in some cases—the early Ozarkers had little choice but to turn increasingly to the church itself for their entertainment.

Baptisms drew large crowds to witness the converts filing into waist-deep water, there to be totally immersed by a minister. Although usually performed during the spring of the year, sometimes it was necessary to break ice in order to accomplish the ceremony.

A newspaper "correspondent" recorded that "the people of New Site, always bent on having a good time, have been attending all the camp meetings, picnics, and so forth for miles around." An elderly Douglas County, Missouri, man allowed that "the church was your outstanding social function because there you met all your neighbors that you hadn't seen for a week."

Barn raising, fence building, threshing, and other necessary chores best done by a crowd of people offered more opportunities for visiting and joking while serious and necessary work was also being done.

"Goin' to mill," likewise a necessary trip, was also an opportunity to visit with seldom-seen neighbors and catch up on the neighborhood news. Since long lines at the mill were common, whole families went along and sometimes even camped out while awaiting their turn. While they took advantage of the enforced rest, they could enjoy the fellowship of their neighbors (see Chapter 18).

In much the same way, a visit to the neighborhood's general store, sometimes at or near the mill, served the dual purpose of acquiring needed purchases and seizing an opportunity to chat and exchange news. Frequently the proprietor of the general store, or his wife, was also postmaster, so customers came and went all the more frequently. Such important business also attracted others; the blacksmith shop, for example, was often near the store.

Stores were located wherever they could most profitably serve the most people. They opened at crossroads, along frequently traveled routes, and at other natural gathering places. Most stores had porches with chairs and benches set out so customers would have a place to stop and rest and, of course, visit. The general stores were the "senior citizen centers" of their day. The older men often spent the whole day at the store, telling tall tales or stories of the old days, playing marbles or checkers, whittling, or pitching horseshoes.

Since by necessity there was a store every few miles—to which area customers walked, rode horseback, or drove a buggy or wagon— many of the old buildings still survive. A very few, in some of the more remote areas, still operate; often the storekeeper is quite elderly and a fund of information about the neighborhood and its history.

Ozarkers were so hungry for fellowship and spectacle that even court trials and hangings were well attended. Both were rare enough to be of particular interest. "Court week" usually occurred only twice a year: in the spring and again in the fall. Political gatherings were enthusiastically attended for the same reasons.

Well before the turn of the century, band concerts became very popular. Every community of any size had its own band and the nearest town was equipped with a bandstand where everyone gathered, usually on Saturday night when the town was full of shoppers. Many years later a member of one of bands recalled, "Even though the kerosene lamps gave off very little brilliance, we thought it very up to date and enjoyed every minute of it. Later the Coleman Company came out with a gasoline-fired floodlight that lit up the whole concert area and was the talk of the community." Some bandstands survive to this day, though they seldom still serve their original purposes.

Baseball was also particularly popular, and the town team could

Like this one near Lebanon, Missouri, the general store was the department store of its day, providing everything the community might need, including a place to socialize. Note the horse-drawn farm implement on the porch. (Courtesy of Bittersweet, Inc.)

Almost anywhere in the Ozarks, visitors are apt to spot old farming machinery, such as this threshing machine, which appears to be merely awaiting the return of its operator to resume its work. Even horse-drawn equipment is frequently seen and, on the back roads, is occasionally still used.

count on enthusiastic support. Silent movies, brought to the area by an advance promoter who distributed handbills at the grocery store and nailed notices on trees along the roads, were shown occasionally, either in the schoolhouse or a tent set up for the purpose.

Medicine shows traveled through the countryside in closed wagons that provided living quarters and a place to transport the patent medicines they sold. There was no charge for the small show they presented to draw a crowd—often including a magician. Their profits were realized from the sale of the medicine that was touted to cure "whatever ails you" as a "commercial" in the middle of the entertainment.

Stock companies performing live shows were sometimes hardy—or hungry—enough to make the trip into the backwoods, especially if the trade area could be counted on to draw a sizable crowd on short notice. One such traveling circus was slated to perform at a neighborhood mill in Ozark County, Missouri, one Saturday in 1923. The bronco riders, cowboys, and other performers rode in wagons and on horseback from the railhead some thirty miles away. Since there were no wagons large enough to haul the trained elephants, the animals had to walk—slowly; the journey took longer than expected. By the time the exhausted roustabouts and performers began to raise the tent in a level field near the mill, the assembled crowd was already impatient. Soon the tent was jammed to capacity; people had walked, rode in buggies and wagons and on horseback for miles to see the entertainment.

But the tired workers began to argue among themselves as they set up the show; soon a full-scale fight broke out. When curtain time arrived the performers were too busy fighting to put on a show. The sharpshooter who was scheduled to shoot a wooden block from his partner's head drank too much moonshine; the partner refused to be a target. "Bronco busters" Pan Handle Pete and Yellow Fever—in a real wrangle between themselves—refused to perform. The circus owner and his wife became embroiled in a heated disagreement over how best to handle the fiasco and she stormed away, with him running after her.

"This was just too much for the impulsive mountain men!" recorded an eye witness. "They shot holes in the top of the tent to show their displeasure. When this did not bring the performers to the tent, the mountain men rode the broncos themselves and put on quite a show."

Always eager for something to break the monotony of their backwoods existence, the fun-loving hill men also played elaborate practical jokes on each other. Occasionally their pranks backfired or had other unforeseen repercussions.

With the coming of the telephone to the Ozarks, folks found another diversion: listening in on their neighbors' telephone conversations. The individual on the party line receiving the call was signaled by a series of short or long rings, or a combination of both, but all telephones along the line also received the signals. Most people, of course, recognized their neighbor's ring as well as their own. At times, several neighbors on the same line would visit, exchanging news and views.

Predictably, the young people embraced the telephone enthusiastically. No longer faced with a long, lonely walk or horseback ride just to talk to his beloved, a fellow could telephone her—if he could manage privacy. Lovers of the early 1900s often formulated their own signaling codes and monopolized the lines.

On Sunday afternoons, when the young people of the neighborhood gathered at one of their homes for recreation to pass the time and as an excuse to be together, one of the games they played was called "ringing through the circle." It began by everyone joining hands to form a circle outside the house near the telephone line entrance. The circle was then broken with the person at one end taking hold of the telephone line and the person at the other end taking hold of the ground wire. Someone inside the house would then give the crank on the telephone a swift turn, generating a startling but harmless shock. (Before the days of electricity, the phone had to generate its own power by means of a simple magneto.) This usually broke the circle. Some would then drop out, and the whole thing would be repeated until finally only a few of the less sensitive would manage to hold the circle intact.

The Music of the Hounds

Another diversion that survives to this day is nocturnal fox hunting —also sometimes called a *fox race* or *chase*. Among gentlemen fox hunters, the fox is never intentionally killed. The object of the hunt is simply to have the specially bred and often highly valuable fox hounds flush a fox and chase him over hill and hollow. As they track the fox, the hounds give voice, and their handlers can follow the race by listening to the baying, or "music," of the dogs. Changes in direction, which dog is in the lead, and much more are all obvious to the excited listeners.

In the meantime, they build a bonfire, perhaps smoke, snack, drink—and talk. Indeed, the comradeship and rapport with other foxhound racers is the driving force behind the sport. And always, the hunters reminisce about the top hounds they have owned and run. Many believe that even the fox enjoys the chase.

As increasing development—not to mention manmade lakes— encroaches on the wilderness, fox racing in the Ozarks is struggling to survive even in remote areas. Most remaining hunters have resorted to fencing in a large area, a few thousand acres if possible, called fox *pens*, wherein they keep a few foxes and can indulge their passion. Most are staunch conservationists, particularly of foxes, and are meticulous about not permitting their dogs to run deer and other wildlife.

"I'd rather hear a good fox race than I would the Grand Ole Opera, and I'm fairly fond of that . . ." says one old-timer.

A similar nighttime pursuit is raccoon hunting, now done legally only in season if the 'coon is actually taken. "Coon hunting is a passion, a pastime that transcends hobby and becomes a way of life for a couple of months every winter," says a writer for the Missouri Conservation Department. "You can always tell where a coon hunter lives by the occasional outburst of hound music from the backyard," says another.

Highly bred hounds are also used in this sport, but they are not the same as fox hounds. In the past the raccoon was taken for his pelt, but the falling price of furs has helped to lessen the practice. Most 'coon hunters nowadays follow the sport for the fellowship of other hunters, the thrill of raising or owning a highly trained (and often very valuable) hound, and for the excuse to be outdoors at night. Often, however, 'coon hunters are not popular with their neighbors because of their habit of ignoring property lines and fences.

Raccoon hunters also participate in "money hunts," in which participants pay an entry fee (sometimes as much as a thousand dollars) and the winner, determined by points scored for proper action and behavior of the dogs, takes the purse. Clubs also compete against each other; the competitions progress to a national level.

Both fox and 'coon hounds are carefully bred. Each has its own breed association, conducts both bench and field trials, and often commands thousands of dollars for a proven stud or bitch. Highly prized is the dog with ". . . that characteristic that coon hunters call 'the spirit of the hound.' Hard to define, but it's what makes a hound be a hound. The heart and desire to hunt and perform. The intense desire to please his teammate [his master]."

Hound-hauling pickups are often seen along roads in the Ozarks, especially "of a morning," when the hunters return to the area of the hunt to collect the dogs that may have lingered there the night before.

Latter-Day Immigrants

Over the years a few Amish and Mennonites found their way into the Ozarks, but the twenty or more Amish and Mennonite settlements in the region today are of relatively recent origin, with most having come to the region since 1960. The two sects are distinctive both as ethnic groups and for their religious beliefs.

Both groups trace their origins to sixteenth-century Europe in the period following Martin Luther and the Protestant Reformation. Persecuted as heretics by both the church and the state, they were sometimes burned at the stake and tortured in other cruel ways. Those who survived fled to the hills of Switzerland and Germany.

In 1683, Mennonite families joined William Penn in Pennsylvania in response to his general invitation to persecuted people in Europe. In the years that followed, most of the Amish and Mennonites still in the Old World fled to America. At first, most located near Philadelphia, where many still live.

Gradually both the Amish and the Mennonites moved into the Corn Belt and Great Plains of the Midwest. The move to the Ozarks is the result primarily of land shortages in the older areas of settlement.

Although both groups maintain some old ways, it is primarily the Amish who adhere most closely to the past. They have clung to the old style of worship including the use of the German language. Their distinctive clothing is suggestive of centuries past. They reject automobiles, tractors, telephones, and electric lights. With few exceptions, the Old Order Amish continue to plow with horses, travel in buggies, and abjure the use of most modern conveniences.

Primarily farmers, the Amish reject most other occupations, particularly those that would require them to live in urban areas. Amish children attend school only through the eighth grade. Parents prefer that their children not be unduly influenced by worldly ways; they need learn only the basic skills of reading, writing, and arithmetic. From then on, learning occurs on the job. In many areas, including the Ozarks, some operate their own schools.

Although the Amish are often characterized as stern people, for whom the work ethic precludes frivolous activities, they do find time to relax and enjoy themselves. Occasionally they can be seen throughout the Ozarks at zoos, public monuments, and tourist attractions such as Dogpatch and Silver Dollar City.

When interviewed, the Amish have given as their reasons for coming to the Ozarks the plenitude of cheaper land, in part because of an economy that depends on livestock as opposed to being crop-oriented, and the general conservatism of the region. Oddly enough, one of the biggest obstacles to their settlement here was the unavailability of windmills, which they ultimately obtained from Indiana.

Near Seymour (on Hwy. 60) are the farmsteads of several Amish families. They build large two-story frame, box-style houses that are always covered with gray roll-type siding. The presence in their barnyards of windmills, outdoor toilets, and horse-drawn farm machinery is reminiscent of times past everywhere in the Ozarks.

CHAPTER 5

The Tri-State District

On January 11, 1863, a six-hour Civil War battle was fought at Hartville by the exhausted and ragged Confederate troops of Brig. Gen. John S. Marmaduke and Federals under the command of Col. Samuel Merrill, garrisoned in Houston, Missouri.

Marmaduke, falling back after an attack on the Federal garrison at Springfield, was on his way to Hartville. He had heard of a mill where he hoped to grind grain for his troops and their horses. Merrill's Union troops were on their way to Springfie'd to reinforce the garrison there, not realizing that Marmaduke had already attacked and fallen back. The two armies literally ran into each other at Hartville.

Col. Joseph Shelby, under the Confederate general Marmaduke, marched into Hartville shortly after 11:00 A.M.; his troops received heavy and accurate fire from the Federals. "Death's black banner is waving there and his best and bravest are falling around him," Shelby later wrote.

The battle raged until sundown, when the fighting was broken off on both sides as each army apparently believed the other was withdrawing. The Confederates lost twelve killed and ninety-six wounded. The Federals claimed the loss of seven killed and sixty-four wounded.

Little House in the Ozarks

Laura Ingalls Wilder and her husband Almanzo came to the Ozarks in August 1894, after a terrible drought in South Dakota. Almanzo's health had been weakened by diphtheria, and they had endured the death of their infant son and the loss of their home to fire. With a hundred-dollar down payment that Laura had saved from work as a seamstress, the Wilders bought the Rocky Ridge Farm near Mansfield, Missouri, and lived in a one-room windowless log cabin there. At first their sole income came from the sale of firewood.

Laura raised chickens and sold the eggs to her neighbors; she often made speeches about how to raise poultry successfully. Once when she was unable to attend a meeting, she wrote out her speech so that it could be read. An editor of the *Missouri Ruralist* was in the audience; he offered Laura the job of home editor. In 1911, Laura Ingalls Wilder became a writer.

Laura's daughter, Rose, a well-known writer, often urged Laura to expand her own writing career. So in 1932 at the age of sixty-five, Laura Ingalls Wilder sent a book to Harper and Brothers entitled, *Little House in the Big Woods*. Her new career had begun. Prompted by Rose, Laura then conceived a plan to develop "an eight-volume historical novel for children covering every aspect of the American frontier."

"I realized that I had seen it all," she explained, "all the successive phases of the frontier, first the frontiersman, then the pioneers, then the farmers and the towns. Then I understood that in my own life I represented a whole period of American history."

The home that Almanzo built for Laura with materials from their own land is now a museum, preserved just as Laura left it, and on the National Register of Historic Places. Her writing desk looks as though she just stepped away from it, and there are the original manuscripts and first editions of all her books. Nearby are Pa's fiddle, Mary's Braille slate and Nine-Patch quilt, the glass bread plate from Laura's and Almanzo's first Christmas, rare old photographs, and other treasures so vividly portrayed by Laura in her books. The house is surrounded by apple, walnut, and dogwood trees, many of which Laura herself planted.

Laura wrote that "there is no other country like the Ozarks in the world." Although their daughter urged them to join her in California, Laura confided to Almanzo that she would not trade "all of California for one Ozark hill." Before her death Laura voiced her regret at the passing of the old ways and the development of a complex, technological society. "At times," she said, "I have a homesick longing but there is no turning back. We must go on. . . ." Laura Ingalls Wilder died in her Rocky Ridge Farm home on February 10, 1957, at the age of ninety. She is buried in Mansfield Cemetery, as are her husband and daughter.

The Laura Ingalls Wilder Home and Museum is located on Route A, one mile east of Mansfield, and is open to visitors from May through October.

The little house in the Ozarks where Laura Ingalls Wilder wrote her famous "Little House Books" was at Mansfield, Missouri. The house is now open for tours, and visitors can see the desk where Laura wrote, her original manuscripts, and much more. (Courtesy of Missouri Division of Tourism)

The eighteen-room Queen Anne-style Bentley House, in Springfield, Missouri, was built as a residence in 1892. The house is known for several architectural features including a turret, half-timbering, shingling, milled porch elements, stained and cut-glass windows, cut stone and brick. It has been restored and furnished in the Victorian style. Now it houses the Museum of Ozarks History.

The Backbone of the Ozarks

Westward toward Springfield, Hwy. 60 follows the high plateau and watershed of the western Ozarks like a finger tracing a backbone. Just west of Mansfield is Cedar Gap, the second highest point in Missouri, only a few feet lower than the highest point, Taum Sauk Mountain in the eastern Ozarks. This highway and its forerunners afford easier traveling than on either side of it, where one quickly re-enters the hills. The road has been a "highway" for a long time; it was the main avenue of trade between the town of Springfield and the far-flung settlements in the 1800s.

By 1892 large orchards had been set out near Seymour. In 1901 there occurred a season especially suited to the production of an extra good apple crop. By contrast, farm crops were generally a failure that year because of drought, and interest in apples increased dramatically. By 1905 orchards of from five hundred to two thousand trees had become common. The period between 1910 and 1940 was the most important for the production of fruit in the area, although the crop failed almost entirely in the drought years of 1934 and 1936. While the war years of the 1940s stimulated a stronger demand for apples, orchardists faced higher labor costs and outright labor shortages during the harvesting season. Fruit acreage gradually declined; by the end of the severe drought of the mid-1950s, virtually all of the large orchards had disappeared. Fruit growing is now highly localized. Apple orchards still survive in the Seymour area, but most of the fruit is sold direct from on-the-farm fruit sheds or from fruit stands along Hwy. 60.

A more recent farming enterprise at Seymour is a buffalo ranch. Frequently the bison are visible along the north side of Hwy. 60. Buffalo burgers are served at a roadside restaurant at Seymour; watch for the huge sign painted on the side of the building on the south side of the road.

Just west of Diggins on Hwy. 60 look for a sign warning of "Horse-Drawn Vehicles." Along the shoulder of the highway in this neighborhood one frequently sees an Amish family in a buggy or horse-drawn farm machinery. Watch on the north just beyond Diggins for a small group of plain, tall gray houses with large barns and windmills—an Amish settlement. Scattered along Hwy. 60, set well back from the highway for a few miles on both sides, Amish farmsteads can be spotted.

The Queen City

Although Springfield is a self-proclaimed monarch, she is indeed "the Queen City of the Ozarks." Strategically located since pioneer days as the hub of trade for a vast area, the city (the third largest in Missouri after only St. Louis and Kansas City) is the crossroads of several highways, the only major airline terminal for some distance in all directions, and the most important cultural and commercial center of the Ozarks region. Most rural Ozarkers look at Springfield as just a big town, where the residents are mostly "just folks" and friendlier than in other big places.

Springfield is easy to get around in, but it is even easier with a map. At the clover leaf where Hwy. 60 joins Hwy. 65, turn right (north) on Hwy. 65 to the Battlefield Exit (watch for the huge McDonald's on your left). Exit and turn left on East Battlefield Road. Across the street from McDonald's is the Springfield Convention and Visitors Bureau, which will gladly supply you with a map showing the points of interest in the city, plus other colorful and helpful brochures and pamphlets. Be sure to ask for the Walking and Driving Tour Maps.

In the 1820s, Delaware and Kickapoo villages occupied the present site of Springfield. The first white families settled here in 1829 and 1830. Probably named for Springfield, Tennessee, the town became the seat of Greene County upon its organization in 1833. Reportedly a small slave market did business in Springfield before the Civil War, probably on or very near the public square, the center of merchandising. Later, those who supported Lincoln did so silently, but these Republicans created signals and secret handshakes by which they recognized each other.

The city was a military prize held by both sides during the Civil War; several key battles were fought in or near it. After the war, as soldiers on both sides were being mustered out, Springfield took on the aspects of a rough frontier town. Eventually, because of the lawlessness, a vigilante group was formed, called the "Regulators."

In 1872 the Springfield Wagon Company was founded, turning out some two thousand famous "Springfield wagons" a year for the next quarter of a century. The strong, durable wagons were made of choice native timber, well able to stand up under hard usage, and many a westward-bound family drove a Springfield wagon to their new homestead site. As the business grew and mechanized, it contracted to make circus wagons and, later, trailers for the auto industry. The second-generation owner of the company lent his name to Fellows Lake, a popular Springfield landmark.

Gray-Campbell Farmstead

One of the few antebellum houses surviving in the Ozarks, the Gray-Campbell house, built about 1854 by the two prominent Greene County families, stood on the Kickapoo Prairie southwest of Springfield on the high ground north of the James River. The Campbells were a substantial farming family who owned ten slaves in 1860 (at that time slaves and land were accepted measures of wealth and prominence). The house possessed two sixteen-by-sixteen-foot rooms, each with a fireplace, plus a two-room kitchen el with fireplaces, and a brick-walled cellar under the el. Outbuildings, including slave quarters, gardens, and an orchard, surrounded the house.

Unused as a dwelling since the 1950s, the house was "discovered" in a pasture—in the direct path of a highway under construction. The main block of the house was saved and moved two miles north to the city's new Nathanael Greene Park. Outbuildings from other old Ozarks farm places have been added: a log kitchen and a log corn crib, which serves for artifact display. The displays and the interpretation at the "Gray-Campbell Farmstead" are excellent. The site is located at 2400 South Scenic Avenue (travel south from West Sunshine past Horton Smith Golf Course; the park is on the left).

Historic Districts Driving Tour

Visitors can drive through two of Springfield's most interesting historic districts. In the north-central section of the city, the Mid-Town National Register Historic District is the largest. Primarily comprised of houses constructed between 1870 and 1925, there is a wide range in the size and architectural design of the homes built by the upper class, merchants, educators, and working class. Behind the houses there remains a large assortment of stables, garages, and other outbuildings. A few churches are scattered in the district, and Drury College, established in 1873, is on the southern edge.

The development of the Mid-Town District is directly related to the arrival of the railroad in 1870. The railroad was constructed one mile north of Springfield, and a new town, North Springfield, developed around it. Division Street was the dividing line between the two towns. North Springfield soon became a thriving and bustling center with the business district along Commercial Street. The two towns settled their differences in 1887 and voted overwhelmingly for consolidation. The Mid-Town District, located between the two rival towns, was subsequently developed during Springfield's railroad era.

The Mid-Town Auto Tour begins at the southwest corner of the district, which is anchored by Drury College and its landmark, Stone Chapel, listed in the National Register of Historic Places. The cornerstone of this Gothic Revival church was laid on November 16, 1880, and work continued until April 25, 1882, when it was ordered stopped for lack of funds. In December 1882, a fire gutted the building. Reconstruction was begun with local contributions and proceeded to completion in 1892. As you travel north on Benton Avenue along Drury's campus, note the brass cannons mounted on stone bases just north of Stone Chapel. The cannons, used in the Civil War, were installed here in 1905 and 1915. Benton Avenue was where the upper class and people of prominence built large architect-designed houses. Hitching posts, carriage steps, and expanses of original brick sidewalk are still visible and help give the Mid-Town District its distinctive character.

If you continue north on Benton to Commercial Street, you will be in the heart of the Commercial Street Historic District. There are many renovated buildings constructed to house the businesses associated with the railroad and the development of North Springfield.

Museum of Ozarks History

At 603 East Calhoun Street, directly north of the Drury College campus, is Bentley House, a Queen Anne-style residence built in 1892 and listed on the National Historic Register in 1980. Authentically furnished, the structure is now the home of the Museum of Ozarks History, a not-for-profit educational and cultural organization dedicated to the collection, preservation, and display of Ozarks history and heritage. Enormous shade trees grace the lawn, and it is easy to suppose they were there a hundred years ago, or perhaps they were planted when the house was built. A parking lot behind the house can be entered from an inconspicuous driveway on its north side.

Walnut Street Historic District Walking Tour

East Walnut Street began taking shape immediately after the Civil War. Lots were platted between 1867 and 1870, and became popular as building sites for Springfield's growing middle class. By 1910 the street was curbed with cut limestone, lined with stone hitching posts, and overhung with the mature trees that gave it its name. Observant walkers who stroll the mile or so of the Historic District on East Walnut Street will note many interesting features representing a century of building styles and changing tastes. The architecture reveals a wide range of influences, from patrician Queen Anne to romantic Moorish, with bungalows and fanciful Victorian "cottages" that more nearly resemble castles. Although some of the fine dwellings that lent the neighborhood its turn-of-the-century elegance are only memories, many others remain as testimony to a time when high-ceilinged rooms, beaded moldings, ornate cornices, long porches, Gothic turrets and towers, leaded and stained-glass windows, shutters that really shut, driveways sheltered to accommodate ladies alighting from carriages in inclement weather, servants' quarters, summer houses, and gracefully reeded pillars were the signs and symbols of gracious living.

Park Central Square

The fifty-acre town plat of Springfield's founder John Campbell was organized around an open square with four streets radiating from the center of the sides rather than from the corners. The square became the principal place of business, and substantial buildings were constructed on its perimeter. The Butterfield Overland Mail stopped at General Nicholas Smith's Hotel on the northeast corner of the square where it exchanged the luxurious Concord coach for a "mud wagon." This sturdier coach was used for the rougher roads of the long journey, and was best for the trip from Springfield to Fort Smith, Arkansas. The wagon was equipped with three leather seats with backs that folded down to make a bed of sorts on which the passengers could take turns sleeping. Canvas curtains dropped from the roof for protection from bad weather. (There is a marker on the site one-half block north of the Park Central Square on Boonville Avenue —the old Boonville Trail). The courthouse was built in the middle of the square, but after its destruction in the Civil War, no building was ever again erected there.

In July 1865, in what some believe to be the first recorded face-to-face gunfight, Wild Bill Hickok met Davis Tutt, formerly of Yellville, on this square. Apparently Hickok and Tutt had known and disliked each other for years. In Springfield following the Civil War, both had been dating the same woman and, to retaliate for Tutt's moving in on his girl, Hickok began courting Tutt's sister. On at least one occasion Tutt confronted Hickok and asked him to stop seeing her. A short time later, Hickok, Tutt, and others were playing poker and a dispute developed over Wild Bill's watch. In some versions, Hickok gave Tutt the watch to keep in pledge until he could raise the money to pay off his gambling losses, with Hickok warning Tutt only to hold the watch, not to wear it. By other accounts, Tutt took the watch off the poker table over Hickok's objection. But apparently the next day Tutt appeared on the street wearing Hickok's watch, to the latter's great displeasure.

According to historian Phillip Steele:

> On July 21, 1865 the confrontation finally came. Tutt's friends notified Hickok that Tutt would be crossing the square at 6 p.m. if he wanted to try to get his watch back. Hickok responded, "He can't take my watch across the square unless dead men can walk." As hundreds of Springfield citizens gathered in doors and alleys around the square to observe, promptly at 6 p.m. Tutt appeared

Threshing with a steam engine is still done annually in at least one location in the Ozarks: the reunion of the Ozarks Steam Engine and Early Day Gas Engine and Tractor Association, Branch 16, at Republic, Missouri, on Hwy. 60 west of Springfield. On the second weekend after Labor Day, the association gathers together their old engines, antique tractors, sawmills, threshing machines—and much more—for a show, parade, and ongoing demonstrations. Here "Proud Mary" shows guests how it was done.

In the path of Civil War, Ray House survived to become the highlight of the automobile tour of Wilson's Creek National Battlefield near Springfield, Missouri. John Ray watched the bloody battle from his vantage point on the front porch, while his wife and children huddled in the cellar.

on one side of the square and Wild Bill on the other. Hickok
yelled out a warning to Tutt. . . . Once more ignoring Hickok's
demands, Tutt started across the square. As he did he drew his
gun. Hickok responded quickly, both guns firing simultaneously.
Tutt fell dead, a bullet through his heart.

Hickok reportedly turned himself in to the local sheriff and stood
trial for murder. The shooting was declared self-defense, however,
and he was acquitted.

For a time in the late 1800s and early 1900s there was a tall bandstand, called Gottfried Tower, in the middle of the square for Saturday-
night concerts. But the tower figured in mob violence in 1906 and was
dismantled by popular request of the citizenry in 1907.

On Friday, April 13, 1906, a young white woman was assaulted. As a
result, three black men were arrested and placed in jail. The following
day a mob formed and first attacked a black club in the downtown
area. Later the mob stormed the county jail, took the three black
prisoners by force to the square, where they hanged them and burned
their bodies, even though the victim insisted they were not her at-
tackers. It is said that five thousand people witnessed the hanging and
burning; many blacks fled the city. Nine companies of the Missouri
National Guard were called and Springfield placed under martial law.

As automobiles began to come into use and street cars were employed, the congested square was the hub of traffic. A "pie" was built
in the center of the square—a large circular elevation that streetcars
could grind around in order to exit the square on the proper street.
Eventually traffic became such a problem that the pie was removed
and the streets were cut straight through.

In the 1960s city planners decided to replace the square with a
pedestrian mall. By that time, much of the merchandising of the city
had moved southward to the new shopping malls. Motor traffic is now
directed around the square about one-half block away and parking
lots surround the area.

A Summer Storm

At the foot of a hill in the peaceful and scenic Wilson Creek valley
south of Springfield, on August 9, 1861, John Gibson's mill had been
busily serving the needs of the neighborhood. The Gibsons made
their living by grinding corn and oats into flour and by carding wool.
But on August 9 the Gibsons and their neighbors found themselves
surrounded by more than twelve thousand Confederate soldiers,
whose camps extended more than two miles south along the creek.

The Confederates had planned to attack the Union forces of Gen.
Nathaniel Lyon on the morning of August 10, but rain on the night of

August 9 changed their plans. The commander feared their powder might be dampened by the march upon the enemy's position. Ironically, the Union general turned the tables and made a surprise attack on the Confederates early on the morning of August 10. The battle was for control of the strategic state of Missouri, which at that moment had two governments: the actual elected government, which had voted to join the Confederacy, and one installed by General Lyon in an attempt to save Missouri for the Union.

Both sides were desperate to win control of the state. Her strategic position on the Missouri and Mississippi rivers and abundant manpower and natural resources—particularly the lead mines—made it imperative that she remain loyal to the Union. But the Confederacy needed her desperately. Some strategists stated flatly that whoever possessed Missouri would win the war.

When Union general Nathaniel Lyon attacked the Confederates in the valley of Wilson Creek and the cannon began to roar on the morning of August 10, the Gibsons took refuge in their cellar.

War came to other settlers in the Wilson Creek valley that morning, too. On a high hill southeast of Gibson's Mill, postmaster and farmer John Ray had built his house in the 1850s. For ten years the Ray House served as Wilson Creek post office and a stopping place on the Old Wire Road from Springfield to Ft. Smith. The house was also a flag stop on the route of the Butterfield Overland Mail. In 1861 twelve people were living in the Ray House: John and Roxanna Ray and their nine children and a mail carrier. Their slave "Aunt Rhoda" and her four children occupied a small cabin to the rear of the house. On August 10, 1861, they found themselves in the path of war.

At the crack of rifle fire and the thunder of cannon, Roxanna Ray gathered her children into the cellar under the house while John stood watch on the front porch. At 6:30 on this hot, humid, and mosquito-ridden morning, soldiers appeared in his cornfield, just beyond the springhouse. When a unit of Louisianans were driven from the cornfield by Union artillery fire, they moved behind the house to regroup. Shells whizzed overhead and exploded nearby.

Losses were heavy in the Battle of Wilson's Creek (called Oak Hills by the Confederates) and about equal on both sides: 1,317 for the Federals, 1,222 for the Confederates. The Southerners, though victorious on the field, were not able to pursue the Northerners. Lyon lost the battle and his life, but he achieved his goal: Missouri remained under Union control.

Not until early afternoon was it safe for the Ray family to come out of their cellar. Then the wounded were brought up and laid in the house, then on the porch and, finally, in the yard. The body of General Lyon, Union commander, was brought into the house before being taken to Springfield. The Ray children carried water to the wounded from their springhouse across the road and down the hill. Surgeons also used the water to wash wounds and to cleanse their surgical instruments.

At day's end, Ray's cornfield was bent and battered, and hungry soldiers had taken much of his grain and livestock. But none of his family was injured. The war had passed over their farmstead like a summer storm.

For the next three and a half years, Missouri was the scene of savage and fierce fighting. The erroneous assumption by the predominantly Northern forces policing Missouri that all its citizens were disloyal secessionists (the majority were neither slaveholders nor abolitionists) led to harsh and often vindictive excesses of martial law. This inflamed the resentments of many Missourians, some of whom were stirred to open rebellion. Guerrilla bands led by men such as William Quantrill and "Bloody Bill" Anderson spread blood and terror across central and western Missouri. The Ozarks endured ravishment by a guerrilla war of revenge, with small bands of mounted raiders—often outlaws only acting in the name of war—destroying anything military or civilian that could aid the enemy or be of use to themselves. A knock on the door at night might mean a visit by bushwhackers or militia, come to search for weapons, conscript the men and boys, or steal and burn.

By the time the war ended in the spring of 1865, Missouri had witnessed so many battles and skirmishes that it ranks as the third most fought-over state in the nation, second only to Virginia and Tennessee. Missouri sent more men to war, in proportion to her population, than any other state.

The Wilson's Creek National Battlefield

Struggling to survive in the face of increasing southward development of the city of Springfield, the Wilson's Creek National Battlefield has so far successfully repulsed encroachment. From I-44 take Exit 70, follow Rte. MM south to Rte. M, then three-quarters of a mile to Rte. ZZ. From Springfield go south on Glenstone or Campbell to Rte. M, then west on M to Rte. ZZ. The park is two miles south on ZZ. (Note that almost all official material refers to the Battle of Wilson's Creek. Many historians and old-timers, however, insist that the correct terminology is Wilson Creek.)

Virtually all of the bloody Wilson Creek battlefield is now a national park intended to preserve its history and integrity—and to share them with visitors. The visitor center features a film, a fiber-optics battle map, and a museum that provides an introduction to the park, the battle, and its relevance to the Civil War. The visitor center itself is also of interest, one of the first such buildings to utilize active and passive solar heating. Archived in the building in a guarded room is a Civil War research library restricted to serious investigators. Historians will, however, answer questions from the general public.

Living history demonstrations are featured at the Ray House and on Bloody Hill on weekends during the summer. Special military demonstrations are presented on Memorial Day, July 4, August 10, and Labor Day. Numerous other events range from programs on Civil War medical practices to Ozarks music. An especially effective program is presented by Dr. Thomas Sweeney, who portrays Dr. Caleb Winfrey, a Civil War surgeon present at the Battle of Wilson's Creek. Karen Sweeney gives performances as Mrs. Roxanna Ray. Write to the battlefield office for a list of events scheduled to coincide with the time of your visit (see the Practical Matters Chart following this chapter).

Winding below the bluff of Wilson Creek, a self-guided automobile tour leads to all the major historic points on the battlefield, now peaceful and lovely, crisscrossed by old rail fences and colorful with wildflowers. There are also several walking trails, with exhibits at Gibson's Mill, the Ray House, and key points of the battle. Still running through the battlefield is the historic Old Wire Road; you can see it, walk on it, and ride horses on it. It is almost overwhelming to stand in the road and know that for a long time men and horses and wagons and the machinery of war moved over it; you almost expect to hear the driver's horn signaling the approach of a Butterfield mud wagon.

The National Cemetery

Following the bloody Battle of Wilson's Creek south of Springfield, the fatalities were not well buried. Because it was oppressively hot, disposal of the bodies was accomplished as quickly as possible. In 1867, because of the critical need for a suitable burial place for the remains, a national cemetery was established at nearby Springfield. It is still one of the few places in the country where Union and Confederate dead are buried in the same cemetery. Other remains of military dead were moved here from battle sites at Forsyth, Newtonia, Carthage, Pea Ridge, and Springfield.

The contractor signed to re-inter the deceased Union soldiers from the Wilson Creek battlefield received payment for 183 bodies: 34 from the sinkhole, 14 from the old well, 135 from other areas of the field. These bodies, so crudely tossed into wells and shallow pits, finally found a suitable resting place at the heart of a soldiers' cemetery. By 1868 a total of 1,514 Union soldiers had received honored burial in Springfield National Cemetery; 719 of them as unknowns.

The exact number of Confederate dead in the cemetery is not known. Of the 501 originally buried here, 238 were killed in the Battle of Wilson's Creek. Most of the remaining 263 died from wounds received in the battle or from sickness. Some were killed in the Battle of Springfield, January 8, 1863. The last burial of a Confederate veteran took place on June 12, 1939.

The burials in the cemetery include the victims of all of the nation's wars, including one Revolutionary War soldier. Several special monuments and statues add to the dignity and beauty of the cemetery. A particularly interesting one is at Grave 245, the resting place of Henry Walters, a scout with the Confederate partisan ranger, John Singleton Mosby, the famed "Gray Ghost" of the Confederacy. In addition to the monuments, there are time capsules, the memorial plaques of various organizations, carillons, and an avenue of flags. When numerous trees were lost during a tornado in April 1983, fifty new trees were planted by The Greater Ozarks Veterans organization.

It is a somberly beautiful place, rows and rows of simple white grave markers making abstract designs against the green of the grass and cedars. City noises seem to swirl over it without touching it. Located at 1702 East Seminole Street in Springfield, the cemetery is easiest to locate by traveling south on Glenstone, National, Jefferson, or Campbell to Seminole.

The "Great Westward Sweep"

The 1941 WPA guide to Missouri declares that, "In one great westward sweep US 60 reveals all the geographic variations of southern Missouri." In that regard, little has changed in the past fifty-plus years. Leave Springfield on Hwy. 60 and drive southwestward across the forgotten plains of the Ozarks through little towns like Billings, Marionville, Aurora, Monett, each with a rich and varied history of its own and all sharing the history of the Ozarks. Mostly bypassed by the craze for water sports—the rush to the rivers and lakes of the region —the little towns live on nevertheless. Kept alive by the fierce loyalty of long-established natives and those who have returned from lifetimes elsewhere, this area, as much as any other in the region, typifies the varied past of the Ozarks.

The railroads, particularly the Frisco, played a role in opening this area to settlement. The railroad owners had acquired large federal land grants and were anxious to attract settlers. They sent executives directly to Germany as recruiters in an effort to dispose of the land to promote growth and prosperity for their lines. A number of different groups came. French Waldenses settled south of Monett; Germans were attracted mainly to the larger towns (Freistatt remains a German enclave); a Swedish colony was set up at Verona.

Although a few fruit trees were a feature of almost every pioneer farmstead, orchards became big business in the Ozarks with the coming of the railroad. Indeed, commercial fruit growing was encouraged by railway officials. As early as 1889, the Iron Mountain Railroad ran special "fruit trains" from St. Louis to Arkansas to accommodate the annual harvest.

Each of the surviving towns along Hwy. 60 has something to offer those who leave the fast-paced highway and venture onto the horse-and-buggy streets and look for living history. At Marionville, where there are vestiges of the vast apple orchards that once flourished here, look for the extraordinary white squirrels found in only one other place in the world. Settled about 1854, Marionville was once a prosperous flour and sawmill town.

At Aurora, which developed along with the lead and zinc mining boom in the area, look for the old Missouri Pacific depot at Olive and Elliott.

Platted as a shipping point on the railroad in 1868, Verona was also the site in the 1870s of a colony of about forty Waldensian families.

Monett, incorporated in 1887 as a railroad town, developed as the shipping center of the strawberry-growing region. This was also tomato country.

A Home-Grown Industry

In the late 1800s tomatoes—which grew well in the rocky, acidic soil of the Ozarks and added variety and provided much-needed Vitamins A and C for the Ozarkers' winter diet—were canned over open fires in the shade of oak trees. Ozarkers "put by" their tomato crops for the winter: they canned them in heavily plated tin pots. A soldering iron, heated in a gasoline firepot, sealed a patch lid over the hole. The cans were then boiled in a big canning tub, and the bulging ends of the cooling cans, pulled inward by the vacuum, sealed with a "plunk." Any extra cans found a ready market in town and, as early as 1885, Springdale, Arkansas, built a community canning factory that could turn out three thousand cans a day.

Always desperate for cash-money, the shade-tree canners found a market with early "entrepreneurs" who traveled from farm to farm, filling their wagons with cans to deliver to the nearest railhead. Then, all along the lengthening railroad, individuals and towns built small canning factories. Gasoline-run power plants provided electricity for

A tomato canning factory must have been the hottest place in the Ozarks. In the midst of summer heat, when the tomatoes were ripe, these folks worked at an assembly line to scald and peel the tomatoes for canning. But they snapped up the twelve- to fourteen-hour days, sometimes camping in tents to avoid commuting on horseback or over rough mountain roads, for the small wages they could earn. This cannery was at Billings, in Christian County, Missouri. (Courtesy of State Historical Society of Missouri)

The Bartlett Block in Carthage, Missouri, dates to 1888 and has been restored to its former glory as part of Victorian Carthage's effort to regain her heritage and her glorious past. Once the richest town, per capita, in America, Carthage boasts many fine examples of Victorian architecture. (Courtesy of Carthage Historic Preservation)

the machinery to run a primitive assembly line. Because commuting on horseback or by car over rough mountain roads was impossible, especially in view of the twelve- to fourteen-hour day at the cannery, workers often camped in tents or rough shelters near the cannery. Wages were pitifully poor, but workers enjoyed the unaccustomed sociability and non-stop conversation. Farmers with contracts for their tomato crop found seeds or seedlings and fertilizer available at the cannery each spring. The whole family worked at raising and harvesting the tomatoes. Wagonloads of tomatoes formed long lines at the canning factories.

While the Depression did not much affect tomato production, the drought years of 1934 and 1936 proved disastrous. World War II meant no replacement parts for the machinery; after the war the plants were worn out. Many canners could not afford to modernize; the new minimum wage laws and Pure Food and Drug Administration regulations forced out many more. Neither could the canners compete with California with its flat land, irrigation, and mechanized pickers. By 1952, the industry was essentially dead in the Ozarks, although a few diehards were able to hang on longer.

Sharp-eyed travelers may yet spot the ghosts of canning factories and their windowless stone warehouses or the concrete cubicles sometimes built to house the workers.

Jolly Mill

Local legend holds that Jolly Mill was built by slave labor in 1837. Land records suggest that it was actually erected somewhat later, probably around 1850. Since the builder did own slaves, it would seem logical that they assisted in construction of the building. Recently restored, Jolly Mill is included on the National Register of Historic Places. It forms the nucleus of a small park; a one-room school has been moved there, placed on the site where the first village school was believed to have been situated. This area, judging by the number of artifacts found here, was once also heavily visited by Indians.

Jolly Mill was first a distillery. An undershot wheel was powered by water diverted from Capps Creek. The three-story mill rested on a foundation of hand-cut limestone slabs—quarried across the creek— that were laid without mortar. The mill's support beams were hand-hewn logs and the siding was pit-sawed boards. These boards or planks were produced by two men using a long ripsaw, one working above the log and the other standing in a pit below the log. No iron nails were used. The logs and boards were mortised and held with handmade wooden pegs or treenails. Its French buhrstones were shipped up the Mississippi River and transported across southern

Missouri by wagon. A more efficient turbine eventually replaced the wooden wheel.

Once the mill was the center of a twenty-acre town known as Jollification. On two occasions in 1862, Union and Confederate forces clashed in the village, and burned it, without destroying the mill. Thereafter, marauders also spared it, although they burned all the other buildings. One has to assume that the presence of the distillery protected the mill.

Although commercial distilling ended at Jolly Mill in 1875, it retained its jolly reputation. It is said that during the mill's best years—from the turn of the century until the eve of World War I—the residents of Capps Creek valley knew that a half-barrel of whiskey and a dipper were located at the door of the mill. A dip of whiskey was free to customers.

Restored by the Jolly Mill Park Foundation, the mill has been substantially rebuilt and a new milldam has been constructed—but the barrel and dipper were not part of the restoration. To visit Jolly Mill, watch for the sign indicating a left turn off Hwy. 60 west of Hwy. 97 between Monett and Granby.

Granby is said to be the oldest of the lead and zinc mining towns in southwestern Missouri. Two years after a Cornish miner discovered lead here in 1853, the "Granby stampede" began. A miners' museum is at 213 Main Street in Granby, open weekends only. Just west of Granby, turn north (right) on Alternate 71 and go north to Diamond and the junction with Rte. V. Turn left on V and watch for signs directing you to the George Washington Carver National Monument.

The Saint-Scientist

In the social dichotomy of the Ozarks following the Civil War, blacks owned mines as partners with whites as well as in their own right. In a few cases Negroes owned mines and employed white men. A native of Granby, William Richard Pilant, said, "A Negro and a white man could have a fight without starting a race riot. . . ." And yet young, black George Washington Carver was not allowed to attend a white school in his own hometown of Diamond, Missouri.

Born a slave on a farm near Diamond, the infant George and his mother were stolen from their owner, Moses Carver, by bushwhackers during the Civil War. Moses hired a Union soldier to track down the marauders and return the mother and child. Pursuing the trail into Arkansas, the soldier returned with George, who was near death from the ordeal; his mother was never seen or heard of again.

Moses Carver raised George and his brother Jim in his own home until George was forced to leave to seek an education. George, possessed of an inquiring mind, learned much about natural science on his own simply from observing nature. When the local school refused to admit him, he left the kindly Carvers and went into the world, making his own living by taking in laundry and doing menial tasks to support himself during his twenty-year struggle for an education.

At the age of thirty, Carver was admitted to Simpson College in Iowa, which later claimed that the great man made the two greatest decisions of his life there. First, he discovered he was a member of the human race, not just a black man. Second, he decided to give up his first love (art and music) and devote himself to agricultural science in the hope of doing "the greatest good for the greatest number" of the "man on the bottom"—the blacks who were chained to the cotton-exhausted Southern soil.

Later, at Tuskegee Institute in Alabama, Carver worked with primitive laboratory equipment (less than that of most present-day high schools). But by discovering and demonstrating some five hundred uses for sweet potatoes and peanuts and becoming known as "the Father of Synthetics," Carver liberated the South. (But rather than acknowledge Carver as their savior, the residents of an Alabama town built a statue to the Boll Weevil.)

But Carver refused riches for his discoveries. Indeed, while the bookkeepers at Tuskegee Institute grumbled because his paychecks often went uncashed, Carver turned down lucrative offers. Thomas Edison reportedly offered him a salary of $150,000 a year and the promise that "together we can remake the world." Henry Ford, understanding that offers of money would not move Carver, offered him unlimited laboratory facilities and assistants for research on the soybean. Carver refused all offers, telling interested people instead, "If I know the answer, you can have it for the price of a postage stamp."

During World War II, when Nazi Germany and the Axis powers criticized America for its treatment of the Negroes even as she pointed to their persecution of the Jews, William Richard Pilant seized upon the idea of establishing a national birthplace monument to honor Carver. Not only was George Washington Carver, the "poor peoples' scientist," imminently deserving, but he was also black. Here was an opportunity to demonstrate to the world that not only could a black man acquire an education and achieve prominence in our country, but he could be recognized and revered for his contributions.

And one suspects that Pilant wanted to help make it up to Carver, whom he describes as ". . . a heart without hate although he had about every reason a man can have for bitterness. For instance on one occasion he had to take the freight elevator and eat alone in the basement before going upstairs to tell white gentlemen how to make more money from their crops."

Carver died in January 1943, and the bill establishing the George Washington Carver National Monument was proclaimed into law by President Franklin D. Roosevelt on July 14, 1943. It is the first national monument to any American for services to agriculture, the first to an American educator, the first to an American scientist, the first to an American Negro, and, says Pilant, the world's first memorial to interracial peace.

The monument at Diamond, birthplace of Carver, offers exhibits on the natural history of the area; photographs, artifacts, films, and displays depicting his childhood and life of service; and picnic tables. On weekends during the season, special programs are offered about the Ozarks, its history and its folklore. For a schedule of these events, write the park superintendent (see the Practical Matters Chart).

Return to Diamond and drive north on Alternate 71 to Victorian Carthage.

A City Built by Millionaires

The dominant landmark in Victorian Carthage is a courthouse that looks more like a castle. Built of Carthage marble in 1894, the towers and turrets of the Romanesque Revival-styled courthouse are visible from the countryside.

Settled in the 1840s, Carthage suffered greatly during the Civil War. By 1866 the town had been burned to the ground and retained only about a dozen families. But by 1890 the population had grown to over nine thousand—thanks to the nearby mining of lead and zinc and to the quarries of Carthage marble. And by 1900, according to an architectural survey prepared for the state Department of Natural Resources, Carthage was considered the richest town per capita in the United States. Built by the fortunes made in the lead and zinc mines, the mansions of these millionaires are still cherished in this lovely small city—and a great many are included in the National Register of Historic Places.

And while they were building their mansions, the mining magnates also invested in business buildings, examples of which can be seen all around Carthage's Victorian Courthouse Square. This grouping of shops and stores, most with relatively unspoiled nineteenth-century facades, is also on the Historic Register.

And now, at the turn of another century, Carthage is committed to keeping its heritage alive and flourishing. "Carthage, more than almost any other town or city, has a population that appreciates its (historic) resources and attempts to preserve them," said Lee Gilliard of the state Division of Parks, Recreation and Historic Preservation.

The quickest way to understand Carthage history is to tour the Jasper County Historical Society's museum inside the courthouse, ride the 1921 elevator to the fourth floor and back, and then tour Powers Museum. This museum highlights an extensive female fashion collection, Civil War artifacts, holiday decorations and greeting cards, quilts and other historic textiles, and a wide range of archival resources such as photographs and scrapbooks (see the chart). With that overview behind you, tour one or more of Carthage's spectacular old houses. Two favorites are Hill House and the Phelps House.

In 1887 when Hill House was built, Frank Hill was president of the Bank of Carthage. He asked the architect to build "the tallest house in town," at 1157 South Main. The house boasts ten fireplaces, seven sets of pocket doors, and the original stained glass. All of the gaslight fixtures remain in place but have been converted to electricity.

Phelps House, at 1146 Grand Avenue, has been restored by Carthage Historic Preservation, Inc. A prominent attorney and Democratic political boss, William Phelps acquired the property in 1868 and developed it progressively through the years. The most striking feature of the three-story home is the huge blocks of Carthage marble used in the exterior construction. The parlor still boasts the original hand-painted wallpaper and a white marble fireplace. Leaded glass bookcases and a circular window seat highlight the formal library.

On the north side of East Chestnut Street, next to Carter Park, is the Battle of Carthage State Park. An undeveloped four-acre tract, the park is the site of the final confrontation in a twelve-hour running battle which began north of town on the morning of July 5, 1861. Missouri's governor Claiborne Fox Jackson commanded the six thousand Southern troops that forced Gen. Franz Sigel and his one thousand Union men to retreat down the stagecoach road to Sarcoxie. The site remains just as it was when the victorious Southern troops camped there on that summer evening after the battle, which had ultimately swirled through the streets of Carthage.

The brick courthouse on the square had become a hospital for the casualties, where some of the townspeople helped as they could. It is said that one of those who volunteered was a teenager named Myra Belle Shirley, whose family owned and operated a hotel on the north side of the town square. Miss Shirley, according to legend, spied for the Confederacy, reporting to her brother. Later in the war, after her brother was killed by Union troops in a guerrilla skirmish, Myra Belle moved to Texas with the rest of her family. Ultimately she gained notoriety as a female outlaw, Belle Starr.

Phelps House in Carthage, Missouri, was constructed of Carthage marble and was the home of William Phelps, a Democratic political boss. An elevator which served all three floors is readily accessible off the hall of each floor. At the time the house was built, elevators were rare in any setting and virtually unknown in residences. (Courtesy of Carthage Historic Preservation)

Most of the town turned out, apparently, to the Main Street of Anderson, Missouri, on May 22, 1909, to be in this photo. Though the street was still dirt, note the grand brick buildings facing it. Still a pleasant little town, Anderson enjoys a picturesque setting. (Courtesy of State Historical Society of Missouri)

A short drive on Hwy. 71 leads to Joplin by way of historic Webb City, where there is a restored electric trolley in King Jack Park.

The Town That Jack Built

Eventually a satisfactory means of processing the Tri-State District's zinc ore was discovered, and by 1872 Joplin began to ship zinc. In 1880, Jasper County zinc production was double that of lead and by 1888 Joplin, with a population of eight thousand, was a nationally recognized lead and zinc center. Miners were paid off in the saloons (forty of them) on Saturday night and spent Sunday nursing heads cracked during drunken brawls. A miner who lacked cash for tickets at the Blackwell Opera House could exchange a wheelbarrow of "jack" for admission. Even groceries could be purchased with lead or zinc.

Originally two separate towns on either side of Joplin Creek that competed in every way—including physically—Joplin was once gaudy with saloons, dance halls, and gambling rooms. Now it is a progressive mid-size city offering amenities unusual in a town its size. Perched on the cusp of the western prairie and the rolling hill country, Joplin looks both ways, as well as to the trade areas to the west in Oklahoma and Kansas.

Two excellent museums are in Joplin's Schifferdecker Park (see chart). The Dorothea B. Hoover Historical Museum emphasizes the Victorian lifestyle and includes photographs of early-day Joplin. The Tri-State Mineral Museum, established in 1930 and owned and operated by the City of Joplin, was rebuilt and dedicated in 1973. Its purpose is to tell the story of the zinc-lead mining industry that resulted in the founding of Joplin and many surrounding communities. The outstanding exhibits cover all aspects of mining, milling, and smelting, the uses of lead and zinc, and the industrial history of the mining district.

Continue south on Hwy. 71 to Anderson, where there is an interesting old railroad depot, and turn right there on Hwy. 59, which leads south to Noel.

The Christmas City

Located on Hwy. 59, nine miles south of the Hwy. 71 junction at Anderson, Noel is beautifully situated on the banks of the Elk River, ringed by timbered hills. It is one of the oldest resort centers in the Midwest and has been a favorite for more than half a century. Some of the most spectacular limestone bluffs in the Ozarks hang over the roadway approaching Noel on Hwy. 59 from the north.

Scientists believe that bluffs like these were inhabited by Ozark Bluff Dwellers from roughly 1000 B.C. to 1500 A.D. In 1922 an expedition into the Ozarks to research the Bluff Dwellers was sponsored by the Museum of the American Indian, New York. Led by M. R. Harrington, whose findings were not published until 1960, the party collected numerous primitive objects in excellent condition, crafted from bone, stone, clay, wood, vegetal material, feathers, and the like.

In the 1930s the University of Arkansas explored the bluff shelters. Much material was gathered, including baskets and mats woven of reeds, and also small quantities of acorns and corn the Bluff Dwellers apparently used for food.

Widely publicized as "The Christmas City," Noel's post office cancels more than a half-million pieces of mail annually at Christmas time. As an added embellishment to the "Noel" cancellation, a tiny Christmas tree is stamped in green ink on every piece of mail by volunteers—an idea credited to a postmaster of the 1930s.

A variety of good fishing awaits the angler in the spring-fed Elk River, which flows to the Grand Lake of the Cherokees in the Oklahoma Ozarks.

From Noel, go east on Hwy. 90 to rejoin Hwy. 71. Turn south on Hwy. 71 and cross into Arkansas. Shortly after crossing the state line, turn east (left) on Rte. 340 to Rte. 94; continue southeast on Rte. 94 to Hwy. 72, which will take you to Pea Ridge National Military Park.

Practical Matters

Chapter 5 — Springfield Plateau

Checking Out	A Sampling	Phone
Lodging	Mimosa Motel, Hwy. 5 & 60, Mansfield MO; University Plaza Hotel, 333 John Q. Hammons Parkway, Springfield MO; Motel 6, 2455 N. Glenstone, Springfield MO; Hallmark Inn, 3600 Range Line, Joplin MO; Super 8 Motel, 2830 E. 36th St., Joplin MO	(417) 924-3531 (417) 864-7333 (417) 869-4343 (417) 624-8400 (417) 782-8765
Bed & Breakfasts	Frisco House Bed & Breakfast, Hartville MO; Walnut Street Bed & Breakfast, 900 E. Walnut, Springfield MO; Grand Avenue Inn, 1615 Grand Ave., Carthage MO; Hill House, 1157 S. Main, Carthage MO; Leggett House, 1106 Grand Ave., Carthage MO	(417) 741-7304 (417) 864-6346 (417) 358-7265 (417) 358-6145 (417) 358-0683
Campgrounds	KOA Campground, Rt. 7, Box 215A (Exit 70 off I-44 west of town), Springfield MO	(417) 831-3645
Restaurants	Hemingway's Blue Water Cafe, 4th Floor, Bass Pro Shops, 1935 South Campbell, Springfield MO; Ebenezer's, 2641 E. Sunshine, Springfield MO; Trotter's, 1155 E. Battlefield, Springfield MO; Pepper's (Ramada Inn), 3320 Range Line, Joplin MO; Maple Leaf Restaurant, 342 Grant, Carthage MO	(417) 887-3388 (417) 887-1245 (417) 883-0366 (417) 781-0500 (417) 358-2528
Outdoor Recreation	Springfield Nature Center, 4600 S. Chrisman, Springfield MO (Nature Exhibits & Walking Trails); Snow Bluff, Rt. 1, Box 293DA, Brighton MO 65617; (Ski the Ozarks!) Schifferdecker Municipal Golf Course, Schifferdecker Park, North of W. 7th St. on Schifferdecker Ave., Joplin MO; Carthage Municipal Golf Course, West Oak St., Carthage MO	(417) 882-4237 (417) 756-2201 (417) 624-3533 (417) 358-8724

Checking Out	A Sampling	Phone
Main Historical Attractions	Laura Ingalls Wilder Home & Museum, Rt. A One Mile East of Mansfield MO;	(417) 924-3626
	Museum of Ozarks History, 603 E. Calhoun, Springfield MO 65802 (Bentley House);	(417) 869-1976
	Gray-Campbell Farmstead, Nathanael Greene Park, 2400 S. Scenic Ave., Springfield MO;	(417) 862-6293
	Wilson Creek National Battlefield, Rt. 2, Box 75 (Postal Drawer C) Republic MO 65738;	(417) 732-2662
	Springfield National Cemetery, 1702 E. Seminole St., Springfield MO 65804;	(417) 881-9499
	Park Central Square, Walnut Street, and Mid-Town Historic Districts, Springfield MO;	
	Phelps House, 1146 S. Grand Ave., Carthage MO;	(417) 358-1776
	Powers Museum, 1617 Oak St., Carthage MO;	(417) 358-2667
	Jasper County Courthouse, Carthage MO;	
	Tri-State Mineral Museum, 7th St. and Schifferdecker Ave., Joplin MO;	(417) 623-2341
	Dorothea B. Hoover Museum, Schifferdecker Park, Joplin MO;	(417) 623-1180
	George Washington Carver National Monument, Alt. US 71 to Hwy. V, Diamond MO	(417) 325-4151
Other Attractions	Bass Pro Shops Outdoor World, Sunshine & Campbell, Springfield MO (Write for Schedule);	(417) 887-1915
	Crystal Cave, 5 mi. N. of I-44 on Hwy. H, Rt. 1, Box 590, Springfield MO 65803;	(417) 883-9599
	Dickerson Park Zoo, 3043 N. Fort, Springfield MO 65803;	(417) 883-1570
	Fantastic Caverns (Hwy. 13 No.) Rt. 20, Box 1935, Springfield MO 65803; (Ride-thru Cave)	(417) 833-2010
	Art Museum, 1111 Brookside Dr., Springfield MO;	(417) 866-2716
	Thomas Hart Benton Mural, "Joplin at the Turn of the Century," Joplin Municipal Bldg., 303 E. 3rd St., Joplin MO	
Where to Write for More Details	Springfield Convention & Visitors Bureau, 3315 E. Battlefield Rd., Springfield MO 65804;	(417) 881-5300 or (800) 678-8766
	Joplin Convention & Visitors Bureau, 303 E. Third St., Joplin MO 64802	(417) 624-0820 (800) 657-2534

SECTION 3

Ozark Mountain Country and "Little Switzerland"

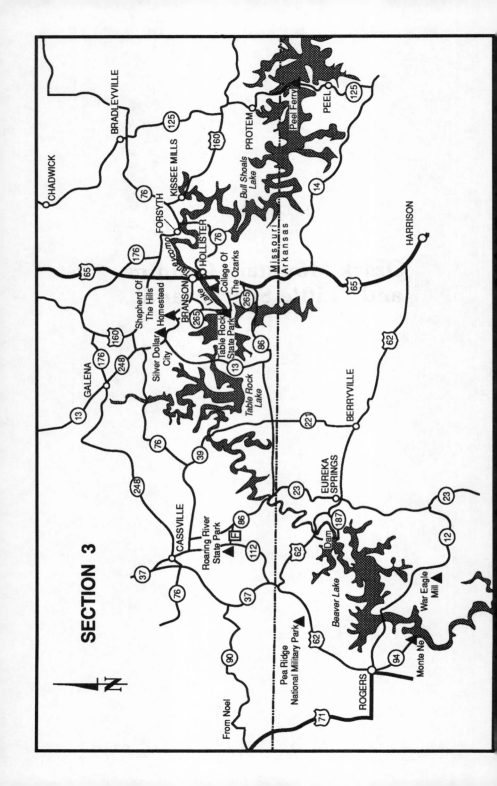

SECTION 3

N

CHAPTER 6

Overview: The Land
of a Million Smiles

In 1919 the Ozark Playgrounds Association, which claimed to be the first regional travel-and-recreation booster group in the United States, was also the first to develop a slogan to market the Upper White River Valley: "The Land of a Million Smiles" adorned picture postcards and appeared on brochures distributed by the Missouri Pacific Railroad in the 1920s.

The visitors came. And still they come—about four million a year to this part of the Ozarks, dubbed Ozark Mountain Country by the successors of the Ozark Playgrounds Association, which disbanded in 1979. Most have found the Land of a Million Smiles to be "as advertised," and most return again and again. Advertising alone, however, is not responsible. The Ozarks sells itself.

But why did this particular corner of the Ozarks become developed while so many other areas of the region remain almost untouched? Many factors have contributed to making "Ozark Mountain Country" synonymous with *Ozarks* to many of the region's visitors.

The Miracle-Cure Spas

Resting and refreshing in the Ozarks probably had its roots in the days of the health spas. By the time the Civil War had been over for a few years, those who could were eager to travel again, particularly to those places that had been off limits because of the war. About the same time, thousands were visiting spas where miraculous cures were being reported.

Since spring water was so abundant, and often so dramatic, in the Ozarks, it is logical that the health craze also reached into this region of "almost mystical proportions and spectacular scenery." The fact that most of these springs had been providing water for unsuspecting settlers and their livestock for decades—without displaying amazing curative powers—was either overlooked or ignored.

Eureka Springs was the most famous of the Ozarks spas, but fabulous resort hotels appeared throughout the region, in both Missouri and Arkansas, within the space of a few years. It seems obvious to us now that the "cures" attributed to mineral water were probably the direct result of the prescribed *manner* in which it was to be used:

> . . . the water (up to four glasses) should be taken slowly, glass by glass . . . and from ten to twenty minutes between the second and third; this latter interval should be passed in walking and a walk of a half mile or a mile at the end is recommended . . . the time which experience has set for a "cure" . . . should be reckoned at not less than four weeks; a shortening of this period by greater daily consumption of water is unwise and sometimes even dangerous.

More than likely, the daily exercise in the Ozarks' outdoors, combined with a more basic diet, a positive mental outlook, and a refreshing change of scene in a resort atmosphere contributed more to an improved physical condition than did the water. And if you did not happen to be sick—well, a grand hotel catering to your every whim and the relaxed atmosphere at the spa made for a delightful spot for a vacation.

But within a few years the novelty wore off, and the actual healing value of the spring water began to be doubted. And the resorts, for the most part, withered and died. Nevertheless, the ultimate result of the spa era in the Ozarks is blessed: Many a spring, partially as a result of its fleeting fame as a cure-all, developed a large following zealously determined to safeguard its existence and availability; most eventually passed into public ownership. As a result, many have been sheltered from destruction and, to the extent possible, from pollution. As a result, the majority of the Ozarks springs continue to flow for the enjoyment, if not the health, of residents and visitors alike.

Floatin' the River . . .

Although the springs brought many for their first visit to the Ozarks, once here they saw the region's other bountiful natural beauty, especially the rivers. It may be that the spa-goers arranged the first organized float trips; almost certainly many of them took advantage of the opportunity to do some hunting and fishing.

By 1904 Southwest Missouri's—and possibly the Ozarks'—first

At Edwards Bluff on the James River, a fisherman—weighted down by his catch—leans on his paddle. The scenic river, rustic camp, and good fishing made the "Galena-to-Branson Float" just one of the attractions advertised for the "Land of a Million Smiles." The slogan was originated by the Rotary Club of Joplin.

On White River soon after 1900, a scene that was repeated many times before the coming of the Corps of Engineers lakes. The guide did all the cooking and camp work, while the paying customers relaxed and enjoyed the scenery. A remnant of this life survives in the guided fishing trips on the White River below Bull Shoals Dam. For the modern floater who can not spare the time for a leisurely week-long float, today's outfitters offer day trips with or without a riverbank lunch prepared by the guide. (Courtesy of Bittersweet, Inc.)

commercial float fishing company had been formed at Galena. Billed as the "Famous Galena to Branson Float," the outing began at Galena, then went south on the James River. At the confluence of the James and White rivers, the route turned east onto the White. It wound a total of 125 miles past the present sites of Cape Fair and Kimberling City. After the week-long odyssey, floaters returned to Galena on the train, a ride of only twenty-one miles.

Even the building of Powersite Dam on White River in 1913 did not impede floaters, who simply moved around the obstruction. An old-timer recalled that ". . . city fishermen could still come in by train, put in at Galena or Branson and float down White River. At Powersite the Empire District Electric Company had a span of white mules to haul your boat from Ozark Beach to the tailrace below the dam and put you back on the river."

"Camps" also developed along the riverbanks of both the James and the White for those who preferred not to spend an entire week on the river, providing scenic vacation spots for the families of floaters. Some offered surprisingly modern comforts.

At first float fishing was a pastime of the relatively well-to-do. It was expensive to organize a safari-like expedition of boats, tents, fishing gear, provisions, and guides to make camp and cook. All these preparations must have been amusing to the "natives" along the rivers, who had always float-fished with little more than a can of worms and a crock jar wrapped in wet burlap to keep it cool. But one outsider recorded that on his trip, ". . . at Pulltight Spring a hillman struggled down the slope to bring us biscuits his wife had baked. . . . We made friends all down the valley that year and they helped us in later voyages. . . . People lived all along the river; it was their highway, and they traveled it in johnboats."

Further, these voyagers learned, as had Henry Rowe Schoolcraft and other explorers before and after him that "the flotsam of a spilled boat is a sad spectacle with wet aftermath."

Early floaters sometimes encountered tie rafts on the rivers. One recorded, "I remember our astonishment on first seeing such a raft heave up its snout and crawl like a snake over a shoal barely under water." Another found ". . . rafts of 1,000 ties, nailed in sections of 50 with saplings, and coupled to bend around the river's curves." When the floaters came upon such tie rafts, they would lash their boats to them, climb aboard, and fish from the ties, then pass in safety when the rafters tied up for the evening.

And once, "Sitting beside our campfire, we saw a pair of natives spearing fish; the steersman sending the johnboat forward with thrusts of a pole, the spearman with his tined weapon poised in the bow beside a torch of pineknots that streaked the water with trembling bars of orange. We watched them pass around a bend of the river—strange, unreal, creatures of a dream, leaving the river silent and dark again under the stars." He wrote of "a dreamlike mingling of tall grass and glassy, sliding water, of towering limestone bluffs, gravel bars white in moonlight and great owls hooting in the forest at night. . . . I saw the rivers as they once were and can never be again."

Not surprisingly, a few traditions begun by tie rafters were passed down to the floaters. At Buttermilk Spring, for example, rafters would drink the buttermilk left in the spring to cool by a neighborhood householder, and leave a coin in payment. Fishing floaters continued the practice.

These early trips were made without benefit of outboard motors. The fishermen drifted silently, poled or paddled along—usually by a guide—a "calloused hillman with a bottomless barrel of stories, jokes, tall tales and priceless fishing information." The guide was also responsible for setting up camp and cooking the outfit's meals. Partially because of the "mystique" of these river-wise and outgoing natives with peppery personalities—and the charm endowed to "hillbilly" culture in general by the outsiders—the guides themselves often became local celebrities. Customers often returned just to further enjoy the guide's company and told others who came seeking a similar experience. Indeed, floaters frequently chose their guides as much for their ability to tell colorful stories and jokes as for their prowess with a johnboat; that was a given. Some rivers had as many as eight or ten outfitters, and most outfitters and guides worked more than one river.

The guided float trip appealed to non-fishing floaters as well. Many floated the rivers who wanted nothing more than to enjoy the peace, the beautiful scenery, and the fresh air of the river. Eventually the rich and famous discovered floating Ozarks rivers; the trips were described in the pages of such magazines as *Life, Look,* and *Sports Afield.*

. . . In a Johnboat

"Wooden johnboats—once they were as much a part of the Ozark streams as the woodducks and the acorns, the hog-mollies and muskrats and caves and springs and rope swings," says Larry Dablemont of Harrison, Arkansas.

In his history of float fishing, Dablemont records that similar boats were used by Louisiana Cajun bayou people and in Canada by French trappers. The Cajuns referred to them as "jump-boats," and it seems likely that their French-dialect pronunciation of "jump-boat" eventually was interpreted as "johnboat" and carried to the Ozarks. The resourceful Ozarker tailored the basic design to his own needs.

The wooden johnboat was characterized by a flat bottom, curved

The silent and stable shallow-draft johnboat was either originated for, or adapted to, Ozarks rivers soon after settlement of the region. Most boaters built their own craft. Frequently the same man might build several boats for himself and others in the course of a lifetime, occasionally modifying or individualizing the design to suit himself. Modern johnboats are usually factory-built and powered by a small outboard motor especially equipped for shallow water. (Courtesy of Bittersweet, Inc.)

The building of Powersite Dam to form Lake Taneycomo at Branson, Missouri, changed more than White River. The new lake changed the lifestyle of those who lived near it, serving as mail and grocery route, easier transportation to the towns along its shores, and as an attraction to bring visitors to the formerly isolated neighborhood. The structure was still called the White River Dam when this photo was taken, about 1911.

sides, a squared bow and stern, and rake at both ends. There were as many types of johnboats as there were boat builders, but each had those common features, despite width or length. Designed for fishing the pools (called eddies) of the area rivers and floating over the swift, shallow riffles, the johnboat floated downstream with the current, paddled by one person in the back using a lightweight (often sassafras) paddle.

Often slightly altered to fit the peculiar demands of the individual river, the design was especially popular for its remarkable stability. A fisherman could stand in the front of the boat—or even fall out—without turning it over.

At the end of the float, in the early days, the boats were usually abandoned. Poling or paddling against the current of an Ozarks river was not worth the effort to retrieve the cheap, easily-constructed johnboats. Later, as the cost of materials to build them increased, especially if there was a road nearby and someone to haul them, they might be loaded onto a wagon and returned to the point of origin. Where the railroad served an area, the boats were loaded onto flatcars for the trip upstream.

But in the 1950s commercial boat builders began to make aluminum johnboats to replace the heavy wooden ones, and floaters could own and transport their own boats. Better roads—and the proliferation of state and federal put-in and take-out points—helped transform Ozarks river floats from a sport for the fortunate few into a family activity.

By the late 1950s and early 1960s the fishing guide business had slowed and canoeing became popular. As the johnboats were replaced by canoes, the guiding business died. "People began to change," said one lifelong guide who was forced to seek other ways of making a living. "The younger generation was not as interested in fishing. It seemed like all they wanted to do was paddle around in them old canoes, fall out of 'em, swim, and play in the water."

Nowadays, the term "float trip" more often means canoeing down the rivers, although outfitters still offer guided johnboat floats—powered by outboard motors—on the White River below Bull Shoals Dam, where the stable fishing craft are still uniquely suited to the trout fishing now done on the White.

(Detailed illustrated plans for constructing a wooden johnboat can be found in *Bittersweet Country*, edited by Ellen Gray Massey, published by the University of Oklahoma Press.)

Among those said to have enjoyed early float trips was Harold Bell Wright, author of the novel, *The Shepherd of the Hills*. History records that Wright made two such trips from Galena to Branson. The first trip lasted about a week and consisted of viewing the scenery and visiting with the people along and adjacent to the river. His second trip lasted about two weeks, with little or no fishing and more neighborhood visiting. On that trip he camped for a time at the mouth of Indian Creek. While there, Wright visited Marvel Cave, Uncle Ike, and other people along the roads and trails that led to the river. It was on these trips, in the opinion of his guide, that he gained the inspiration and formulated the plot for his most famous book.

The Shepherd of the Hills

And that book, *The Shepherd of the Hills*, unquestionably played a major role in the development of the "Land of a Million Smiles." Published in 1907, it became an instant best-seller. Advertised in the *Saturday Evening Post* and the Sears Roebuck catalog, the idyllic portrayal of the Ozarks and its people found its way to major cities and to Europe.

The book triggered a phenomenon. Set in the unfictionalized settings of the White River Hills and inspired by real, breathing human beings (some of whom could still be identified in the community), *The Shepherd of the Hills* unleashed an explosion of tourism into southwest Missouri. It helped to further the idea of "taking the cure" in the Ozarks. Its timing was perfect. At about the same time the novel was published, access to the Ozarks was dramatically improved by the coming of the White River Line. Thanks to the new railroad, the book's readers could visit the setting for themselves.

Further, the railroad made it possible for many to take advantage of the many recreational resources that had previously been used by only a hardy few. The line ran 254 miles from Carthage, Missouri, to Newport, Arkansas, and generally followed the course of the White River. It provided comfortable, affordable access to the White River Hills, where terrain had previously discouraged travel. Development for outsiders by outsiders began almost immediately.

For many years the railroad itself publicized the whole White River region, offering special excursion rates to weekend and holiday visitors and summer tourists. Photography was important in promotion, and souvenir postcards spread the image of the Ozarks far and wide. In the service of tourism, amenities such as electricity, decent roads, and indoor plumbing were introduced into the Upper White River Valley.

Lake Taneycomo

The craze for the White River Hills might have subsided, after a time, had it not been for the building of Powersite Dam and Lake Taneycomo (named for *Taney Co*unty, *Mo.*). A small lake formed by a small dam (by modern standards), the impact of Lake Taneycomo was gigantic.

Using the region's plentiful water power to run machinery was a familiar idea in the Ozarks, where virtually every creek that flowed during the harvest season had, at one time or another, been harnessed to drive a flour or gristmill. But the idea of damming the White caused considerable furor. Some objected for "conservation" reasons, and others vigorously opposed licensing a private company to profit from a public waterway. A local newspaper editor wrote that the government was "giving away franchises worth millions of dollars to greedy corporations for nothing," and argued that the government should control the streams. The desire for electric power and the dream of bringing industry to the Ozarks, however, won the debate. The dam, authorized in 1911 and completed in 1913, was said to be the largest power dam in the country when it was built. It is twelve hundred feet long and fifty feet high.

It is doubtful whether the developers of the dam had any idea that they were in the vanguard of changes that would literally remake the map of the Ozarks in the next half-century. The dam brought more than a change in the river and the geography of the region; it brought changes in lifestyle, population, and channeled development.

Hundreds of men worked on the dam, built virtually by hand with only the aid of mules, horses, large scoop shovels, and the most basic of tools. For many of them, transportation was a problem; there were no autos in the county at that time. Bunkhouses and mess halls were constructed where men could eat and sleep, as well as a commissary where the laborers could purchase goods and pay by the week. Some moved their families to the site and lived in tents or constructed inexpensive shacks. The area just northwest of the building site became so populated it was named Camp Ozark.

Forsyth attorney Douglas Mahnkey remembered watching the construction as a nine-year-old boy. "We lived at Kirbyville," he says, "and it was such a project that Dad would rent or borrow a hack, Mom would pack a picnic lunch, and we'd ride over to the bluffs at Powersite and watch them work. They had one dredge pulling gravel, and the rest was men, mules, horses, and shovels."

Water pouring over the completed dam created the area's newest scenic view—and safely submerged the shoals upstream as it deepened water in a twenty-two-mile stretch where boats of considerable size could freely navigate the river. Even more tourists came to see the lake and ride the boats; now there were more reasons to vacation in the Ozarks. Lakeside resorts were built to accommodate the visitors and, gradually, roads were improved to make their coming even easier.

"Them Tourists Ain't Nothin' But People"

Awakened to the beauty and charm of the "Shepherd of the Hills Country" by Wright's novel, the promotions of the railroad and the Ozark Playgrounds Association, and drawn to the fascinating new Lake Taneycomo, the trickle of visitors to the Ozarks increased to a flood. Entrepreneurs rushed to provide them with more and more to see and do.

Visitors could tour Marble Cave (later Marvel Cave and part of Silver Dollar City) and Fairy Cave (today operated as Talking Rocks Cavern). Or they could participate in local festivities such as bronco-riding exhibitions; camping-out celebrations featuring nationally known traveling vaudeville troupes, plays, and musicals performed in Marble Cave; fiddling contests; art exhibits and competitions; and picnics. And always there was the lake for swimming and fishing—and the float trips.

So many people came that discussion of the visitors reached all parts of Taney County. Emmett Adams remembered that people were curious about these "tourists":

> A couple, Uncle John and Aunt Mary, who lived twenty-five miles from Forsyth, heard so much about the tourists that they decided to come and see one. Uncle John hitched the team to the buggy and in due time they reached the county seat. Aunt Mary sat in the buggy while Uncle John visited with a few old timers he knew. Pretty soon, Aunt Mary got out of the buggy, went over to Uncle John, took him by the arm and said, "Come on. Let's go home. Them tourists ain't nothin' but people."

Cruisin' Down the Lake

Following completion of the dam, the ferries that had crossed the river were eliminated. But boat traffic thrived on the new lake. In the first ten weeks after Lake Taneycomo filled, six excursion boats began operating out of Branson. They offered sightseeing trips downriver to the dam, moonlight rides, and later, dance trips complete with orchestra.

Sightseers and other travelers began to leave the train in Branson to take a boat ride on the lake to enjoy the view or as an aid to finding a shoreline resort of their choice.

Because the roads were so miserable, whenever possible everything —passengers, mail, freight—went by boat. Anything bound for Forsyth was hauled there from Ozark Beach, where the boats were docked. Much later a resident recalled, "The big event of the day was when the boat from Branson arrived. Besides bags of mail, there were boxes of groceries, huge cakes of ice, cases of pop, big boxes of bread." Boats on

Lake Taneycomo were the *Sadie H.*; the *Sammy Lane*; the *Jim Lane*, a freighter; a paddlewheeler, *Virginia May*.

The pride of the line was *The Shepherd of the Hills*, "a beautiful boat with pilot house at the top," remembered a lady who was a teenager at the time. "On summer moonlight nights the *Shepherd* pushed a dance barge for a special evening cruise for dancing. Once the *Shepherd* made a special trip for a boat load of the young men of that area who were leaving for service during World War I. Their families gathered there at Ozark Beach to see them off." *The Shepherd of the Hills* washed over the dam in the flood of 1927.

Even after roads were completed around Taneycomo in the 1940s, the line continued to carry mail and passengers. "The roads were in such awful shape," remembers a resident, "a lot of people preferred to take the boat because it was smoother, and sometimes a shorter ride." The water route mail service continued into the early 1960s, when the contract went to rural carriers.

Descendants of the *Sammy Lane* still carry tourists on Lake Taneycomo—upwards of a hundred thousand of them annually.

The Megalakes

Part of the mystique generated about the White River country was that the pure mountain air had a special, almost magical ability to induce good health. Promoters of the healthy Ozarks boasted of its effects on sickly Harold Bell Wright.

Pearl Spurlock, who operated an early taxi service in the area, also emphasized the wholesomeness of the climate. She recounted the tale of some great-great-grandsons who wanted the family patriarch, aged 145, to die so they could finally receive their inheritance. They took him from the Ozarks to Chicago, where he promptly expired. When the family brought him back home to be buried, however, the Ozarks air resuscitated him. When he finally died of natural causes, the heirs interred him in Chicago to prevent another resurrection.

To sum up the reasons why this corner of the Ozarks was so popular so early: visitors began to flock to "Ozark Mountain Country" to look at the scenery, to visit the storied "Shepherd of the Hills" setting, to play in Lake Taneycomo, to float the rivers, to hunt and fish, and to enjoy the magical pure air.

Then, in the generation after World War II, another factor entered the equation: The Corps of Engineers built more than a dozen "megalakes" on Ozarks rivers. Suddenly, there were lakes—and the recreational opportunities they offer—dotted virtually around the whole Ozarks. And one or more of them were within a day's drive of millions of potential visitors.

Early automobile tourists often discovered, to their dismay, that Ozarks roads were not ready for the horseless carriage. These travelers required the assistance of a local farmer and his team to negotiate this stretch of road. (Courtesy of State Historical Society of Missouri)

Although the Corps had no intention of creating a tourism industry when it built the lakes, in effect that is exactly what happened. The close proximity of several of these lakes in the southwest Missouri Ozarks added fuel to the fire of tourism and fed a blaze that has become an inferno.

New Destinations

And there is one other major facet of the history of Ozarks tourism to be considered. Until quite recently, "tourist attractions" in the region were intended primarily to offer visitors something *else* to do while they were here—to fill a rainy day or provide a quiet evening with the family after a day on the lake. But within the past couple of decades, some of the attractions have themselves become *destinations*: people come into the region specifically to visit them, rather than use them as a backup pastime when too sunburned to boat or to wile away an evening without television.

Silver Dollar City is a prime example, of course. And so is what is now being called the *music show industry*, as though the music shows constitute an industry of their own separate from the industry of tourism.

Perhaps they do. In 1985 a six-mile stretch of Hwy. 76 was dubbed "76 Country Boulevard" in a contest sponsored by the Branson/Lakes Area Chamber of Commerce. Indeed, Branson has begun to boast of having more music shows and big name stars—many of whom are building their own theaters in this neighborhood—than Nashville. Now the "industry" is capable of seating more than fifty thousand people in the Branson area on a given day. Called "the strip" by most residents, 76 Country Boulevard is home to more than two dozen country music shows, making it a vacation destination for travelers who appreciate "country music, country crafts, country cooking, and country fun" all in one location.

Not all that long ago, live music in Branson began and ended with "Presley's Mountain Music Jubilee," the "Baldknobbers," and a local family band. But the emphasis has shifted from the tenacious locals who started it all to imported "national" performers; the music in Ozark Mountain Country has all the glitz and glitter of Las Vegas. Not so many people, apparently, still want to hear "the music of the Ozarks"; those who do go to Ozark Folk Center at Mountain View, Arkansas, and to the pickin' and grinnin' on the square there (see Chapter 15) and in a few other isolated hamlets throughout the Ozarks.

There is still another magnet drawing visitors to the Ozarks these days, one that is often overlooked. That is the plethora of heritage crafts available here, often made from native materials, and the products of local looms, spinning wheels, kilns, tanneries, and the like. One has only to witness the growth and popularity of a crafts outlet such as Engler Block in Branson and those of the Arkansas Craft Guild to see evidence of this phenomenon, to say nothing of the astonishing popularity of the Ozark Arts and Crafts Fair at War Eagle that has now grown to two giant events annually.

Taken all together, and adding all the individual reasons why people visit the Ozarks, there seems little doubt that the region's guest list will continue to grow—and with it the facilities to accommodate them.

Taneycomo Today

The building of Table Rock Lake upstream changed Lake Taneycomo. Now its water comes from deep in the larger lake and is extremely cold—less than 50 degrees. This changed habitat is far too cold for the native fish, but not too cold for trout.

Anticipating the change, the Missouri Department of Conservation began stocking rainbow trout in Lake Taneycomo in 1958 when Table Rock Dam closed. Now Taneycomo trout are numerous and easy to catch.

The trout hatchery for Missourians was part of the mitigation for Table Rock Dam, and today Shepherd of the Hills Hatchery feeds fish into what has become the premier trophy trout fishing lake in Mid-America and arguably the best in the entire country. And, in turn, the nationally famed trout fishery has been yet another major factor in the continued development of the Branson area as a retirement and tourism community.

Almost as a bonus, the White River lakes dominate all bass records, despite the many other impoundments in Missouri and Arkansas.

CHAPTER 7

Northwest Arkansas City

Six months after the battle at Wilson Creek near Springfield, Missouri, the same Confederate Army met a slightly different Union Army in another—decisive—battle for the strategic control of the key state of Missouri. The side that held Missouri and her natural resources also stood to gain control of the entire West. Many believe the Battle of Pea Ridge to be the most important Civil War engagement west of the Mississippi. It was certainly the strangest: The South attacked from the north using some French-speaking soldiers and more than a thousand Cherokees; the North fought from a defensive position on Southern soil using some troops who spoke German.

The Battle of Pea Ridge marked the end of a campaign that began on Christmas Day, 1861, with the appointment of Brig. Gen. Samuel R. Curtis to head the Federal Southwestern District of Missouri. Acting with more zeal than his predecessors, Curtis at last began pushing Confederate and pro-Confederate forces out of the state. By mid-February 1862 he and his troops had chased their main opponents, Maj. Gen. Sterling Price and the Missouri State Guard, into Arkansas.

In the Boston Mountains south of Fayetteville, Price joined forces with Brig. Gen. Ben McCulloch's Confederates. There Maj. Gen. Earl Van Dorn took command of this combined sixteen-thousand-man force and on March 4 headed it northward, intending to strike into Missouri and capture St. Louis.

It is said that the Southern army burned the rail fences along the road at night to light their march. "The night of March 6 was quite windy, cold and snowy," according to a soldier's diary. The marchers were exhausted, hungry, and chilled to the bone. But dug in across

149

Van Dorn's path on the bluffs overlooking Little Sugar Creek, not far from Elkhorn Tavern and nearby Pea Ridge, were Curtis's 10,500 Federals.

Van Dorn knew that a frontal assault against Curtis's troops would be suicidal, so he swung north to come in behind them. He planned to strike at dawn on March 7, but his troops, weary from a difficult three-day march, arrived hours behind schedule. This gave Curtis time to pull his men away from Little Sugar Creek, face about, and prepare to receive the assault.

Van Dorn then decided to launch a two-pronged assault, hoping to catch Curtis in the middle. First, he sent McCulloch's troops, including two regiments of Cherokee Indians under Brig. Gen. Albert Pike, west of Pea Ridge and the hill known as Round Top to drive down upon the village of Leetown. They ran into an intensive fire that resulted in the deaths of McCulloch and Gen. James McIntosh and the capture of the ranking colonel. With their command structure practically destroyed, McCulloch's men scattered from the field.

The other prong of the attack fared considerably better. Attacking east of Pea Ridge, Price's Missourians slowly but steadily pushed the Federals back until, at nightfall, the Confederates held Elkhorn Tavern and the crucial Telegraph and Huntsville Roads. During the night the survivors of McCulloch's Leetown fight joined them.

On March 7, 1862, when the war came to Elkhorn Tavern, their own home, the Cox family and others fled to the cellar of the building. Historian Elmo Ingenthron wrote, "Almost at once the building above them was impressed into use as a hospital where the wounded and dying were brought for treatment. Pools of blood soon trickled through to the cellar, which then became a sickening and wretched place."

On the morning of March 8, Curtis counterattacked in the tavern area. His massed artillery severely punished the Confederates and his concerted infantry and cavalry attacks began to crumple their defenses. Desperate to hold the site at the junction of the two vital roads, the Confederates stood firm. By mid-morning, however, Van Dorn realized that his ammunition was running short; he ordered his troops to withdraw. The battle of Pea Ridge was over, and the key state of Missouri was still in Union hands.

The diaries and letters of the defeated Confederates tell of more privations suffered on the way back to their refuge in the Boston Mountains. One captain wrote his wife that the retreat was made in the most miserable weather and over the most miserable roads that had ever fallen the lot of man to travel. His command arrived in Van Buren with its horses and men nearly starved to death.

Estimates of the cost of Pea Ridge: the Federals suffered 203 killed,

In Hog Scald Hollow a creek flows across an expanse of bare rock; where it has the added power of a short fall, the water has gouged deep depressions into the stone. In the neighborhood these basins are called "kettles." Foraging Civil War soldiers who had come by a wild hog to butcher but had no kettle in which to scald it (to soften the hide for easier removal of the hair) heated the water in the natural kettles by dropping in red hot stones. Reportedly settlers in the area continued the practice for several generations. Located south of Eureka Springs, Arkansas, a few miles off Hwy. 23, the hollow is on private property.

At the junction of the crucial Huntsville and Telegraph Roads, both important in the Civil War, stood Elkhorn Tavern, home to Jesse Cox and his family. But when war came to Elkhorn Tavern, Cox and his family found themselves in the middle of the Battle of Pea Ridge. Now restored on the grounds of Pea Ridge National Military Park near Rogers, Arkansas, Elkhorn Tavern—and the still-visible imprints of the wartime highways—help visitors visualize the battle that saved Missouri for the Union.

980 wounded, and 201 missing, while the Confederates suffered 1,000 killed and wounded and approximately 300 captured. Some reports consider these figures too conservative. Pike's Indians were accused of scalping their victims, and the Confederates countered with the claim that "Sigel's Germans" were guilty of committing atrocities.

As at Wilson Creek, the fallen were inadequately buried. Said one historian: "Many of the dead were buried on or near the battlefield. For ten miles along the roads by which the Rebels retreated, farm homes were full of the wounded, and those who died in the hastily outfitted hospitals were interred in nearby fields and local burying grounds."

The Pea Ridge National Military Park

A forty-three-hundred-acre unit of the National Park system, the Pea Ridge battlefield has been preserved. (Access is from Hwy. 62 a few miles northeast of Rogers; there are signs directing traffic to the park.) A visitor center is open daily, and a picnic area is nearby. In addition to audio-visual presentations of Civil War history west of the Mississippi and specific to the Battle of Pea Ridge itself, there is a museum of muskets, cannons, uniforms, and other artifacts. There are also hiking trails and a trail for horseback riding.

A self-guiding auto tour leads to key points of the battle, where displays and "sound stations"—tape-recorded information about what he is seeing—help the visitor to visualize and understand the battle. A map furnished at the visitor center places the sequence of events in perspective on the landscape. In addition to the sites on the main battlefield, the time-eroded Federal earthworks are still visible on the crest of the Little Sugar Creek bluff about three miles west of the military park entrance (see the Park Service brochure map).

Elkhorn Tavern

The battle was known as the Battle of Elkhorn Tavern by the Confederates. (In those days *tavern* was synonymous with *inn*.) The two-story building, which tradition dates to 1833, was built of logs. A Federal commander who used the tavern as his headquarters in the fall of 1862 described the building as an ". . . old-fashioned structure, consisting of two apartments and a lean to, on the Virginia model of a century and half gone." He noted, however, that ". . . its overhanging roof and capacious chimneys built up sturdily from the outside gave it an air of comfort."

Jesse C. Cox bought Elkhorn Tavern and the land around it in

1858, and it stayed in his family until 1959. Then it was sold to the state of Arkansas and subsequently donated to the federal government to become part of the Pea Ridge National Military Park. In addition to housing the Cox family, the building served as a post office, a stage stop, and a church before the war. The first Benton County Baptist Society was organized in the building in 1842 and it continued to be a part-time place of worship until 1862, when the congregation moved because of the noisy parties and dances the Federals held in the building during their occupation. Although not an official stop along the Butterfield Overland mail route, individual travelers and those traveling on local stage lines used the tavern for overnight stops.

Cox improved the appearance of the building by weather-boarding it with lumber sawed at Blackburn's mill on War Eagle Creek. Apparently it was Cox who named the building Elkhorn Tavern. A neighbor gave Cox the horns and skull of a large elk he had killed and Cox mounted them and placed them on the ridgepole of the building. The elk horns identified the building until shortly after the Battle of Pea Ridge, when they were reportedly carried away by a Federal colonel, Eugene Carr. Some years after the war, the horns were returned and replaced on the roof of the rebuilt tavern.

After the battle, the Federals stayed in the vicinity for another month. It is presumed that during this time, the tavern served as headquarters for one of the Northern commanders. It is known that by November of 1862 the building was the headquarters of Lt. Col. Albert W. Bishop, commander of the First Arkansas Cavalry Volunteers (Union). During the time of Bishop's occupation of the tavern, it was the last station on the military telegraph line running from St. Louis.

The tavern was particularly important during early December when communications were being transmitted regarding the impending battle at Prairie Grove, Arkansas. According to tradition, when the Federals left to join that battle, bushwhackers burned the building. After the fire only the two rock chimneys and the rock walls of the basement remained.

Joseph Cox, son of Jesse, was in the basement of the original tavern during the Battle of Pea Ridge, and it was he who constructed the present building in 1886—against the original chimney. The present Elkhorn Tavern, therefore, shares the heritage of the original structure.

Numerous alterations were made on the rebuilt tavern prior to its donation to the National Park Service in March 1960. But in 1965, following extensive research, the National Park Service restored the building to closely resemble photographs of the tavern at the time of the Civil War. In a ravine below Elkhorn Tavern is a spring and a cave, and there is a walking trail. There was also a tannery nearby. You can still see the indentation in the ground of the Old Wire Road.

Across the road from Elkhorn Tavern are monuments to the dead of Pea Ridge. One was dedicated on September 1, 1887, in a special ceremony with both Confederate and Union veterans participating. The other, the Goddess of Liberty, was set in 1889 during a soldiers' reunion, and is dedicated to the "Reunited Soldiery" and restored friendship between veterans of both the blue and the gray.

Northwest Arkansas City

Dr. Milton Rafferty, university professor, geographer, and author of *The Ozarks: Land and Life*, refers to the Standard Metropolitan Statistical Area (or "metropolex") of Benton and Washington counties in extreme northwestern Arkansas as "Northwest Arkansas City."

Because the individual small cities of Bentonville, Rogers, Springdale, and Fayetteville have "grown together" along Highway 71 for a distance of some thirty miles, it is difficult to know when you have left one of the towns and entered another. As Rafferty points out, the traffic on Hwy. 71, "the main street of Northwest Arkansas City," is ". . . the frenzied scramble of a big city string street." And for that reason, "There is little to distinguish the strip from scores of others that have grown up throughout the United States except that the roadsides are strewn with feathers blown from semitrailer loads of chickens that are hauled into the food-processing plants in Springdale."

There is plenty of visible history, however, in "Northwest Arkansas City." The best course would be to request information from the local chambers of commerce (see Practical Matters Chart) and chart your own path according to what interests you. Major attractions are listed on the chart. If you would prefer to bypass the metroplex, drive east on Hwy. 62 from Pea Ridge Battlefield to Eureka Springs.

Monte Ne

"The real brains behind William Jennings Bryan and his free silver crusade," is how Vance Randolph referred to William "Coin" Harvey. Harvey came to national prominence in 1894 with the publication of *Coin's Financial School*, a small book advocating bimetallism. It sold more than a million copies in one year and converted vast numbers of Western and Southern farmers to the free-silver doctrines.

Harvey was crushed by the defeat of William Jennings Bryan and Free Silver. According to Randolph, "He intimated profanely that civilization was going to hell in a handbasket, and the honest men would do well to hide their heads in the wilderness."

Harvey turned his back upon a gold-mad world and retired to the Arkansas hills, where he bought six hundred acres in a secluded valley four miles out of Rogers, Arkansas. He decided to call the place Monte Ne. *Monte*, he said, means mountain, and *Ne* is the Cherokee word for water.

Randolph, who met Harvey about this time, remembered him as ". . . rather insignificant to one who could remember the vast mouth and sonorous trumpetings of William Jennings Bryan. Harvey was a lean, well-dressed fellow with gold eye glasses, rather like a prosperous schoolmaster except that he had a weakness for red neckties. There was a cool, remote look in his gray eyes, and he spoke precisely with what the Midwestern newspapermen called a Harvard accent."

Convinced that civilization could not be saved, Harvey planned to preserve a record of progress in science, industry, etc., so that when another culture arose the people could benefit from such progress as ours had made. He planned to build a pyramid at Monte Ne which would house something far more important than corpses.

There were to be four separate vaults in the pyramid, each containing a great number of pictures showing people, animals, machinery, and scientific instruments. Another room was to contain many articles, from needles and safety pins to phonographs and an automobile, all coated with grease or wax to prevent deterioration. In each of the four vaults were to be placed many books dealing with the principal industries and scientific attainments of our society. Each was to contain one copy of a special book written by Harvey himself; it was a report on the rise and growth of the present civilization, complete with his opinions regarding the causes of its collapse. The book was to be specially preserved to last forever.

Harvey envisioned an obelisk 130 feet tall so as to be still visible to future archaeologists as they dug in the rubble and sediment of a bygone society. At the top of the obelisk would be a plate of "the most enduring metal known," and on the plate would be an inscription: *When This Can Be Read, Go Below And Find A Record Of And The Cause Of The Death Of A Former Civilization.*

Entombed along with the other artifacts in the base of the obelisk would be a guide to unlocking the secrets of the English language— since the tongue would be dead by the time civilization rose from the ashes of gold worship. Harvey never explained, however, how the diggers of the future were going to decipher and obey the inscription at the top of the obelisk if the key to the language lay sealed in its base.

An expert from the Portland Cement Association stated that a pyramid built according to Harvey's specifications "would last a million years, and longer."

Harvey's warnings about the fall of civilization seemed nonsense in the early 1920s when the United States was the most prosperous nation on earth. Solid citizens laughed at his prophet-of-doom stance for years. Then came 1929 and the economic collapse which shook the whole country. People wondered if Coin Harvey and William Jennings Bryan had been right all along. In the emergency Harvey returned briefly to public life, organized the Liberty Party, and ran for president in 1932 as its candidate, receiving some fifty thousand votes.

Then, convinced that the American people, who had twice rejected his message, could not long survive, Harvey, now past eighty, returned to Monte Ne obsessed with his plans for preserving a record of their cultural achievements in the great American pyramid.

And it was all good publicity for Monte Ne, where Harvey had established a resort. He persuaded the Frisco railroad to run a spur track to his valley, where he built a railroad station and a big frame hotel called the Frances House. Nearby he built two clubhouses of squared logs with red tile roofs also to house guests of the resort. A gondola carried hotel guests from the railroad depot on a canal he had constructed in the spring valley. He even platted a town, built some civic buildings, and sold a few lots. Humorist Will Rogers met his wife Betty at Monte Ne, where her family lived.

Harvey also did a great deal to promote good roads in Missouri and Arkansas. There were no highways in the Ozarks at that time and automobiles were almost unknown. As early as 1913 he launched the Ozark Trail movement, which marked a motor highway from St. Louis to Las Vegas, New Mexico. Harvey and his party traveled over this road, held public meetings in all the towns, and made careful notes of just what grades, fills, and culverts would be required. This route was later taken over by U.S. Highway 66.

But the number of customers coming to Harvey's resort at Monte Ne slowed to a trickle. And construction on the great pyramid, begun in 1925, came to a halt when Harvey ran out of money. He died in his sleep on February 11, 1936.

Virtually all of Monte Ne was subsequently inundated by the waters of manmade Beaver Lake. All around the cove of Beaver Lake are modern homes and boat docks. When the lake is abnormally low, as in times of severe drought, the bulk of the ruins becomes visible. Constructed to last a million years, they still wait at the bottom of Beaver Lake. And once every couple of decades, when the lake level drops, visitors return to Monte Ne.

Just before the junction of Hwys. 94 and 94S, heading south toward

Monte Ne, there is a long, low building made of logs and stone, with a red-tiled roof—the remains of one of the rustic lodge buildings moved to high ground before the lake filled.

(For a perspective of the Ozarks mill scene, do not overlook a visit to War Eagle Mill. Drive east from Rogers on Hwy. 12 and watch for the sign indicating the turn south to War Eagle.)

War Eagle

The name *War Eagle* appeared and disappeared from postal records and maps from the time of an 1830s settlement on War Eagle Creek until 1880, when it was listed at today's mill site. A romantic legend of the origin of the creek's name is that War Eagle, a young Cherokee warrior whose sweetheart was stolen by a white man, died along the creek while searching for the girl. The stream was then named for him.

A less romantic probability is that the creek is called for an Osage, Hurachis the War Eagle, who signed treaties with the federal government during the 1820s.

Despite floods (past and present), the Civil War, and fire, the big wheel keeps on turning at War Eagle Mill. The first mill on the creek was part of the settlement in the 1830s. When it was washed away by a flood, another was built in 1848, but it was destroyed during the Civil War. In 1873 a new mill was erected on the same foundation; it was consumed by fire in 1924.

The present mill was built in 1973, a replica of the 1873 mill—on the same foundation adjacent to the historic one-lane War Eagle Bridge. Fortunately, photographs of the earlier mill were available to guide the builder. Native lumber was milled by a veteran sawmiller at nearby Pea Ridge. The two sets of buhrs came from a millsite at Old Alabam in Madison County. Collected from many places, most of the milling machinery had to be put back into working condition. The wooden counters and showcases are also worn. Like the 1897 cash register, the merchandising fixtures came from old general stores in the Ozarks.

The mill grinds and sells several different types of grain, and cookbooks for their use are also available. In addition to the stone-ground products, the first two floors of the structure are strongly reminiscent of an old-fashioned mercantile. There are sacks of cornmeal; jars of jam, jelly, sorghum, and honey from the area; herbal teas; tinware and tole items; cutting boards, ironware, and baskets made from Ozarks hardwoods; Christmas ornaments; and much more. Among the country decor offered are beautiful crocheted tablecloths, afghans, and placemats, and a great many other attractive crafts—

Just across War Eagle Creek from War Eagle Mills Farm is the War Eagle Mill, near Rogers, Arkansas. War Eagle offers splendid Ozarks scenery, stone-ground grains and cookbooks, exquisite handmade afghans and tablecloths—and many other handcrafted articles, numerous items for country decorating, and beans and cornbread and other toothsome delights. Or you can simply stand and watch that big wheel keep on turning.

Although it is charmingly off the beaten path, the world comes to War Eagle Mills Farm near Rogers, Arkansas, twice a year during the semi-annual Ozark Arts and Crafts Fair held on the grounds. Hundreds of thousands of Ozarkers and their visitors count on doing their Christmas shopping at War Eagle—and decorating their homes, supplying their gift shops, and being delighted by the handmade wonders, antiques, and collectibles waiting there. The old house has grown around the nucleus of a log cabin.

including handwoven goods—all made by local artisans. Also offered is a collection of original paintings and prints.

On the third floor of War Eagle Mill is the homey Bean Palace Restaurant, where the visitor can indulge in beans and cornbread, buckwheat pancakes, and old-fashioned goodies for the sweet tooth. The daily bill of fare is listed on blackboards. Surrounded by feed sacks and a collection of antiques, diners sit at handmade tables covered by checkered tablecloths. From the high windows of the mill-house there is a view of the dam and the undershot waterwheel.

The power to turn the wheel is furnished by wide and swift War Eagle Creek. Spanning the creek is a single-lane, wooden-plank bridge. And War Eagle Creek still periodically floods the millhouse. In 1984 the water was seven feet deep in the first floor of the mill and four inches over the floor of the one-lane bridge over the creek.

War Eagle Mills Farm

The founder of the first mill at War Eagle, Sylvanus Blackburn, also built a log house across the stream from the mill. The log cabin has been enclosed in the farm house, which has grown over the years as its uses and needs have changed.

War Eagle Mills Farm has always had a goodly number of people who came to fish, camp, and relax by the peaceful stream when the crops were "laid by." For a couple of decades in the first half of this century, choice spots along the War Eagle were lively with vacationers from late spring until early fall.

At one time the old farmhouse saw duty as the War Eagle Hotel, which catered to drummers who called regularly on the merchants of the two country stores. The hotel also kept out-of-town fishermen and boarded the country schoolteachers during the school term.

In 1935 War Eagle Mills Farm was sold to Oklahomans who developed Pine Grove Camp, adding rustic log cabins to the pastoral creekside scene. But the flood of 1943—when the water was nine inches above the floor of the bridge—washed the cabins away.

Today War Eagle Farm is a home again, but with an important difference.

"War Eagle is the kind of place where the dogs do most of their sleeping in the road," said an article writer recently. But certainly not during the Ozark Arts and Crafts Fair, which draws thirty-five or forty thousand people *a day* for four days. This fair is by no means the only crafts fair in the Ozarks, but it is generally acknowledged to be the biggest and most important. In a region known for its arts and crafts, this is the fair to which all others are compared.

It may even be the oldest, as for almost forty years it has been held annually in October. Several years ago the fair had grown so large that it added a second event in May. Staged without commercialism or pretentiousness, the fair provides one of the most exciting markets for handcrafted goods in the Ozarks. More than five hundred booths are housed in a building and five enormous tents. The quality of exhibited goods is strictly regulated by a board of directors, and there is a waiting list of contenders.

The idea for the fair sprouted after members of the Benton County Rug Weavers Association held a successful weaving school in the spring of 1954, and an exhibition of the weavers' work climaxed the school. The rural War Eagle Farm seemed a natural setting for an arts and crafts fair, so the group decided to organize the first fair. The autumn date was set to coincide with the beautiful color of the changing seasons.

Although all the roads from the nearby towns of Rogers, Springdale, Fayetteville, and Eureka Springs were still gravel then, carloads of people braved the bumpy trip. And the fair was such a success that it has been held every year since then.

Because of the large crowds drawn by the event at War Eagle, other fairs are held simultaneously in the neighborhood, and individuals along the nearby roads also take advantage of the traffic and the crowds to hang quilts on the clothesline or fence, and set up racks to display their own wares on their driveways, yards, and porches.

The Springtime War Eagle Fair is smaller, with about 60 percent as many arts and crafts exhibitors as the fall show, but it also includes antiques and collectibles, providing a unique display of pioneer skills and artifacts in one place. Either in the spring or the fall, the War Eagle Fair is a shopper's paradise for the home decorator, collector, buyer for a gift shop or museum, or the individual who likes handcrafted items or antique treasures for herself or to use as gifts.

The Springtime Fair lasts three days, beginning the first Friday in May.

The Ozark Arts and Crafts Fair Association, sponsors of the two annual fairs, also produce a yearly educational seminar. In the summer the War Eagle Seminar encourages others to learn many of the same arts and crafts that have been revived by the fairs. Top-quality instructors are recruited for the faculty. Enrollment fees are modest and the association subsidizes a portion of the annual expenses from funds generated by the fairs.

Beginning on the second Monday of June each year, the seminar runs for two weeks—with the exception of a few week-long "short courses"—Monday through Friday. Classes are taught beneath large tents, in the barn loft, in the rustic exhibits building, or under the trees beside the War Eagle River (see the Practical Matters Chart for where to write).

The Fall War Eagle Fair lasts four days, beginning the third Thursday in October. All events are held rain or shine; no event has ever been canceled in the history of the association.

War Eagle Mill is no closer to town than it was in 1954, but the roads are much improved. More than a hundred acres are available for daytime parking, supervised by experienced attendants. Wrecker service and a first-aid station are also provided. Because of traffic congestion on the one-lane iron bridge across War Eagle Creek, the Ozark Arts and Crafts Fair Association recommends that visitors approach from the south via Hwys. 412 and 303. Both pedestrian and vehicular traffic are extremely heavy at times, and in the interest of safety and convenience, it is preferable to use the ample parking and trained personnel of War Eagle Mills Farm. This route has the added advantage of being the best road—and the most scenic.

All the while you are in the "Northwest Arkansas City" and War Eagle areas, of course, you are skirting around and over Beaver Lake —which offers all the usual fishing, boating, swimming, skiing, diving, and camping facilities of a large Corps of Engineers lake (see the chart). The lake is highly accessible from this vicinity.

To reach Eureka Springs, return to Hwy. 23 from War Eagle (Hwy. 12 east to Hwy. 23 *or* Hwy. 303 south to 412 then east to 23) and turn north on Hwy. 23.

Practical Matters

Chapter 7 — Northwest Arkansas

Checking Out	A Sampling	Phone
Lodging	Best Western Inn, Hwys. 62 & 71, Fayetteville AR;	(501) 442-3041
	Days Inn, Hwy. 71N., Bentonville AR;	(501) 273-2451
	Town & Country Motor Inn, 2102 S. 8th, Rogers AR 72756;	(501) 636-3820
	Best Western Heritage Inn, 1114 W. Sunset, Springdale AR 72764	(501) 751-3100
Bed & Breakfasts	Arkansas Discovery B & B, 1801 Hwy. 12E, Rogers AR 72756	(501) 925-1744
Campgrounds	Withrow Springs State Park, Rt. 3, Huntsville AR 72740;	(501) 559-2593
	Fox-Fire Camping Resort, Hwy. 12 & 45E, Hindsville AR;	(501) 789-2122
	Numerous Corps of Engineers Campgrounds at Beaver Lake (see Where to Write)	
Restaurants	Ozark Mountain Smokehouse, 215 W. Dickson, Fayetteville AR 72701;	(501) 442-2152
	The Old Post Office, Number One Center Square, Fayetteville AR 72701;	(501) 443-5588
	Crumpet Tea Room, 107 W. Elm, Rogers AR	(501) 636-7498
Other Attractions	War Eagle Fair, War Eagle Mills Farm, Rt. 1, Hindsville AR 72738;	(501) 789-5398
	War Eagle Cavern, Rt. 5, Box 748, Rogers AR 72756 (Hwy. 12 east of Rogers);	(501) 789-2909 or (501) 756-0913
	Wal-Mart Visitors Center, 105 N. Main, Bentonville AR 72712;	(501) 273-1329
	Poor Richard's Gift & Confectionary Shop (1907 Drugstore), 116 S. First St., Rogers AR 72756	(501) 631-7687
Outdoor Recreation	Fishing and Canoeing in War Eagle River, access at Withrow Springs State Park (See Campgrounds) and at Beaver Lake (Write Resident Engineer, Drawer H, Rogers AR 72756); Hiking and Backpacking at Devil's Den State Park (Write Park Superintendent, West Fork AR 72774)	

Checking Out	A Sampling	Phone
Main Historical Attractions	War Eagle Mill, Rt. 5, Box 411, Rogers AR 72756;	(501) 789-5343
	War Eagle Mills Farm, Rt. 1, Hindsville AR 72738;	(501) 789-5398
	Pea Ridge National Military Park, 10 miles northeast of Rogers AR on Hwy. 62;	(501) 451-8122
	Arkansas Air Museum, 4290 S. School, Drake Field, Hwy 71 S. Fayetteville AR 72632;	(501) 521-4947
	Headquarters House & Grounds, 118 E. Dickson St., Fayetteville AR 72701;	(501) 521-2970
	The University Museum, Univ. of Arkansas, Garland Ave., Fayetteville AR 72701;	(501) 575-3555\
	Many Other Historic Sites in Fayetteville; See C of C, 123 W. Mountain, for Maps or Write for Information--see Where to Write)	
	Prairie Grove Battlefield State Park, P.O. Box 306, Prairie Grove AR 72753;	(501) 846-2990
	Johnson Mill, 1835 Greathouse Springs Rd., Johnson AR 72741;	(501) 443-1830
	Rogers Historical Museum, 322 S. Second, Rogers AR 72746;	(501) 621-1154
	Vinson Square, First St. & Elm, Rogers AR;	(501) 636-4580
	Poor Richard's, 116 S. First St., Rogers AR;	(501) 631-7687
	Shiloh Museum, 118 W. Johnson, Springdale AR;	(501) 751-8411
	Prairie Grove Battlefield State Park, P.O. Box 306, Prairie Grove AR 72753	(501) 846-2990
Where to Write for More Details	War Eagle Crafts Seminars, Ozark Arts & Crafts Fair Association, Inc., War Eagle Mills Farm, Rt. 1, Hindsville AR 72738;	(501) 789-5398
	Pea Ridge National Military Park: Superintendent, Pea Ridge AR 72751;	(501) 451-8122
	Corps of Engineers, Beaver Resident Office, P.O. Drawer H, Rogers AR 72756;	(501) 636-1210
	Scenic Hwy. 12 East Assoc., 2018 Hwy. 12 East, Rogers AR 72756;	(501) 925-2222
	Fayetteville Chamber of Commerce, 123 W. Mountain, Fayetteville AR 72702;	(501) 521-1710
	Bentonville/Bella Vista Chamber of Commerce, 412 S. Main St., Bentonville AR 72712	(501) 273-2841

CHAPTER 8

"Little Switzerland"

If you yearn to visit a time when ladies wore bustles and twirled parasols while strolling along shady sidewalks, when gents wore stickpins in their cravats and listened to time ticking by on gold pocket watches, where you might have viewed opera through mother of pearl glasses and dined by gaslight and traveled on a "cabbage head" locomotive to a fashionable spa to "take the baths"—then visit Eureka Springs, Arkansas.

While theme parks everywhere strive to capture the essence of the Victorian Age and erect props and imitations to simulate the ambiance, Eureka Springs offers the real thing: real Victorian mansions and buildings, not facades, and real stone walls and time-worn marble sidewalks and narrow, winding streets built for surreys and electric trolleys.

And Eureka Springs is the classic example of how the Ozarks' perceived "backwardness" now works in its favor. Bypassed by the "progressive" world, left in the backwash of the rush to bigger and better, too poor to modernize or compete, Eureka Springs remained as though frozen in time. Until now, when the lovely spa is once again in vogue. Brigadoon-like Eureka picked herself up, dusted herself off, restored a few down-at-the-heels aging buildings, and put a smile on her new-old face.

The Healing Spring

With the suddenness of a Western gold rush town, Eureka Springs came into existence almost overnight. In a matter of weeks it changed

165

On Spring Street in Eureka Springs, Arkansas, at the foot of a bluff about halfway down the mountain from the Crescent Hotel, is Crescent Spring. In the early days water from this spring was piped up the hill to the hotel. The gazebo over the spring was built in the 1890s to replace the original one that burned in 1888.

from a spring flowing in the wilderness to a community of several thousand residents.

It is said that for centuries the Indians had known about the "great healing spring," but few white men visited it, even when the Indians were pushed on into Indian Territory. Then, in 1856, Dr. Alvah Jackson found the spring and believed its waters cured his long-standing illness. The "Indian Healing Spring" was also known as Basin Spring because the water flowed into a small natural stone basin.

During the Civil War, Dr. Jackson established a hospital in the "Rock House," a cave near the spring, where he treated the wounded of both armies. Many concluded they were returned to health by the curative waters of the spring, but essentially it remained hidden in the wilderness until 1879.

The first permanent dwelling at the spring was a small frame house built by Judge L. B. Saunders of Berryville, prominent in legal and political circles, who came at the urging of his friend, Dr. Alvah Jackson, discoverer of the spring. Saunders was so delighted by the relief he obtained after using the spring water that he began to "proclaim abroad the news of his healing." People began coming to the spring.

They came by horseback, in carriages, and by simple farm wagons. They came with families and household belongings or with a single valise containing their "buryin' clothes," but come they did during the summer of 1879. By July 4, 1879, more than four hundred people were camped nearby; they decided that July 4 would be an appropriate day to name their new community. The name *Eureka Springs* is attributed to Burton Saunders, the judge's young son.

The new town grew on four "mountains," with Basin Spring at its center. To furnish lumber for the houses being built around the spring, sawmills developed all around the area. The hillsides themselves were quickly stripped of trees to provide building sites and materials.

The hills were so steep and the houses so close—stacked in layers up the sides of the steep slopes—that one historian claimed that "some residents could step from their gardens to the roof of the house, while others must climb stairways to their vegetable patch." A local story claims that the first lawsuit in Eureka Springs was caused by a woman who lived in one of these terraced homesites. She carelessly threw dishwater out of the back door and down a neighbor's chimney, damaging the furniture.

The first two streets provided for were Main Street (nicknamed Mud Street because of its condition in wet weather) and Spring Street. A stagecoach line began in the autumn of 1879, providing service to larger settlements in all directions and to the railhead ninety miles away at Pierce City, Missouri.

Daily and weekly newspapers began publication in February 1880, heralding the news of a city of healing waters with ten to twelve thousand persons already in residence. Two thousand dwellings had been completed by May 1880; daily mail service was established. Churches and schools were organized; there were some thirty physicians in the community in 1880. Fortunately, there were six photographers among the early settlers, providing for a well-documented visual history of the town.

Basin Spring water began to be sold and shipped to destinations far and wide. All over the United States the face of the "Ozarka Girl," a trademark, was seen as a symbol of the pure spring water shipped from Eureka Springs.

But by 1882 the hillside acres which flanked the deep gulch called "Main Street" were tied up in a four-way court fight that took five years to settle. The original townsite had been platted and claimed in forty-by-forty-foot lots, but there were conflicting homestead claims on the sites of all the springs, and both miners and farmers demanded various portions of the same areas.

The battle was resolved with the assistance of a group of big city promoters, whose knowledge of political processes and access to capital were to determine the future of the town. The Eureka Springs Improvement Company, led by politician and financier Powell Clayton, not only brought the litigation to a successful conclusion, but dreamed up, financed, and brought into being civic projects which, by the turn of the century, made the town a popular and elegant vacation spot for the nation's wealthy.

A happy result of the court fight was that "public preserves" were created around the springs.

Extensive excavation was necessary to bring the railroad to town, but it reached Eureka in February 1883. Connections with the Frisco at Seligman, Missouri, assured the success of Eureka Springs as a health spa catering to visitors from all over the United States. Twenty-three thousand passengers rode the trains into Eureka that first year. Early in 1882 Eureka Springs became "a City of the First Class" with five thousand legal residents: the fourth largest city in the state of Arkansas.

During the late 1880s the city fathers not only installed sidewalks and gaslights, but had the foresight to plant maple and sycamore trees on most of the major streets. By 1891, the rutted dirt streets had been graded and equipped with three miles of tracks so that horse- and mule-drawn streetcars traveled from the train to downtown and up the hills past the doors of the thirty largest hotels. You could also ride the streetcar just for fun—all day for a nickel. The streetcars were electrified by 1899.

By 1885 the city streets were gas-lighted. Sprinkled daily in summer to keep down the dust, the principal streets were widened and graded in 1892. In 1894 the town put into service a municipal water system and a modern sewage disposal system. The fire department was established that same year. In 1895 the community began enjoying the telephone. The Board of Improvements worked diligently to bring into being better streets, board sidewalks—later replaced by stone walks—and public parks. Native stone retaining walls became an attractive feature of the town's landscape; miles of them were completed before the turn of the century.

Victorian Health Spa

From 1885 until about 1910 the town peaked in popularity as a health resort. Proclaimed the "Siloam of the Afflicted," it attracted visitors who flocked on the Eureka Springs Railroad, which scheduled six trains a day. The Frisco advertised Pullman sleeping cars on the direct route to Eureka Springs. Water from Basin Spring was served to guests in all Frisco dining cars. The railroad advertised to the very wealthy, and palatial homes were built in Eureka.

Businesses of every description lined the busy streets, meeting almost every imaginable need in goods and services. Visitors thronged to purchase souvenirs of local onyx, cedar walking sticks—and the now-famous water, conveniently bottled or in kegs.

Visitors were met at the depot by handsome horse-drawn tallyhos and carriages and conveyed stylishly through the streets to well-appointed hotels. Parties on horseback and tallyhos loaded with sightseers were constantly in the streets and nearby countryside. Livery stables abounded. In 1910 electric street lights were installed and a Carnegie public library was under construction.

In addition to seeking his health, the visitor could enjoy a busy social life of style and elegance at the grand musicales and literary evenings. Theatrical productions were staged at the opera house on the corner of Main and Spring Streets. Concert bands performed daily in the pavilion at Basin Spring Park.

Perhaps not surprisingly for a town founded upon water instead of stronger drink, Carry Nation spent the last years of her life in Eureka. Reportedly she blasted an "ice box" out of solid rock to use a spring—which still bears her name—as cold storage. She died here in 1911 after a stroke following a "fire and brimstone" temperance speech at Basin Park.

But the city that grew like wildfire paid the price. In 1883 seventy-five homes and businesses went up in flames. A second major fire occurred in 1888, destroying the majority of the Spring Street business district. Beginning in the Perry House hotel, a third fire burned in 1890; and in 1893 the fourth big burn claimed a number of hotels as well as homes.

The next stage in the city's development ensured it against more than fire; it ensured its longevity. Much more permanent structures were built of native stone quarried near the White River. The new stone buildings also greatly improved the city's appearance. By now, however, the crowds coming to the springs had begun to dwindle and some hotels were never replaced.

By 1904, the permanent population was recorded as five thousand. Fourteen physicians and six dentists were in residence and at least one sanitarium offered treatment for chronic diseases. But by this time people generally had begun to rely heavily on medicine and surgery for the healing of physical ailments. The reliance upon and faith in natural cures diminished rapidly, and individuals no longer visited the health spas in such numbers. Gradually visitors changed from health-seekers to those looking for rest and relaxation in beautiful surroundings.

Several livery stables still flourished, meeting the needs of visitors for riding horses and transportation by carriage. The electric street railway was the most popular means of transport within the city itself. Then in 1906 the automobile arrived in Eureka Springs; within a decade local residents owned twenty-five of these modern vehicles. By 1916 there were only twenty-five saddle horses for hire in a community which had at one time required hundreds. By 1920 the street railroad ceased operation. In 1928 the tracks were removed and the principal streets were paved.

And convict labor had built Highway 62, enabling visitors to arrive by private automobile. With the motorcar an era arrived that exists to this day. By 1929, fifty years after the founding of the town, visitors arriving by automobile found accommodations in several remaining hotels and two rustic "tourist camps."

In 1929 it was estimated that the automobile brought five hundred thousand people to the Ozark Mountain area annually. The era of motor tourism had begun.

Into the Twentieth Century

From the beginning in Eureka Springs, unfortunately, the drive to supply the town with expensive civic luxuries in order to promote its salability to visitors had saddled it with debts that, in 1907, threw the town into a depression from which it had not recovered when the national Depression hit in 1929.

During the first fifty years of Eureka Springs' history, more than fifty hotels of differing capacities came and went. By 1930, only three of those—the Crescent, the Basin Park, and the Wadsworth (later to be called the Allred, the Springs, and the New Orleans)—were still doing business.

Then the Missouri and North Arkansas Railroad, formerly the Eureka Springs Railroad, relocated its shops; its loss was devastating to Eureka. In 1913 the company had built a spacious new stone depot, but by 1920 passenger service to the resort had decreased to the point that the line was no longer profitable. In 1921 a fraudulent oil well scheme raised the hopes of local citizens—until the derrick mysteriously burned and the stockholders lost their investment. In the autumn of 1922 the last remnant of the old Henry Starr gang attempted to rob the Bank of Eureka Springs. After a brief shoot-out with local businessmen the criminals were either killed or captured, and the affair became a sensation in the press across the country.

The elegant years faded like a dream.

But gradually artists and writers were drawn to the quaint little town nestled in the enduring hills. And with all the new-found freedom of their family cars, families began vacationing in Eureka Springs and the rest of the Ozarks in increasing numbers. After World War II and the end of gasoline rationing and scarce tires and repair parts, tourism increased appreciably, providing funds for more individual restoration efforts.

When the Corps of Engineers completed Beaver Lake in the 1960s, the keystone was in place. Now visitors to Eureka Springs also have access to water sports. From drinking the water to playing in it, "the town that water built" has come full circle.

Eureka Springs Today

Today's visitors still seek relaxation and recreation in a refreshing atmosphere. Located in the midst of a scenic area of rugged hills and deep gorges, Eureka Springs has earned the nickname of "Little Switzerland." True, instead of riding up the mountain from the train station in a horse-drawn tallyho and changing into silk and satin for dinner, today's visitor—wearing shorts and Reeboks—arrives in a private car and has likely already eaten at McDonald's.

But still heard in the valley of the springs is the pealing of a church bell; it echoes through the hills as such chimes must do in the real Switzerland. Vying for notice is the homesick whistle of a steam engine, the crowing of a rooster, the barking of a village dog. Standing on the summit of East Mountain, the visitor can catch a glimpse of the locomotive's headlight, as it wheezes into the twilighted yards below, and watch the setting sun rouge the windows of the Grand Old Lady, the Crescent Hotel, across the valley on the summit of West Mountain.

Nothing has really changed in Eureka Springs. The elegance may be behind her, but the glory days are at hand.

People still congregate around Basin Spring, though instead of covered wagons or pedestrians with cedar walking canes, you will find a concrete-and-rock-walled courtyard with shaded benches for resting from the climb up Spring Street. The exaggerated tales continue to be told about the "crazy quilt" town. There is the fellow, for instance, who does not need a picture window in his house to observe the scenery. He merely looks up the chimney. You may still hear the story of the well digger who was digging a well on East Mountain. When down about forty feet, the bottom of the well fell out and he landed on his feet right in the middle of Main Street. He had to change his plans and dig the well up instead of down.

Made famous many years ago by Ripley's *Believe It Or Not*, several sites in Eureka Springs are no less enjoyable today: Basin Park Hotel, "eight floors and every floor a ground floor"; St. Elizabeth's Church, "entered through the steeple" (actually a separate bell tower); and Pivot Rock, sixteen inches in diameter at the base and thirty-two feet across at the top.

In both the residential areas and the downtown Historic District there are located a great many examples of fine late Victorian architecture. The stone business and public buildings were constructed by skilled craftsmen in a time when much of the work was laboriously done by hand. The many fine old Victorian homes were well made and embellished with picturesque wooden "gingerbread." In fact, the entire town is listed on the National Historic Register. Nowadays the decorative stone buildings house myriad shops and stores, many of them featuring decor and costuming appropriate to the Victorian character of the downtown area. Artists and craftsmen at work in their studios add color and interest as they create beautiful and unique pieces.

You can choose between century-old accommodations and dining rooms and modern motels and restaurants. In addition to the Historic District with its shops, galleries, artists' studios, crafts workshops, Victorian tour homes, and antique dealers, there are many other interesting attractions in the town and its vicinity which are widely advertised.

The easiest way to become acquainted with Eureka Springs is to request the lavish brochure offered by the Chamber of Commerce (see Practical Matters Chart). The booklet includes maps, advertisements of hotels, motels, restaurants, and attractions so that you can

In the "crazy quilt" town of Eureka Springs, Arkansas, built on the sides of four mountains, the streets were designed for pedestrians and people on horseback—not cars. The city runs a fleet of open-air trolleys to help alleviate congestion. Somehow the trolleys seem right at home on streets once plied by electric trolley cars. (Courtesy of Arkansas Department of Parks and Tourism)

plan your visit in advance. There is a lot to see and do; one day is not enough.

While it is not advisable to just "stop by" Eureka Springs without advance reservations—at least from Memorial Day through October —you can also pick up the brochure at the Chamber of Commerce office on Hwy. 62 West.

Often referred to as the "Stair Step Town" because of its steep hills and the wooden stairways between levels, Eureka Springs is a walking town. The streets were laid out to accommodate pedestrians and horseback riders, not multilanes of automobile traffic. Walking puts you in touch with the beauty, charm, and history of Eureka Springs like nothing else. To guide your walks, the Eureka Springs Preservation Society has published a Scenic Walking Tours booklet which divides the city into six different walking routes. Tours show you popular points of interest and scenic areas in the Historic District as well as landmarks in outlying areas. A comprehensive description of each tour is included along with a map. A master map of the city also relates walking tours to color-coded trolley routes.

The second-best way to see Eureka Springs is by open-air trolley, a tradition since early visitors arrived by train, though today's cars are rubber-tired rather than electric. Request a trolley map showing the color-coded routes that correspond with the individual trolley cars so that you know each car's destination and route. They make the rounds of all the major hotels and motels and tourist attractions. You can leave your car parked—at your hotel or at municipal parking lots in various places throughout the town—and see the sights without hunting for nonexistent parking spaces in the crowded downtown area. A paved park-and-ride lot is adjacent to the Chamber of Commerce office. You can purchase a single-ride ticket or an all-day pass.

Accommodations in Eureka range from elegant Victorian hotels receiving guests in the grand manner to gingerbreaded bed-and-breakfasts (dozens to choose from!) to rustic log cabins dating back to "tourist camp" days to modern motels with swimming pools and water beds to cabins, cottages, and tourist homes.

Restaurants are just as eclectic. Favorites are the Victorian Sampler Tearoom, featuring outstanding food, service, and atmosphere; the Victorian splendor of the Crystal Dining Room at the Crescent Hotel; and Dairy Hollow House, where reservations are necessary sometimes weeks in advance.

As is happening in other highly developed tourist areas in the Ozarks, the "season" is being extended to include several weeks between Thanksgiving and Christmas. To help entice visitors, Eureka gets dressed up for Christmas. Outlined in lights, the ornate porches of the Victorian homes and the turrets of the grand old buildings downtown are even more breathtaking.

While there are attractions enough in and around Eureka Springs to sustain an extended visit, there follows just a mere sampling of the more history-oriented.

Whether you are walking, driving, enjoying the trolley, or a rented motor bike available on the highway, be sure to travel the Historic Loop (Hwy. 62B) in Eureka Springs. But be careful; the street is extremely narrow and curving. And the temptation is strong to stare at the hundreds of Victorian mansions lining its curbs. The route also passes by the long-famed Crescent Hotel ("the Grand Old Lady of the Ozarks") constructed at the outrageous sum of a quarter of a million dollars at a time when a house and three city lots could be had for a hundred dollars and eight hundred dollars was a handsome annual income.

The Grand Old Lady of the Ozarks

In 1886 the "Castle in the Wilderness" opened with a grand ball attended by the socially elite from several states. The prominent and wealthy came to enjoy their "Season at the Springs." Four hundred prominent citizens, including the chief justice of Arkansas, and several judges, attended the gala opening ball. In a day when travel was slow and tedious, famous names registered from as far away as New York, Chicago, New Orleans, and Dallas. The *St. Louis Globe Democrat* later described the attire of the ladies, who appeared in velvets, silks, and lace accessorized with diamonds and ostrich tips.

That day the local newspaper reported that an Irish stonemason, imported to help build the limestone-marble structure, predicted that ". . . the eighteen inch thick walls of the Crescent, fitted without the use of mortar, would withstand the destructive forces of time and retain its original beauty for many years to come." He was right.

The hotel maintained its own orchestra. It provided a sun parlor, tennis courts, pool rooms, a bowling alley, a swimming pool, saddle horses, nightly dances in the large ballroom, and a supply of fresh spring water for drinking and bathing on every floor. The telephone directory listed four numbers for the Crescent, but warned, "Calls not answered in thunderstorms."

By 1902, however, the hotel needed a face lift. Leased by the Frisco Railroad, which advertised it widely, the Crescent reopened on July 3, 1902. But after five years as a year-round resort, the hotel went into the same decline that had afflicted Eureka Springs as a whole. The Grand Old Lady lost her international reputation and prestige.

Since 1886 the Crescent Hotel in Eureka Springs, Arkansas—the Castle in the Wilderness—has looked down upon the rest of the town like a benevolent monarch. Despite the size of this grand old hotel, it manages a homey coziness along with its air of faded elegance. The halls fairly reek of history.

At the depot of the Eureka Springs & North Arkansas Railway in Eureka Springs, Arkansas, this Railway Express cart seems to be waiting for the next train. The depot is an experience in déjà vu for those able to remember those halcyon days, an education for those too young—and a delight for all. Visitors can ride the train pulled by a steam locomotive and dine in a restored dining car.

From 1908 to 1932, to supplement lagging winter hotel business, the hotel was rented to a Conservatory for Young Women from September to May. In 1912 the tuition was $375 a year including room and board. *The Crescent College Bulletin* for the academic year 1916-17 touted the Eureka Springs climate (". . . every breath drawn is life-giving . . .") and the healing waters of its springs. Water from Crescent and Congress Springs stood in bottle fountains on all floors. But Crescent College closed its doors in 1924, according to its newsletter, ". . . because of lack of interest, lack of funds, and lack of backing by the citizens."

A junior college operated in the hotel for a couple of years during the Depression, but it also folded. The grand old lady struggled along as a seasonal hotel for a few more years.

In 1937 the building was sold to "Dr." Norman Baker, who had just finished serving time in a Texas prison for fraud. A flashy dresser (purple was his color, over a bulletproof vest), his specialty was miracle cures for cancer, although he did also transplant goat glands for those wanting "renewed sexual vigor." He was a protégé of the infamous "Dr." John Brinkley.

Inasmuch as Baker claimed to cure cancer in promotional literature he mailed throughout the nation, he was convicted of mail fraud in 1940. The hospital was then abandoned and the building—which had undergone some irreversible changes during Baker's tenure—deteriorated badly while it stood empty during the years 1940 to 1946.

In 1947 a group of Chicago businessmen acquired the property, restored it back to a fine hotel and promoted the Crescent as "A Castle in the Air High Atop the Ozarks." Through various owners and managers, the hotel is again one of the Ozarks' most enchanting.

Adding to the charm and personality of the "Grand Old Lady," the Crescent is reputed to be haunted by several ghosts. Whether or not you wish to share your accommodations with possible ghosts, do at least visit. Ride the hydraulic elevator to the Top of the Crescent Lounge. Step out on the observation deck four stories above the summit of West Mountain and gaze—between the gaslights—at the Ozark hills and down at Eureka Springs. Ride a horse-drawn carriage from the sweeping entrance of the hotel through the Victorian elegance of another day.

The lobby is furnished in period furniture, and the front desk appears the same as in old photographs of the hotel, as does the magnificent fireplace. Huge wooden columns, fan-shaped transoms over the doors, hardwood floors that gap a little and squeak as you walk on them bespeak the Crescent ambiance. Be sure to notice the ceiling fans and the chandeliers and the design carved into the

wooden banisters and the way the carpeted stairwell forms a mesmerizing design as it winds upward.

Say hello to "Morris," the hotel's mascot—once a stray kitten taken
in by the cook and now a cherished member of the staff. Morris has
his own door, complete with its little staircase and exit sign.

Indeed, so much history and tradition swirls around you in these
mahogany-columned halls that it would be easy to believe they are
haunted. They are haunted, at the very least, by their past.

The Eureka Springs & North Arkansas Railway

If you remember when steam locomotives ruled the rails—or would
like to—visit the Eureka Springs & North Arkansas Railway north of
town on Main Street (Hwy. 23 North). The original native stone railroad depot nestles in a narrow valley that it shares with several other
old buildings.

Even if you elect not to ride the restored train, do visit the native
stone depot that has been authentically restored inside and out. Watch
the engines turned around on the turntable and take on water at
the tank. The collection of rolling stock at these yards is one of the
Ozarks' largest. All the railroad memorabilia is authentic and graph-
ically illustrates how it was when rail service brought its first passengers to Eureka Springs in 1883. From the first chug of the engine
and clanging of the bell to call boarders, it is an exciting adventure
and the ultimate nostalgia trip right down to the last whistle.

What's more, you can even return to the opulent era of railroad
dining on the Eureka Springs & North Arkansas. White-jacketed
waiters, elegant place settings with fine crystal, and all the atmosphere
of "The Eurekan," an authentic restored dining car, are yours to
enjoy for lunch or dinner—1920s style (see the chart).

Blue Spring

As are most routes in the Eureka Springs vicinity, the paved road to
Blue Spring is narrow and scenic; it offers some long-range views of
the hill-ringed White River Valley, homes perched on the bluff above
the river, and split-rail fences.

Blue Spring itself is situated in a bend of the White River, and to
reach it one must descend into the river valley from the ridge followed
by the access road. Two *long* flights of steps (with a handrail) wind
down into the gorge. Once in the spring's narrow valley, the ground is
flat and one can enjoy the rest of the complex without exertion. If you
are able to manage the steps, it is a lovely spot and worth the climb
back up the hillside.

Not far from the parking lot on the level ground far above the
spring, the multimedia slide show is accessible to all. Without question

the excellent audio-visual program offered in a small theater building at the Blue Spring complex is alone worth the price of admission, even if you can not negotiate the steps down to the spring itself. Indeed, this presentation affords an excellent orientation to Eureka Springs and its history and makes a good place to begin one's tour for that reason.

After a general discussion of how the springs were discovered and Eureka was named, an excellent commentary accompanies a "seven-projector slide/sound/motion picture show" explaining how Eureka Springs grew from a primitive camp in the woods. Included are many fascinating old photographs of the area and the early growth of the town, including the convict labor used in construction of Hwy. 62. You will learn a great deal not in the tourist brochures.

Blue Spring itself rises in a pool about seventy feet in diameter at the surface, the top of a funnel-shaped rise pool. Although a sign nearby states that "geologists report that it is glacier water and that it comes from the Pacific Northwest. . . . Blue Spring belched silt following the Alaskan earthquake of 1964," most scientists seriously dispute that origin of the water.

More than likely, the experts say, the water of Blue Spring originates under the precipitous ranges of "Little Switzerland," which certainly does not render it any less mysterious or attractive.

Similarly, a local man "translated" what he believed to be Indian "hieroglyphics" on the rocks around the spring recording visits by De Soto's men, Frenchmen, Daniel Boone, and other early explorers to the spring. Vance Randolph, the noted folklorist and historian of the Ozarks, wrote, "I have seen these markings, and I do not believe they were made by human beings. . . ."

Obviously, however, the visitor does not have to believe the signs posted on the property to enjoy the spring itself and its lovely, peaceful lagoon. Trout are visible in the basin of the spring. Machines dispense food to feed them and the large number of resident ducks and geese there. But if you do so, be prepared to be ganged by fifty large birds, all of them vocally demanding more as they follow you around the complex.

A lovely bluff overlooks the spring branch, and a path traces the branch to the old milldam. The first mill at Blue Spring was built in the 1840s and burned during the Civil War. In 1879 a second mill was constructed, which stood until the 1940s. The location of the mill is marked by an old buhrstone and a turbine.

Beaver Lake

West of Eureka Springs is the terrain that earned the town the nickname, "Little Switzerland." Take it slow and easy and enjoy the

Hills that once towered over the White River still tower above Beaver Lake near the dam not far from Eureka Springs, Arkansas. Beaver is the first of three large Corps of Engineers lakes on the river; below it are Table Rock and Bull Shoals. Between the latter two is riverine Lake Taneycomo, formed in 1913 by a dam built by private enterprise.

Built by the CCC half a century ago, this landmark building in Roaring River State Park near Cassville, Missouri, was originally the lodge of the then-new state park. Now it serves as park headquarters. Other CCC-built structures serve the trout hatchery located here. Partly because of the trout fishery and partly because of the superb Ozarks scenery, Roaring River State Park is one of Missouri's most popular.

views. For a brief side trip that offers some of the area's very best Ozarks scenery and the recreational opportunities of a lake to boot, drive out Hwy. 62 West past the first junction with Hwy. 187. At the next junction with Hwy. 187 (just after crossing the White River), turn left and follow Hwy. 187 across Beaver Dam. The highway makes a loop and rejoins Hwy. 62, where you head east (right) back to Eureka Springs.

Beaver Dam was completed in 1964; the lake has a shoreline of 445 miles and offers twenty-eight thousand surface acres of water. For fishermen, there are gigantic striped bass, black bass, walleye, and many other species. Beaver Lake is also popular with swimmers, water-skiers, scuba divers, and all kinds of boat enthusiasts. Surrounding the lake are Corps of Engineers campgrounds, swim areas, boat launching ramps, and full-service marinas where you can rent boats, motors, and scuba gear, and hire fishing guides (see the Practical Matters Chart).

Beaver was the last of the White River dams and the smoothest to construct. When work on Beaver began in November 1960, no towns had to be moved. Only a few structures required relocation. Aggregate was readily available from a cliff at the dam site, and that—coupled with safer, more efficient construction techniques—allowed the $46.2 million dam to be completed in June 1966 without a single fatality.

Below Beaver Dam the cool waters of the White River provide perfect habitat for rainbow and brown trout. Outfitters and guides have located here, and there are campsites and resorts to serve you. At the overlook at Beaver Dam, there is Dogwood Hiking Trail two miles long, the first part of it straight up the bluff.

Get a Bang Out of Berryville

Berryville likes to describe itself as being "Where the Old South Meets the Old West," and the description is surprisingly apt. The history of both regions is still visible here, as is much that is uniquely Ozarkian. The town is nationally famous with blackpowder muzzleloaders as a favorite rendezvous campground and site of muzzleloader matches and the annual Arkansas State Championship Muzzleloader Shoot.

By the outbreak of the Civil War, Berryville had fifty-one houses and a population of two hundred. Ill-used by both the Confederates and the Federals, by the war's end only the Mother Hubbert Hotel remained near the town square. It is said that the building was spared because the Masonic records and regalia were stored in the upper story where the lodge had held their pre-war meetings.

Now the charming turn-of-the-century town square is a tree-shaded park with a fountain, old-fashioned street lamps, and lots of benches for relaxing. All around it are interesting shops, restaurants, and museums. There is an old-time five and dime store, a dry goods and hardware store, and a working village blacksmith shop.

Visible to your right as you enter the square on Hwy. 62 from Eureka Springs is the Heritage Center Museum. Built in 1881, this three-story, red-brick building, now on the National Historic Register, was the Carroll County Courthouse until 1977. It houses hundreds of historical items, including a moonshiner's still, and both a pioneer school room and funeral home. Two blocks west of the square is Pioneer Park, home of a vintage log cabin and other artifacts. On the northeast corner of the square, look for Fulton's drugstore. There is an old-fashioned soda fountain with authentic light fixtures and other accoutrements.

A block north of the drugstore is Saunders Museum. C. Burton Saunders is the fellow who is credited with naming Eureka Springs in 1879 while still a teenager. As a man, Saunders made a fortune in mining and real estate on the West Coast. He achieved a reputation as a sharpshooter, winning a world championship for pistol marksmanship in Paris in 1910, and toured the country with Buffalo Bill's Wild West Show. He also traveled the world collecting antiques and firearms. When he died, he bequeathed his collection—which many experts claim is the finest in the country—along with the money to build a museum to house it, to his hometown of Berryville.

"You can educate yourself in the development of the handgun just by starting at the first case and working through the exhibit," said a museum director. Included is the complete line of Colts, which shows all of the important steps in the development of this line, beginning with the Patterson-Colt of 1836, which revolutionized the design of pistols.

Each gun has a card bearing an explanatory note. One weapon, the card informs you, was used by Jesse James to kill five officers who tried to arrest him in Joplin, Missouri. Here, too, is Cole Younger's Colt, which was taken from the renegade when he was captured while robbing a bank in Minnesota, and those of Billy the Kid, Belle Starr, and numerous other desperadoes.

And, "We've got several firearms that used to belong to colorful characters on the other side of the fence," says the director, citing handguns that once belonged to Buffalo Bill, Wild Bill Hickok, Annie Oakley, Sam Houston, and famous old-time law enforcers. Also preserved here is the Colt .45 which, on June 22, 1889, fired the noonday signal opening the last remaining areas of Oklahoma Territory to settlement. All the guns are kept cleaned, oiled, and in firing condition.

Besides its famous gun collections, the Saunders Museum also has a great variety of other artifacts, including American Indian relics. Clyde Barrow's hat (lost in a running gun battle with law officers near Reeds Spring, Missouri, in February 1934), an Arab sheik's tent, antique lace, shawls, feather fans, Geronimo's scalp belt, Sitting Bull's war bonnet, and many more exotic, unusual, or rare items can be found in this museum.

Roaring River

From Eureka Springs, drive north on Hwy. 23 only a few miles to the Missouri state line and the short distance from there to the junction with Hwy. 86. Turn northwest (left) on Hwy. 86 through Eagle Rock. Turn left again on Rte. F and follow it into Roaring River State Park. This road, constructed on the hillsides, was established in 1948 and improved in 1958. An earlier road from Eagle Rock to Roaring River followed the river; there were thirteen crossings in a distance of some six or seven miles, and early-day cars often had to be towed across the fords by a team and wagon.

Roaring River rises as a spring, far back in a cool, shady grotto. A dam was built prior to 1880, and since then the waters have emerged into a lake. Before the construction of the dam, the waters rushed from the grotto down the rocks "with a sound and splash which merit for the stream its name. . . ."

The first mill to use this power was built about 1836. Another mill built in 1845 was destroyed during the Civil War. The steep terrain and canyonlike gorges near Roaring River provided excellent hide-outs for bushwhackers.

Rebuilt in 1866, the second mill was located at the site of the present park lodge. Roaring River power has carded wool, ground grain, and sawed huge logs. Because the mill customers often had to wait days for their grain to be ground or their woolen or cotton products finished, the spring at Roaring River became a favorite "vacation" place.

In fact, when the milling business fell off, the last mill was converted to a hotel. By the early 1920s, the river had been discovered by residents of Kansas City and St. Louis as an ideal place for fishing retreats. Subsequently the inn was destroyed by fire. A private resort and trout hatchery was established at the site, but it came to an inglorious end at a foreclosure sale. The buyer at the sale, a wealthy soap manufacturer from St. Louis, owned the property only a short time before he presented the entire tract of twenty-four hundred

Far back in a grotto at the foot of a towering bluff, Roaring River Spring in Roaring River State Park near Cassville, Missouri, forms a small lake and waters a trout hatchery before racing away to become Roaring River. Once these waters powered gristmills and a sawmill. A footpath climbs to the top of the bluff.

acres to the state of Missouri. Roaring River State Park came into being.

During the 1930s the Civilian Conservation Corps (CCC) did extensive work on the park and the trout hatchery, and most of the structures are still used today. Notable among them is the former lodge building, now the park office, which was completed in 1938.

The 2,075 acres of Roaring River Hills Wild Area provide a superb example of the White River Hills landscape. Numerous plants and animals are protected here; some are found nowhere else. Bobcats and an occasional black bear make their homes in the wild areas. In the winter, bald eagles are often spotted sailing over the Roaring River Valley.

Besides the Missouri Department of Conservation's trout hatchery, there is a nature center where interpretive displays help visitors better understand the park's natural features. The park's naturalist presents programs and slide shows year-round. Approximately ten miles of hiking trails wind through the park, through dense, hardwood forests, small Ozarks streams, and scenic views atop open dolomite glades. There are campsites along the river, cabins with kitchens, and a modern three-story motel (see the Practical Matters Chart).

Leave the park on Hwy. 112 for the short drive into Cassville. In a distance of three miles the road climbs five hundred feet up the slope of the Springfield Plateau. Once on top of the escarpment, the terrain becomes gently rolling rather than dramatically rugged.

The first cars had trouble with the steep incline up the face of the escarpment, and a few local residents can still remember backing up the hill from Roaring River (the early cars had more power in reverse). Others recall hopping out to "scotch" the wheels by putting rocks under them as they slowly wended their way up or down the hill. After a heavy rainfall, the road washed away to simply one rocky ledge after another. The highway was begun in 1936.

Turn east (right) on Hwy. 76 just short of Cassville for the trip around Table Rock Lake. Be on the lookout for the early-day "tourist camps," or "cabin courts," a few miles outside of town on Hwy. 112. Once, complexes like these dotted the Ozarks for the use of the "city folks" who came to rest and relax near the springs and rivers.

At the junction of Hwys. 112 and 76, it is only another mile into the pleasant town of Cassville, which was a stop for the Butterfield Overland Mail and—briefly—the Confederate capital of Missouri. The pro-secessionist governor and members of the Missouri general assembly, fleeing before Union troops, met here the first week of November 1861 to consider the ordinance of secession, approved at Neosho by eleven senators and forty-four representatives. Both the

This lovely old home in Cassville, Missouri, is typical of the thousands that still stand in the Ozarks in towns large and small, in both Missouri and Arkansas. Most are still private residences. Many that were once converted into apartments are being restored to their former glory. Cassville was briefly the "Confederate Capital of Missouri."

ordinance and act of affiliation to the Confederate States were signed here and the Confederate flag was hoisted above the courthouse.

During the war, Cassville was ravaged first by one side, then the other. County records were hidden in a cave southeast of town until the war was over. The old courthouse suffered from its use as a fort and horse stable, and it was torn down in 1910. The present courthouse replaced it in 1913. Quite a number of old buildings still surround the square, although some have been remodeled to look modern.

After the war when the town was rebuilt, a bell was placed on the square to be used, among other things, to call worshippers to church. Reportedly the bell pole was used to lynch an accused murderer. It is now a permanent fixture on the school grounds.

Drive east on Hwy. 76 through Mark Twain National Forest to Reeds Spring. Along the way, the highway skirts the edge of Piney Creek Wilderness, which offers excellent opportunities for hiking, backpacking, and birdwatching. No vehicle traffic is allowed (see the chart).

Practical Matters

Chapter 8 — Little Switzerland

Checking Out	A Sampling	Phone
Lodging	Roaring River State Park, 7 Miles South of Cassville on Hwy. 112, Cassville MO; Best Western Inn of the Ozarks, P.O. Box 431, Eureka Springs AR 72632 (Hwy. 62 West); Victorian Inn Resort Motel, Rt. 1 Box 9, Eureka Springs AR 72632; Table Rock Resort, 95 Woodsdale Dr., Holiday Island AR 72632	(417) 847-2330 or (800) 334-6946 (501) 253-9768 or (800) 528-1234 (501) 253-6262 or (501) 253-9922 (501) 253-7733 or (800) 255-9381
Bed & Breakfasts	The Association of Bed & Breakfasts, Cabins & Cottages, P.O. Box 27, Eureka Springs AR; Bed & Breakfast Association of Eureka Springs, P.O. Box 213, Eureka Springs AR	(501) 253-6767 (501) 253-6657
Campgrounds	Wanderlust RV Park & Campground, Rt. 1 Box 946, Eureka Springs AR 72632; Green Tree Lodge RV Park, Rt. 2 Box 30, Eureka Springs AR	(501) 253-7385 or (501) 253-9332 (501) 253-8807
Restaurants	The Eurekan, ES&NA Railway, Eureka Springs; Victorian Sampler Tea Room, 44 Prospect, Eureka Springs AR 72632; Crystal Dining Room, Crescent Hotel, 75 Prospect, Eureka Springs AR 72632	(501) 253-9623 (501) 253-8374 (501) 253-9766 Ext. 114
Main Historical Attractions	Saunders Memorial Museum, Berryville AR; ES & NA Railway, P.O. Box 310, Eureka Springs AR 72632; The Castle & Museum, 5.5 Miles West of Eureka Springs AR on Hwy. 62 (Rt 2 Box 375); Blue Spring, 5.5 Miles West of Eureka Springs on Hwy. 62; Abundant Memories Heritage Village, Rt. 5 Box 759, Eureka Springs AR 72632; Carroll County Heritage Center, 1880 Courthouse on the Square, Berryville AR	(501) 423-2563 (501) 253-9623 or (501) 253-9677 (501) 253-9462 (501) 253-9244 (501) 253-6764 (501) 423-6312
Other Attractions	Cosmic Cavern, Rt.4, Box 392, Berryville AR; Ozark Emporium, 65 S. Main, Eureka Springs AR; Onyx Cave Park, Rt. 4 Box 420, Eureka Springs AR; Ark. Craft Gallery, 33 Spring St., Eureka Springs AR	(501) 749-2298 (501) 435-6070 (501) 253-9321

Checking Out	A Sampling	Phone
Outdoor Recreation	Hiking: Piney Creek Wilderness, Mark Twain National Forest (See Where to Write); Fishing, Hiking, Nature Study: Roaring River State Park, P. O. Box D, Cassville MO 65625; Excursion Boat on Beaver Lake: Belle of the Ozarks, Starkey Marina, Hwy. 62 West (Rt.1, Box 182-A) Eureka Springs AR	(417) 847-2539 (501) 253-6200
Where to Write for More Details	District Ranger, Mark Twain National Forest, Cassville MO 65625; Berryville Chamber of Commerce, P.O. Box 402, Berryville AR 72616; Eureka Springs Chamber of Commerce, P.O. Box 551, Eureka Springs AR 72632; Beaver Lake: U.S. Corps of Engineers, Hwys. 62 & 94 Jct., Rogers AR 72756; Table Rock: Shell Knob Chamber of Commerce, P.O. Box 193, Shell Knob MO 65747	(417) 847-2144 (501) 423-3704 (501) 253-8737 (501) 636-1210 (417) 858-3300

CHAPTER 9

Table Rock

Heading east on Hwy. 76, you are treated to long-range views of the hills and Table Rock Lake. This general route has been a travelway a long time; it appears on very early maps of the area. The road is particularly scenic at dogwood time and during the "Flaming Fall Review" you hear so much about. (It is not oversold, by the way.) At both of those seasons, there are fewer leaves on the trees to hide the vistas.

But brace yourself. At Reed's Spring you leave the deeper peace of the countryside behind. With the possible exception of the Lake of the Ozarks area, there is no more highly developed neighborhood in the rural Ozarks. In Stone and Taney counties you will encounter some of the worst congestion in the region—but some marvelous scenery and fascinating history.

To help gear you up for the more fast-paced high-traffic areas, you may first want to visit peaceful Kimberling City on Table Rock Lake. Turn south onto Hwy. 13 at Reeds Spring.

Table Rock Lake

Table Rock Dam casts a long shadow behind it. As early as 1901 a dam at Table Rock Mountain was eagerly touted. Discussed and disputed for more than half a century before it was finally completed, the lake caused the demise of several villages (with all the memories and heartaches attached thereto), the relocation of twenty-two miles of roads, and the loss of a few large and many small farms. It also drowned several good-sized creeks, flooded a number of splendid lost valleys and some historic rivers.

But no one can deny that the lake itself is magnificent. Occupying approximately seventy-nine miles of the original White River channel, the lake spreads out over some fifty thousand acres and has a shoreline of 745 miles at the top of the conservation pool. But place names like Naked Joe Bald Mountain and Sow Coon Mountain are all that remain of once thriving mountain communities and inhabited hollows. Take, for example, Oasis on Long Creek.

At Oasis, once known as Cedar Valley, stood a three-story mill and store; the milldam was built by hand. Also used as the polling place, the bright-red mill served the community for half a century. In the valley's prime bottomland grew small grain, corn, melons, cotton, and tobacco. Virgin pine forest blanketed the hills to the west. A row of catalpa trees lined the road into the valley, and the peaceful scene must have called to mind an oasis. Roads from Arkansas and from the north converged at the mill, and within a quarter-mile there were two fords on Long Creek—Deep Ford and Shallow Ford. In response to the traffic in the valley, Taney County spent several thousand dollars to construct a bridge across the creek just below the mill dam.

But the bridge stood unused for years as there were no funds to build approaches to it. Because the northern approach to the bridge was against the high bluff, considerable blasting would have to be done. Eventually, the approaches were built and the one-lane bridge became a connecting link for Hwy. 86.

Douglas Mahnkey, whose parents once owned and operated the mill and store at Oasis and who cast his first vote there in 1924, recalls that:

> . . . We had a baseball team that played in the field back of the store. We matched games with Blue Eye and Hollister. The U.S. mail came by horseback. . . . Then the great Table Rock Dam came. The waters of Long Creek were impounded and the farms, the school, the mill, the store, are all covered in some 100 feet of water. The remains of those sleeping in the little cemetery were moved to the new Cedar Valley Church site on U.S. 65. Speed boats now race over the pleasant spot where Oasis once stood. Strangers may never know that once a happy and busy community of mountain people lived where now a small island lifts its head above Table Rock Lake.

If you cross the Long Creek arm of Table Rock Lake on Hwy. 86, look for the small island some distance to the north. The island is the top of Goat Hill that once looked down upon Oasis. Says Mahnkey: ". . . I grew up on the river, and I miss the river, and sometimes I just can't help feeling sad about it."

Kimberling City

Once buffalo migrated along your route on Hwy. 13 from the Kickapoo prairie at Springfield to winter grazing on the north Arkansas prairies. They followed the ridges, thus making a trail along the way, which was also followed by Indians going from one hunting ground to another. Later, white men found that the old buffalo trail through the wilderness was the easiest route south from Springfield. They called it the Wilderness Road.

Early wagon freighters followed in the footsteps of the buffalo and the Indians to ford the White River at the twin shoals, where the water was shallow just below the present Kimberling Bridge. The ford at this location remained in use until Mabry Ferry was established shortly after the Civil War.

Then the Kimberlings acquired the ferry, and it was operated under their name until the first bridge was built across the river here in the 1930s. Visitors and neighborhood residents alike crossed the White on the ferry. The late Fred Kimberling once told a friend of taking the Daltons and other infamous night riders across the river as a child. Others spoke of how, in times of high water, you could see a hundred wagons lined up on each side of the river, waiting for the flood waters to go down.

The area contained some of the finest white oak timber anywhere, and white oak was in great demand for railroad ties. Delivery was made along the old Wilderness Road to Reeds Spring. When the supply of trees was exhausted, it was discovered that tomatoes—Red Gold of the Ozarks—grew well here and canneries sprang up. Look for the derelict at the Reeds Spring junction.

Another historic landmark is the log cabin still standing on the Kimberling Hills golf course. The structure was built before the turn of the century and occupied by tie hackers, hunters, trappers, and others seeking a temporary home.

On December 10, 1933, the old Kimberling ferry, at last replaced by a bridge, made its last trip across the White. There are actually two Kimberling City bridges: one under the lake and the new, higher one built to span the lake. The old bridge had been sold for scrap iron and was to be removed once the new bridge was completed, prior to the flooding of the lake. But for some reason the old bridge was not removed in time and still stands below the lake. It is now a favorite fishing spot.

The present Kimberling Bridge is said to be the largest bridge span of its type in Missouri. Near the site where buffalo drank and waded the river, the bridge carries Hwy. 13 across the heart of Table Rock Lake.

Return to Hwy. 76 and turn southeast (right) toward the Shepherd of the Hills country. Soon after you make the turn, watch for the gateway to Silver Dollar City.

Marvel Cave

Part 1880s theme village, part amusement park, part crafts community, Silver Dollar City is one of the major attractions for travelers in the Ozarks. Acres of rides, shops, theaters, craft demonstrations, festivals, performances, and restaurants draw tourists to this mountaintop—a tradition which began in 1894, when Marvel Cave, now a National Natural Landmark, was opened to visitors as Missouri's first commercial cave.

A story that is told about the early history of the cave holds that during the reign of the Bald Knobbers, the dreaded vigilante group, a former bushwhacker returned to his White River home. When the Bald Knobbers learned the identify of the former guerrilla—who had committed many atrocities during the Civil War years—they abducted him. With his legs hobbled and his hands tied, the offender was escorted on horseback to "the Devil's Den," as the cave was then known.

Here the vigilantes stood on the rim of the craterlike opening and peered into the mouth of what was then believed to be a bottomless pit. The prisoner was seated on a rock which, without a word from his captors, was knocked out from under him. He plummeted to his death in the darkness below.

Later in the 1880s the mining community of Marmaros was founded over Marvel Cave to exploit the copious bat guano found there. William Henry Lynch, a Canadian businessman who had helped explore the miles of cave passages, became fascinated by the cave and bought it. Lynch called it Marble Cave because he thought it contained marble.

After his death, Lynch's daughters, Genevieve and Miriam, ran the cave. By 1906, the trickle of visitors to the cave become a slow but steady stream with the inauguration of passenger rail service through Branson and a "whistle stop" at Garber, three miles away. By the 1920s, improving roads brought tourist traffic almost to the mouth of the cave. But picture postcards of those days still show only a yawning, black pit in the ground.

And touring the cave remained an ordeal for visitors. Hollister resident and writer Edith McCall says that when she visited the cave in 1934 she was given coveralls to wear over her clothing, rubber galoshes for her feet, and a tin cup from which to drink the water flowing there.

All such early adventurers spoke of the ordeal of climbing back up the long ladder to emerge from the cave. Said Flo Tidgwell, "We . . . came out into the hot summer sunshine. The sudden reversal of temperature left us gasping for breath but immeasurably thrilled with our adventures, the kind of feeling one might experience upon a visit to another planet."

In 1946, while on vacation in the Ozarks, Mary and Hugo Herschend decided to tour the cave. A few years later they signed a ninety-nine year lease with the Lynch sisters and became tour cave operators. Within a year of the construction of a cave exit railway system in 1957, the boom began. And something was needed to keep the crowds of visitors entertained while they waited to tour the cave.

"We put up a blacksmith shop, general store, doll shop, candy store, and print shop, and we had a surrey ride," says Peter Herschend, executive vice president. "That was Silver Dollar City."

Silver Dollar City

The name was coined by Don Richardson, Silver Dollar City's director of publicity for thirty years. "We gave out real silver dollars in change, and that was the gimmick for the customers," Richardson later remembered. "When the crazy things started circulating around town, we got the attention of the merchants, too."

Much of the charm of the city has always been its "citizens"—the people who work and entertain there. It is easy to believe, if only for a moment, that they really did step out of the past. The men are often bearded and wear the rugged clothing of mountain men of yesteryear. The women dress in simple, yet almost elegant, long skirts and aprons.

Nineteen sixty-nine proved to be a watershed year for the City. The cast and crew of the television comedy "The Beverly Hillbillies" came "from the hills of Hollywood to the hills of Branson" to film five episodes at Silver Dollar City. In addition to shots of the theme park, the shows were peppered with references to actual people and places of the Ozarks.

"The immediate impact of those shows being aired was phenomenal," says Peter Herschend. Of the millions who saw the shows, thousands decided to come see Silver Dollar City for themselves. "Those five shows collectively were the best single piece of publicity ever to hit this area," Herschend says.

From the beginning Silver Dollar City has been involved in perpetuating the heritage crafts of the Ozarks. Now almost fifty unique shops offer crafts and other decorator items. You can choose a guided tour of the crafts area or explore on your own. Almost anything that was produced by the technology of the 1880s is for sale here.

Violet Hensley, one of Silver Dollar City's most beloved "citizens," made her first fiddle at age fifteen and had completed three more by age seventeen. Then she paused for twenty-seven years to marry and raise nine children. She has appeared regularly at Silver Dollar City for twenty years, demonstrating the making of fiddles—and playing them to the delight of everyone. For many visitors to "the City," chatting with the people who work, perform, and demonstrate their crafts there is the most pleasant of all the fun things to do. (Courtesy of Silver Dollar City)

All of the several craft demonstrations are performed with the same sort of tools that were originally used. This means that instead of an electric drill, you may see a craftsman using an antique steam lathe. There are spinning wheels, looms, candle dipping, broom making, glassblowing, quilts and quilters galore, and much more. Since the "citizens" are encouraged to interact with guests, the crafts folk will happily explain the tools they use and the history behind their particular craft. You can visit with a poet-knifemaker, a sixth-generation gunsmith, an Amish buggymaker, and many others.

As you wander around the City, you are likely to encounter a fast-talking snake-oil salesman and other types of "characters" that might have been encountered in an 1880s Ozarks town—or the mayor or the sheriff. For those with small children, the City offers baby strollers and baby-changing areas. Wheelchairs, electric carts, and easy-access areas are also at hand.

In the fall the City hosts a National Crafts Festival when the regulars are joined by crafters from all over the country. The event is a six-week exposition where hundreds of craftspeople share their talents. Visitors are mesmerized as woodcarvers chisel the faces of the past, dollmakers bring to life the dolls of grandmother's attic, metal spinners mold the essential utensils of yesteryear, and so much more. Especially during the festival, the feeling of rustic, romantic Early America fills the streets of the turn-of-the-century theme park.

And there is food—most of it traditional, even nostalgic. Bakers, candy makers, and cooks stirring apple butter over an open fire tempt you with samples. Everywhere you look someone is eating something delicious-looking; most of it is for sale to take home. And there are a dozen restaurants, with a wide variety of offerings, to feed you on the spot.

All day and all evening, there is music. Most is "good ol' country music" and bluegrass, but there are also some ragtime and jazz. Regularly scheduled shows are performed at bandstands throughout the park and at an indoor theater. Saturday night affords an opportunity to do some square dancing during an old-time barn dance. The City also hosts the National Clogging Competition, drawing colorful, high-stepping dancers from across the country.

The physical setting is beautiful. The buildings and other structures are quaint and appealing. Look especially for Sullivan Mill, a reproduction of an 1880s flour mill, and for the Wilderness Church. The old log church came from Wilson Creek near the site of the great Civil War battle there. The lectern, as a tree, stood on the ground now occupied by the building. The McHaffie Homestead, an 1843 log cabin, was disassembled on Swan Creek near Forsyth, transported to Silver Dollar City, and rebuilt log by log, as was the church.

Only one of the dozen or more themed rides at Silver Dollar City near Branson, Missouri, is the Lost River of the Ozarks. On the shores of Table Rock Lake and minutes from the music shows and other attractions of the area—including the scenery—Silver Dollar City entertains more than 1.5 million visitors annually. The story of "the City's" phenomenal growth and its impact on the Ozarks has become part of the region's history. (Courtesy of Silver Dollar City)

From Inspiration Point at The Shepherd of the Hills Homestead, a guide points out the landmarks made famous by Harold Bell Wright's novel, The Shepherd of the Hills. *The jeep-drawn tour familiarizes guests with the layout of the Homestead so that they can fully enjoy the sights to be seen there, including some things that would have astonished "Old Matt," such as Inspiration Tower. (Courtesy of The Shepherd of the Hills Homestead)*

As at other theme parks, amusement rides are part of the fun. Those at Silver Dollar City seem to revolve around water, perhaps as the influence of the numerous rushing rivers, waterfalls, and lakes of the region. And when the Silver Dollar City folks warn that you will get wet on their rides, they are not kidding. All emphasize the turn-of-the-century theme. (Silver Dollar City also owns White Water, "the urban surf park," featuring giant waterslides, tube rides, and an artificial tidal wave pool, located on Hwy. 76.)

Now almost two million visitors are entertained at Silver Dollar City annually, by far the majority in the regular season from late April through October. In the past few years the park has celebrated an old-time Christmas on weekends in November and early December. During this time Silver Dollar City is transformed into a brilliantly lighted playground—paths outlined in seventy miles of tiny, twinkling white Christmas lights that resemble the candlelight of years ago, plus animated lighting displays on Lake Silver. Whether or not this is what Christmas used to be like a hundred years ago, it is lovely: carolers and bell choirs, wassail and cranberry chicken, a living nativity, and carriage rides in the crisp winter night.

History Old and New

Anyone who doubts the power of the written word has only to witness the world that has been created around the novel, *The Shepherd of the Hills*, to be convinced of the potential of a book to bring about change. The Shepherd of the Hills country is a phenomenon: real history strongly influenced by fiction.

The history of how Wright's novel came to be written is itself novel-like. In 1896, during one of the floods that often ravaged Ozarks river valleys, Wright, a minister and landscape painter, rode on horseback into the hills north of the White River near Branson. His plan was to cross the river into Arkansas, where his father and brother had fallen ill on a trapping expedition.

But when Wright reached the river, the operator of Compton Ferry refused to carry him across. The water was too high, the current too swift. Wright retreated up the hill in darkness and found lodging for the night at the cabin of John and Anna Ross. When he awoke the next day, he got his first glimpse of a breathtaking vista, a view extending south across more than forty miles of mountains and valleys. Like countless other visitors who would come later, Wright fell in love with the Ozarks.

Having befriended the Rosses, Wright corresponded with them and sent them a copy of his first book, *That Printer of Udell's*. Reportedly he returned for periodic visits over the next several years. Then in July

1904, ailing from tuberculosis, Wright decided that a lengthy stay in the mountain air would be good for his health, so he returned to the Ross homestead and received their permission to camp on a knoll in their cornfield, the location now known as Inspiration Point. The Rosses' son Charles (the basis of "Young Matt" in the book) acted as Wright's guide and traveled with him around the countryside.

Living in a large tent, Wright gathered material and made notes for the novel that was to become *The Shepherd of the Hills*. Over the next three years, writing by hand, Wright wrote a novel based on his experiences with the Rosses and others he met on his travels through the hills along the White River. The book was published in 1907, and within three years tourists began taking advantage of the new White River Railroad to visit the locations described in the book and to meet the people who had inspired Wright's fictional characters. They could visit with Levi Morrill, upon whom Wright was said to have modeled "Uncle Ike," at the Notch post office. And they found the homestead —Old Matt's Cabin—of Mr. and Mrs. J. K. Ross.

The book became so closely identified with the locale that it came to define the sub-region: it created a geographical region west of Branson known to this day as "Shepherd of the Hills Country." Almost a hundred years after its publication, the impact of *The Shepherd of the Hills* is still apparent. Attractions in the region, businesses, restaurants, and motels are named for characters in the book; in a few cases, physical locations have been named or renamed to coincide with the novel.

And for most of that century, critics have been saying that *The Shepherd of the Hills* was not all that well written and marvel at its enduring popularity. But the simple basic truths of the story are as real today as they were at the turn of the last century, which surely must account for the book's enormous and continuing popularity—as well as for the perpetuation of its setting as beloved and revered, almost hallowed, ground.

In the novel, the protagonist comes into the hills looking for something that was not here, but found something far better. He expected to find people that never existed, a population of simple, gentle "natives." Most of the people he encountered had also come into the area from somewhere else, a condition that is still true. And now, as then, the *essence* of the region—clearly definable on a map though it may be—is nebulous and longingly sought by all who come here.

The remarkable thing about the story (and probably what accounts for its astonishingly long-lived popularity) is its enduring timeliness. To re-read *The Shepherd of the Hills* today is to be struck by the *continuity* apparent in its pages, for all its gentle, old-fashioned tones. Scenes described by Wright a century ago are still experienced by

"Jim Lane's Cabin" near Branson, Missouri, is an authentic log cabin—said to be the home of Jim Lane, a character from Harold Bell Wright's The Shepherd of the Hills*—now on the historic register. Ironically, the superhighway that has evolved from the old foot trail over Dewey Bald is virtually at its door. (Courtesy of Bittersweet, Inc.)*

"Old Matt's Cabin," probably the most renowned landmark in the Ozarks, is a real log cabin built by a real Ozarker. Now part of The Shepherd of the Hills Homestead near Branson, Missouri, it was in this home that Harold Bell Wright took refuge when the flooded White River interrupted his trip to Arkansas. Mr. Wright predicted that many changes would come to the hills, but it is doubtful that he foresaw Table Rock Lake and the superhighway crossing Dewey Bald. Certain it is, however, that he would find today much of what he loved almost a century ago. (Courtesy of Bittersweet, Inc.)

modern Ozarkers. Who among us has not witnessed "a company of buzzards" and the lowering of a mist that leaves the forest "dim and dripping"?

Not surprisingly, over the years the lines between fiction and reality have blurred. For example, "Jim Lane's" cabin is now an historical landmark, as is "Old Matt's" cabin and "Uncle Ike's" post office. Old Matt, Jim Lane, and Uncle Ike never existed, but the buildings are real; they are historic in their own right. Wright himself invented many of the locales in the novel; we call them today by the names he gave them—not, in all cases, the way they were when he immortalized them in his book. But that we should do so is, in itself, remarkable, and historic.

Uncle Ike's Post Office

"Uncle Ike's" post office is at Notch on Hwy. 76. It is believed that Notch postmaster Levi Morrill was the model for Wright's "Uncle Ike." Morrill was born in Portland, Maine, graduated from Bowdoin College, was a personal friend of Longfellow and Hawthorne, and set type with Horace Greeley. It is said that he had been a newspaper publisher in Kansas and that his brother had been governor of that state. Told by his doctor that he had only a short time to live, Mr. Morrill, like Mr. Wright, hoped the fresh mountain air would prolong his life. He died in August 1926 at the age of eighty-nine.

The Morrill homestead, circa 1895, is the oldest clapboard house in the immediate area and is a registered Historic Landmark. The house and the post office, according to a neighbor who loves and worries about them, are "almost lost to the bustle and highway widening that comes dangerously close to their location on West Hwy. 76."

The Shepherd of the Hills Homestead

Much of the fascination of The Shepherd of the Hills Homestead is its *own* history—the unbroken line of many different people very nearly obsessed with this story and these characters and, above all, this setting.

In 1884 J. K. Ross (accepted to be the inspiration for the "Old Matt" of the novel) built the log cabin that has become a symbol of tourism in the Shepherd of the Hills country. John K. Ross was not a "native" Ozarker; he was born and raised in eastern Pennsylvania and came to the Ozarks by way of Kansas and Iowa. Widowed young, John then married a Kentucky girl and they migrated to West Plains in Howell County, Missouri, and then to Springfield. Then, in the 1890s, the Rosses homesteaded public land in Taney County. A skilled carpenter, Ross, with the aid of his son, Charles, built the single pen log house, some twenty by fourteen feet, of hand-hewn logs. Sawn lumber for the house came from Ross's nearby sawmill. The barn is also original and is held together with wooden pins.

Scarcely had the Rosses settled in the new house in the spring of 1896 when Harold Bell Wright found shelter there.

Soon after the book's publication, the Rosses' home became one of the most visited and photographed houses in Missouri. We know, therefore, that the house originally had no fireplace; it was equipped with a more modern stove and flue. Reportedly the curious tourists annoyed the Rosses to the point that they abandoned their cabin in 1911 and moved to Garber. It has been said that they never forgave Wright for "betraying their friendship."

M. R. Driver, a physical education teacher at a college in Wichita, Kansas, bought the Rosses' farm. Driver was a promoter who made "Old Matt's" a wayside inn for tourists. He expanded the property and hired caretakers to operate it. In 1913 he added a screened dining room on the north. A chimney with flanking windows was added on the east, along with stone porch pillars, as part of Driver's interpretation of a rustic summer resort.

In 1926 Driver sold the 160-acre parcel to Mrs. Lizzie McDaniel (King), who rode horseback the fifty or so miles to visit the cabin. Indignantly she reported it "overrun with pigs and squatters." She remodeled all the buildings at the farm, reclaimed furniture original to the house, and converted the barn into comfortable sleeping quarters for tourists. Her associates in the venture opened the Twin Pine Inn at the fork of the Dewey Bald and Compton Ridge roads two miles west of Old Matt's Cabin.

McDaniel joined other promoters in calling for improved roads and more accessibility to the area for tourists. Working for the WPA, local men began building a modern highway between Branson and Reeds Spring, following the rocky trail which wound around Dewey Bald and Inspiration Point. In 1936 Lizzie granted a fifty-year lease on Inspiration Point to the state of Missouri—at a dollar a year—for a public roadside automobile park. For the next half-century the tiny state park on Inspiration Point hosted travelers who rested in the shade and gazed afar.

When McDaniel died in 1946, the Civic League of Branson assumed ownership of the house and Dr. and Mrs. Bruce Trimble acquired the remainder of the estate. The Trimbles maintained the Ross homesite and opened a coffee and novelty shop and a museum on the property. Well preserved and maintained, "Old Matt's Cabin"—the original tourist attraction in this area—remains a Taney County treasure. "The story, so very old, is still in the telling," Wright wrote about his novel. And it still is.

Passion and Pageantry

Wright's novel has been made into four motion pictures of varying quality, and theatrical stage productions were seen as early as 1912. In 1960 the Trimbles began producing a dramatized version of *The Shepherd of the Hills* in the original setting of the story. The first show was held with 435 folding lawn chairs for the audience. The first sound system was installed in 1975 and by 1976 the seating capacity was increased to twenty-five hundred. By 1979 more parking space was needed, and the tunnel and lot across the road were built.

The problems of staging a performance of this magnitude are mind-boggling. In addition to the eighty-five performers, most of whom are equipped with wireless microphones, each evening's production calls for thirty-six horses, ten wagons and buggies, a flock of sheep, fifteen Colt .45 pistols, and several rifles and shotguns—all of which fire more than two hundred rounds of ammunition each performance. On a stage as large as a football field, the show includes an old-time country square dance with a live band, "a knock-down, drag-out fight" between "the two strongest men in the hills," the actual burning of a log cabin, and a dramatic shoot-out.

Throughout the daylight hours, while you are waiting for the spectacle to begin, you can enjoy the homestead's other offerings. A jeep-drawn tour will help to orient you to the entire farm, including Old Matt's Cabin and steam-powered mill. There are bullfrog races, street shows, a blacksmith shop, a moonshine still, a traveling "medicine show," a general store-museum, craft demonstrations, music, and much more. At Aunt Mollie's Restaurant you can have breakfast, lunch, or dinner. (Incidentally, to native Ozarkers the noon meal is dinner; they eat "supper" in the evening.)

The Shepherd of the Hills Homestead and Outdoor Theater earns high marks for its accommodation of the handicapped. For once, these special people do not have to be left out of the fun. Tram drivers help load and unload wheelchairs and their occupants, and there is a separate section for seating them in the theater. Inspiration Tower, the restaurant, the Country Church, the Trading Post Museum, and gift shops are all handicapped accessible. One can only hope that more public facilities will emulate the excellent example set by this attraction and its personnel.

A Born-Again Church

In 1901 the Lutheran congregation at Morgan, Missouri—not far from Lebanon—built a trim white church with a boxed-entry bell tower. By the late 1980s, the scattered survivors of the congregation held their annual reunion at the church, but they mourned its rapid deterioration. Although they could not restore it themselves, they were grieved to consider its destruction.

Then the owner of The Shepherd of the Hills Homestead read of their reunion and was struck by the similarity of the church to those in which Pastor Harold Bell Wright had preached. He decided that the little white church and Inspiration Point needed each other. Because of its deterioration, the church building was not moved to Taney County intact. With the help of many photographs and measurements, the walls, floor, and roof were duplicated with new materials. But its windows, doors, inside woodwork, the bell tower, pews, and pulpit were salvaged and installed in the new shell. Writer Kathleen Van Buskirk calls it "a church born again."

Now the little church seems quite at home on Inspiration Point, where it helps visitors to the homestead visualize life in the Ozarks at the turn of the last century.

The Tower on Inspiration Point

In 1985 Mr. and Mrs. Gary Snadon purchased the "homestead." Snadon had held one of the roles in the outdoor pageant for several seasons in the 1960s. When the state's fifty-year lease on Inspiration Point expired, the Snadons erected Inspiration Tower on the site. Opened in 1989, the 225-foot prestressed concrete structure houses two glassed-in elevators to whisk visitors to an air-conditioned "Observation Auditorium." Even more spectacular is the open-air viewing deck. Both afford a 360-degree panorama from one of the highest points in Southwest Missouri, including Table Rock Lake, Compton Ridge, Dewey Bald, even the Boston Mountains in Arkansas. A recorded commentary describes the panorama and sites of particular interest.

Harold Bell Wright Museum
in Mutton Hollow

Even the life story of novelist Wright is now an attraction. In Mutton Hollow, a "crafts village" east of The Shepherd of the Hills Homestead on Hwy. 76, is the Harold Bell Wright Museum and Theater operated by the writer's youngest and only surviving son, Norman. There are enshrined Wright's original handwritten manuscripts and the first editions of his books. Hundreds of photographs tell the story of his life, and a film acted by members of his own family and written by his son are features of the museum. A corner is set up as Wright's study, with the actual furnishings. Other items from Wright's home and collections are also there: valuable antiques, paintings, Indian artifacts, flintlocks, a silver-mounted saddle, bronze statues, and much more. Although Harold Bell Wright wrote eighteen other books, many of them highly successful, he is most remembered for introducing the world to the Ozarks in *The Shepherd of the Hills*.

Mutton Hollow, part of the inspirational view Wright overlooked while camped near "Old Matt's Cabin," is now the site of a picturesque crafts village where you can also find the likes of old-time photographers, candle shops, candy makers, broom factories, woodcarvers, pie and ice cream parlors, antique shops, and potters (see the Practical Matters Chart).

And on your right soon after you leave Mutton Hollow is the "Jim Lane Cabin," with the widened roadway virtually at its doorstep. Designated an Historical Monument, the cabin is authentic. The contrast between the ramshackle old structure and the busy highway rushing by it could not be more dramatic and is more evidence of the coexistence of Old and New in the Ozarks.

White River Balds

Also on Hwy. 76 east of the Homestead is the Henning State Forest that features the Ozarks landscapes known as *glades*. The view from the overlook affords visitors a good look at a glade (sometimes called a "bald" for the absence of trees) with little investment of effort. Two trails begin here for those who wish to walk through the forest area and up the side of Dewey Bald Mountain (a locale from Wright's novel). The forest's parking area is located on the north side of Hwy. 76 approximately a half mile west of the Mutton Hollow Campground.

A 1.6-mile trail covered with wood chips offers a close-up look at the White River Balds Natural Area, a section of the state forest. It also goes through Boulder Bald, where an overlook provides a look at a good example of a glade, and down to Dewey Cove. The second, paved, trail takes visitors about half a mile to the top of Dewey Bald.

The Engler Block

Still headed eastward on Hwy. 76 toward Branson, not long before the junction with Hwy. 65, watch on your left for Engler Block—an entire "city block" of shops under one roof—offering woodcarvings and other art and Ozarks crafts. Engler's entire complex was intended to hark back to an earlier time.

Quite simply, there is nothing like Engler Block anywhere in the Ozarks. If you have even the slightest interest in Ozarks crafts or woodcarving, do not miss it. Watch especially for the clocks carved by Jesse Kuhs at Branson Clockworks. His grandfather clocks, some of which are hand-carved out of an entire tree trunk and may even look like a grandfather, will haunt you forever.

All along Hwy. 76 are multitudes of other attractions designed to interest, entertain, and accommodate tourists. Locals frequently refer to the highway as "The Strip," and indeed it is strongly reminiscent of the glittering Las Vegas strip, both in the numbers of attractions and for general gaudiness. But there is a difference in this Ozarks strip: By far the majority of these establishments advertise "family" entertainment.

Besides the overwhelming number of country music shows from which to choose, and the crafts outlets of widely varying quality, numerous restaurants offer everything from barbecue, fried chicken, and steak to Cajun cuisine, Italian, prime rib—and everything in between, including a winery. There are miniature golf courses, go-kart tracks, and video arcades. There is Waltzing Waters: a show of waterfalls, sprays, fountains and rainbows set to music and bathed in ever-changing colored lights. There is the Ozarks Auto Show that features eighty-five vehicles representing America's love affair with the automobile. There are bumper cars, helicopter rides over the lake, horseback rides, a Factory Merchants Mall, and excursion boats. There are even sightseeing ducks—1945-vintage Army amphibious vehicles that take sightseers over land and lake.

Unlike Peter Engler's block of Ozarks crafts, however, there is little else on the "strip" that represents the real Ozarks. Virtually all of it was attracted to cash in on the popularity of Silver Dollar City and The Shepherd of the Hills Homestead.

Hard Work U.

Just south of Branson on Hwy. 65, turn right on Rte. V to visit "Hard Work U."—the College of the Ozarks. The campus has many sites of interest to visitors, including a nationally known museum and "Point Lookout," an overlook affording a panoramic view of Lake Taneycomo and the White River Valley.

Originally known as School of the Ozarks, the institution was founded to meet the needs of young people in the hills of the Ozarks, where schools were few and inaccessible to many families. It was the brainchild of a young evangelist, who envisioned a residential school where students could work for their room, board, and tuition. In 1907 a faculty of four opened the school to thirty-five boarding students. As the educational needs of the Ozarks changed over the years, so did the School of the Ozarks. It grew from a boarding school for youngsters to a high school, then a junior college, and finally in 1964, it became a fully accredited four-year college of liberal arts: "the college that works." The school changed its name to the College of the Ozarks in 1990. The work-scholarship plan has long been an integral part of the overall program of the college.

The entire campus is lovely, but visitors are especially drawn to the Ralph Foster Museum, which exhibits hundreds of Indian artifacts, Rose O'Neill's famous Kewpie Dolls, Western memorabilia, numismatics, guns, and even the car from the television series, "The Beverly Hillbillies." It houses hundreds of thousands of objects representing archaeology, antiques, natural history, fine arts, geology, and mineralogy. The museum collects, preserves, and exhibits artifacts of the cultural history of the Ozarks. It gathers information that will better enable present and future generations to understand the land, climate, and people of the region.

Near the museum building is Star School, a one-room rural school building moved to the campus from its site on Flat Creek in Barry county and restored in the late 1970s. Star School is an excellent example of an Ozarks schoolhouse from the era of the turn of the century. It is folk architecture and, as such, a significant component of Ozarks material culture.

When Edwards Mill—the other must-see building on the campus—was dedicated, an old-timer remarked, "My, my, what an immaculate mill. The ones I remember as a lad were completely draped in flour dust and cobwebs with the building vibrating and machinery complaining at every turn of the wheel accompanied by definite odors of flour, river water, and frayed belts."

But Edwards Mill, named for major donors who made it possible, is otherwise authentic. And it is no ordinary water mill. Taney County historian Elmo Ingenthron pointed out that the mill is actually a sort of milling hall of fame, with many of the components—such things as beams, shafts, bearing blocks, buhrstones, and more—coming from a number of old mills over a wide area of the Ozarks. Built in 1972 by an expert in old-time gristmills who scavenged equipment and machinery from throughout the region, Edwards Mill stands as a virtual replica of the thousands of long-gone buildings it represents. You can still purchase stone-ground products there, too, and upstairs is a weaving studio where college students produce the handwoven textiles also offered for sale in the building.

Table Rock Dam Area

From the College of the Ozarks main entrance, turn right on Rte. V and go another mile or so to its junction with Hwy. 165. Turn right on Hwy. 165 to visit the Table Rock Dam. (From Silver Dollar City take Hwy. 265 south of Hwy. 76; from The Shepherd of the Hills Home-

Though it dates only to 1972, Edwards Mill on the campus of the College of the Ozarks is a veritable hall of fame for many departed mill buildings, as it incorporates parts from mills throughout the region. The college welcomes visitors and is the site of the superb Ralph Foster Museum, caretaker of many artifacts of Ozarks history. (Courtesy of Public Relations Department, College of the Ozarks)

The "Y Bridge" across the James River at Galena was built of reinforced concrete in 1926 during the good-roads movement in Missouri. An early example of Classical Moderne, a form of the Deco style, it has been named to the National Register of Historic Places. The junction of the two arms of the "Y" was the scene of many accidents as cars became larger and faster. No longer used, the bridge may be viewed by driving north to Galena on Hwy. 13. Turn left at the junction with Hwy. 176 and then left again at the "Business District" sign; watch for the entrance to Y-Bridge Park. And do drive around the square of historic Galena.

stead or Mutton Hollow, take Hwy. 165 in order to avoid the traffic on Hwy. 76 west of Branson.)

Along the way watch for the scenic turnout affording a spectacular view of Table Rock Dam, Lake Taneycomo, the College of the Ozarks, and the towns of Branson and Hollister. At this scenic point you are standing on one of the "table rocks" that gave the lake its name.

Farther on you will see on your left the vast Table Rock State Park, where there are campgrounds, a marina, and scenic picnic areas overlooking the lake. A few miles farther west, the Dewey Short Visitor Center—at the Table Rock Dam—is located on the lakeshore at the south end of the dam, just off Hwys. 165-265. A four-room exhibit area depicts the seasonal changes in the Ozark hills. Artwork, mounted wildlife specimens, photographs, artifacts, and sound effects capture the activities of animals, birds, and plants of the area—and the dependence of the early settlers on nature's resources. Multimedia programs and films about nature and the history of the White River Valley are presented in the 175-seat auditorium during the day (May through October). A nature trail is here too; it begins at the observation deck and winds through the woods and along the shoreline of the lake. The first section of trail is paved to accommodate those who cannot negotiate the more difficult terrain. The trout hatchery is nearby.

Return to Branson via Hwys. 165 and 65 for a visit to Bald Knobber country.

Practical Matters

Chapter 9 — Table Rock

Checking Out	A Sampling	Phone
Lodging	Captain Hook's Cove, P.O. Box 792, Kimberling City MO 65686 (Caters to Handicapped & Elderly);	(417) 739-2845
	Shore Acres Resort, Rt. 4 Box 2010, Reeds Spring MO 65737;	(417) 338-2351
	Trail's End Resort & RV Park, HCR 1 Box 1149, Branson MO 65616;	(417) 338-2633
	Sleepy Hollow Resort, Rt. 3 Box 348, Kimberling City MO 65686	(417) 739-4525
Bed & Breakfasts	Ozark Mountain Country Bed & Breakfast Service, Box 295, Branson MO 65616	(417) 334-4720 or (800) 321-8594
Campgrounds	Tall Pines Campground, HCR 1, Box 1175, Branson MO 65616;	(417) 338-2445
	Compton Ridge Campground, SR 1, Box 1180, Branson MO 65616;	(417) 338-2911
	Old Shepherd's Campground, P.O. Box 97, Branson MO 65616;	(417) 334-3447
	Table Rock Lake: Missouri State Park and U.S. Corps of Engineers Parks (See Where to Write)	(417) 334-4101
Restaurants	Garden Terrace Restaurant, P.O. Box 159, Hwy. 13, Kimberling City MO 65686;	(417) 739-4311
	Jack's Clubhouse, HCR 2, Box 1035, Hollister MO 65672;	(417) 334-4995
	Devil's Pool Restaurant at Big Cedar Lodge, 612 Devil's Pool Rd, Ridgedale MO 65739 (1 mile West of Hwy. 65 on Hwy. 86);	(417) 335-2777
	Mary Jane's (Lunch Only), Rt. 6, Box 630, Reeds Spring MO 65737 (Hwy. 13 North of Kimberling City);	(417) 272-8908
	Friendship House, College of the Ozarks, Point Lookout MO 65726	(417) 334-6411
Main Historical Attractions	Harold Bell Wright Museum & Theater, P.O. Box 1420A, Branson MO 65616;	(417) 334-0065
	Ralph Foster Museum and Edwards Mill, College of the Ozarks, Point Lookout MO	(417) 334-6411 Ext. 407 or 408
Other Attractions	The Shepherd of the Hills Homestead & Outdoor Theatre, Rt. 1 Box 770 (W. Hwy. 76), Branson MO 65616;	(417) 334-4191
	Mutton Hollow Craft Village, (W. Hwy. 76), Branson MO 65616;	(417) 334-4947
	Silver Dollar City, W. Hwy. 76, Marvel Cave Park MO 65616;	(417) 338-8100
	Dewey Short Table Rock Lake Visitor Center; Table Rock Dam Powerhouse;	
	Shepherd of the Hills Trout Hatchery, P.O. Box 427, Branson MO 65616;	(417) 334-4865
	Engler Block, 1335 W. Hwy. 76, Branson MO 65616	(417) 335-2200

Checking Out	A Sampling	Phone
Outdoor Recreation	Table Rock Lake (see Where to Write); Water Slides, Horseback Riding, and Much More (see Where to Write); Hiking: Henning State Forest, W. Hwy. 76, Branson MO; Golf: Kimberling Hills Country Club, Hwy. 13, Kimberling City MO	(417) 739-4370
Where to Write for More Details	Table Rock Lake: U.S. Army Corps of Engineers Resident Engineer, P.O. Box 1109, Branson MO 65616; Table Rock State Park, Branson MO 65616; Branson/Lakes Area Chamber of Commerce, P.O. Box 220, Branson MO 65616; Kimberling City Area Chamber of Commerce, P.O. Box 495, Kimberling City MO 65686 (See Also the Chart Following Chapter 10)	(417) 334-4101 (417) 334-4704 (417) 334-4136 (417) 739-2564

CHAPTER 10

Shepherd of the Hills Country

As late as 1850, this region of the Ozarks was still a raw frontier competing for settlers against a multitude of well-advertised regions between the Mississippi River and the gold fields of California. Although the population along the Missouri portion of the White River was probably double that of ten years before, only thirty-six hundred people were recorded in Taney County.

Today's family historians can, therefore, accurately write of "pioneering ancestors who came to Taney County" as late as the 1890s, when there still were 96,500 acres of government land available for "cash or homestead entry."

The custom was to name a new political unit to honor an important national government official. But since the names at the top of the then-current list had already been given to other Missouri counties, the new county was named Taney (rhymes with *rainy*) after Roger B. Taney, chief justice of the Supreme Court from 1837 until his death in 1864. Justice Taney handed down some earth-shaking decisions during his long tenure—including the Dred Scott Decision. The folks of Taney County, however, without benefit of televised newscasts or radio broadcasts to tell them otherwise, pronounced the chief justice's name incorrectly. His Philadelphia family has always pronounced it *Tawney* (rhymes with brawny).

A large brick courthouse was built on the town square in Forsyth in 1855. Not only was Forsyth the county seat, it was the only "town"— the home of eighty-eight people. Around the square were six stores,

213

two doctors' offices, and the businesses of a druggist, a painter, a carpenter, and a blacksmith. But the Civil War wiped out all progress and depopulated the region. Living off the land, the troops of both sides took livestock, crops, and entire stores of grain and other food from families struggling without their husbands and fathers, who had either gone off to war or been killed by bushwhackers.

For the Ozarks, the Civil War was a guerrilla war, with all the horror surrounding such a free-for-all. To make matters even worse, bands of outlaws—often posing as patriots from one or both sides—were free, in the absence of any deterrents, to murder and maraud. Those residents who could, fled. Many never returned.

But after the war, population along White River rebuilt rapidly. Veterans came seeking land to claim with their new bounty rights. Southern families came too, hoping to rebuild their lives in the isolation of the Ozark hills.

In Taney County, however, a complete state of anarchy existed. There were no county officials and no civil government. As many Union and Confederate sympathizers and participants returned to their homes, there were many old scores to settle, and for a time numerous vengeful acts of violence occurred. The old wounds were slow to heal. There followed two decades of lawlessness that brought shootings at family picnics, the fiery destruction of the county courthouse at Forsyth, beatings, hangings, and a general breakdown in law and order. By and large the population mistrusted the county officials who had been installed, and there were charges of large-scale graft and corruption in county government. Civil authority was weak at best; often little or nothing was done to combat the endless train of criminal events.

Between 1865 and 1884, somewhere between thirty and forty murders were committed in Taney County; no one was convicted. Since Taney was a border county, criminals often escaped merely by crossing into Arkansas. In those days there was no provision made for reciprocal law enforcement across jurisdictional borders. This state of lawlessness spawned one of America's most publicized vigilante organizations, the Bald Knobbers.

Historians Lynn and Kristen Morrow have suggested that the Bald Knobbers were ". . . revolutionaries trying to bring their brand of order and capitalism to a land that had little of either." In order to broaden the tax base, they were trying to drive out "squatters" and close the open range. "They were Republicans who looked down on traditional southern mountain lifestyles." To others, they were civic-minded vigilantes stepping in to right wrongs where officialdom was powerless to cope with rampant and repeated lawlessness. One of them cites Mark Twain as stating, "The West could never have been settled by civilized people had it not been for the vigilantes."

Three events, in retrospect, can be seen as triggering the birth of Taney County's Bald Knobbers. The first was the arrival of Nathaniel Kinney, a giant of a man and a natural leader, a war veteran who had later ridden shotgun on Western stagecoaches and had been a special agent for the Santa Fe Railroad in the West. Kinney deplored the conditions under which the entire population lived in fear of violence. About the same time, the corrupt courts freed a known murderer. Finally, the county was being repeatedly terrorized by two brothers, Frank and Jubal Taylor, who had robbed and murdered virtually with impunity.

Under the leadership of Nathaniel Kinney, many of the county's "best men"—lawyers, doctors, prominent farmers—formed the Law and Order League in an effort to put an end to the anarchy. Because the group met on the treeless mountaintops known as "bald knobs," the populace quickly dubbed the group the *Bald Knobbers*.

"The Distant Signal Fire"

Kinney was quoted as declaring, "The best men in the country gradually drifted to my side, and it became a war between civilization and barbarism."

Once a child who rode behind Kinney to Sunday School, Mary Elizabeth Mahnkey—a rural newspaper correspondent for almost sixty years and a prize-winning poet—wrote of the vigilante meetings around "the distant signal fire," which must have been visible for miles from the high bald knobs. It was around one of these fires that the Bald Knobbers decided to lynch Frank and Jubal Taylor. That act, on April 15, 1885, unleashed years of terror and near-warfare between the Bald Knobbers and the Anti-Bald Knobbers, another group of upstanding citizens, who organized to oppose vigilantism.

Ultimately the vigilante organization spread to both Christian and Douglas Counties where the bands of men were soon joined by the dark side of society who, under the umbrella of vigilantism, robbed, terrorized, and killed. Eventually three Christian County Knobbers were hanged—in a horribly botched execution—virtually ending the Knobbers' power.

Meanwhile, Taney County Bald Knobbers had voted to officially disband at the request of the governor. And, after years of almost total sway in Taney County, Kinney was shot down on August 20, 1888. Lacking a leader, the Law and Order League ceased to ride. (For a complete treatment of the grisly history of the Bald Knobbers, see the books recommended on the suggested reading list in the appendix.)

"No one was neutral about Captain Kinney," says Mary Hartman. "They either despised him or they idolized him." And the memory of the chasm between them yet lingers. Undoubtedly, a sensation-seeking press fanned the flames of violence. "As so often happened during this era," say Hartman and Ingenthron, "William Randolph Hearst and his imitators compounded the widespread publicity with their new brand of irresponsible, inaccurate yellow journalism."

Further, as pointed out by Douglas Mahnkey, grandson of one of the original thirteen organizers of the vigilantes, "Harold Bell Wright in *The Shepherd of the Hills* gave the Bald Knobbers a bad name, and the theatrical play shown each summer west of Branson continues that misconception of the purpose and work of the Committee for Law and Order."

Although there is little left to see of Bald Knobber history, visitors can drive through the area where the organization was formed and held their meetings. East of present-day Branson on what is now Hwy. T, visitors can see where Captain Kinney's property was located, although some of it is now under Lake Taneycomo. Look for the highest hill; that is Snapp's Bald, where the Knobbers met and had their "signal fire." Also on this road is Oak Grove Church; although the church has been relocated slightly, it was the scene of pivotal events.

In the Meantime . . .

Then, as now, life in the Ozarks went on. People still struggled to make a living, and the coming of the railroad had opened up new opportunities.

More than anything else, the forested hills had always been the settlers' greatest resource. Wood was used for almost everything. It provided logs for building the pioneer's cabin and then heated it. The ashes were used to make his soap and to hull his hominy, and charcoal heated his forge. Oak bark rendered the acid for tanning hides, maple trees yielded sap for manufacturing syrup and sugar. Ash made grain cradles, white oak was chosen for wagon parts, black oak for clapboards, and hickory for tool handles. The oaks and cedars fenced his fields. Even hollow trees were used to make bee gums, stock troughs, and watering tanks. Cedar was chosen for buckets, churns, and tubs, while white oak was best for barrels and kegs. Walnut produced strong and beautiful gun stocks and furniture. And the products of the forest trees—the berries, fruits, and nuts—were eaten by both the pioneer and his livestock.

Fashioned at first by hand, the settler's tools were later made with

In the late 1890s a new source of power came to the Ozarks to help with the heavy work of threshing, crushing rock, grinding grain. And when a steam-driven sawmill came to the neighborhood, settlers could have frame homes rather than log. The first steam engines were stationary—the work had to be taken to them. Then came the "traction engine" that could run under its own power: "About two or three miles an hour downhill with a good wind behind it." But the steam engines were insatiable. In return for threshing up to a thousand bushels of wheat a day, the engine could use as much as a ton of coal or a cord of wood—and drink fifteen hundred gallons of water. This engine is powering a sawmill in Christian County, Missouri, in 1908. (Courtesy of State Historical Society of Missouri)

About 1910 the American Pencil Company in Branson, Missouri, made heavy use of the native cedar in this area. At its height more than a hundred wagonloads of cedar logs passed daily over the company scales. In one year alone, the American Pencil Company bought over fifty thousand dollars worth of logs—a considerable sum in those days. This company and the Eagle Pencil Company at Cotter, Arkansas, bought the bulk of the virgin cedar in the Upper White River Valley. The heavy cedar harvest lasted about twenty-five years, although cedar is still cut in the region for closet linings, pet bedding, and other modern uses.

the aid of water-powered sawmills that produced rough planks and saved a great deal of time and work. Even the mills themselves, with the exception of the metal saws and cowhide belts, were largely made of wood. Even though most houses were still built with logs, lumber was used for floors, doors, and window facings. Wagons, farm implements, boats, and more could be built better and more easily with lumber than with hewn timbers.

With the coming of the railroads in the early 1900s, markets for lumber products developed outside the immediate community. Settlers found buyers for fence posts, pilings, poles, tool handles, wagon parts, and crossties. Since Chadwick had a railroad earlier than Branson, great quantities of crossties were hauled by wagons to Chadwick. Cedar logs by the thousands were floated down the White River to Cotter and Batesville, Arkansas, before the railroad came to Branson.

With the completion of the rail lines to Branson, the rafting of crossties and cedar logs continued at an accelerated rate from Upper White and James rivers, with Branson serving as a terminal point where they were retrieved from the river, processed, or shipped elsewhere. The American Pencil Company built a factory at Branson to process the cedar into rectangular slats measuring about three by three by eight inches; these slats were shipped elsewhere to be manufactured into pencils. For about twenty-five years this plant and the Eagle Pencil Company at Cotter, Arkansas, bought the bulk of the virgin cedar in the Upper White River Valley. In one year alone, the American Pencil Company bought over fifty thousand dollars worth of logs. In later years postyards were established for the purchase and shipment of cedar for fence posts.

King Cotton

Cotton also heavily influenced the economics of the Upper White River country. Cotton was grown in the bottomlands of the White River and its major tributaries, now mostly inundated by the man-made lakes. From 1870 to 1920, cotton dollars were as important as tourist dollars are today.

The first cotton in this region is thought to have been grown from seed brought by settlers from the cotton-producing states east of the Mississippi. At first, it was picked and seeded by hand for domestic use in the manufacture of homespun clothing and for quilt batts. As such, it was associated with family gardens and truck patches. "In order to have clothes," said one who remembered those days, "they had to process their own cotton, beginning with removing the seeds. Each kid had to remove his shoeful of seeds every night if he wanted to have any new clothes."

Before the Civil War, flatboats and steamboats laden with cotton bales descended the White River on the way to distant markets. Most of the region's smattering of slaveholders owned only a few slaves each, however, and many of them did not work in the cotton fields. The chief cotton growers were white settlers; their large families provided ample labor for growing and harvesting the cotton. Historian Elmo Ingenthron reported that "the customs, traditions and heritage of the people were of southern origin. Cotton was king of the cash crops; yet, it was not Dixieland."

Cotton growing came to a complete halt during the Civil War, but was revived after the conflict. The coming of the railroad to Springfield in 1870 and to Ozark and Chadwick in the early 1880s provided additional markets and shipping points—an added incentive for cotton growing and ginning. In the mid-1870s a cotton gin was established in the bend of the White River below Forsyth. It is estimated that Taney County produced and sold a hundred thousand dollars worth of cotton that year. During the 1880s cotton sometimes brought forty dollars a bale. As a result, cotton growing continued to increase. The cotton gin, like the blacksmith shop, store, post office, and gristmill, was a part of every town and village in the White River region. Some gins were powered by water, others by steam or horsepower. If a farmer and his family owned no suitable land to grow cotton, they could earn cash during picking season—about 2.5 cents a pound for seed cotton—by hiring out to the neighbors. School was dismissed for two or three weeks in the fall to allow the pupils to help their parents pick the cotton and get it to the gin.

But the price of cotton dropped from a hundred dollars a bale during World War I to fifteen dollars a bale in the Depression years of the early 1930s. By 1940 there were only twenty-five acres of cotton in Taney County.

Hazel Splitters

Another little-known aspect of Ozarks agriculture is the wild hogs that once roamed these hills. Because of the settlers' tendency to let livestock run loose and fend for themselves off the land, feral hogs—sometimes called *hazel splitters* locally—became a menace to the neighborhood. Domestic sows would stray, find sustenance in nuts, and roots, and acorns (mast). Litters would be farrowed in the hills and the pigs could grow to be two or three years old before seeing their first human being. If unmarked pigs were found with marked sows (usually a farmer used a distinctive ear marking), they were considered the property of the stockman whose mark the sow bore. The marks could be recorded at the county seat.

Owners preferred to bring the range hogs in alive to be fed corn for a period of time to "harden the fat." "This was due to the fact that mast meat will drip badly when hung up to cure." But rounding up the hogs for butchering required ingenuity and not a little bravery. Said one who remembered those days, "Needless to say that these wild hogs couldn't be caught by sprinkling salt on their tails. They were most adept at fighting and/or running, and the choice was always theirs."

When the stock laws were passed requiring animals to be confined, stockmen gradually turned to purebred hogs. The hazel splitter became extinct.

Indeed, many things have changed in the White River Hills. The remarkable thing is how much they have stayed the same. And, while the little towns in the region share a common history of lumbering, tie hacking, cotton, wild hogs, travel and trade on the White River— and much more—each of them has a distinctive personality as well. And knowing the past of a community helps us understand—and empathize—with it today.

Branson: More Cement Sidewalks Than Any Town in the County

Historian and writer Kathleen Van Buskirk, in trying to unravel the history of Branson, admitted: ". . . when a town has a history as complicated as Branson's, it pays to be vague. . . ."

Nevertheless, with the help of her research and understanding, as well as that of Elmo Ingenthron, author of *The Land of Taney*, we know that when the first pioneers arrived in the 1830s and 1840s, the present town site of Branson was a place of inspiring beauty. Stands of oak and cedar crowded the flood plain of the White River and the hillside on the west bank, backed by forested mountains rising ridge upon ridge. Thick growths of cane, taller than a man's head, engulfed the swampy mouths of creeks such as Roark, producing natural fishing poles but making travel difficult. Upstream, the wide flats at the mouth of Turkey Creek also invited heavy growths of trees and cane. By the beginning of the Civil War, settlers had cleared homesites and established pioneer industries, only to see it all wiped out by the war and by the outlaw violence accompanying the conflict.

Branson, like most Ozarks towns, began as a country store and post office. An enterprising river traveler, Reuben S. Branson, established a center of trade here in 1882. About twenty-five years later, the coming of the railroad introduced the first tourists to the area. As businesses sprang up almost overnight, streets were laid out so quickly that buggy drivers were advised to "watch out for stumps." A cotton

"The first automobile in Branson" posed in front of the bank (top). Commercial Street (bottom) is now called Main Street.

gin was located at the foot of the hill where the White River encircled the waterfront. There was a gristmill "up on Roark Creek." Men earned hard cash by hacking out railroad ties to be floated downriver to market.

Formed soon after the turn of the century, the Branson Town Company financed and platted a town. In 1902 the name was changed to Lucia (pronounced Loosha), then back to Branson again in 1904.

Local businessmen, seeking a way to get some cash into farmers' pockets, put up the necessary capital to incorporate the Branson Canning Factory. Farmers could pick up free tomato seed at the drug store, and the cannery would buy all the tomatoes raised. The factory, just north and across the street from the railroad depot, began operation on August 30, 1907; twelve thousand cases of canned tomatoes were sent to market that year.

New merchants moved in and a school district was organized. In 1912 Branson's business district was almost completely destroyed by a fire that began in the early morning hours in the newly enlarged Commercial Hotel at Commercial and Pacific. Verbal reports attribute the blaze to an accident involving overheated flatirons and a wood-burning kitchen range.

The only four business buildings which survived that fire are the Branson Hotel, the railroad depot, the bank building at the corner of Main and Commercial, and the gabled structure near the depot, first known as Sullenger's Saloon. But the town immediately rebuilt and continued to grow. In Branson's youth, blocks of wood had studded the streets to serve as stepping stones across the mud, but soon downtown Branson boasted more "cement sidewalks than any other town in the county."

Most of downtown Branson's existing brick buildings date from the years after the fire. Sullenger's Saloon was the first business building to appear in Branson after it was platted in 1903 and is the oldest building still standing. Built at Third and College, it was relocated in 1909 to Sycamore and Main. The men who built the railroad made Sullenger's a lively, raucous place. Over the years the building has seen many uses. For a time Sullenger ran a billiard and pool hall there. In 1946 it was a boarding house. Inside, the walls are uncovered studs and rough wooden planks—a reminder of the time when frame frontier buildings were common in small Ozarks towns.

With the completion of the railroad in 1906, growth became rapid. And now visitors could arrive from Kansas City or St. Louis in a matter of hours. But sometimes the one hotel was full. Then it was not uncommon to see travelers unrolling their blankets and tents to set up camp on the lawns of local residents. As trainloads of sightseers continued to arrive regularly at Branson's new depot, enterprising land-

The hub of activity in early-day Branson, Missouri, was the riverfront, as seen in this photo. Reportedly the bridge rumbled ominously when crossed. Later it was swept away by a flood.

An "English Village in the Ozarks," Hollister was a planned community designed to be unique enough to attract visitors in the heyday of railroad travel. Today's visitors will want to see the lobby of Ye Olde English Inn and tour the other old buildings on Downing Street—and the interesting shops they now house—treasures of antiques and the workshops of fine craftsmen. Indeed as picturesque as an English village, even Hollister's water tower is lettered in Old English.

owners laid out campgrounds which later would become permanent resorts.

On the lakefront of today's Branson is a seawall capped with wide sidewalks, green areas with park benches, ample parking, public fishing docks, rest rooms, and a picnic area. Ducks and Canada geese roam freely along the shore begging for corn. You can take a horse-drawn carriage ride or play a game of tennis. There are two excursion boats, and two full-service marinas rent all types of boats, motors, and stalls, and offer guides, tackle, and fishing information.

Hollister-On-Turkey Creek

Seven thousand years ago Indians lived at the confluence of Turkey Creek and White River. Now there is an English-style village there, fronting a thoroughfare called Downing Street; it was listed in the National Register of Historic Places in 1979.

Officially named for Hollister, California, in June 1904, the town's early buildings were of wood, false-fronted, and apparently thrown up along the trail with little forethought or planning. Roads were alternately muddy and dusty. Then, fortuitously, the railroad scheduled a meal stop at Hollister (a boxcar served as depot until 1910), and to meet that need the first tourist establishment opened.

In fact, the White River Railway (which became the Missouri Pacific after a 1917 merger) was active in establishing the area as a tourist mecca. Unlike many towns that sprang up along the track, Hollister became a planned community—a collaboration between a Springfield developer and the railroad. The idea was to establish an English village in the Ozarks. Appropriate materials were at hand, for Turkey Creek held plenty of building rock and the neighboring forests were full of timbers that could be cut by the region's skilled woodsmen, already expert in hand-hewing beams. The railroad assigned a landscape engineer to beautify the town.

But the adjustment from stock town to tourist center was not easy for the area ranchers. When their cattle and hogs, while awaiting shipment on the railroad, ate the flowers and trampled the shrubs, an ordinance was passed requiring the penning of animals. Rebels destroyed the pen. But eventually peace came with acceptance—and the employment of a local man, "known for his ability to handle his peers," as town marshall.

Two trains every day brought the tourists, and Hollister had already gained fame as a lovely vacation spot by the time the impounding of Lake Taneycomo added an extra boost. Another local industry flourished briefly with the establishment of a canning factory that turned out Flint Rock brand canned tomatoes.

Thanks to the rapid runoff of Ozarks "gully washers," or downpours, streams in the region often rise rapidly and dramatically, rendering them unfordable on foot or horseback and unnavigable even in johnboats. Several early communities solved the transportation problem by erecting swinging footbridges that could carry folks across the creek except in times of most severe flooding. This swinging footbridge was across Turkey Creek at Hollister, Missouri. Note the homemade johnboats. (From English Village in the Ozarks *by Edith McCall.*

On the old Springfield to Harrison Road, now Hwy. JJ, still stands Pine Top School. Pine Top community, in its heyday, was the site of a dram shop *(saloon) that served the workers building the St. Louis and Iron Mountain Railway (later Missouri Pacific) across western Taney County about 1903 to 1905. The coming of the railroad accelerated the cutting and sawing of the pine woods which once clothed these hills. Lumber was loaded on railroad cars at the Pine Top Switch, a flag station on the railway. Now no sign remains of the dram shop or the switch and few pines are left to remind us of the lush pinery that flourished here.*

But flooding plagued the unique little town, also hard hit by the Depression, as did a highway relocation. A severe decline in tourism accompanied the gas rationing and worn-out tires and cars of World War II. By 1955 Front Street (later Downing) was shabby and desolate. Cedar slabs were nailed over the large front windows of the half-timbered hotel building. The government threatened to close the post office.

Then, with the promise of Table Rock Dam, leadership began to stir the determination to revitalize the little community. The depot, no longer in active use by the railroad since passenger service had ended, was repainted and occupied as the Hollister City Hall. The old English-style buildings were restored and reopened. Now, with the patina of age, they are even more strongly reminiscent of the structures that inspired them.

Forsyth: Dimple Spot on the Face of Nature

Forsyth's post office was established at the mouth of Swan Creek in the autumn of 1837. By the time of the Civil War, Forsyth had become an important river port. It was the head of navigation for steamboats on the White River, the point where cargo was reloaded onto smaller boats to go farther up river or on wagons to travel overland (see Chapter 16).

Both sides alternately occupied Forsyth during the Civil War. In July 1861, Union general Nathaniel Lyon ordered Gen. Thomas W. Sweeny to take a force to Forsyth to remove the Rebels. Earlier attempts by the Taney and Christian County Home Guards had failed. On July 22, 1861, General Sweeny accomplished his assignment in one hour with twelve hundred Union troops and some artillery with twelve-pound howitzers. Three cannon balls breached the courthouse, and there were several casualties. On April 22, 1863, the Federals, who had fortified the town, put it to the torch rather than have it fall into the hands of the Confederates. They left behind the smoldering ruin of a town.

After the war the courthouse was repaired; but it was burned again in 1865, destroying most of the records. In 1890 a stone building was built of limestone quarried nearby and set by a local stonemason.

Forsyth had problems in common with those of other towns in the region. Livestock ran at large, with the courthouse lawn and business district as part of the open range. By the mid-1890s the indignant townspeople had been enraged by scourging swine and embarrassed by unfavorable publicity when range hogs had mutilated the body of a corpse retrieved from a hangman's noose and laid on the ground in front of the courthouse to serve as an example to others. (The unfortunate lynchee had murdered his wife, mother of his four small children, and was snatched from jail and hanged—with the rope from the community well on the square—by a drunken mob, believed by many to be one of the last acts incited by the Bald Knobbers.)

When the city election was held in April of that year, among the usual candidates for city office and ordinances to be considered was a proposition to invoke a "hog law" designed to bring an end to the animals' depredations. Candidates took stands on one side or other of the hot issue. After the election, the *Aurora Argus* commented on the outcome. "Forsyth, Taney County, had an exciting city election, the question being hog in or hog out. They elected one hog and four anti-hog councilmen. Forsyth is very progressive."

Following completion of the Powersite Dam in 1913, Forsyth began to enjoy the visits of tourists. In 1926 the Lake Taneycomo Chamber of Commerce published a brochure which claimed, "Forsyth offers you a spot where man has not yet marred the glory of the firm set hills. . . . Forsyth is the dimple spot on the face of nature."

But in the late 1940s Forsyth residents learned that the Corps of Engineers planned to build a dam in Arkansas which would result in Bull Shoals Lake—and flood their town site and many of their homes. The Corps agreed to reimburse the town for demolition of its church, lodge hall, courthouse, and all public buildings and to buy the land of the affected individuals—*if* a majority of the residents could agree to move in one direction. Ninety percent of the town's residents agreed to move "up the hill," where they had extended their corporate limits to enclose a farm and a golf course. The entire town of Forsyth moved west to the top of Shadow Rock, once used by the Indians as a lookout. A Corps of Engineers campground on the shores of Bull Shoals Lake is near the site of the old riverfront.

The former town site is now Shadow Rock Park, at the junction of Hwys. 160 and 76 West. Standing in front of the towering bluff that is Shadow Rock, one can almost feel the ground vibrate with the dramatic history it has known. This site was once occupied by prehistoric Indians and was later the hunting village of Osages. A group of Delawares lived here in 1806, and a tribe of Miamis occupied it in 1825. In the early days of white settlement, there was a swinging bridge across Swan Creek, the stream that flows at the foot of Shadow Rock. The park was the site of four of the county's former courthouses, including the stone building erected in 1890.

The first military engagement in the Upper White River Valley during the Civil War occurred here in July 1861. Federals fired on the town from the north, across Swan Creek. Much of the drama of the Taney County Bald Knobbers took place here as well. The jail stood on the slope of the hill to the east of the park, about where Shadow

Rock Motel now stands; it was from that location that the Bald Knobbers seized the victims of their lynchings. In 1968 an 1886 log home and smokehouse were moved and reconstructed in the park on the site of the 1890 courthouse.

When Forsyth moved up the hill, the stone from the courthouse and from the Union Church, "the stone chapel," built in 1893, was salvaged by the College of the Ozarks and used in construction on their campus at Point Lookout. The old church had enjoyed a bell mounted on a tall pole at a corner of the building. A telephone wire was used to ring the bell, which could be heard all over the village, and "it was rung loud and long for Sunday School, church and other meetings."

Upon completion of the new church up the hill in the new town, its congregation wanted to move the precious bell to peal in the new building. But when the Corps of Engineers bought the old building for ten thousand dollars, the bell became their property. Its retrieval from the federal bureaucracy, the townspeople discovered, would require the untangling of miles of red tape.

"It seemed as though it was going to take an act of Congress for local people to again possess this relic of years past," remembered Douglas Mahnkey, a Forsyth attorney and elder of the church. But, "One dark night, while the other villagers slept, two of the elders of the church drove a pickup to the [old] church site, picked up the bell and hid it in the barn of one of the church deacons. There it remained for some years." Eventually the bell emerged from hiding, and it now stands on the front lawn of the Presbyterian church—the "new stone chapel"—in new Forsyth.

For a look at Powersite Dam and an excellent level fishing area ideal for the elderly or handicapped, leave Shadow Rock Park by driving toward the campground and turn right to cross the old (1932) bridge across Swan Creek. When the road forks, bear to the left. At Ozark Beach, besides the easy access to Lake Taneycomo for fishing, is a shady picnic ground and rest rooms. Canada geese and other water fowl make the park their home. Ozark Beach is the site of Camp Ozark, the construction town that sprang up during the building of the dam.

There are several places in Forsyth to see a spectacular view of Lake Taneycomo, the valley of the White River, and the hills and bluffs of the surrounding countryside. Scenic turnouts with safe parking are on Hwy. 160 on the west side of town, and on Hwy. Y south of Hwy. 160.

On the site of the present Methodist church in Forsyth, there was once a giant tree; it was there that Bald Knobber violence first erupted in the lynching of Frank and Jubal Taylor.

Rockaway Beach: A 1920s Postcard

Immediately upon its impoundment, Lake Taneycomo triggered development all along its shores. One of the largest projects was Rockaway Beach, platted in 1914 as a pleasure resort. Originally the town was named Taneycomo, but the founder renamed it after visiting Rockaway Beach in New York. By 1925 the thriving resort town boasted a dance pavilion for the big bands from Kansas City and St. Louis, new summer cottages, and the addition of sixteen rooms to the Taneycomo Hotel. Newly installed electric lights illuminated the bathing beach and diving tower.

But when Table Rock Lake was built and Taneycomo changed so drastically from a warm water lake popular with families and swimmers to a cold water lake suitable for trout, Rockaway Beach changed too. It became a trout fisherman's resort and a home base for vacationers. "The Pavilion" now houses a flea market, but boat docks still bob on the waves and the forested hills still enfold quiet waters.

Rockaway Beach is on Hwy. 176 south off Hwy. 160, and virtually on the shores of Lake Taneycomo. The old resort town is still picturesque and has the ambiance of a 1920s postcard, as if frozen in its heyday past.

Kirbyville: Murder Rocks

From earliest settlement, the wagon freighters' road from Springfield to Harrison turned down Bear and Bull Creeks to cross the river by way of Hensley's Ferry several miles downstream from Roark Creek. By 1875 from fifty to one hundred wagons a day were using Hensley's Ferry.

The teamsters liked to camp about five miles south of the White River, where the road pulled out of the river hills onto a level upland. Soon a town grew up around the campground. Platted as Warnersville in 1870, Kirbyville got a new name when it got a new postmaster in 1872. Some of the worst Bald Knobber violence occurred near here.

In the 1880s and 1890s, lead, zinc, and onyx mines were located near Kirbyville and the community boomed, its population swollen to more than twice that of Forsyth, which numbered two hundred at the turn of the century. In 1900 the thriving community included a hotel, a gristmill, and a cotton gin; it was a mail distribution point. But when the railroad went to Branson rather than Kirbyville or Forsyth, prosperity followed it.

The countryside is beautiful south of Kirbyville on Hwys. J and JJ. And steeped in history. Bald Knobbers rode these hills in the late 1880s, and at a spring near Kirbyville—during a Fourth of July picnic attended by families—men were shot and killed.

And nearby Murder Rocks provided an ideal place for outlaws to ambush travelers on the road between Arkansas and Missouri. The cluster of rocks was large enough to conceal several men and horses as they waited for their unsuspecting victims. Sometimes the giant boulders were called Bolin Rocks for Alf Bolin, the most vicious and feared bushwhacker in this border region; they were the scene of many of Bolin's most horrible crimes. Bolin and his men pounced on freight haulers and stole their oxen, mules, horses, wagons, anything of value. From here they roamed near and far, killing old men, women, and young children. Bolin was finally killed—stories vary as to who actually accomplished the deed—as he stooped before a fireplace to light his pipe. Soldiers charged with taking his body to Springfield cut off his head and took it to Ozark to collect the reward for killing the outlaw. The body was taken to Forsyth and buried in an unmarked grave on Swan Creek.

In Alf Bolin's time, the roadway was level with the base of Murder Rocks; now it passes above them, which severely limits their visibility. An outcropping of great gray boulders on a hillside, the main group covers an area about twenty by thirty feet. At the end nearest the road is a giant boulder forming the complete frontage and rising about fifteen feet. A mighty cleft in the giant boulder two or three feet wide at ground level made an open passageway—a hidden corridor for ambushers—and provided protection. The danger to be faced at Murder Rocks was well known, so for many years travelers dreaded the spot and could not breathe easily until it was behind them.

About one and a half miles after you turn onto Hwy. JJ from Hwy. J, watch for Murder Rocks on your right. Only their summits are now barely visible through the pines. The rocks are on private property along the side of a hill as the roadway ascends it, so you will only be able to get a glimpse of them. You will, however, enjoy the drive through the scenic—and historic—countryside.

Protem: Nobody Close at All

A Union captain named Christopher Columbus Owen settled in the Protem area after the Civil War, where he was the first postmaster. Owen had some difficulty in selecting a name for the village. Every name he submitted to Washington had already been taken elsewhere. The post office department, however, wrote that he could use any name *protem* (Latin for "temporarily") until he made up his mind.

Located at the forks of Shoal Creek on the Yellville-Chadwick road, near a ferry across the White River, Protem began as a pleasant camping point for the freighters of both Missouri and Arkansas. The road ran north and south through the town as the main street. The busi-

At Protem, Missouri, where the business district lined the freighters' road from Chadwick, Missouri, to Yellville, Arkansas, many doorways were elevated above the dusty road. Wooden stairs—or in this case, stone—rose to platforms that doubled as porches. Other than this store building, very little remains of the old town of Protem. But now the road through town is paved, and it leads to popular Bull Shoals Lake.

Named for the Arkansas county it serves, The Lady Marion is one of two highway ferries left in Arkansas. The rest have been replaced by bridges. Often called "The Peel Ferry," it is the Hwy. 125 link across Bull Shoals Lake and is one of three ferries left in the Ozarks. Another is at Akers in the Ozark National Scenic Riverways, and one is across the Gasconade River southwest of Hermann. Once there were hundreds. This ferry survives because traffic in this remote location does not justify the huge expenditure that would be required to bridge the mile-wide crossing of the lake.

ness section was located along this route for several hundred yards: three general stores, a doctor's office, two blacksmith shops, a drug store, several cotton gins, and a cabin for drying tobacco. At the north edge of town—still standing but partially hidden by vines—was a two-story school building.

A sweeping curve in the White River, now filled with lake waters, then contained many acres of fertile, almost level land. Old-timers tell of seeing as many as one hundred wagonloads of cotton lined up to cross the ferries, and many times a like number at the gins in Protem. Corn, wheat, and tobacco were also grown in the upland fields north of Protem and along Big Creek.

The crossroads village had grown considerably by the turn of the century. And in 1901 lead and zinc were discovered nearby. Amid considerable speculation and advertising, the Golden Eagle Mine was opened, but mining—as in all Taney County—fizzled quickly. As with other towns in the area, Protem reached its peak of growth and prosperity between 1890 and 1920.

A bank was chartered about 1920 and was doing well, a great asset to the neighborhood. On August 6, 1924, a country picnic was in progress by the big spring at the old campground, with the usual dancing platform, doll racks, lemonade and general stands. Most of the citizens were at the picnic grounds. About 11:00 A.M. two strange young men, unmasked, armed with pistols, entered the bank, held the owner at gunpoint and took $125 of the bank's cash. They came and went on foot. Leaving on a dead run, they disappeared into the timber just west of town. The cry soon went out that the bank had been held up.

Although an accomplice had apparently waited in the woods nearby with the getaway horses, that individual was spooked by the general alarm and deserted his or her post. The bandits were forced to flee on foot and were seen by a former neighbor who recognized them. On the morning of August 12 one of the fugitives shot and killed Sheriff Newt Boles, who was attempting to take him into custody. The killer was later apprehended, convicted, and incarcerated in the Missouri State Penitentiary.

Gradually new farming methods made small cotton acreages unprofitable, and by 1930 the total cotton acreage in the county had fallen to almost nothing. Even so, the cotton industry continued longer in this area than elsewhere. When Brightwell's gin at Protem closed in the mid-1930s, it was the last.

The years-long drought of the early 1930s and the simultaneous nationwide depression took a heavy toll of the rest of the farmers around Protem. Many who had survived the '30s left for the service during World War II, or moved to work in war industries. Few returned after the war. From those who were left, the lake took the rich bottomland. Sturdy stone homes that had endured for several generations were dismantled and moved to higher ground or buried under the lake waters. Cemeteries were dug up and moved above the project flood line.

"When we moved here in 1921 there were houses all around. You could see the smoke coming out of the stove pipes and chimneys," said a Protem old-timer not long ago. "And now there's nobody close at all."

The Lady Marion

Just south of Protem is one of the last remaining automobile ferries in the Ozarks. A fair-weather link serving Hwy. 125 from south of Protem, Missouri, to Peel, Arkansas, the "Peel Ferry" crosses an arm of Bull Shoals Lake.

Running a ferry quickly became a feasible occupation—and an honorable profession—in the early Ozarks, land of rivers and streams. Almost anywhere a river was too deep to ford conveniently, an early-day entrepreneur set up as ferry operator. Probably it was pleasant enough work, especially in nice weather: outside in the fresh air, being on the river, enjoying nature and the scenery, visiting with folks who crossed.

Toll fees were meager unless the route was unusually busy or heavily traveled. At the turn of the century, rates averaged ten cents for a person on foot, twenty-five cents for a man on horseback, and fifty cents for a team and wagon. Livestock was assessed by the number on each crossing.

But ferryboating could also be dangerous—especially when the rivers became choked with logs and railroad ties that could overwhelm and crush a fragile vessel. Suddenly swollen by heavy rains, the White River brought death to James H. Breeden on April 14, 1906, when his small boat was swamped as he returned from the day's last run.

This was the approximate site of Brown's Ferry, a cable ferry that once spanned the White River. But after the lake was completed, Brown's Ferry was discontinued. Nearly twenty years later in the mid-1960s, businessmen living on both sides of the lake created a shareholding corporation and initiated the present ferry as a private operation. In 1968, after it was proven to be an essential service, Marion County, Arkansas, ran it as a toll ferry until December 1969. Then the Arkansas State Highway Department took over its operation and continues to operate it toll free.

Aside from being transportation across the water, *The Lady Marion* offers a pleasant ride and uncluttered views of Bull Shoals Lake. Bald

eagles can sometimes be seen in the wintertime, and it is not uncommon to see deer and beaver swimming across a cove. The ferry runs
every forty-five minutes from each side, operating only during the
day. Powered by a small tug boat alongside, the craft can carry six cars
or their equivalent in boats or travel trailers. It does not make the
crossing in a high wind or fog.

On the Arkansas side of the lake, the white settlement that preceded Peel was named, at least by legendary account, Need More.
Settlers were said to have felt that the place needed more people. In
modern times the construction of Bull Shoals Lake and the modest
influx of retirees and visitors to this remote area has awakened in both
Protem and Peel the hope of new growth.

As you enjoy the ferry ride across the cool blue lake, give some
thought to the Ozarkers in the cotton fields and on the snake rafts
and the steamboats that once plied the river beneath your feet. Look
around you at the hilltops and the bluffs and remember that where
you see fifty or a hundred feet of land above the water, that much and
more is beneath it. Consider the towering trees that were skidded to
the edge of those bluffs and sent crashing into the river below, and be
aware that most of the forest you see around you is relatively new,
working to heal the scars of former "harvesting." Think of the men
and the women and their children who scratched out a homeplace on
the fertile land that is now lake bottom and clawed for a living here
among the rocks.

On the Arkansas side of the ferry crossing, Hwy. 125 joins Hwy. 14,
the route to Buffalo National River.

Practical Matters

Chapter 10 — Taney County

Checking Out	A Sampling	Phone
Lodging	Big Cedar Lodge, 612 Devils Pool Rd., Ridgedale MO 65739;	(417) 335-2777
	Lakeshore Resort, P.O. Box 537, Branson MO;	(417) 334-6262
	Dogwood Park Hotel, P.O. Box 309, Branson MO;	(417) 334-1985
	Best Western Branson Inn, P.O. Box 676, Branson MO	(417) 334-5121
Bed & Breakfasts	Ozark Mountain Country Bed & Breakfast (Reservation Service for more than 50 B&Bs), P.O. Box 295, Branson MO 65616	(417) 334-4720 or (800) 321-8594
Campgrounds	Branson City Campground, East on Main St., Lake Taneycomo, Branson MO;	(417) 334-2915
	Cooper Creek Resort & Campground, HCR 5, Box 2202B, Branson MO 65616;	(417) 334-4871 and (417) 334-5250
	Presleys' Campground, 2910 76 Country Blvd., Branson MO 65616;	(417) 334-3447
	Shadow Rock Park, Hwys. 106 and 76, Forsyth MO;	
	River Run Park at Forsyth, and other Corps of Engineers Campgrounds on Bull Shoals Lake (See Where to Write)	
Restaurants	Candlestick Inn Restaurant & Lounge, Hwy. 76 East Atop Mt. Branson, Branson MO;	(417) 334-3633
	Dimitris, 420 E. Main, Branson MO 65616;	(417) 334-0888
	The Farmhouse, 119 W. Main, Branson MO;	(417) 334-9701
	Outback Steak & Oyster Bar, P.O. Box 576, Branson MO	(417) 334-6306
Main Historical Attractions	The Shepherd of the Hills Homestead & Outdoor Theatre, Rt. 1 Box 770 (W. Hwy. 76), Branson MO 65616;	(417) 334-4191
	Silver Dollar City, W. Hwy. 76, Marvel Cave Park MO 65616 (See Also the Chart Following Chapter 9)	(417) 338-2611
Other Attractions	Lake Queen Sightseeing Tour (Handicapped Accessible), Lake Queen Dock at the Lake Front, Branson MO 65616;	(417) 334-3015 (800) 492-4661 MO (800) 641-4374
	Stone Hill Winery, HCR 5, Box 1825, Branson MO 65616 (Hwy. 165);	(417) 334-1897
	Factory Merchants Mall, W. Hwy. 76, Branson MO 65616;	(417) 335-6686
	Table Rock Helicopters, P.O. Box 101, Branson MO 65616;	(417) 334-6102
	Waltzing Waters, P.O. Box V, Branson MO	(417) 334-4144

Checking Out	A Sampling	Phone
Outdoor Recreation	Hercules Glades Wilderness, Hwy. 125 near Kissee Mills MO (See Where to Write); Fishing, Boating & Other Water Sports: on Bull Shoals, Taneycomo and Table Rock Lakes, Numerous Corps of Engineers Campgrounds and Private Facilities, including in this area Hwy. 125 Marina on Bull Shoals Lake, Rt. N, Box 53, Peel AR 72668 (Near Peel Ferry);	(501) 436-5390
	Indian Point Boat Dock, HCR 1, Box 1137, Branson MO 65612;	(417) 338-2891
	Table Rock State Park Marina, HCR 1, Box 911, Branson MO 65616 (Near the Dam);	(417) 334-3069
	Branson Trout Dock, Lake Taneycomo, 305 St. Limas, Branson MO 65616 (Near Campground);	(417) 334-3703
	Taneycomo Golf Club, Rt. 1, Box 196-1, Forsyth MO 65653;	(417) 546-5454
	Holiday Hills Golf Course, Rt. 3, Box 282, Branson MO 65616	(417) 334-4443
Where to Write for More Details	Ava Ranger District, Mark Twain National Forest, Ava MO 65608;	(471) 683-4428
	Rockaway Beach Chamber of Commerce, P.O. Box 1004, Rockaway Beach MO 65740; (See Also the Chart Following Chapter 9);	(417) 561-4280 or (800) 798-0178
	Forsyth Chamber of Commerce, Box 777, Forsyth MO 65653;	(417) 546-2741
	Corps of Engineers Resident Engineer, Mountain Home AR	(501) 425-2700

SECTION 4

Buffalo National River and Greers Ferry Lake

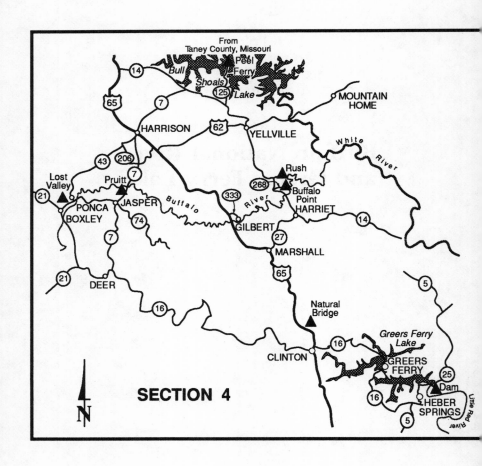

From
Taney County, Missouri

Bull
Shoals
Lake

Peel
Ferry

14

65

7

125

MOUNTAIN
HOME

HARRISON

62

YELLVILLE

White River

43

206

268

Rush

7

333

Buffalo Point

Lost
Valley

Pruitt

PONCA
BOXLEY

21

JASPER

Buffalo

River

River

HARRIET

14

GILBERT

74

27

7

MARSHALL

65

21

DEER

16

5

Natural
Bridge

Greers Ferry
Lake

16

GREERS
FERRY

CLINTON

16

25

Dam

Little Red River

16

HEBER
SPRINGS

5

SECTION 4

N

CHAPTER 11

Overview:
A National Treasure

If all the beauty and charm of the Ozarks could be distilled and poured out in a single stream, the resulting brew would probably be very much like the Buffalo National River.

Actually unremarkable as a waterway, relatively short, narrow, and too shallow for sizable boats, the Buffalo is nonetheless a singular river. Represented in its jewel-green waters are all the other American rivers previously sacrificed to the gods of "progress." Echoing in its verdant valley and from its soaring bluffs are memories of other beautiful rivers now drowned beneath manmade lakes.

And when, by popular demand, the Buffalo was rescued from a similar fate, more than a river was saved. In its canyon is preserved all that makes the Ozarks special: the grandeur of rugged hills, primeval flora and fauna, history—both ancient and modern—and a unique folk culture and its artifacts. And something else: an almost palpable sensation of great age, a sense of being haunted by the memory of the bustling human activity that once occurred in the river's watershed and by a nostalgic—even poignant—yearning for the time out of mind. Standing on the bank of the Buffalo, it is impossible not to feel connected to history.

The river itself is timeless. Though fluctuating with the seasons and the rainfall, the Buffalo seems always the same. Yet, somehow, it yields up new secrets on every visit; new facets of its character remain always waiting to be discovered. Even the National Park Service, official custodian of the Buffalo, waxes poetic about the river: "Time resonates along its ancient, carved-out hills, but the present moment also dances like a twig down its rain swollen rapids. The Buffalo . . . an island of space and time. . . ."

From its source in the Boston Mountains, highest of the Ozark hills, to its confluence with the White near Buffalo City southwest of Mountain Home, the Buffalo flows entirely in the state of Arkansas. But there is little doubt that the river and its watershed constitute a national treasure.

Especially popular with campers, hikers, and canoeists, the protected river corridor can also be enjoyed by those who seek only a restful respite somewhere along its beautiful shoreline. On the upper river, from Ponca to Pruitt, steep drops, hairpin turns, and swift chutes provide challenges for whitewater fans. The average drop of the river along this stretch is ten feet per mile, but it can usually only be floated in the spring.

In contrast, the drop along the lower river is about three feet per mile, but except in very dry weather, it can be floated year-round. Adding to the attractiveness of this lower portion of the river is the presence of official and virtually unpeopled wilderness.

Names on the Land

The Buffalo River was probably named for the bison that apparently thrived along the northern and western portions of the Arkansas Territory until about 1820. (Bison bones have been unearthed in the numerous bluff shelters in the Ozarks.) The river's name seems to have been in common use by shortly after 1800, and the term "Buffalo Fork of the White River" first appeared on a map in 1807. Although the bison were gone by the time the first permanent settlers began arriving in the 1830s, the name of the river persisted.

Tributaries of the river bear the names of some of the earliest families to settle here: Arrington, Clark, Edgmon, Whiteley. And like rivers elsewhere in the region, each of the Buffalo's eddies, shoals, and fords was named after local events or people. Everyone along the river knew every such spot—and exactly how the feature gained its title. Swindell Ford, for example, was so called because a man named Swindell tried to cross there during high water on horseback. He was swept away and drowned. Nearby Lost Hill Eddy earned its name when two children were lost overnight on a hill overlooking the eddy.

But the names of geographic features are often repeated from one place to another, making it almost impossible for visitors to follow local directions. There are two Big Creeks, two Mill Creeks, two Bear

Words attempt to describe and photos to reflect the elusive quality of the Buffalo National River, but both fall short. One must experience the Buffalo firsthand to comprehend its unique qualities. Even if you are not a canoeist or an outdoors person, take a moment to walk along the riverbank or to sit in contemplation of its towering bluffs. You cannot help but be enriched by the time you spend with the Buffalo. The easiest place to make its acquaintance is here, at Buffalo Point Recreation Area south of Yellville, Arkansas.

One of more than two hundred structures of historical significance—houses, barns, a gristmill—listed on the National Register of Historic Places as the "Big Buffalo Valley Historic District," this community building dates to the last century. Often known as "Boxley Valley," the exceptionally scenic neighborhood is still shown on Arkansas maps as Boxley.

Creeks, and three Brush Creeks. What's more, a single feature is frequently called by two or more differing names, depending upon local preference.

The Coming of the White Man

The journals of early travelers—before the coming of white settlers—tell us of rolling upland prairies where big bluestem grass grew head high. Roaming bands of buffalo and elk mingled with deer in vast acreages of wildflowers. Giant oaks grew in parklike groves on the hillsides, while ancient cedars furred the drier slopes and pines towered over the ancient bluffs.

After the Indians were pushed farther west, the white settlers, for the most part, lived off the land. But often they killed more than they needed; some even killed for love of killing. They slaughtered bears in great numbers—to the point of extinction in the region. By 1830 the buffalo and elk were also killed off, as well as many of the small fur bearers and birds like ruffed grouse and wild turkeys. One Jim Villines earned the nickname "Beaver Jim" because he killed so many beavers.

Unable to withstand the relentless slaughter, it was not long before the wild game dwindled drastically. As a natural result, predators turned in desperation to the domestic stock running free in the woods. Their inroads, in turn, unleashed another blood bath; all animals not directly useful were killed on sight. When county officials offered bounties on wildcats, panthers, and wolves, those animals were soon eradicated.

By 1850 the settlement had grown large enough to support a gristmill just north of the present hamlet of Boxley. A village grew up around the mill and was called Whiteley, or Whiteley's Mills. In 1860 the rugged valley was home to almost fifteen thousand souls. Many tilled the fertile bottomlands, while others built gristmills and sawmills on the swift tributaries of the river. But towns were still few and far between.

While there was little in the region for the military to fight over during the Civil War, the countryside suffered from guerrilla warfare. Troops and partisans of both sides plundered the land and victimized the women and children left to fend for themselves. By March 1864, the commander of a Federal force encamped at Yellville reported that there was no forage available within twenty miles of that town. Jasper, Yellville and Buffalo City had been either totally or partially destroyed by fire, and a large number of survivors took shelter in caves or other temporary homes. In April of 1864, there was a skirmish near Whiteley's Mills. Most of the fighting took place near the present junction of Hwys. 21 and 43.

As they did elsewhere in the cave-rich Ozarks, Confederates mined the nitrogen-rich earth from numerous local cave floors to extract potassium nitrate, or saltpeter, for making gunpowder. Collected and hauled in wagons over the mountains to the Arkansas River for shipment to arsenals of the Confederacy, the saltpeter was vital to the war effort. The Federals, of course, waged continual war against these operations. One Union Army officer's report of such a raid inventoried a number of the huge iron kettles broken by his men against further such use. It is typical of the continuity in this country that, a century after the kettles were last inventoried in that officer's report, all remained in the neighborhood and were still in use for various other purposes: wash tubs, rain barrels, and stock tanks.

Boxley

After the Civil War, a merchant named Boxley moved into the valley. In 1883 he established another post office, and the community took its name. Whiteley's Mill continued in use for a few years after the Civil War, but by 1870 the community needed a larger mill. The new three-story frame millhouse built of hand-hewn timbers served the neighborhood for almost a century. But by 1950 nearly everyone had turned to store-bought meal and flour, and the machinery was in bad repair. When the flume caved in, the miller at last shut down the old mill.

Log construction techniques in Newton County were among the best in the Ozarks and are still represented in a few surviving buildings of fine craftsmanship. New log buildings were erected in the valley until at least World War II. Many buildings were made with wooden pegs whittled at night before the fireplace. Thus prepared in otherwise idle moments and stockpiled, the pegs were ready when needed for a house raising.

By 1905 there were some twenty-seven thousand people living in the river's 1,338-square-mile watershed. Because of its limited carrying capacity, the land was overpopulated. Everywhere a few sloping acres could be cleared, and in every hollow, families scratched out a living. Area farmers grew wheat, corn, potatoes, oats, and even some tobacco and rice.

But getting their crops to market was a major undertaking for the isolated settlers. The few roads were exceedingly poor and treacherous, what with the ever-present danger of wagons rolling off the narrow, rough paths. And always there was the Buffalo itself to contend with. Dependent on ferries to cross the river, residents were constantly aware that after a heavy rain, crossing at all might be either impossible or extremely difficult. They lived with the problem until bridges were finally built, beginning in the 1930s.

As in much of the rest of the Ozarks, at least a portion of the populace enjoyed debating societies, town bands, and newspapers. In 1898 Searcy County boasted of 1,004 carriages and thirty-four pianos. But the Methodist Church, during its efforts to organize churches in the hills, characterized the hillfolk by their "independence, self-reliance, and individuality, which often runs to eccentricity."

The 1880s were boom years for the growing of cotton, and gins throughout the Buffalo valley processed and baled the fiber. But the soil-sapping plant had done long-lasting damage by the 1890s, and in its wake agriculture was effectively dead. There was no new tillable land available for new generations of people.

To make a living, area inhabitants turned to lumbering. And because the railroad did not penetrate the Buffalo valley until 1902, the river itself provided the early means of transporting the logs to market. For several months, while the river was too low to float, men cut the timber. Then, during flood stage, the stockpiled logs were dumped into the water and formed into rafts that were then floated downstream to the White River and eventually reached the lumber yard at Batesville.

By 1920 most of the easily accessible cedar and walnut stands were gone; the industry became a victim of its own shortsightedness. Cattle, hogs, and goats ran free in the woods, overgrazing, eating everything, even killing young trees. Gravel choked the creek beds. By the time of World War II, a massive exodus had begun. Caught between diminishing resources at home and the desire for a "better" way of life, entire families packed up and left. And because there were few other buyers for their exhausted land, most sold out to the Forest Service. From the 1930s on, the government bought up hundreds of old homesteads and tracts of cut-over woodland to fill in gaps around its original national forest holdings. By 1965 there were fewer than half as many people in the valley than at the turn of the century.

The Controversy

Long interested in "improving" the Buffalo River, the Army Corps of Engineers in 1939 recommended the construction of a dam one mile above the river's mouth. But while they were perfecting their plan, World War II began. For some years the project appeared to be forgotten, or at least shelved. But in 1954 the Corps recommended that *two* dams be built on the river: the Lone Rock dam 3.5 miles above the mouth and a second near Gilbert. Either or both of the proposed dams would drown many miles of river—pools, picturesque shoals, bluffs, caves, historical and archaeological sites. There appeared to be little or no opposition to the Corps' plan.

For decades johnboat fishermen had enjoyed the river in solitude. Then, in the late 1950s and early 1960s, people—many of them outsiders from beyond the confines of the valley—began to discover the pleasures of floating the river in canoes. Strangers arrived in increasing numbers, and all of them became aware of the unique qualities of the river and started to think about and speak of what would be lost if it were dammed.

As had happened so frequently elsewhere, local promoters of the dams saw only the short-term gain: a few years of much-needed jobs and lucrative contracts while the dams were being built and a continuing income from tourists and users of the resulting lake. They overlooked the long-term loss with the same mentality that had caused their forebears to overtimber, overgraze, overcrop, overhunt, and bulldoze pastures from the rocky slopes.

Opponents questioned the dam's supposed benefits: flood control where there was little need for it, electric power that could be produced more cheaply elsewhere, another recreation lake when there were already several in the area. Many locals deeply resented that outsiders would come into their neighborhood and decide how their resources and their historic wilderness—so long shunned by everybody else—should be used.

It seemed to many that the battles for the Buffalo and for two similar rivers in the Missouri Ozarks, the Current and the Meramec, all being waged more or less simultaneously, were somehow part of the larger struggle to save what was left of our heritage. Of course, "heritage" meant something different to each participant in the struggle. For the natives of the valley, it might be the right to fish and trap on the river—a basic question of whether they could continue their very way of life. As might be expected, most of the landowners along the banks of the river opposed the dams. But for the outsiders who became involved, usually city dwellers—many of whom had never even seen the Buffalo—the cause was no less vital.

For ten years there raged the battle of the Buffalo. Both sides organized and waged war with publicity and propaganda. Eventually the Corps of Engineers agreed to settle for one dam near Gilbert, but the price of the project continued to escalate.

As an alternative to damming the river, some opponents proposed that a national park be established along its shores to preserve its beauty and character. A survey team from the National Park Service spent ten days on the river and agreed that it should be preserved.

Their report said in part, "Here lies the last opportunity for preservation of a river typical of the Arkansas Ozarks and, indeed, the opportunity for preservation of a river considered by many to be the most outstanding free-flowing stream in the Southwest."

In the meantime, the controversy heated up. Memorial Day, 1965, saw violence erupt. That weekend extremist advocates of the dam cut eighteen large trees along the banks and dropped them across the channel at what came to be called *Crisis Curve*, in order to stop the Ozark Wilderness Waterways Club from completing their float to Pruitt that weekend. Most of the club canoeists took out upstream, and a few days later a group of Boy Scouts sawed and chopped through the downed trees to reopen the channel.

Also that weekend, barbed wire was strung across the river ahead of a publicized canoe race. At least one canoeist was cut as he maneuvered through the wire, and all were threatened. Other canoeists—who had been warned off the river by anonymous phone calls—were fired upon as they floated. Although no one was seriously injured or killed, the battle had become one of more than words and opinions.

Meanwhile, many who had previously opposed the national park came to believe that it was a necessity, not only to stop the Corps' dam, but to halt the damage being done to the river by some of the property owners along its banks. In Newton County large landholders were bulldozing trees from the banks, dredging the river itself, and clearing steep slopes that washed into the stream.

At last the tide began to turn in favor of the river when Arkansas governor Orval Faubus stated publicly that he opposed damming the Buffalo and endorsed the National River, an endorsement reaffirmed by the state's next two governors as well. In 1967 the Arkansas senators and a new congressman introduced bills to authorize a national river, followed up by supporters' letter-writing campaigns and testimony at congressional hearings. Years passed while Congress deliberated and became preoccupied with Vietnam.

The Victory and the Challenge

Finally, on the one-hundredth anniversary of the signing of the act to establish Yellowstone National Park on March 1, 1972, the president signed an act authorizing the creation of the Buffalo National River. The law specifies that the Buffalo is to be kept a free-flowing stream and includes a narrow strip of land along 132 miles of the river from above Boxley all the way to its mouth. The park varies in width from less than a half-mile to four miles, averaging about 1.8 miles. Boundaries were drawn to protect the river and its scenery while keeping land acquisition to a minimum. The Park Service, at the behest of constant urging by the people, says it has a mandate to "keep the river as it is" and not to "spoil it with overdevelopment."

Predictably there are still many who are bitter about the status of the Buffalo. On the other hand, as Larry Dablemont, an outdoor writer in Harrison, Arkansas, has written, "But few people wander from the river, canoes don't leave tracks, and it's a sight better than summer homes and wave-washed lake shores. . . . The National Park Service, after all, is the best chance the Buffalo has to remain wild and free and natural. The native settlers wouldn't have destroyed it willingly. But the developers who come to get rich quick surely would have ruined it."

For yet a while longer the Buffalo flows as it has since the Ozarks was born. Instead of marinas and jetboats along its shores, there is solitude. Deep in the renewed woods clothing the hills, log cabins return to the soil, their graves marked by the spring jonquils still blooming around their door stones. Ruffed grouse still drum there in the spring, and once again a hungry bear just awakened forages with her cubs.

An Introduction to the Buffalo

Roughly 150 miles long and with a watershed of 1,388 square miles, the Buffalo can really only be seen well from its surface. It is possible, however, to get a sense of it at several easily reached "access points" that will be described later. The second-best way to see the river is by hiking the trail along its shore. But you can certainly appreciate the scenery even from the ridgetop roads, and the valley vistas are memorable. The range and depth of the offerings of nature in the watershed are staggering: fifteen hundred species of plants, fifty-nine species of fish, and a birdwatcher's heaven. Among the myriad of mammals are the white-tailed deer, raccoon, opossum, bobcat, mink, and beaver. Bear and elk have recently been re-introduced; mountain lions are sometimes reported.

A total of ninety-five thousand acres of public land are protected in the Buffalo's corridor. Along its course the river descends nearly two thousand feet through layers of sandstone, limestone, and chert— which translates to mean spectacular bluffs, some of the highest in the Ozarks, at nearly every bend. And hidden away along its length are other marvelous sights: springs, caves, waterfalls, natural bridges, and box canyons.

Possibly the best way to get a feeling for the entire Buffalo River country, an introduction to the beauty and tranquility that will bring you back for more exploration, is to drive from Harrison (particularly if you have crossed Bull Shoals Lake on Peel Ferry as suggested in the last chapter) to Boxley and Ponca via Hwy. 43, see Lost Valley, then drive Hwy. 74 over the mountains to Jasper, and then south on Scenic Hwy. 7 at least to Cliff House. (For information about canoeing the river, see the Practical Matters Chart following the next chapter.)

One can explore more deeply from the scenic drives in the Ozark National Forest, particularly Hwys. 21 and 23 via Hwy. 16 west of Hwy. 7. (At the tiny town of Deer, Arkansas, on Hwy. 16, the high school team is known as the Antlers.) Hwy. 16 follows a ridge and affords long-range views in both directions where not blocked by tree leaves. Hwy. 21 is an official Scenic Byway through the Ozark National Forest. Ozarks scenery does not get any better.

Do be sure to stop at the picnic ground and river access at Pruitt, on Hwy. 7 about five miles north of Jasper. There are restrooms, a ranger station, a striking bluff, a wide beach, and picnic tables under towering shade trees. Watch for the turnoff just south of the bridge across the river. The access is paved, and there is a parking lot. Just across the flat picnic ground, a short, easy walk, is the river. Though not accessible to the handicapped all the way to the riverbank, there is a good close-up view of the river from the picnic ground.

Jasper and Pruitt

Nestled in a mountain valley, Jasper is a definitive little Ozarks town. Settled, platted, and named by its first postmaster, John Ross, a Cherokee, Jasper was designated as the county seat of Newton County soon after the creation of the county in December 1842. In 1938 a suspiciously convenient fire destroyed the courthouse and all the county's records. Suspected of embezzlement, the sheriff fled. The present courthouse was built in 1940 of stones from the nearby Little Buffalo River; the floors are cement and each room is a fireproof vault.

Until about 1940 Jasper was surrounded by cultivated plots of corn, vegetables, and feed crops. Nowadays, however, agriculture is limited and is almost exclusively devoted to raising beef cattle. Newton County has never had a railroad. The highest summits in the Ozarks, with elevations of more than twenty-four hundred feet, are here. Vance Randolph once met a man who claimed that if Newton County were ever "smoothed out, it would be bigger'n the whole state of Texas."

Three miles south of Jasper is famous Scenic Point; an observation tower—and the see-forever view of the Buffalo River Valley—are free. A few miles farther south is Cliff House, a famous restaurant sharing the panorama. And just south of Cliff House is a roadside picnic ground offering yet another vantage point to admire the scenery.

All along its length, Scenic Hwy. 7 south of Jasper offers turnouts where motorists can safely stop to admire the view. Called "one of the most fun-to-drive highways in America" by *Car and Driver* magazine, the route offers curves and dips as it meanders through the wondrous countryside. Although it seems almost like gilding the lily, Hwy. 7 was recently designated an official National Scenic Byway.

The Parker-Hickman Farmstead

For a peek at the way life was lived along the Buffalo for more than a century, visit the Parker-Hickman farmstead. Home to successive generations of Hickmans for 125 years when the National Park service purchased it in 1982, the 195-acre farm is now "an outdoor museum of the Ozarks rural vernacular" on the National Register of Historic Places. Eight buildings on the farm are "superior examples of the craftsmanship displayed in fine log structures."

Part of a group migration from Tennessee, the Parker family came to the Ozarks in the 1830s. They sold their farm to the Hickmans, another antebellum immigrant family, in 1857. The house was probably built within a few years of the sale, but whether by the Parkers or the Hickmans is uncertain. Historians say the joinery in the half-dovetail corners of the house displays "the closest tolerances of any log building yet identified by preservationists in the Ozarks." Built of red cedar, the house is a departure from the more common oak or walnut. At various times the Hickmans kept a store and post office in their home. Behind it is a Works Project Administration privy.

To reach the Parker-Hickman farmstead, follow the directions to Erbie campground, six miles off Hwy. 7 north of Jasper. A trail system at Erbie connects the Parker-Hickman farm with other historic sites in the area.

Big Buffalo Valley Historic District

Sharing the slender valley with the river and enfolded by the hills, the village of Ponca is now a collection of canoe outfitters and lodges serving visitors to the Buffalo National River. Old buildings, many abandoned, lend the little town a slightly haunted air.

South of Ponca is the "Big Buffalo Valley," also sometimes referred to as Boxley Valley. Although warned to be prepared for its drama, the unsuspecting traveler is almost overwhelmed upon descending the last long hill to the valley floor. Long mountains with bluffs carved into their sides form a deep bowl whose rim pushes up on all sides.

But aside from its loveliness, the valley is a distinctive cultural landscape, and as such it was included in the National Register of Historic

Places in 1987 as the "Big Buffalo Valley Historic District." More than two hundred structures of historical significance—houses, barns, the gristmill, and a community building—are "fine examples of regional vernacular architecture." Many date from the last century.

Unlike earlier national parks that did not recognize the cultural landscapes that pre-existed the parks, the legislation that set up the Buffalo National River explicitly provided for the retention of Boxley Valley's living community and its lifeways. Although it often seemed to embittered locals that the Park Service's intention was to acquire all the valley and get rid of the people, in 1982 the park superintendent announced a plan to preserve and perpetuate the valley's cultural landscape. The Service hopes to preserve a population with distinctive ties to the land. Since the plan's approval, negotiations have proceeded with a dozen families interested in buying back their old farms and homes.

But not all the valley is to be returned to private ownership. Along a one-mile stretch at the valley's north end there are no occupied farms. Open fields surround uninhabitable historic buildings, including two log houses pre-dating the Civil War. Near the valley's center stands the two-story gristmill built in 1870 and the log house and barn of the first miller. The lands associated with these structures will be kept in Park Service ownership, maintained, and made accessible to visitors.

Several of the old buildings are currently being restored, including Whiteley's Mill. Eventually the mill race will be repaired, and an interpretive walking trail around the mill pond is planned. The millhouse is listed individually on the National Register of Historic Places, and is included as part of the cultural landscape of the Historic District. It is located on Hwy. 43 one mile north of Boxley.

Another outstanding example of the old structures in the valley is the boyhood home of Beaver Jim Villines on Hwy. 43 south of Ponca. This shell of a pre-Civil War log house was remade into a barn and is typical of the settlers' efficient reuse of old structures.

Lost Valley

Three miles north of Boxley, Hwy. 43 crosses a small stream coming down from a hollow to join the Buffalo. An unobtrusive sign marks the turnoff to Lost Valley, but the uninformed visitor hurries past, unaware of the surprises hidden up the tiny valley of Clark Creek. A short distance up a narrow ravine choked with boulders, at the bottom of a two-hundred-foot bluff, is a cave—150 feet deep, 50 feet high, and 160 feet from end to end—that is really a natural bridge. Geologists believe that the cave—and the wonders beyond it—are parts of a collapsed cavern system.

The first pioneers found the unique valley, but because it was "just home," they took it for granted. The year 1898 marks the first recorded time that outsiders were led to the cave. Although the visitors were suitably impressed by the valley's beauty, they gave it the prosaic name of Corn Cob Cave because of ancient corn cobs littering the floor. For many years the valley and its cave remained a picnic place for local Sunday schools and a curiosity to be shown to visitors. Then in 1931, drawn by the evidence of ancient habitation in the cave, including the corn cobs, the University of Arkansas conducted an archeological excavation.

The little four- and five-inch corncobs, along with pieces of gourds, sunflower and other native seeds, were evidence of early Indian habitation. Preserved by the dryness on a ledge along one side of the cave, woven work and basketry were discovered. Under layers of dust, leaves, gravel, stones, and heavy slabs of limestone that evidently had fallen from the ceiling of the cave, scientists found a cache of baskets and basket fragments estimated to have been placed there between one and two thousand years ago. But still Cob Cave, as it is now known, was little known to the outside world.

Then, in the spring of 1945, a *National Geographic* photographer, guided by Arkansas's publicity director, Glen Green, and a group of Harrison high school students, hiked up the gorge to see the cave for themselves. Green later reported that the explorers first encountered a beautiful waterfall, then the huge cave, through which the creek flowed. Making their way inside the cave, they discovered they could walk through it and out the other side, where there was a series of waterfalls—four of them coming in steps down a two-hundred-foot gorge—then another cave, inside of which the high school boys discovered an underground waterfall. Overwhelmed, Green named the place Lost Valley and the stair-step waterfall, Eden Falls.

Many species of trees thrive in the narrow valley, including a number of unusual beeches, several kinds of oaks, American elm, shagbark hickory, chinkapin, white and blue ash, blackgum, American basswood, yellowwood, cucumber magnolia, carolina buckthorn, and papaw. A profusion of wildflowers, including wild orchids, bloom almost year around. On the rocks and bluffs are columbine, ferns, and all manner of lichens and mosses.

In 1960 and '63 loggers invaded Lost Valley, bulldozing a road and stripping the woods to within sight of Corn Cob Cave—for a few hundred dollars worth of timber.

But Lost Valley became a state park in 1966, and in 1973 Arkansas donated it to the Buffalo National River. Although protected from woodcutters, the valley now has many more visitors; and the Park Service struggles to avoid "human erosion" in the scenic area. Primitive camping is permitted along the road near the entrance, but walk-in campsites back in the woods afford an opportunity to really get away from it all. The wet-weather creek tumbles beside the camp-ground under enormous shade trees.

In the Wilderness

When traveling in Buffalo River country, remember to take the opportunity to fill your vehicle's gasoline tank in the little towns you drive through. There are often no service stations along the back roads.

In addition to the sparsely populated near-wilderness throughout the region, the Buffalo National River offers three congressionally designated, official wilderness areas totaling approximately thirty-six thousand acres. The only way to enjoy the land areas of the wilderness is either on foot or on horseback. No motorized vehicles are allowed. Trailheads are available on both sides of the river if you have your own horse. Topographic maps and other information are available at the ranger station at Buffalo Point.

There is also a licensed outfitter equipped for horse trailriding and packing on the Buffalo National River. Fully guided trips are offered, complete with meals. Or you can be taken into the wilderness, dropped off, and then picked up at a predetermined time and place. Such trips offer the opportunity to experience the wilderness as the pioneers did. Instead of a ringing telephone and the blare of television, you will hear only the creak of saddle leather and the sounds of nature.

The Buffalo River Hiking Trail is still under development, and eventually the trail will extend the entire length of the river. The finished portion follows a twenty-five-mile segment of the river popular with canoeists, from Ponca to Pruitt. But while floating is possible on this section only during high water, the trail is available for hiking all year.

A word to the wise: Try to hike from late fall to early spring. You will not only avoid the worst of the ticks and chiggers, but you will also be able to see more without leaves on the trees to block the views. A section-by-section description of the trail and its features is available from park headquarters (see Practical Matters Chart following the next chapter).

For more hiking opportunities, there are several other developed trails throughout the park, most of them short and suitable for day use. Self-guiding brochures on these trails are available at ranger stations or from the park headquarters in Harrison (see chart). Guided hikes led by park rangers are also available.

Gilbert

When the railroad finally came to Gilbert (at the end of Hwy. 333, three miles east of Hwy. 65) about 1901, large timber and railroad tie yards opened almost immediately. Pencil companies located offices there and bought thousands of cedar logs along the river. The rafts were corralled, placed on flatcars, and shipped nationwide.

Before long Gilbert became a major departure point for investors and prospectors headed for the Rush Creek mining area and a major shipping point for Buffalo River zinc. A local resident later recalled that ore wagons often lined up two abreast for almost a mile waiting to unload. According to a local historian, a copper nugget the size of a water barrel was taken from nearby Mud Hollow and shipped to St. Louis for display at the 1904 World's Fair.

In the early 1920s a religious colony was founded near Gilbert. Its leader, John Battenfield, taught that a great war between Catholics and Protestants would desolate the world in 1923 and that the Millennium would begin in 1973. Battenfield claimed to be able to cure various diseases and even to raise the dead. He started a newspaper called *The Kingdom Harbinger* to spread his message, but it was short-lived. Many of the colonists came from the upper Midwest and their descendants still live in the area today.

When the railroad tracks were pulled up in 1949, the town suffered but survived. Today there is a two-mile trail on the old railroad bed along the riverbank. The community outfits camping and float trips on the Buffalo National River.

For a taste of the mercantile flavor of another era, see the general store, which dates to about 1901 and is on the National Historic Register. Along with the general merchandise and a "pigeon-hole" post office is memorabilia from the early 1900s. Rental canoes and housekeeping cabins are also available there.

From Gilbert the shortest, most scenic route to Buffalo Point and Rush—obligatory destinations for visitors to the Buffalo National River—is to return to Hwy. 65, turn south to Marshall. At Marshall turn east on Hwy. 27 to Hwy. 14 and north on Hwy. 14. Where Hwy. 14 crosses the Buffalo, there are access to the river, rest rooms, and a stunning look at both the river and a bridge built to withstand a "hundred-year flood."

Alternatively, one can travel east on Hwy. 62 to historic Yellville and then south on Hwy. 14 to Buffalo Point.

CHAPTER 12

Buffalo Point
and Rush Ghost Town

Yellville, Arkansas, is probably best known for its annual fall event, the Turkey Trot, and its feature attraction, the National Wild Turkey Calling Contest. Of course there is the choosing of Miss Turkey Trot, game and craft booths, an art show and sale, a parade, dances, a talent show, and—you guessed it—a gigantic turkey dinner. But more importantly, when at Yellville the visitor is very near Bull Shoals Lake to the north, the White River to the east, and the Buffalo River to the south.

Once included in Indian lands, Yellville was first called Shawneetown. Because it was on the main northern road between Batesville and Fayetteville, it was chosen as county seat in 1836 and named for Archibald Yell, a governor of Arkansas who died in the Mexican War. Local legend has it that Yell offered the town's founding fathers fifty dollars to name the town in his honor. They did, but the money was never paid.

During the Civil War the Federals established a hospital in the Berry house, which still stands one block southeast of Yellville's square. Another historic building is the beautiful Cowdrey House, on the National Historic Register. Now the Red Raven Inn, a bed-and-breakfast, the house was begun in 1900 and occupied from 1904 to 1976 by the Cowdrey family. It dominates the junction of Hwys. 62 and 14.

From the Red Raven Inn it is seventeen miles to Buffalo Point via Hwy. 14, a lovely drive. The highway was paved over the decade of the 1950s, with the last section, to the Buffalo River bridge and the Searcy

255

From high atop the bluff at Buffalo Point Recreation Area, the river probably looks much the same as it did when Indians camped here during their semi-annual buffalo hunts. Rustic CCC-built cabins and campsites with hookups are at Buffalo Point, just off Hwy. 14 south of Yellville, Arkansas.

County line, not paved until 1959. The Hwy. 14 bridge soars over the Buffalo on concrete pylons more than fifty feet tall—high enough to let the biggest flood of record pass beneath the roadway. When the bridge was built in the late 1950s, it replaced a ramshackle wooden ferry.

The Buffalo Point Recreation Area and river access is only three miles off Hwy. 14 on Hwy. 268, which is paved all the way to the riverbank.

Buffalo Point Recreation Area

If places were prescribed like medicine, Buffalo Point would be an antidote to an overdose of the modern world. Take as needed for refreshment of the soul, to cleanse the psyche, to relax the nerves. But one does not need a prescription to. enjoy the benefits of Buffalo Point, and its effectiveness never fails. Best of all, it is available to everyone at little cost.

Camping on the riverbank (in developed sites, complete with hook-ups) is the quickest way to a cure. Even the shouts and laughter of people swimming, fishing, and beachcombing near the campground seem somehow right and natural, as humans have surely enjoyed therapeutic spots like this since the beginning of time. And something primeval inside us responds to the sight of overturned canoes lined up along the beach at night and the strangely distant booming sound, almost like thunder, that echoes from the river's bluff when one of them is launched or landed.

One can canoe, hike, join the frolickers in the clear water, admire or photograph driftwood, or simply sit and sift the fine, white sand on the shore and watch the way the mist slides down the bluff in the evening to hover over the river like a blanket. In the blackness of a night far away from city lights, illumined only by the reflection of starlight on the water, lulled by the hushed whispers of a liberated river, you will sleep as our more natural ancestors probably did. You will awaken to the soft *bump-slush* of a canoe on the sandy beach and rise to watch the mist straggle away to greet the sunlight.

But if you are the type who prefers a more substantial roof over his head, the Civilian Conservation Corps provided for your comfort a half-century ago. This recreation area began as an Arkansas state park in March 1938. From 1939 to 1941 the CCC operated a camp here and developed the area; the structures they built are now on the National Historic Register. The concessioner-operated cabins, a picnic pavilion, and much of the existing roadway rock work were constructed by the CCC. The foundation rock was quarried at the "fossil quarry" on the Indian Rockhouse Trail, a hiking trail available to visitors. The cabins, although maintained as historic structures, are available for rental (see the Practical Matters Chart).

Arkansas donated the park to the Buffalo National River in 1973, and the Park Service rechristened it as Buffalo Point Recreation Area. For many it is the showplace of the Buffalo; and it is the canoers' favored put-in point for the most popular stretch of river floatable year-round. In season a restaurant operates out of a rustic building overlooking long-range views of the river and its hills.

The Ghost Town of Rush

The stretch of Buffalo River from Buffalo Point to Rush is very popular with floaters. It is scenic, just about the right length for a leisurely float, and—except in the very driest summer—floatable the year around. And "Rush Landing" is the very last of all canoers' take-outs on the river; downstream the river flows through miles of official wilderness where no cars are allowed. If a floater elects to bypass Rush, he must continue all the way to the river's confluence with the White, then struggle upstream on the White for a mile to the first available take-out or turn downstream on the White for several miles to Norfork. There are pit toilets at Rush and "open" camping; that is, there are no developed sites or hookups, just an open area where canoers may pitch their tents near the riverbank.

Indeed, "development" is a thing of the past at Rush. Rush itself is a ghost, a derelict mining town in the process of being reclaimed by nature. To reach Rush by land, turn east off of Hwy. 14 south of Caney and north of the turnoff to Buffalo Point. The junction is marked by a small sign. The road to Rush, six miles from Hwy. 14, is paved most of the way. Once you cross onto Buffalo National River property, however, the road becomes gravel—and rough and steep and very beautiful. (It would not be advisable to pull a travel trailer down into Rush Creek Valley.) Watch for the few signs directing you to Rush Historic District.

From ancient Indians to zinc miners, the story of Rush is the familiar one of the progression of human occupation in the Ozarks. In the hills and hollows of the valley is buried evidence of centuries of use. Ancient Indians once walked the riverbanks and hills, leaving signs of their passing buried deep in layers of soil left by centuries of floods. Artifacts from Archaic, Woodland, and Mississippian periods—about 8000 B.C. to 1350 A.D.—have been found in the area. In the 1840s and 1850s white settlers penetrated the Rush valley and turned the fertile bottomlands of creek and river into farms.

Now the hills to the east of Rush are nearly deserted, a hundred square miles of wilderness; the "lost corner of the Buffalo watershed."

The general store at Rush, Arkansas, now a historic district on the Buffalo National River, once supplied a mining boom town with the necessities of life. Freight was hauled to the town over impossibly difficult roads or—under optimum conditions—up the Buffalo River on keelboats. The ruins at Rush will not be visitable much longer if they continue to be vandalized for their weathered wood.

The former occupants of this modest house in the ghost town of Rush probably considered themselves lucky to have such grand accommodations. All around them in the hills—because people were coming into the boom town faster than homes could be built—families were living in tents. So many tents, in fact, that an early nickname for the community was "Rag Town."

But here, too, there was once a family living down every ridge and creek and within every bend of the river. The countryside is laced with their wagon trails and cemeteries, and the foundations and the chimneys of forgotten towns.

The first relics encountered at Rush are the ruins of homes. Vandalized for their weathered wood (prized for picture frames), some are missing walls and doors. Nearby a livery stable is recognizable, and a store building leans tiredly, as if considering whether to give up and sprawl into the road. If you leave your vehicle and stroll down the narrow lane and listen closely, it seems as if—just on the edge of awareness—you can hear neighbors calling to each other across the yards, catch the excited laughter of children, and even, perhaps, the echo of a dynamite blast in the nearby mines.

Then the visitor catches a glimpse of a small smelter on the side of a hill, seeming oddly out of place. It is the first visual clue that in this creek valley once boomed a mining town of some five thousand people. Now only the memories—and the ghosts—remain of Rush. Just a few yards farther on at the Rush canoe access, there is a sign warning of bears in the area, and detailing how to avoid encounters with them.

The Mines at Rush

The first commercial mining began in north-central Arkansas in the early 1850s near Lead Hill in Boone County. In the Buffalo River region some limited mining began before the Civil War. When the demand for lead increased during the war, Confederates worked a number of mines in the area. But it was not until the 1870s that lead mining on a large scale commenced in the Buffalo River basin. Local legend says that two girls out looking for lost cows led to the establishment of the first zinc mine on Rush Creek, when they found some "glitter stones." According to the legend, the girls found the stones in front of an old stone smelter "of Spanish design" and thought they were silver.

Legend, too, may be the origin of the name *Rush*. Flash floods rushing down a creek past the point where the town later would be built are said to have inspired white settlers to name the creek Rush. Others believe that the community was named because of the "rush" that ensued when zinc was discovered. The Rush post office was established in 1886.

Old mining reports say the first known prospectors in the Rush area were looking for silver. After spending several months in 1882 digging ore which they believed to contain silver, based on an erroneous assay, they built a small rock smelter in which to reduce the ore. Alas, the first run of the smelter "produced colorful rainbows

Centerpiece of Rush Historic District, this smelter, built in 1882, was the site of bitter disappointment for the first prospectors at Rush, Arkansas, who thought they had been mining silver. Although it turned out to be lead, it was a rich strike. From then on until after World War II, lead was mined from the hills along what is now the Buffalo National River. Rush ghost town is accessible from Hwy. 14 south of Yellville, Arkansas.

over the blast, which represented the zinc going off in fumes, but the expected silver did not collect in the sand molds at the bottom." It is said that the discouraged prospectors offered to trade their prospect, with the smelter thrown in, for a box of canned oysters worth $2.50; the offer was rejected. The old smelter still stands near the road. The prospectors held the claim for a few years then sold it to the organizer of the Morning Star Company in 1891.

Reportedly the Morning Star Mine was named by claim holder Jim McCabe for the moon's early morning position over the mine. The Morning Star became Rush's most famous mine and nationally respected. A community quickly grew up around the mine: residences, stores, a hotel, livery barn, and even a doctor's office intermingled with the mining facilities. The name of Rush became synonymous with the entire mining area.

And constantly the mountain serenity for miles around was disturbed by the noisy operation of the huge oil engines that ran the mills. The parade of wagons out of the valley was almost continuous. In bad weather three-mule teams were required to move a ton of ore from the camp to the railroad at Summit.

Eventually some of the ore was floated down the Buffalo to the White and thence to Batesville on barges. The river traffic led to the prominence of Buffalo City, near the confluence of the Buffalo and the White, as the center of supply for the Rush Creek Valley and neighboring areas. Steamboats on the White River regularly replenished Buffalo City with merchandise and supplies.

Actually, there were two towns called Buffalo City. The earliest was on a peninsula-like point between the White River and the mouth of the Buffalo; its vanished site is virtually inaccessible today. The second Buffalo City, relocated to greet the railroad in the early 1900s, is still a small cluster of buildings on the north side of the White. Today the tiny community on the riverbank is the location of a popular river access for float fishermen.

The *Dauntless*

Unlike other large rivers in the Ozarks, most notably the White, the Buffalo was never used extensively as a river-road. Too shallow for boats other than flatboats and rafts, its depth also depends directly upon the amount of rainfall in the watershed—too undependable for transportation. But recorded history details a single dramatic exception, a river adventure appropriate to the reputations of daring and determined steamboat captains and crews. When, in the rainy April of 1896, the Buffalo ran bank-full, Capt. William T. Warner of the steamboat *Dauntless* seized the opportunity to attempt a voyage upstream to the mining community at the mouth of Rush Creek. The boom town needed mining equipment, but hauling the heavy machinery on mule-drawn wagons over rough trails through the wilderness was, to say the least, extraordinarily difficult.

From the mouth of the Buffalo upriver to Rush Creek is only about twenty-four miles, but the *Dauntless* and her crew struggled for two days to make the trip. In the dense forest through which the river flowed, overhanging tree limbs snagged on the steamer's smokestacks. Even at this time of high water, numerous barely submerged rocky shoals blocked the vessel's passage, and the crew was forced to winch the boat laboriously over them. When at last the *Dauntless* cleared the turbulent waters at the mouths of Clabber and Rush creeks and attained Rush Landing, she unloaded her cargo and immediately turned downriver for the return trip, lest she be stranded upriver indefinitely by falling water levels.

Jumbo

One day the miners at the Morning Star pried from its ore face a single mass of pure zinc carbonate weighing 12,750 pounds. They moved "Jumbo" (the name given the huge rock by the miners) on a logging wagon drawn by sixteen oxen to a flatboat for its trip down the Buffalo to the White River, where it was transferred to a steamboat and taken to Batesville and the railroad for its trip to the 1893 World's Fair in Chicago. Jumbo went on exhibit, won a gold medal— and speculators hustled to Rush. When zinc ore from the Morning Star Mine also won the first award at the St. Louis World's Fair in 1904, more miners poured into the valley.

And for the next decade, the mines flourished; seventeen of them operated in the Rush Creek District. Rush became a swarming, noisy camp town. Various estimates of the total population range from two to five thousand people. But the ore occurred only in scattered, irregular bodies, and the hills became honeycombed with empty tunnels. Finding new ore often proved expensive.

Then World War I began and the price of zinc skyrocketed. Further, the demand for higher quality zinc became urgent. Bigger and more modern mining machinery and equipment made the rigorous trip to Rush. Such freight came by rail to Summit, just north of Yellville, but the remainder of the trip still had to be made by wagon and team. Within a matter of a few months, a hundred mines were in production; the quantity of mined ore burgeoned.

New Town, a boom town of World War I, filled an area from Rush Creek to the present campground. In its heyday there were three hotels, a hardware store, a pharmacy, restaurants, a bakery, and several other business establishments. Seven barbers put in long days in front of the several pool halls. The post office was in Old Town (Rush). A telephone exchange served 165 phones.

As the people poured into the area to find work in the mines, a housing shortage developed. Many of the newcomers bought tents; eventually tent homes sprouted over the hills like mushrooms. People began to call the place "Rag Town," a name not at all acceptable to the oldest residents of Rush.

Reportedly, Rush was relatively orderly and not as rough as most mining boom towns. "Only" two or three killings were reported, plus a few near misses. History also records that three serious accidents occurred at the mines. At the Morning Star a large rock fell in a shaft, crushing two men. Many years later a former resident of Rush reported that she could still recall hearing the whistle blow at the mine, signaling a fatal accident. Hurriedly people gathered to learn what had happened. Another fatality occurred at the Morning Star when a man fell from the tramway to the ground several hundred feet below.

At the White Eagle Mine, a vein of zinc extended under the bed of the river. While the miners were working in this tunnel, water began to pour into the diggings. The evacuation of the tunnels was so hurried that all the equipment was left where it lay and the men barely escaped with their lives by clinging to pipes being pulled from the shafts by the ground crew.

The Naked Hills

The lumber business also boomed in the Rush Creek Valley as it sought to provide an endless supply of fuel for the steam boilers of the smelters and for the heating of the homes and stores. An average mill consumed eight cords of wood per day during the winter. The inevitable result of such an insatiable demand for wood was the denuding of the forest surrounding the valley. Local farmers and woodcutters provided the bulk of the fuel wood under contract with the mine operators and the miners themselves for one dollar per cord plus fifteen cents per hundredweight hauling costs. And hauling the wood on a regular schedule depended directly on the condition of the roads. A heavy cargo of cord wood often sank a wagon up to its hubs in mud.

But a reliable source of fuel was not the only problem facing the miners at Rush. Aside from the hazardous working conditions in and around the mines, the extremely crowded housing conditions and inadequate sanitary facilities (the outdoor toilets of four to five thousand people) led to epidemics of typhoid and related diseases. Fortunately there was an abundance of springs in the area, although at least one was declared contaminated and condemned.

The Bubble Bursts

But it was the end of the war that finally sealed the fate of Rush. As the demand fell off, the price of ore slumped badly, and by 1920 it was hard to sell at any price. The population of Rush—and the entire valley—began to decline.

In the 1920s the boom of dynamite was heard less and less frequently and the few remaining residents of Rush returned to subsistence living. Finally, during World War II, the once-proud ore concentrating mills were converted to scrap iron for the war effort. Although the Morning Star Mining Company held its land until the 1960s, the property was then sold and many of the remaining buildings removed. Nature went to work reclaiming and restoring the damaged land. For years afterward the abandoned mines were a mecca for collectors and rockhounds.

The importance of the region to Arkansas' mining period earned Rush's ruins a place on the National Historic Register. Scattered throughout the valley, the abandoned buildings and old foundations still speak of the once-bustling activity.

Hiking trails are popular at Rush, and they are of varying lengths and difficulties. The Morning Star Trail leads straight up the steep side of a hill of mine waste. There are some ruins at the top of the hill, including the foundations of some of the mine buildings. Eventually the trail passes the old smelter where the original prospectors at Rush were so sorely disappointed to learn they had not found silver.

The confluence where Rush Creek flows into the Buffalo is beautiful once again, and the visitor must work hard to visualize the area as it was at the turn of the century. Sharp eyes, however, will spot an occasional reminder in the new forest. For example, near the present rest room at Rush Landing, look for a lonely chimney still looming from the undergrowth.

Leaving the valley of the Buffalo behind for another legendary Ozarks river, the Little Red, return to Hwy. 14 and turn south on Hwy. 65 for the short drive to Clinton.

Incidentally, if you plan to do much fishing, boating, or just plain exploring in the state of Arkansas, you would do well to acquire *Fishing in Arkansas*, an enormous book (eleven by seventeen inches) published by the Arkansas Game and Fish Commission. The Commission calls the book "an unashamedly single-purpose book," but it is useful for more than just knowing where to fish. Based on the individual

A remnant of the Morning Star Mine, on the Morning Star Hiking Trail from Rush ghost town on the Buffalo National River. While the few remaining ruins of mine buildings in the area seem innocuous enough, some waste from the mines still bears mute testimony to the presence of humankind.

county maps of the whole state furnished by the Arkansas Highway and Transportation Department—and published in a size to make them readable—the book affords in supremely useful detail just what you need to know to go gypsying along Arkansas' wonderful back roads. That it also shows you where you can launch a fishing boat or a canoe along the way is icing on the cake. Of course, remember to also inquire about a fishing license.

For current ordering information, write to: The Arkansas Game and Fish Commission, 2 Natural Resources Drive, Little Rock AR 72205. The same address can be used to request a "Floater's Kit" intended to make it easy to locate access to canoeable rivers in Arkansas.

Practical Matters

Chapter 12 — Buffalo River

Checking Out	A Sampling	Phone
Lodging	Cabins at Buffalo Point, HCR No.66, Box 388, Yellville AR 72687; Buffalo Outdoor Center Log Cabins, P.O. Box 1, Ponca AR 72670, Jct. Hwys. 43 & 74; Numerous Motel Chains in Harrison AR	(501) 449-6206 (501) 861-5514
Bed & Breakfasts	Red Raven Inn, Hwys. 62 & 14 South, P.O. Box 1217, Yellville AR 72687; Anna's House, P.O. Box 58, Gilbert AR 72636; Cliff House Inn, Hwy. 7 SO, Jasper AR 72641	(501) 449-5168 (501) 446-2292
Campgrounds	Numerous campgrounds in Buffalo National River Park, including Buffalo Point, where there are hookups: Hwy. 268 off Hwy. 14 south of Yellville AR; Sherwood Forest Campground, HCR 66, Box 260, Yellville AR 72687	(501) 449-4311 (501) 449-4260
Restaurants	Buffalo Point (May 21-Labor Day), Hwy. 268 off Hwy. 14 south of Yellville AR; Cliff House Inn Restaurant, HCR 31, Box 85, Jasper AR 72641, Hwy. 7 South; Deli 1 Block North of Courthouse in Jasper	(501) 449-6206 (501) 446-2292
Main Historical Attractions	Parker-Hickman Farmstead near Erbie Campground off Hwy. 7 north of Jasper AR; Big Buffalo Valley Historic District, Hwys. 21 and 43 near Boxley AR; Beaver Jim Villines Boyhood Home, Hwy. 43 south of Ponca AR; Rush Historic District, 6 miles off Hwy. 14 south of Yellville AR; Gilbert General Store, Hwy. 333 east of Hwy. 65, Gilbert AR; Robinson's Museum of the Ozarks, 12 miles S.E. of Harrison off Hwy. 65, Rt. 1, Box 324, Everton AR 72633	(501) 429-5855
Other Attractions	Pendergraft Ozarks Crafts, Hwy. 7, 6 Miles South of Jasper AR; Top of the Mountain, HCR 31, Box 110A, Jasper AR 72641, Hwy. 7 South; Hot Air Ballooning at Buffalo Outdoor Center, P.O. Box 1, Ponca AR 72670	(501) 446-5267 (501) 428-5540 (501) 861-5514

The natural bridge north of Clinton, Arkansas, just off Hwy. 65, was formed by the erosive power of a small stream of running water. Admission is charged to the privately owned scenic wonder, but the setting is dramatically beautiful, and a gentle path ends at a bluff-shaded picnic table. A gift shop and a small museum—housed in a log cabin— add to the charm of the site.

A native-stone band shell dating to 1933 adds historic ambiance to Springs Park at Heber Springs, Arkansas, on the shores of Greers Ferry Lake. The pleasant little town is well equipped to serve travelers and is picturesque and historic, especially the park.

Checking Out	A Sampling	Phone
Outdoor Recreation	For a list of Canoe Concessions and Guides on all sections of Buffalo River, Schedule of Ranger-led Activities, Information on Hiking Trails, Maps, etc., write Buffalo National River, HCR 66, Box 387, Yellville AR 72687 or Administrative Headquarters, P.O. Box 1173, Harrison AR 72602;	(501) 741-5443
	Wilderness Horse Packing: J & J Outfitters, P.O. Box 236, Flippin AR 72634;	(501) 453-8359
	Hot Air Ballooning over Buffalo National River, Buffalo Outdoor Center, P.O. Box 1, Ponca AR 72670	(501) 861-5514
Where to Write for More Details	See "Buffalo National River Guide," $4.25, and/or "Buffalo River Canoeing Guide," $2.50, from Buffalo National River, P.O. Box 1173, Harrison AR 72602; Wilderness Areas: Buffalo Ranger District, P.O. Box 427, Jasper AR 72641;	
	Yellville Chamber of Commerce, P.O. Box 369, Yellville AR 72687;	(501) 449-4676
	Harrison Tourist Commission, P.O. Box 939, Harrison AR 72602;	(501) 741-2659
	Jasper Chamber of Commerce, P.O. Box 250, Jasper AR 72641; Scenic Hwy. 7, P.O. Box 374, Dardanelle AR 72834; For Information About "Arkansas Floater's Kit," write Arkansas Game & Fish Commission, Information & Education Div., 2 Natural Resources Dr., Little Rock AR 72205; For More Information about Scenic Hwy. 7 or other places in Arkansas, write: Arkansas Dept. of Parks & Tourism, One Capitol Mall, Little Rock AR 72201	

CHAPTER 13

Greers Ferry

The natural bridge located about three miles north of Clinton off of Hwy. 65 was reportedly once used by covered wagons as an actual bridge when the creek was too high to ford. If there is any truth to this tale, the drivers of those covered wagons must have been very brave indeed, as were their teams.

The turnoff to the privately owned natural bridge is marked by a prominent billboard. The unpaved access road is spectacular; absolutely no trailers! At the foot of the mountain the setting is rustic and lovely. A small log cabin museum houses "primitives" that visitors can inspect; do not miss the moonshine still tucked under the cabin. Take a picnic lunch and follow the trail along the natural bridge to a table under the huge bluff.

Also on the premises at the natural bridge attraction are a couple of the curious round boulders found near Prim, Arkansas. Although the smoothly rounded rocks appear to be artificially formed, they are of natural origin and have been studied by the Arkansas Geological Commission (see the section on the Heber Springs Park).

Greers Ferry

Designated a scenic drive by the state of Arkansas, the route from Hwy. 65 to Greers Ferry Lake on Hwy. 16 is ever-green, thanks to an abundance of pines lining the road. "The third time you come back, you'll bring your furniture!" folks in these parts tell their visitors. And one does not have to linger long before that prophecy begins to be attractive—or worrisome, depending on your point of view.

A five-hundred-foot cone-shaped "mountain," capped by a rock formation reminiscent of a sugar cube, first gave the area its name. Dr. Heber Jones found that the seven "Sugar Loaf Springs," though closely spaced, exhibited different "medicinal properties." Because the springs offered seven mineral waters for the treatment of different ailments—and since the area was more accessible because of its gentler terrain—the "Sugar Loaf Springs" became one of the most popular of the health spas.

The town of Sugar Loaf was incorporated in 1882 and, at the same time, the Heber post office was established. After confusion in mail service, and to emphasize the town's prominent reputation as a spa, the two names were consolidated in 1910 to Heber Springs. When the Missouri & North Arkansas Railroad came to town in 1908, the future seemed assured (despite the fact that the M&NA was also referred to as the May Never Arrive).

Heber Springs' "Spring Park"

Scattered throughout a ten-acre site that is the Heber Springs city park, each of the seven springs is labeled to indicate its mineral agents: black, white, and red sulphur; iron; arsenic; magnesia; and "eye." Their individually constant temperatures vary from 54.5 to 61.7 degrees. The springs are sheltered by small native stone sheds dating to the 1920s. Each spring is enclosed in a concrete vat equipped with spigots. The spring fills the vat, which can then be tapped at will by the turn of a faucet—minimizing the wait for each user to fill his container. Overflow trickles into a drain at the base of the vat.

The park itself is an enchanting reminder of the slower pace at the turn of the century. A band shell, "Erected by the Women's Community Club 1933," still awaits the town's musicians. Pedestaled picnic tables and benches, embossed in the decorative style of yesteryear and showing the effects of long use, are yet shaded by venerable trees. Joggers and strollers smile and nod to the stranger, and the ambiance of small-town peace and contentment is palpable.

Also of interest in the park near the old band shell are a number of large boulders, each as round and smooth as a huge beachball. Found near Prim, the "round rocks" are something of a local legend. Long used as adornments around old house places, at least one also serves as tombstone for a grave.

In response to numerous inquiries as to their origin, the boulders received cursory examination in the 1960s by the Arkansas Geological Commission. But lamentably, because "no economic significance is assigned these rocks; their only importance lies in their curious nature," the geologist did not take the time for a complete study. He did

Old-timers still fill plastic jugs at the mineral springs in Heber Springs, Arkansas. Scattered throughout the ten-acre city park, each of the seven springs is labeled to indicate its mineral agent: black, white, and red sulphur; iron; arsenic; magnesia; and "eye." The individually constant temperatures of the springs vary from 54.5 to 61.7 degrees.

determine, however, that the "spheroidal boulders . . . fall under the category of concretions," consist of sandstone, and were "liberated," or eroded, from the parent formation, some 300 million years old, by natural weathering. Some of the smoothly rounded boulders are reportedly up to seven feet in diameter.

A few blocks from the park, the handsome restored courthouse, seat of Cleburne County, was finished in 1914. Not only is the building picturesque, it is quite grand for a small Ozarks county seat. The buildings facing it around the town square are old, but most appear refurbished and have been updated with modern awnings, plate glass windows, and the like.

Still on the wall in the Heber Springs post office, 102 East Main Street, is a dramatic mural painted in the "heroic style" during the Great Depression. Often termed a "WPA mural," the project was actually financed by the Treasury Department under a fine arts competition. The mural, one of the last of its kind in Arkansas, was painted by Louis Freund and represents the pioneer spirit in the state.

Winkley Bridge

Dependent on ferryboats and the whims of the Little Red River for years, early residents of the Heber Springs area were delighted in the early 1900s by the building of three suspension bridges. The most famous was erected in 1912; 550-feet-long, one-lane Winkley Bridge superseded Turney's Ferry across the river.

No longer were residents cut off from stores and services in town when the river proved too high for safe crossing. But it ". . . felt as though a spring bounced the floor of the bridge" under the traveler, reports area writer Arline Chandler. Then, too, "If the load being transported was heavy, ripples of flooring like an ocean wave rolled before the driver and prevented a view of the end of the bridge until the vehicle progressed across the suspended passageway near the opposite side."

Nevertheless, Winkley Bridge was beloved. For many years after it was replaced by a modern highway span, the people of Cleburne County clung to "Old Swinging Bridge" as a part of their heritage. Stone markers prevented all but pedestrian traffic and recorded the structure's history. In 1984 the bridge was named to the National Register of Historic Places.

But the story of Winkley Bridge ends in tragedy. The weakened structure, although it had known only foot traffic for many years, was more dangerous than anyone realized. Overstressed by a large group of people who had set it to swinging, the aged structure collapsed into the Little Red River; five persons lost their lives. Only the towers remain.

Little Red River

Stephen H. Long, that intrepid explorer whose name is so often linked with the Ozarks, was one of the first white men to explore and describe the Little Red River country. In 1819 Long's expedition set out to chart the great Western frontier. On his steamboat, the *Western Engineer*, were scholars and soldiers; in its cargo, everything from garden seed to gun powder. Although they were heading into Indian country, the boat's passengers probably feared getting lost in the interior of the wild Ozarks more than they feared the Indians.

At times Long and a small party from the ship broke off into overland mule trains. On one of these expeditions, Long first sighted the Little Red River. He noted that, judging from the high water marks along its shores, the river was "subjected to great and sudden floods." Indeed, the Indians in the area had passed down tales of great floods on the river.

In the 1880s Bud Greer established a ferry near the present location of the dam named for his venture. Greer shuttled mountain men and mules and the wagons of settlers across the Little Red. With the coming of the railroad and the new suspension bridges, the ferries retired.

But the Little Red still rolled and occasionally rampaged. In 1921 the Doniphan Lumber Company purchased most of the timber rights in the Greers Ferry area and used the river to float the tall hardwoods downstream to a mill. Hill farmers, lumberjacks, and entrepreneurs moved into the region and built mountain towns and traditions.

In April 1927 disaster struck. Rain fell steadily for more than a month and turned the Little Red—as well as most rivers in the Ozarks—into a raging torrent. When the flood waters subsided, the horrendous damage inspired cries for a series of dams on the rivers. Support for the dams gradually intensified and in June 1936, Congress passed the first bill authorizing six flood-control dams in the White River Basin (of which the Little Red is part).

Greers Ferry Lake

But politics and World War II stalled the project until the 1950s, when newcomers brought fresh enthusiasm and energy. The Greers Ferry Dam Association was formed and fought hard to make the dream a reality. In 1957 major construction began on the six-story dam. The Corps of Engineers had the task of relocating more than a hundred miles of utility lines, forty-two miles of roads, ten cemeteries, numerous houses, and five entire towns. They also ringed the 31,500-acre lake with fifteen park-and-camping areas along its nearly three-hundred-mile shoreline. Unusually shaped, the lake has two huge arms connected by a constricted, four-mile-long channel called "The Narrows."

President John F. Kennedy dedicated the Greers Ferry Lake project in October 1963—his last public dedication. A bust of Kennedy stands near an observation point overlooking the dam and the Little Red River below it. The pleasant road to the overlook is a welcome relief from the highway. Virtually a trail, the narrow pavement curves away from the concrete glare. Trees press in on both sides and meet overhead like a tunnel. Hiking trails branch off from this road and skirt the edges of the river bluffs. Numbered posts along the Mossy Bluff Trail, the longest (1.6 miles) of these trails, are keyed to a brochure explaining the plant life to be seen at that point. The Corps warns that this trail is rough and moderately difficult.

But noteworthy at Greers Ferry is the Buckeye Trail, which was constructed ". . . to provide a quality trail experience for persons who are not physically able to negotiate the more difficult areas. The trail is accessible to wheelchairs and its smooth, level surface is easy to walk. Two picnic tables enable trail users to enjoy a meal under the forest canopy. Two vista points provide lofty views of the area downstream of the dam. Interesting features are interpreted on plaques alongside the trail. For the seeing impaired, a large print guide and a braille guide are available at the Visitor Center." One can certainly hope that more such trails will be constructed for the enjoyment of the disabled and the elderly, who also treasure the opportunity to enjoy leafy bowers and less well-beaten paths. (Another braille trail is at Elephant Rocks; see Chapter 23.)

A third—and spectacular—hiking opportunity is at Greers Ferry Lake on Sugar Loaf Mountain. Actually, there are three Sugar Loaf "Mountains" in the Heber Springs area: one is east of town near the site of the old swinging bridge on Hwy. 110; another is in the middle of the lake; and the third is *under* the lake. Spiraling around the mid-lake Sugar Loaf Mountain is the Sugar Loaf Mountain National Nature Trail. Part of the fun is the boat ride to reach the island; you disembark at a courtesy dock near the trail's beginning. Offering outstanding scenic vistas of the lake from the summit of the mountain, the trail itself is a living exhibit of the flora and fauna in the region.

Back on the lake shore, the beautifully landscaped visitor center at Greers Ferry is one of the most interesting in the Ozarks. The 6,100-square-foot redwood-and-native-stone building is designed for active and passive solar heating and cooling. An adjacent grove of pine trees is studded with benches, a drinking fountain, and cobbled paths for an enchanting interlude just steps from the busy highway. Featured inside is an exhibit of fossils, Indian arrowheads, and other artifacts, and an impressive and comprehensive exhibit depicting the history of whites in the region. Because the dams along the state line on the White River are also under the jurisdiction of the Little Rock District of the Corps of Engineers, there is much in this museum about the rest of the White River Valley as well.

During the summer season, the visitor center offers an assortment of free programs on Saturday evenings. These presentations range from folk music concerts and magic shows to a special Eagle Awareness Program featuring live eagles and owls. Also available are tours of the dam and its powerhouse, as well as a National Fish Hatchery on the grounds. A boat launch is on Little Red River near the hatchery. Other river accesses are available at five commercial boat docks downstream and at several ramps maintained by the Arkansas Game and Fish Commission (see Practical Matters Chart for this chapter). Trout is stocked in the Little Red River below the dam, and there is no closed season on trout fishing.

For a notion of just how much impact the Corps of Engineers has had on the Ozarks, visit next the Ozark Folk Center. Travel north on Hwy. 5 to Mountain View.

Practical Matters

Chapter 13 — Greers Ferry Lake

Checking Out	A Sampling	Phone
Lodging	Lindsey's Rainbow Resort, 350 Rainbow Rd., Heber Springs AR 72543; Colonial Motor Inn, 2949 Ark. 25 N, Heber Springs AR 72543; Red Apple Inn and Executive Conference Center, P. O. Box 192, Heber Springs AR	(501) 362-3138 (501) 362-5846 (501) 362-3111 or (800) 255-8900
Bed & Breakfasts	Oak Tree Inn, Ark. 110 at Ely St., Heber Springs AR 72543; The Anderson House Inn, 201 E. Main, Heber Springs AR 72543	(501) 362-8870 (501) 362-5266
Campgrounds	Golden Pond RV Park; Hwys. 330 & 16, Heber Springs AR; Swinging Bridge Trout Dock & Campground, Hwy. 110, Heber Springs AR; Numerous COE Campgrounds--See Address Below	(501) 723-8212 (501) 362-3327
Restaurants	The Pot O'Gold Restaurant, 350 Rainbow Rd., Heber Springs AR 72543; Katherine's, 603 W. Quitman, Heber Springs AR	(501) 362-3130 (501) 362-3963
Main Historical Attractions	WPA Mural, Post Office, 102 E. Main, Downtown Heber Springs AR; Greers Ferry Lake Visitors Center, Hwy. 25, 3 Miles North of Heber Springs AR; Cleburne County Courthouse and Spring Park, Heber Springs AR	
Other Attractions	Greers Ferry Lake Dam & Powerhouse, 45-Minute Tour; Greers Ferry National Fish Hatchery: Aquarium and Tours, Hwy. 25, 5 Miles North of Heber Springs AR; Natural Bridge, Hwy. 65 North of Clinton AR	
Outdoor Recreation	COE Hiking Trails: Sugar Loaf Mountain National Nature Trail, Mossy Bluff and Buckeye Self-Guiding Trails; Big Creek Nature Area; Walk Railroad History Trail, P. O. Box 129, Shirley, AR 72153 (M&NA Railroad Bed); Lake and River Fishing; Red River Trout Dock, Wilburn Route, Heber Springs AR 72543; Numerous Marinas on Greers Ferry Lake	(501) 723-4675 (501) 362-2197

Checking Out	A Sampling	Phone
Where to Write for More Details	U. S. Army Corps of Engineers, P. O. Box 310, Heber Springs AR 72543;	(501) 362-2416
	Greers Ferry Lake & Little Red River Association, P.O. Box 1170, Fairfield Bay AR;	(501) 723-8332
	Greers Ferry Area Chamber of Commerce, P.O. Box 354, Greers Ferry Lake AR 72067;	(501) 825-7188
	Heber Springs Chamber of Commerce, 1001 W. Main, Heber Springs AR 72543;	(501) 362-2444
	For Information About "A Fisherman's Guide to Public Access Facilities in Arkansas Counties" and a "Floater's Kit," write Arkansas Game & Fish Commission, Information & Education Div., 2 Natural Resources Dr., Little Rock AR 72205	(501) 223-6351

SECTION 5

White River Hills

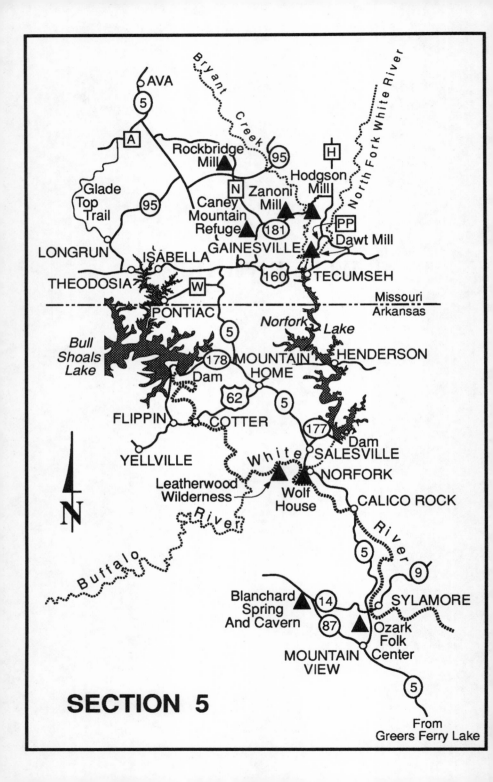

SECTION 5

CHAPTER 14

Overview: Folk Culture of the Ozarks

By and large the culture of the Ozarks has been influenced predominantly by the Scotch-Irish. By the time they came to the Ozarks, the Scotch-Irish were Americans of several generations' standing. They entered, and remained in, mostly the "interior" of the Ozarks: in the rugged terrain that traces the routes of the major Ozarks rivers and their tributaries.

Because an overland journey laden with household goods—the wagon train of westward expansion—was extraordinarily difficult in these rougher regions of the Ozarks, most came via the river highways, on keelboats and on steamboats. Disembarking on the river's shore, they liked what they saw, moved up- or downriver, mostly via foot trails and stream beds because there were no roads, to vacant land and settled in.

Clannish and ultraconservative by the traditions of hundreds of years, even reaching back for generations in the old country, the Scotch-Irish found the Ozark hills quite suited to their already well-established way of life. They mingled more freely with the Native Americans than with "outsiders," and occasionally married them. Few outsiders entered the tortuous country.

Although steady progress was made toward modernity prior to the Civil War, that conflict and its horrendous effects and aftermath plunged the region into a kind of dark ages that surpassed anything experienced by the rest of the country, and from which it took much longer to recover.

For generations the Ozarks society of the Scotch-Irish perpetuated itself with little alteration. Even in the face of changes wrought by two World Wars and the Great Depression—which brought relief workers, social programs, and much more from the outside—the folks in the most isolated of the hills immediately bordering the White River adamantly resisted "modernization." The geography of their homeland aided and abetted their determination to remain aloof from the outside world. Because many roads remained unpaved until the middle of the twentieth century, fewer visitors came their way. (In Marion County, Arkansas, mail continued to be delivered on horseback into the 1950s; the postman could simply negotiate the rocky roads and ford the numerous streams more easily and quickly on horseback than he could in a car.) Telephones were used, mostly at central locations such as the local general store, but were not allowed to really effect much change.

Eventually radio brought music and news, but judicious programming offered the audience mostly an extension of their own. It is debatable whether radio broadened horizons or assisted in walling them up. News broadcasts only served to reinforce what many already knew: they were well off where they were.

Probably the most frequently misunderstood characteristic of these Ozarkers is their willingness to be content with so little. They, in turn, are often scornful of the "furriners'" need for material goods, and sometimes see such possessions as worldly—even sinful.

Perpetuating the Frontier

It may increase one's understanding to consider this nucleus of change-resistant Ozarks in a geographers' term: an *arrested frontier*. As the frontier straggled into the Ozarks, it ground to a halt in the tortuous terrain. With little encouragement from behind, and with settlers content with the status quo, the frontier stalled out in the Ozarks. Those counties bypassed by the railroads, in particular, were stranded in the past. Even the timber and mining industries passed them by.

The thoughtful observer will recognize to this day numerous elements of the "Western cowboy culture" in the rural Ozarks, characterized by "Life in the Outdoors" and all its accoutrements: Western dress, guns, horses, and rodeos; hunting of all kinds; a lingering closeness to, understanding of, and dependence upon nature; and even the music and the dance. Social customs, too, have more in common with frontier times: pie suppers, square dances, and other opportunities for homespun music, school and church programs. And, because the population remained at or below 1900 levels for so

"Mountain cabin and family ca 1885," according to the State Historical Society of Missouri. For obvious reasons, life was lived out of doors except in the most inclement weather. When the nearest neighbor might be twenty or thirty miles away, a couple was limited to the size of house they could build alone despite the fact that raw materials were abundant and there for the taking. Upon first arriving in the area, their most immediate need was for shelter of any sort, to be improved later as possible. (Courtesy of The Ozarks Mountaineer)

Constructed of logs squared by hand, this outbuilding—like virtually all of the Ozarker's farm buildings—was utilitarian and no more complicated than was needed to serve the purpose. The Ozarker was never interested in show. Homey buildings such as this one are becoming extremely rare. (Courtesy of Bittersweet, Inc.)

long, most of the turn-of-the-century architecture is not only still standing, it is still in use.

It is no exaggeration to say that, in some areas or in some hearts, at least, there still remains the desire to deliberately *perpetuate* the frontier—to fend off the effects of modernity for as long as possible, especially those seen as undesirable.

The Ozarks: Folk Region

A chief of the folklore section at the Library of Congress has defined *folklore*: "*Folklore* includes folk architecture, craft and art; folk industry (lumbering, fishing, farming); folk speech and language, folk literature (tall tales, proverbs, rhymes); folk history (local legends, the reminiscences of old-timers); folk medicine and weather lore; folk law (the Western code, vigilantes, kangaroo courts); and folk belief and custom (knock on wood, a handshake, and Fourth-of-July picnics). It is considerably more than Grandma Moses, Burl Ives and Paul Bunyan."

In the case of Ozarks folklore, it is also considerably more than hillbillies and good ol' boys. And since its folklore is so complex, the casual or one-time visitor will not be able to fully comprehend the intricacies of the Ozarks way of life.

Vance Randolph, the region's revered folklorist who probably really *knew* the Ozarks and its folks as well as anyone, did so imperfectly and only after a long lifetime of living among Ozarkers, marrying into an Ozarks family, working alongside them, playing with them, listening to them, learning from them, and studying them. How then can outsiders who visit only briefly feel so free to analyze and criticize that which they understand so poorly and know not at all?

Human beings are said to be naturally ethnocentric; that is, we not only cling to our own ways, we also believe our ways are better than everybody else's ways. We tend to judge other people by how well they measure up to our own ways. Whether our ways fit the other fellow's needs or desires is not taken into consideration. We just automatically consider him inferior to us because he does not do things our way.

But the simple—if not so obvious—truth is, another's ways can only be properly understood by taking into consideration the tools and resources he has to work with, the problems and pitfalls in his path, and the traditions and adaptations that have made him the way he is. Folk wisdom calls this "walking a mile in the other fellow's shoes."

"Walking a Mile" in an Ozarker's Shoes

Imagine yourself as an American settler in the Ozarks of about 1840.

If you are a man, you are probably accompanied by your wife and at least two small children; you are solely responsible for their safety and well-being in this raw, often inhospitable new land. As you disembark from the keelboat that has just landed you at a tiny, crude outpost somewhere along White River, you and your family are tired and hungry. As you look around you, you see only incredibly dense wilderness that appears to offer no shelter or food for your family. Only a narrow trail through the forest leads away from the river landing.

Although you come from a tradition of linen weaving in Ulster, where farming was merely a sideline for your family, linen weaving is not a practical option in this Ozarks wilderness. Land, however, is cheap. Several million acres of land are available at twenty-five cents an acre, and some for only 12.5 cents an acre.

If you are a woman, you are no doubt following your land-hungry husband into the wilderness, chasing his dream of independence and self-determination. Although he admits to not being much of a crop farmer, by working together you hope to raise enough livestock and crops in this poor, rocky soil for your family's sustenance, augmented by what you can harvest from nature's bounty on the land.

Clinging to your long skirts are a couple of frightened, exhausted children who need to be fed and sheltered for the night. Although you are grateful to be free of the cramped, miserable conditions you endured on the interminable trip upriver, you fear that the boat has landed you out of the frying pan and into the fire. Towering, forbidding rock bluffs rise above you, and all around you presses a terrible forest, probably full of wild beasts and savages.

How—and why—on earth did you come to be here? Although your family first came to America from Ireland in the early 1700s, they were not really Irishmen, but Scots who had immigrated to Ireland a century earlier in the quest for land. Since they had kept to their own kind in the Ulster section of Ireland, they had become known as the Ulster Scots, or the Scotch-Irish. The majority of the Scotch-Irish had entered the American colonies through the port of Philadelphia, attracted by the promises of William Penn, who offered land to those willing to work for it—and religious freedom. Hard-working but poor, many Scotch-Irish arrived in America as indentured servants. Once their obligations were discharged, most acquired land on the new frontier. But they were quick to sell out to newer immigrants and push the frontier west and south. It began to be said that no Scotch-Irish family felt comfortable until it had moved at least twice. For whatever reason, the Scotch-Irish thrived on the frontier.

In order to avoid paying taxes on land in the wilderness, these sturdy pioneers often simply settled on vacant land and waited, sometimes many years, until the land had been surveyed and came up for government sale. Then, if they could, they bought it. If not, they were forced to move when others claimed the property legally. Because the Scotch-Irish were usually cash poor, this happened to them frequently. As a result, they acquired a reputation as squatters.

By the time of the Revolutionary War, during which they were some of America's most ardent patriots, the Scotch-Irish made up fifteen percent of the population of the colonies. The beginning of the war brought a halt to immigration from Ulster.

As livestock farmers, and hunters and gatherers, the Scotch-Irish had no need for expensive valley soils. They could be content with the less desirable hill country that reminded them of their ancestral homes in Ulster and in southwestern Scotland. They were self-sufficient, fiercely independent, often anti-government. In short, they were unimpressed by, and not dependent upon, organized society. Following the frontier, being free and independent, became a way of life for the Scotch-Irish. They have furnished this country with fourteen presidents.

Eventually they came to the Ozarks. The first to arrive sent back word to their families and were followed by the rest of the clan. By the time of the Civil War, the interior highlands of Missouri and Arkansas were settled by Scotch-Irish Americans from the hill country of Kentucky and Tennessee, leaving the better lands of the Ozarks borders to others. (As the generations progressed, many families eventually left the Ozarks and continued their migratory movement into the Texas Hill Country, the northern Rockies, and the Cascades of Oregon and Washington. Although Scandinavians brought the log cabin to America, it was the Scotch-Irish who took it to areas west of the Atlantic seaboard.) Because they spoke English, the Scotch-Irish faced no particular difficulty in being assimilated in America. In fact, many of their modern descendants have no knowledge of their ethnic background.

Today the folk culture of the Ozarks, at least that of the interior Ozarks, is founded upon many of their traits and the traditional music and folktales they brought with them from Scotland and Ireland. Even the long tradition of distilling whiskey for home use dates back to seventeenth-century Scotland.

The first need is for shelter. You find a small cave on the face of the river bluff that promises interim protection from the night and its beasts. Since there is plenty of raw material, you can build a log cabin with logs you yourself cut and drag to your chosen homesite. Since neighbors, if any, are likely to be twenty miles away, the cabin can be no larger than the length of logs the two of you can manhandle into place—probably no more than twelve or fourteen feet square. At first the floor will be the good earth, but eventually—if you have access to a sawmill or someone to help with more rudimentary methods—you may have time to fashion puncheon flooring. As your family grows you will build a second cabin of the same dimensions, connected to the first by a "dogtrot," or breezeway. For warmth and light, there appears to be a plentiful supply of firewood and abundant rock with which to build a fireplace.

Wildlife is everywhere—a largess of food and raw materials for the taking. As you get settled in, you will begin to hunt and trap wildlife for your family's needs and for the market. By selling your game to others, you can supplement your family's diet with salt, coffee, flour, and perhaps a bit of sugar. From the many rivers of the land you will harvest fish, mussels, and crawfish, and from the springs you will take watercress and other marine life.

Nature also provides fruits, berries, and nuts, and you have learned to dry and preserve them to sustain your family through the winter. You have also learned to use the vegetables and greens provided by the land, and to prepare them in nutritious ways with the materials you have at hand. Long generations of living close to nature has unlocked for you many of her secrets, and you also understand which of her plenitude of plants can be used for medicine and poultices—for there are no doctors in this wild land. By wasting nothing, it is to be hoped, you will want for nothing.

Once the cabin is up and a supply of food assured, you will clear the giant timber from a few acres using only your strong back and an ax. A few rows of corn, some gourds and pumpkins, perhaps a few potatoes, can help supply the family larder. These you will store in a root cellar of your own construction and hang from the rafters of your cabin.

Eventually you can barter furs or a jug of homemade whiskey for a mule to help you plow the rocky ground and for a cow—milk for the children, as well as homemade butter and cheese—a few hogs, chickens, and ducks to supply meat, eggs, and feathers for warm bedding. Because the domesticated animals are not likely to wander far in the wilderness, and because natural foods are also available for them in abundance, your livestock remains nearby unbidden. You erect a few rough fences of stone or logs—a back-breaking and time-consuming task—but to keep the animals out of your precious gardens and fields, rather than to confine them. Your time and effort are more wisely directed to providing for your family.

The cool waters of the spring in the hollow will provide safekeeping for the butter, eggs, and milk, and all the fresh, sweet water you need—although it will mean a long walk to the spring from the cabin several times a day. For this reason you build your home as near to the spring as practical.

Since there is no other way to preserve them, you erect a smokehouse in which to cure meats. The preparing and curing of game and domestic meat becomes another in the unending and vital work to be done on the homestead. All animal skins, domestic and wild, are carefully saved and tanned for their leather.

Because it is a long tradition of your people and, you believe, your God-given right, to make whiskey from the corn of your fields, grown by the sweat of your brow, you sometimes distill liquor. The practice, after all, was not always

Even a simple wood cook stove and cast iron utensils were better than cooking over a fireplace or other open fire. Notice the flat irons that were heated on the cook top—sometimes also called "sad irons," because you were sad when you had to use them! Some member of the family had to prepare a continuing supply of "cook wood"—wood cut short enough and split fine enough to fit into the relatively small firebox of the cook stove. It was not unusual for the cook to prepare her own cook wood.

Before the advent of efficient refrigeration and easily available canned foods, the homes of most Ozarkers included a cellar used to store the fruits of their own orchards and gardens. Sometimes the fruit cellar doubled as a refuge from violent storms. (Courtesy of Bittersweet, Inc.)

against the law. Except for the years 1791-1802 and for a few years following the War of 1812 when a federal excise tax on whiskey was collected, it was completely legal. But beginning in 1862 (1868 in Arkansas), it became a crime to distill alcohol without a federal permit. Long accustomed to being isolated and relatively insulated from the legal whims of city people, however, you continue to produce corn whiskey in secluded wildcat stills. You believe the government has no right to interfere in matters of daily life and what you do with your land and your labor. Moreover, the profits are ten times greater than farming and logging and you are often desperate to provide for your family. But now you are forced to work in secret and at night, often by only the light of the moon; the practice becomes known as "moonshining."

The family's clothing needs are simple and secondary in importance to the providing of food. By washing them frequently in the local stream, using homemade lye soap made with ashes from the fireplace, a couple of garments each will suffice. You can wash, card, and spin the wool of your own sheep and goats, perhaps raise a few acres of cotton to spin or sell, and you will weave your homespun yarns into the cloth for your garments. Hats are fashioned from animal skins, and the men will wear buckskin shirts and leather britches much of the time. If time permits, you may gather walnut leaves, yellowwood, and other natural materials and from them you will make a dye to color your threads and clothes, for all human beings love and need beauty, even in simple, utilitarian things.

Of course you make your own bedclothes, and the making of bedcovers from the leftover scraps of garments and linens will give rise to the art form of quilting. As time permits, and as you are able to acquire the materials, you will indulge your innate sense of beauty and love of color by fashioning multi-colored and intricately patterned quilts.

Other household needs are also homemade: from cornhusks you fashion brooms and mattresses. During the Great Depression many backwoods families will replace the lumpy "cornshuck" mattresses with cotton mattresses made at home from instructions and materials furnished by county agents.

Occasionally you are able to supplement the foodstuffs you raise and harvest from the land and its creatures. You earn a bit of cash from the railroad for ties you have hacked with a broadax from the forest trees. In some areas, you eventually hire out—for long, hard hours and very little pay—to work in the lumber camps and the mines and the quarries and the canneries owned by outsiders who exploit and plunder your homeland with little returned.

By working together eighteen hours a day your family is able to provide for most of its own needs. The strict division of labor between the sexes arises primarily to ensure survival of the family group. Even in play, boys are the hunters, while girls "play house" in preparation for their role as nurturers and keepers of the hearth.

And as the children get bigger, their contributions of time and effort are also required to support the family. If later a schoolteacher should come among you,

If the cook needed to supplement the meal under preparation, she would go to the cellar, where she could choose from the supply of foodstuffs she had "put by" during the summer and fall harvest season—often working outdoors over an open fire. Also stored in the cellar were potatoes, carrots, turnips, and other root crops (sometimes it was called a "root cellar"), and perhaps a few apples which were ordinarily canned or sliced and dried. Before the days of refrigeration, meats were also canned or cured in the smokehouse. (Courtesy of Bittersweet, Inc.)

perhaps you can spare the children for a few weeks of the year; perhaps not, if you are all to continue to eat.

God forbid that the hard life should take one of their parents before your time, though if that should happen one of your extended family—or one of your closest neighbors, whom you often call "aunt" or "uncle"—will help to care for those who are left. You will take care of your own. But before you have been long in this country, you will recognize that your only important possession is life itself. In 1850 life expectancy stands at 38.3 years for a man, 40.5 years for a woman—and that without the added stress of wilderness living. On the frontier, cholera, pneumonia, influenza, or smallpox appears unexpectedly, leaving a few of the stronger to bury most of their family.

Because family is so vital to your survival and kinship so important to your way of life, the enemy of any one of your relatives is the enemy of your entire family. You will protect your own and your rights even if it means conflict with a neighboring family, because that is the way of this rough land in which you must survive. There is no other social structure on which to depend, no law and no authority taller than the head of your own family.

Since you have few roads and your trails through the wilderness are long and rough, your family lives in virtual isolation and toils almost constantly for your daily sustenance. Electricity to lighten your load or to power a radio is late in coming to the Ozarks. In particularly rugged areas, it will not arrive until well after World War II.

But because by playing together you enhance your relationships with your neighbors, promote cooperation and group solidarity among the few who brave this wilderness—and because you are human—you manage to take a few hours occasionally for lighter moments.

Being a pragmatic people, you and your fellow Ozarkers have learned to play even in times of work. You make a game of erecting a barn, building a fence, or threshing a hay field. By working together in the spirit of fun, you can achieve much and enjoy its accomplishment.

Because human play is expressed in the arts, you sing, dance, stage dramas, recite poetry, have formalized debates, and perform music. Music is, indeed, your most prized possession, a natural part of your lives, one of the primary ways you express the universal need for beauty and emotion. You also recognize that music and dance are particularly helpful in making a group from individuals, for drawing people together. Even in worship, singing is of paramount importance and a social event. When no building is available, in warm weather, or just for the fun of meeting outside, you construct an arbor of saplings, shaded by green branches, and sit on split-log benches.

If you can squeeze a bit of cash money from the sale of furs, eggs, or watermelons, you may buy a guitar from a roving peddler. If not, and you are driven to make music, you fashion your own instruments from whatever materials are at hand, often inventing new ones in the process.

Using the materials at hand—wood was always abundant—the Ozarker himself fash-ioned most of what he needed. Fences were used to keep the livestock out *of gardens and fields, rather than* in *pastures or pens. Stock wandered freely on open range until the middle of this century in some places. "Fences" were also frequently constructed of stone. (Courtesy of Bittersweet, Inc.)*

You have remembered and still perform the ballads and other music from your ancestral homes. You often still sing of kings and queens, castles, knights, and fair maidens, even as you share the songs of others—the railroad men, the cowboys, the Negroes. Most of your fellow musicians play "by ear" and tunes are passed down from generation to generation though few can read music.

In this new land you find much to mystify and frighten you: natural phenomena that are commonplace here but are unexplainable to you and new to your experience can be daunting in the wilderness. And so you and your neighbors make up stories to explain them, somehow comforted by these homemade explanations; in time, they pass into the lore and superstitions of your people.

Because you live so close to nature, her whims are of vital importance to you. And, by long and careful observation, you have developed a body of knowledge about the weather in your sometimes violent new land. Although you are made fun of because your weather lore sounds like ignorant superstition, it helps you keep track of the proper times to plant and to harvest and to recognize the changing of the seasons.

By the time of the Civil War, you have established post offices and counties, courts and sheriffs, settled towns, started newspapers. Schools and colleges are springing up everywhere, and a well-ordered social system is emerging.

Then the war brings disaster. Social control collapses. Both Southern and Northern sympathizers are living in close proximity, and this leads to terrible tension.

But much worse are those who take advantage of the anarchic conditions— often hiding behind the guise of soldiers—to settle old grievances or plunder and prey on the innocent and helpless. In a land depopulated by the war, left defenseless by the forced conscription of its men and boys, this grievous condition persists for a long, painful time after the close of hostilities.

Vigilante groups determined to better the deplorable conditions eventually only make them worse. You watch your husbands and sons and babies murdered, you endure starvation and homelessness and other privations beyond human endurance. And you learn to be suspicious and fearful in the presence of strangers.

You become even more clannish, drawing to yourself those you know and trust, and determined to remain aloof from the world.

Over time you have evolved a dialect, a spoken form of language that is partly a result of the language you brought with you to these shores hundreds of years ago and partly the result of living in isolation for so long in these hills. Your dialect and its use by your close neighbors makes it easy to know when a stranger has come among you. The use of words in your dialect unknown by the stranger allows you to communicate secretly even in his presence.

If this stranger who has come among you should think you are strange, or even make fun of you because you are different, your only defense is in remaining aloof from him and his kind. Outsiders do not understand the forces that

Until the days of running water in the home—quite late in this century in some areas, this little building was a necessity on the farmstead. This particular one is actually quite grand; most were simple, unfinished sheds. Called variously the backhouse, the outhouse, the privy, or even, perhaps, the two-holer—if you lived in the country, you had one. It disappeared quickly from the scene once its usefulness had been served. Derelicts are rarely seen these days. (Courtesy of Bittersweet, Inc.)

have shaped you or how living in a harsh and unforgiving land has made you different. Not inferior; only different.

Much as fishermen belong to the sea they curse, and ranchers love the harsh land and hard climate that sometimes defeat them, you backwoods Ozarkers reflect the rugged freedom of your lonely hill country.

And when others look at you now, they see only ". . . blighted men and women who seemed never to have known youth, but only toil; people lost in solitary wilderness, like the lonely ones of Chaucer."

They cannot understand.

Ozark Folk Center

Stone County, Arkansas, remained a quiet backwater of the Ozarks until the middle of the twentieth century. Because there were no paved primary roads until then, the county received virtually no tourists and few travelers or sportsmen. Almost unapproachable from the north and east because of the difficult terrain and a nearly impenetrable wilderness, Stone County remained uninfluenced by a railroad or the Corps of Engineers. "Progress" flowed around it.

Then, about the time that Stone County highways were finally paved and outsiders began to discover the natural beauty there, the nation began to experience a resurgence of interest in its various folk cultures. In Stone County there existed an almost perfect sanctuary of another time. To help safeguard this culture, the Ozark Folk Center was built with three million dollars in federal grants and loans and dedicated to the preservation and the sharing of the Ozark Mountain way of life.

Preserving Ozarks Folk Culture and Music

Like a time capsule buried deep in the guardian hills, the Ozark Folk Center at Mountain View, Arkansas, preserves the Ozarks folkways from 1820 to 1920—the "cabin crafts," the music, the folklore, and the food. There are no carnival rides, pop music, nor cotton candy. Authenticity is the key word. You will find only the essence of a bygone era, unique in America. Since you leave the modern age behind in the parking lot and ride a motorized tram up the steep hillside to the crafts and the music, it is easy to lose yourself in the Ozarks past.

Throughout the May-to-November season you can smell the aroma of hot peach pie, cheer the old-time fiddle championships, or witness a muzzleloader shoot. You can see the old crafts done in the time-honored ways: spinning, weaving, candlemaking, basketry, woodcarving, and many more. Listen to storytellers, have your picture taken on

At the Ozark Folk Center in Mountain View, Arkansas, the visitor will see—besides examples and demonstrations of heritage crafts—antique farm equipment such as this horse-powered hay baler. In the background is a sulky rake.

Virtually all of the musicians and performers at the Ozark Folk Center are local folks. In the afternoon, shows are given at this outdoor theater on the grounds. Evenings, except Sunday, the show is indoors in the octagonal cedar-and-stone auditorium. Pictured are, left to right, John Taylor, and Elaine and Hank Blumenthal, all popular Folk Center musicians.

tintype, view an Indian lore exhibit, log cabins, frontier games, an herb garden, a harness and saddle shop, a blacksmith shop, and a cook shed where fruit, jellies, and peach butter are "put by."

All of these activities celebrate Ozarks folkways and allow visitors to experience the living history of the area, so recent that this simpler way of life is still enjoyed by many in the surrounding hills. Now operated as an Arkansas state park of about nine hundred acres, the crafts-and-music complex consists of several buildings on eighty acres.

A magnificent domed, native-stone-and-cedar auditorium seats a thousand people for the nightly folk music concerts. Only nonamplified instruments—guitars, Autoharps, banjos, and locally crafted dulcimers—are played, and only pre-1941 music and lyrics are allowed. Featured throughout the season are many special musical events, including fiddle competitions, gospel concerts, string band jamborees, bluegrass festivals, and much more. Fascinating performances are offered by hammered dulcimer, mountain dulcimer, and Autoharp virtuosos. In addition to the music program presented in the auditorium every day except Sunday throughout the season, music is performed in an open-air amphitheater on the grounds every afternoon for several hours.

And anywhere the old music is played, anyone who feels like it is welcomed on the stage to do his or her own version of the jig. Performed by an individual dancing alone, the *jig* is probably related to clogging, which dates far back in the annals of folk dance. Usually fast and high-stepping, the dancer jigs on first one foot and then the other, transferring the body's weight in the air, as in running, in time to the music. Differing from region to region and highly individualistic, the step is loose and performed primarily with the feet. The body above the knees is relaxed but held mostly stationary and the arms are usually allowed to hang motionless, giving the dancer a limber, almost disjointed appearance in motion. No description is adequate; the jig must be seen to be understood. (In contrast, *clogging* uses ritualistic steps taught to the dancers and is performed in unison.)

Safeguarding the Heritage Crafts

The Ozark Folk Center is also dedicated to ensuring that the heritage crafts are not forgotten. A teaching program ensures that today's masters pass along their skills and experience to the younger generation. Apprentices are selected from applicants over eighteen years of age who live within a sixty-mile radius. Top priority is given to historical crafts in immediate danger of extinction, but of equal importance is the economic potential of the craft as apprentices are encouraged to learn skills by which they can earn a living. And, in fact, several craftsmen have developed home-based industries in nearby Mountain View.

Even visitors can spend some time learning the Ozarks folkways and heritage crafts. A "unique and extensive crafts workshop program," Folk Center workshops include the teaching of such skills as spinning and weaving; jewelry, lace, or basket making; blacksmithing; quilting; and woodcarving. As a very flexible alternative to being unable to attend a workshop with a fixed date, the Folk Center allows you to "build your own workshop." Interested individuals can establish their learning time based on their own schedules; contact the Ozark Folk Center (for details see the Practical Matters Chart after Chapter 15).

Not Just a Museum

The Ozark Folk Center is more than just a museum of a former lifestyle, it is a representation, albeit to a lesser degree, of the way many rural Ozarkers still live in the more isolated areas. In important new ways the Folk Center is perpetuating that lifestyle: By encouraging the apprenticeship of heritage crafts and fostering cottage industries, the Center is helping to make it economically feasible for young people to stay in the hills. Already the crafts demonstrators at the Center are more often the one-time apprentices themselves, rather than the old-timers as was once the case. And, no doubt, the influence of newcomers and the tastes of travelers are certain to have an effect on even the heritage crafts.

Also on the grounds at the Ozark Folk Center are duplex-style lodges for overnight accommodations and a conference center to serve up to a thousand.

For a brief moment visitors to the Folk Center can turn back the clock and be down-home in the Ozarks. Now, linger in Stone County for yet a while longer.

CHAPTER 15

The Land That
Time Forgot

Included in the Cherokee Indian Reservation between 1817 and 1828, Stone County was designated in 1873 and named for its abundant stones. Mountain View was established as the county seat and in 1874 the name of the post office was picked from a hat. Built by a local stonemason, the courthouse dates to 1922 and was listed on the National Register of Historic Places in 1976.

Heritage of Music

Mountain music is heard everywhere in the Mountain View vicinity, both formally and informally. The courthouse square is the focal point on weekend afternoons and evenings for jam sessions—"pickin' and grinnin'." Folks bring their instruments and lawn chairs to hear or make music, dance, visit, and enjoy each other's company after a week of hard work and isolation in the hills. They are often joined by company from afar. In fact, the music of Mountain View is now a major attraction for travelers in the Ozarks. Bring your lawn chair.

Diagonally behind the courthouse is an old house that is home to a music store, the Signal Hill Music Shop, chock full of instruments, sheet music, tapes, instruction books, and mountain musicians. If you have the slightest interest in the music of the Ozarks, do not miss this establishment.

Additionally, there are a number of music shows in and around Mountain View that you may want to attend, including the Friday and

Sunday performances at Jimmy Driftwood's Barn (see the Practical Matters Chart). A famous songwriter and singer of Ozarks songs, Driftwood was pivotal in the formation of the Rackensack Society, largely responsible for the perpetuation of mountain music in the area. And do not forget the nightly (except Sunday) music shows at the Ozark Folk Center.

Heritage Crafts

Whatever else you do in the Mountain View area, be sure to stop by the local craft outlet of the Arkansas Craft Guild. One of several permanent outlets, and the headquarters of the Guild, is about two miles north of Mountain View on Hwy. 5. In addition to their shops throughout Arkansas, the Guild sponsors spring and fall shows that include, besides crafts, folk music and dance.

Formed in 1962 just in time to revive the traditional crafts—and undoubtedly to rescue some of them from oblivion—the Guild has provided an outlet for the crafts of Arkansans who can qualify. Each must apply for admission to the Guild, submit samples of her or his wares for jurying, and meet the established criteria of excellence. To assure an ever-increasing level of quality, members' works are reviewed every five years on the basis of craftsmanship, materials, design, and originality. Without a doubt the members of this professional guild are producing some of the finest crafts in the Ozarks.

Do be aware, also, of the shops on the square. All around town are the stores of local craftsmen, from blacksmiths to spinning wheel makers to rug weavers. If you do not see what you are looking for, ask anyone.

The Old Mill And Other Antiques

For antiquers, the Mountain View area is paradise. The problem is in deciding where to start. A favorite is Dogwood Hollow, which offers china, glass, quilts, stoneware, all types of kitchenware, furniture, porcelain dolls, and handwoven fabrics. Also of interest at the same location, a half-mile north of the Folk Center road on Hwy. 5, is a museum of antique hand tools and fine antique needlework. There are several interesting flea markets, too, and these are usually good spots to meet and visit with the locals.

As you stroll through town, the Old Mill, just one block west of the courthouse square, will draw you like a magnet. Built in 1914 and opened on July 4, the mill supplied local residents with fresh cornmeal and flour for many years. The millhouse sat idle from 1942 until it was restored in 1983, except for its use as a location for the movie *The Bootleggers* in the 1970s.

The Old Mill in Mountain View, Arkansas, ceased to mill grain for its customers in 1942. From then until 1983 it waited—like a time capsule. Then the mill was unlocked, restored, and opened to the visitors who were flocking to the Ozark Folk Center. Now it is one of the most evocative-of-the-past old mills in the Ozarks.

Now the Old Mill once again grinds meal for visitors on weekends (Thursday through Saturday) during the Folk Center season, still powered by its original ten-horsepower, one-cylinder kerosene engine, a 1916 International Harvester weighing twenty-three hundred pounds. It and a companion collection of other old-time engines are rare; most such vintage machines were collected for scrap during the World Wars—unless they were still in use, as was the case in time-warped Stone County. In the rodent-proof "keeping room," a cozy gift shop displays the wares of local crafters. Fascinating vintage photographs of the Mountain View area are displayed in the mill's one-time "holding room." Tools of a bygone era add interest here and there, so that no matter where you look in the old building, there is something unique.

Another without-fail stop in the Mountain View area is the Dulcimer Shoppe on Hwy. 5 just north of town. Dulcimers are handmade at this location (in a glassed-in workroom visible from the retail section of the shop), and there are many other wonders there: hand-tooled leather belts, oak-splint baskets, spellbinding one-of-a-kind pottery creations, books about the Ozarks, sock dolls, the tapes of local musicians, and much more. Almost invariably, someone sits down to try out a new dulcimer.

When you need a break, a pleasant place for a picnic in Mountain View is the city park. Located a few blocks north of the square, its location is well marked by signs along the route. A scenic hiking trail, far removed in spirit from the busy highway, leads from the park to the Ozark Folk Center.

Ozark National Forest

Established by the proclamation of President Theodore Roosevelt on March 6, 1908, Ozark National Forest was not altogether popular with area residents. In fact, the new forest was a political hot potato for many years and the total land area fluctuated as sometimes successful pressures were applied to decrease the acreage included. Much of the land had been clear-cut and abused, and it included some former farms. Remains of homesteads can still be found along forest trails, and here and there an old general store or church building reminds the visitor that areas now reclaimed by wilderness once supported thriving communities.

Some of that once-homesteaded land in the Ozark National Forest has been designated an official wilderness area. There is very little truly "wild" wilderness left in the Ozarks—that is, "virgin land" that has not at one time in its history been lumbered, farmed, mined, or otherwise disturbed. But because some of the land knew the heavy hand of man only briefly, it is recovering its once-wild demeanor. In the Sylamore District of the forest, visitors will find another official wilderness—the Leatherwood—which can be explored only on foot or by horseback. No motorized vehicles are allowed. This wilderness adjoins the Lower Buffalo River Wilderness.

Blanchard Spring and Cavern

The longer one stays in the special place that is the Ozarks, the more one becomes conditioned to *expect* beauty. Not jaded, but so accustomed to the level of enchantment that when one unexpectedly encounters a scene of even more charm, the effect is breathtaking. Such a place is Blanchard Spring.

You leave your car in the modern world, in a small parking lot ringed by sheer limestone bluffs and serenaded by the brook, and walk up a narrow, bluff-walled hollow. The path parallels the spring branch sparkling in sunlight softly filtered through a tangle of under-story trees—exhibitionistic dogwoods in springtime and a flamboyant mantle in autumn—and verdant mosses and lichens thriving in the protected, humid environment.

The approach to the spring is level and easy, even for wheelchairs and the elderly. At one point a wooden footbridge spans the spring branch, known as Mill Creek, and seems to suspend you in the air between the crystal water and the leafy bower. A bench is situated invitingly and strategically within full view of the spring, so that one may sit and marvel. Watch closely and you may see a swallow darting over the water to disappear into the mouth of the spring itself. For the young and agile, the stream and the spring are easily accessible, the fifty-eight-degree water delightfully chilling, and the whole scene exhilarating.

At Blanchard you are witnessing the egress of an underground stream—Lost River—that meanders through the underground passages of a vast cavern to leave the mountain as a spring. Like most such springs in the Ozarks, this one (named for the builder of the mill) once powered a gristmill and anchored a small community. But its (white) human history is very recent.

Following his release as a prisoner of the Union Army, John Blanchard left his Kentucky home in 1865 in the aftermath of the Civil War. Finding these solacing hills, he homesteaded 160 acres. Besides being a miller, he served the new community as county treasurer for two terms before his death in 1914. There does not seem to be any evidence that Blanchard knew of the existence of the cavern. If he did, he had no time for exploration.

But certainly by the 1930s the existence of the cave was known.

Unlike many such wonders in the Ozarks, Blanchard Spring is easily accessible to those who are unable to hike or backpack into the wilderness. Green Thumb workers have constructed a footbridge and a path—that even wheelchairs can negotiate with care—into the lovely hollow, where an observation deck commands a good view of the spring. Those more agile can clamber over the rocks and get a really close-up view.

The White River from the bluff at Calico Rock, Arkansas, on the Sylamore Scenic Byway through Ozark National Forest.

Local residents called the cavern Half-Mile Cave. They suspected that a large sinkhole, half a mile up and around the mountain from the spring, might be connected to it. To prove it, they dropped corn cobs into the sinkhole and heard them splash in the stream far below. And the cobs did indeed emerge at the spring, but only after taking an astonishing twenty-four hours to travel the apparent one-half mile.

The young and vigorous members of the Civilian Conservation Corps who worked and lived in the Ozark National Forest during the Depression no doubt made a few abortive attempts at exploration. The only natural entrance to the cave, however, is through the sinkhole, with a seventy-foot drop to the floor of the first room. Extensive time, equipment, and expertise would be required to explore properly, though some of the earlier explorers had left their mark.

In 1955 spelunkers descended into the depths of Half-Mile Cave and began some five years of exploring. And, as is appropriate to all unfathomable caverns, this one has its mystery. One of the first discoveries was the skeleton of a human being and the remains of bundles of reeds he might have taken into the cave for torches. Carbon dating of the reeds and scientific analysis of the human skull placed their ages at about a thousand years. That very early explorer is believed to be a Bluff Dweller Indian, a young male, and we can only speculate about his mission in the cave—and his death. He is believed to have died of a skull fracture.

Eventually the Forest Service, having seen for itself what wonders lay below the surface of the mountain, decided to develop the cave for the enjoyment of visitors to the National Forest. Meanwhile, exploration continued. Spelunkers and speologists made further discoveries and mapped miles of passages on three levels. In the autumn of 1971 scuba divers entered the cave system through the spring itself. From the water's outlet to the natural entrance of the cave is about four thousand feet—a fourth of that distance through chambers completely filled with icy water.

Due in part to funding that became available only in fits and starts, development of Blanchard Springs Caverns was slow and careful. Then, too, the cave is still "living": that is, still in formation. The home of endangered species of bats and other cave dwellers, the vast cavern is a delicate ecosystem that could easily be destroyed by humankind's intervention. But eventually the Forest Service established a visitor center complete with interpretive films and exhibits about the cave and the life within it, and two guided tours of the cavern. First opened to the public in 1973, Blanchard Springs Caverns is the only underground tour in the U.S. Forest Service.

Assured by the Forest Service that every precaution has been taken to ensure the safety and enjoyment of the public, visitors descend into the depths of the mountain via elevator. One of the tours, the Drip-stone Trail, is said to be accessible to wheelchairs with assistance and suitable even for those with a heart condition or respiratory problems. The Discovery Trail, on the other hand, is much longer, both in time and distance.

Experts agree that Blanchard Springs Caverns has a wider variety of colorful formations and unique features than many of the world's famous caves. Cave connoisseurs—those who have seen most com-mercial caves, as well as many undeveloped ones, in the region—agree that this cave is the most magnificent of them all.

Among the features seen along the trails is a seventy-foot calcite column that looks like ice, a 160-foot flowstone that resembles a frozen waterfall, and walls that nature has draped with colorful stone curtains. Illumination of the dramatic geology was arranged by the same designer who planned the lighting systems of the Metropolitan Opera in New York and the Kennedy Center in Washington. In order to fully appreciate the cavern and its fascinating natural history, watch the Forest Service's informative audio-visual program and view their *Life in the Dark* exhibit in addition to touring the cave.

More Outdoor Enchantment at Blanchard Spring

"The best swimming hole in the Ozarks" is at the Blanchard Spring complex, and this is probably not much of an exaggeration. Clear, clean, with a gravel bottom and a gentle flow, backed by picturesque bluffs, Sylamore Creek and its sloping shore is undeniably inviting. To top it off, there is a modern bathhouse and a lifeguard's tower—neither of which is usually associated with an Ozarks "swimming hole." According to an 1877 newspaper article, Sylamore Creek took its name from an outlaw Indian, "one old Syllamo . . . (who) generally stayed a little out of town and spent a great deal of his time" on the creek.

Just around the bend of the creek is the campground. Shady and quiet, but with limited hookups and accessibility for really big rigs, the campground seems to appeal to families in tents and smaller trailers. There are rest rooms and showers and centrally located water faucets.

Other attractions at Blanchard Spring are an amphitheater nestled against a towering bluff, a shelter cave that just might have been the home of the ill-fated cave explorer of long ago, and a small lake stocked with trout. The dam that forms Mirror Lake was built of native stone by the CCC. Not fully visible from the road, the dam—which forms enchanting waterfalls from the little lake—is worth the short walk, and is much better viewed from a small observation deck nearby.

Additionally, numerous hiking trails wind through the forest from Blanchard Spring. Several isolated, primitive campgrounds are nearby in very scenic surroundings in the Ozark National Forest (see the chart).

The Sylamore Scenic Byway

Well underway nationally is the establishment of the U.S. Forest Service's network of scenic byways. The Forest Service defines a scenic byway as "a road or highway, or segment thereof, which traverses a scenic corridor of outstanding aesthetic, cultural, historic, and/or interpretive forest values."

Many roads designated as National Forest Scenic Byways are in the Ozarks: Mt. Magazine Scenic Byway, Ozark Highlands Scenic Byway, Pig Trail Scenic Byway, and Arkansas Highway 7 Scenic Byway, all in the Ozark-St. Francis National Forests in Arkansas (phone 501-968-2345). In Missouri, the Glade Top Trail in Mark Twain National Forest also has been officially designated a Forest Service Scenic Byway (see Chapter 19).

In the present neighborhood, the Sylamore Scenic Byway, in Ozark National Forest, runs from Blanchard Springs Caverns along Forest Service Road 1110 for three miles to Arkansas State Hwy. 14, then 6.7 miles to Allison, Arkansas, and the intersection with Arkansas State Hwy. 5, then 16.8 miles north to Calico Rock, Arkansas, our next destination.

Practical Matters

Chapter 15 — Stone County

Checking Out	A Sampling	Phone
Lodging	Ozark Folk Center Lodge, Box 500, Mountain View, AR 72560; American Inn, Mountain View AR; Fiddlers' Inn Best Western, Mountain View AR; Dogwood Motel, Mountain View AR	(501) 269-3871 or (800) 243-FOLK (501) 269-3775 (501) 269-3332 (501) 269-3847
Bed & Breakfasts	The Commercial Hotel, Mountain View AR; The Inn at Mountain View AR; Owl Hollow Bed & Breakfast; Mountain View AR; Arkansas Ozarks Bed & Breakfast Reservation Service, Rt. 1, Box 38, Calico Rock AR 72519	(501) 269-4383 (501) 269-4200 (501) 269-8699 (501) 297-8764 or (501) 297-8211
Campgrounds	Blue Sky Travel Park, 2 Mi. N. Mountain View AR; Whitewater Travel Park, Mountain View AR; Jack's Fishing Resort, Mountain View AR; Ozark National Forest (May 15-Sept. 15)	(501) 269-8132 (501) 269-8047 (501) 585-2211 (501) 757-2211 or (800) 283-CAMP
Restaurants	Ozark Folk Center; Catfish House & Mtn. Music Dinner Theater; Hearthstone Bakery, NW Corner of Square; Rainbow Restaurant, SW Corner of Square; Leatherwoods Music Theater; (All Mountain View AR)	(501) 269-3139 (501) 269-3820 (501) 269-3297 (501) 269-8438 (501) 269-2100
Main Historical Attractions	Ozark Folk Center, Mountain View AR; The Old Mill, 1 Block West of Square; Dogwood Hollow Primitive Museum, Half Mile North of Folk Center Road on Hwy. 5 (All Mountain View AR)	(501) 269-3851 (501) 269-3354
Other Attractions	Blanchard Spring and Cavern, Ozark National Forest, P. O. Box 1, Mountain View AR 72560	(501) 725-2213
Outdoor Recreation	River Floating and Fishing: Custom Expeditions, Mountain View AR; Trout Fishing, Blanchard Spring, Ozark National Forest; Swimming and Tennis: Recreational Complex North of Square, Mountain View AR	(501) 269-8167 (501) 269-8400

Checking Out	A Sampling	Phone
Other Recreational Opportunities	Mountain Music Shows: Ozark Folk Center; White River Hoedown HCR 72, Box 44, Mountain View AR;	(501) 269-4161
	Jimmy Driftwood Barn, 2 Miles N. Mountain View AR;	(501) 269-8042
	Crafts and Antiques: Mountain View AR	
Where to Write for More Details	Tourist Information Center, 1/2 Block West of Courthouse Square in Mountain View AR;	(501) 269-8098
	Stone County Council on Tourism, P. O. Box 253, Mountain View AR 72560;	(501) 269-8098
	Mountain View Area Chamber of Commerce, P.O. Box 133, Mountain View AR 72560;	(501) 269-8068
	District Ranger, Ozark National Forest, P.O. Box 1, Mountain View AR 72560;	
	For Information About "A Fisherman's Guide to Public Access Facilities in Arkansas Counties" and a "Floater's Kit," write Arkansas Game & Fish Commission, Information & Education Div., 2 Natural Resources Dr., Little Rock AR 72205	(501) 223-6351

CHAPTER 16

Two Rivers

The White River was once a highway. The surrounding terrain was so rugged and the forest so dense it only made sense to travel by boat. Not only did settlers come into the country by boat, they neighbored, shipped their produce, did their shopping, and took their dead to cemeteries—by boat. When they did travel overland, on roads little more than footpaths, ferries crossed every river and sizable stream. Dozens of ferries served local neighborhoods along the river. As roads gradually improved, there were fewer ferries more widely spaced.

The Legendary White River

If the White River were anywhere but in the isolated Ozarks, its fame would rival that of the Mississippi, the Missouri, the Ohio, the Colorado. Geologists guesstimate that the White is about a hundred million years old. Although the river's straight-line distance from source to mouth is only 225 miles, almost eight hundred river miles snake from its elusive, multipronged source to its confluence with the Mississippi. Flowing north from near Boston, Arkansas, to the Missouri state line, the White makes a wide detour through three southern Missouri counties and then swoops back into Arkansas to race southeastward toward the Mississippi.

Along the way, its waters are swelled by those of the James, Kings, Buffalo, Little North Fork, Big North Fork, Black, Little Red, Cache, Current, Spring, Eleven Point, and Strawberry rivers—and many creeks and streams large and small. As a result, the periodic rampages

A tie yard similar to this one was at Sylamore, Arkansas, on White River. Railroad ties, floated down the river to the railhead, were "banked" in the yards awaiting shipment. At the time of rapid railroad expansion, white-oak ties from the Ozarks crisscrossed the country—some three thousand of them per mile of track. (Courtesy of Bittersweet, Inc.)

An Ozarks morning, particularly in the spring or fall, is often greeted by fog hovering over the rivers. When one climbs out of the river valley into the sunlight, he can look back—and down—on the river below and follow its meandering through the hills by the trail of mist that marks its course. In this case, two rivers—the White and its North Fork—come together at Norfork, Arkansas.

of the White are legendary in the Ozarks. Because its network of tributaries drains almost thirty thousand square miles (three-fourths of that total in the Ozarks) into a relatively narrow valley frequently constricted by gigantic bluffs, the river collects and funnels unbelievable amounts of water. Damaging floods that devastated homes, businesses, and crops one year out of three had, by the mid-1930s, reached epic proportions. Old-timers in the area still remember seeing the White brimming bluff-to-bluff between Cotter and Norfork. One has only to stand at the foot of those towering bluffs to gain some appreciation for the river's destructive power.

The most powerful miles of the White are now impeded by a chain of dams forming lakes Beaver, Table Rock, Taneycomo, and Bull Shoals. Norfork Lake is formed by a dam on the Big North Fork of the White, a few miles upstream of the confluence of the two rivers at Norfork, Arkansas. To this day, however, the gigantic White River Basin is capable of reasserting its mastery. Infamous Ozarks gully washers occasionally remind puny mankind and his dams that they are but minor impedances to the forces of nature: the river and its tributaries can yet overtax the flood control system.

About a river mile up the White from its confluence with the North Fork, near the town of Norfork, is the mouth of another major tributary, the Buffalo, which carries its own load of folklore to mingle with the White. The history and legends of the great rivers, coupled with the awesome natural beauty of the area in which they come together, make this region of the Ozarks—still relatively undisturbed—perhaps the most entrancing of all. The dawn mists over the rivers, the views of their lustrous ribbons winding through steep, forested hillsides, all contribute to the traveler's sensation that he has dropped down through a pass in the cloud-impaled hilltops into a pocket of the past.

It is possible that the Spanish explorer Hernando de Soto was the first white man to see *Rio Blanco*, but the French voyagers were probably first to make much use of the river highway. Like the Spaniards and the Indians, who called it *Unica* or *Niuskah*, meaning "white water," the early French explorers of the 1730s called the river *La Rivière au Blanc*. Most of the numerous foaming whitewater shoals that gave the river its name have since been obliterated by humankind, either to facilitate passage of steamboats or inundated by the lakes. Most shoals are remembered in place names only (Bull Shoals Lake, for example), but a few—including Wildcat Shoals—remain below the dam.

A few scholarly explorers came to the White River highway around 1820, and to a man they left us glowing descriptions of the river and the wildlife along its banks. The most famous of these, Henry Rowe Schoolcraft, was a geologist who came looking for evidence of minable metals. He wrote that the White River contained "the clearest and purest water possible," adding that when frozen the ice was as transparent as window glass. Leaving the Ozarks in January by canoeing down the White River, Schoolcraft noted in his journal that he floated swiftly "down one of the most beautiful and enchanting rivers . . . possessing the purity of crystal and the most imposing and delightful scenery."

Although Schoolcraft found few settlers in the river hills in 1819— and most of them more interested in furs than homes—the next several decades saw many newcomers poling their way up the river in pirogues (large dug-out canoes), keelboats, flatboats, and, eventually, steamboats.

Calico Rock

The Scenic Byway follows a high, piney ridge until it once more intersects the White at Calico Rock. One of the most pleasant and scenic drives in the Ozarks, Hwy. 5 from Sylamore to Calico Rock should be savored. Along the way, watch for the old Optimus General Store building on your left about nine miles south of Calico Rock. Virtually all that remains of a once-thriving community of a hundred families clustered around a tomato cannery (Optimus was a variety of tomato), the village, first called Forest Home, also boasted vineyards, a sawmill, and a post office. Weakened by the Depression, Optimus was finished by mass exodus during World War II.

At length the traveler rounds a curve, tops a hill, and is confronted by the "calico rock": a towering river bluff famous since the days of early explorers for its beauty and wonder. *Calico*, a multicolored fabric, was widely used to make both dresses and shirts. Schoolcraft described the bluff as ". . . a lofty smooth wall of stratified limestone rock, presenting a diversity of colour in squares, stripes, spots, or angles, all confusedly mixed and arranged according to the inimitable pencil of nature."

Early travelers referred often to the "calico rock" landmark on the river for some time before a town was established on the bluff. Indian artifacts have been found along the riverbanks. The first white men in the area were probably the Frenchmen who came upriver from New Orleans to harvest forty-foot cedar trees for boat timbers. Steamboats began landing at the calico rock in the 1830s, and gradually a settlement grew up around the landing.

Although the original face of the bluff was blasted away to make room for the railroad bed, Calico Rock kept its colorful name. And over the years since, nature has been busy repairing the damage. Once more multihued mineral stains are leaching onto the face of the bluff, and in a few more centuries the calico effect should be fully restored.

Peppersauce Alley (so called because of the "peppersauce," or moonshine, once available there) was the site of "the wagon yard" and the center of community activity. There the blacksmiths and the wheelwrights plied their crucial trades. When farmers came to town on their semi-annual (spring and fall) buying trips, they slept in their wagons at the wagon yard for the two or three days required to accomplish their trading and buying of supplies.

When the railroad arrived, it paid its workers in cash. In response to the change to a cash economy, the Bank of Calico Rock was organized and built up the hill from Calico Creek to avoid the frequent floods. That structure is now the city hall. Soon the more prosperous merchants followed the bank's lead and moved from the crowded steamboat landing to the top of the bluff. The Riverview Hotel, still a prominent building, was built in the 1920s to serve the railroad trade.

The area along Calico Creek, first site of the town's stores clustered around the steamboat landing, later became a warehouse district. Goods brought upriver by steamboat, and later the railroad, were stored here for distribution over a hundred-mile area. Here also were a cotton gin, an ice house, and an electric station that supplied electricity to Calico Rock long before it was available in neighboring towns.

After a disastrous fire that destroyed the business district in 1897, the town rebuilt, though it was frequently battered by floods. Then, on April 7, 1923, a spark from a passing locomotive ignited a fire between Main Street and Peppersauce Alley. In two hours more than twenty buildings were destroyed. The railroad paid for their restoration, and this time the buildings were constructed of brick and stone.

Built on three levels up the side of the hill from the river landing, the sixteen structures downtown—dating from 1902 to the 1930s—are on the National Register of Historic Places. So little has the business district changed over the last three-quarters of a century that movie companies have used it as a backdrop for stories set in the 1930s and earlier.

Visitors intrigued by history should not miss a tour of the old-time hardware store on the southeast corner of Main Street next to the railroad tracks.

Aside from the abundant visible history in Calico Rock, there is much else of interest. Docks on the river offer guided trout fishing and float trips and the rental of johnboats and canoes. The annual IRA Championship Rodeo is held here the second weekend in June. One of the largest IRA-sanctioned contests in Arkansas, the three-day rodeo attracts some of the top cowboys in the sport. In addition to two modern motels, this area offers some of the most charming bed-and-breakfast establishments in the region (see Practical Matters Chart following this chapter). Numerous resorts cluster around the nearby lakes.

For a view of the river and its bluffs missed by most visitors, drive west—up the steep hill—on Bluff Street. High atop the "City Bluff," where the pavement gives way to the red dirt and rocks of a country road, is a floor of multicolored stone—acres of solid rock that is cushiony underfoot—carpeted by gray-green lichens and velvet, viridian mosses and fringed by pines clinging to crevices, softening the edges of the magnificent cliff. At the Cedar Ridge Campground, make a left turn onto a narrow dirt road and edge out onto the calico rock itself. Go slowly; there is no stop sign and no barrier between you and the rim of that soaring bluff. But just beyond the campground there is room to safely park your car and for you to stand and look down on the river and its valley and outward to the surrounding hills.

Norfork

North of Calico Rock, Hwy. 5 continues to parallel the White River, mostly out of sight in the valley below. Then, just south of the town of Norfork—and the confluence there of the White with a major tributary, the Big North Fork—the highway begins to wind sharply and descend steeply, affording magnificent views of the surrounding hills and the river valley. Often, until dissipated by the morning sun, fog marks the rivers' routes and settles over the valley floor so that as the road descends into the cloud the traveler can not be sure where—or if—the rivers of mist become distinct from the rivers of water.

Although they do not attain a lofty elevation even here, the blue mountains seem almost alpine in their close-set beauty. Towering over the two rivers, the hills are often cloaked in clouds, which lends a magical quality to the scenery. And the little hamlet of Norfork, although it is one of the oldest settlements in Arkansas and the Ozarks, still seems to be perched tentatively on the river bank.

Once the Izard County seat, from the forming of the county in October 1825 until 1830, Norfork was first known as Liberty or Izard Court House. Named in honor of George Izard, governor of Arkansas Territory from 1825 to 1829, Izard County once contained most of north-central Arkansas; later counties were broken off as population increased. Mail arrived by canoe and horseback about every two weeks; later it came by steamboat.

Until the advent of powerful steamboats, water craft could not proceed upstream beyond this point. Shoals and rapids at the confluence of the White and the Big North Fork rendered the river impassable for any craft heavier than a flatboat. So at Norfork homeseekers disembarked from keelboats, piled their belongings into ox-drawn wagons, and creaked into the wilderness.

With the arrival of the steamboats in the mid-1800s, Liberty's importance increased. Loads of salt and other necessities were freighted from the river port through the hills as far as Springfield, Missouri, over the "Old Salt Trail," a route essentially followed by modern Highways 5 and 160. After the opening of military roads, Liberty slowly began to lose some of its prominence, but it remained a busy river port as long as the great steamboats plied the White.

When the railroad came, the town's name was changed to Devero in honor of a handsome French railroad engineer, Devereaux. Devero became the timber and tie center of the county; timber from all over the Buffalo, White, and North Fork River basins was floated downriver and shipped from the depot there. And the old settlement and popular trading center became a real town, finally incorporated in 1907 as Norfork, a contraction of North Fork, for the river. Many of the first businesses were false-front stores, like the Western boom towns. In 1927 the town still wore the air of earlier times, and a movie set in Civil War times, *Souls Aflame*, was filmed there. Later brick and stone buildings replaced the temporary stores. Much of the social life of Norfork centered around the railroad depot and the town pump.

Prior to construction, in the late 1930s, of a bridge across the North Fork, a current-powered ferry established in 1902 still served residents. After the building of the railroad, pedestrians often preferred to walk across the railroad bridge rather than wait for the ferry. Old-timers recall that it was especially exciting on the tracks during flood time when the murky waters lapped over the railroad ties and the ferry could not run.

Norfork boomed briefly in the 1940s during the building of Norfork Dam a few miles upstream, then returned to the peaceful routine established soon after the turn of the nineteenth century.

Wolf House: A Log Mansion

When the interior of the Arkansas Ozarks was being settled by pioneers who arrived mostly by water, the confluence of two major rivers—the White and the Big North Fork—was an extremely strategic location. And because the land on its southern shore had been set aside for Indians removed from east of the Mississippi, the White River represented the far edge of civilization in the early 1800s.

Evidence suggests that the Wolf family came west because Jacob Wolf had been appointed agent for the Indians. They established a community, first known as Izard Court House and then Liberty, along the north shore of the White River soon after the turn of the nineteenth century.

With the help of his slaves and the Indians, Major Wolf (he acquired his title, which he used throughout the remainder of his life, on De-

At a time when most other log cabins were little more than huts with dirt floors, Major Wolf's home, at Norfork, Arkansas, was two-storied and complete with hand-sawn plank flooring. The logs were dovetailed for a weather-proof fit; fireplaces formed from handmade and sun-dried bricks warmed all four rooms. Because the cabin was so grand for its time and place, the first Mrs. Wolf always referred to her home as "the mansion." The building is considered to be the oldest log structure still standing in Arkansas.

The Ozark Queen was the last steamboat to operate regularly on the Upper White River. She was 135 feet long, had a thirty-foot beam, and could run on only twelve inches of water "light," or without a load. Her schedule called for two weekly trips from Batesville to Buffalo City and beyond. She made her last trip in June 1903. (Courtesy of State Historical Society of Missouri)

cember 3, 1825, when he was commissioned a major in the Seventh Regiment of the Arkansas Territorial Militia) built a log home near the confluence of the two rivers. So well did they build that the structure still stands today, overlooking much the same view.

The yellow pine logs for the building—and the several others that once formed Wolf's complex on this site—were cut in the surrounding hills. Lime for the fireplace and foundation mortar and for chinking between the logs was obtained by grinding the shells of mussels found in the rivers. A skillful blacksmith, Major Wolf himself is thought to have fashioned the door hinges and square-headed nails for the building.

While most other log cabins in the region were little more than huts with dirt floors, Major Wolf's log home was two-storied and complete with hand-sawn plank flooring. The logs were dovetailed for a weatherproof fit; roof rafters were fastened with sturdy wooden pegs. Fireplaces formed from handmade and sun-dried bricks warmed all four rooms. Because the building was so grand for its time and place, the first Mrs. Wolf always referred to her home as "the mansion."

Just exactly when the log mansion was constructed is not certain, but the Department of Anthropology at the University of Arkansas has concluded that the house was built during the fall and winter of 1827 and 1828 and no earlier, though it might have been later. In any event, Wolf House is believed to be the oldest log structure still standing in Arkansas.

Widowed twice, Major Wolf and his three wives raised sixteen children in the house, and it was the scene of cotillions, weddings, an occasional church service and, no doubt, funerals. One of the upstairs rooms served as Izard County's courthouse while the other was occupied by the county clerk, a brother of Sam Houston of Texas fame, who visited the house, as did Davy Crockett, many judges, governors, clergymen, trappers, and Indians. From very early on, the house also served the developing territory as post office. In 1844 the name of the post office was changed to North Fork and Wolf was appointed postmaster.

It was Major Wolf's son, William, who was master of the first steamboat to make its way up the White as far as its confluence with the North Fork. The arrival of steamboats on the White River ushered in a new era of trade with ports downriver and a measure of prosperity for the settlers.

Major Wolf was seventy-five years old when the Civil War began. In the early summer of 1861 when a Union officer attempted to commandeer the house for his headquarters, the Major beat him with his cane. Imprisoned at Batesville, Wolf was released a year later because his health had failed. He died on January 1, 1863.

The location of his grave is a mystery. Although the whereabouts of the Wolf family cemetery is known and graves have been found dating back to 1823, the Major's is not among them. It is recorded that a deep snow blanketed the ground on the day of his death, and because of the war, there were few men to help with the burial. It is probable that his body was not taken to the cemetery for interment.

Like all antebellum structures, Wolf House has its Civil War ghost. Local legend holds that for years the steps of the house were stained by the blood of a Confederate soldier killed there. The moans and strange noises within the old building are believed by some to be manifestations of his still-suffering spirit.

When Major Wolf's estate was settled, Confederate currency was accepted in payment. The ravages of war completed the ruin and disbursement of the Wolf holdings. Thereafter a store operated in the Wolf House for a time. A grandson of the major re-acquired the house from 1900 to 1910, but it soon passed out of the family again. With the coming of the railroad, Wolf House served as a kitchen to prepare meals for railroad employees. Converted later to a two-family apartment, its dogtrot, or breezeway, was enclosed to make another room. During the Depression the stately old house seriously deteriorated almost to the point of no return.

Just in time the citizens of Norfork decided they could not let this important part of their heritage slip away. The town purchased the property and, with the aid of the National Youth Administration (NYA), a Depression-era job program, renovated the building as a memorial to Jacob Wolf and opened a museum with volunteer help and local contributions.

Although the front of the house had originally faced the river (the "highway" of pioneer Norfork), the "back" of the house became the front when the modern highway was constructed behind it in 1937. A bronze marker was erected in front of the house by the Arkansas Centennial Association in June of that year, on the same day that the first local bridge over the North Fork River was dedicated.

In the mid-1960s, Wolf House was adopted by the Elna M. Smith Foundation of Eureka Springs, who took over the complete restoration of the building. They restored the original lines to the house, landscaped the yards, and completely furnished the rooms with authentic period pieces. It is believed that handmade bricks still form the upper part of the right chimney.

The Wolf House Memorial has been named to the National Register of Historic Places and is one of Arkansas' most significant historical structures. Once again, the city of Norfork and a committee of volunteers has assumed management of the building and its museum of pioneer settlement. The only known photograph of Major Wolf hangs in the house, and it is furnished with more than four hundred items dating from the 1700s. Tours are offered for a nominal fee from April to October; tickets are available at the craft shop next door.

Without question the currents of the past still swirl around Wolf House, just as do the mists on White River. One can stand on the lawn below the house, out of sight of the highway at its door and, although the noises of traffic are clearly audible, gaze across the river and imagine the plumes of smoke rising from the cooking fires of the Indians in their village. If you listen very closely, you may yet hear an echo from the river bluff—the clang of Major Wolf's anvil, the bell of a steamboat laboring upriver, or the excited shout of the children and slaves hurrying to the landing.

Steamboatin' on the White

The date of William Wolf's arrival at Norfork with the first steamboat is not known. But by the mid-1840s, steamboats unloaded cargoes at Dubuque, two miles below the Missouri-Arkansas state line. From then on until completion of the railroad after the turn of the twentieth century, steamboats plied the Upper White River from late fall, when the river rose to a reasonable depth, and continued throughout the spring until the summer drought lowered the water level.

Special shallow-draft "packets" were designed for White River navigation. People joked that Arkansas steamboats would run anywhere that the ground was a little damp. The boats were powered by steam boilers fired by wood, preferably pine knots. Wood yards were located at all landings and at several points in between. The sternwheeler (paddlewheel at the rear) had more power and speed, but the sidewheeler (paddlewheel on the side) could turn more quickly, making navigation easier.

Steamboating was not without dangers: snags, sandbars, shoals, and boiler explosions were some of the reasons that riverboats averaged only about five years afloat. And the swift current, rapid fluctuation in water level, and rocky shoals and chutes of the White River—where even the Indians had portaged their canoes—offered some of the greatest challenges for riverboat crews. But daring men rose to the challenge, pushing farther upstream in quest of trade and adventure. Often the boats traveled at night, sparks from their stacks showering into the darkness and reflecting on the water like fireworks.

The safety of the boat—and that of its cargo—depended upon the pilot's knowledge of the river. Also called "Captain," the pilot had to know every shoal, snag, and rock by heart. Buffalo, Wildcat, and Bull Shoals were especially dangerous, testing every pilot's skill. The shoals near the mouth of Bruce Creek were called Trammell's Chute because Captain "Rasp" Trammell, unlike the other pilots, went through the shoals, not around it. It is said that he dared this feat to regain the respect he had lost from his fellow Confederates when he agreed to pilot Federal boats on the Mississippi rather than suffer in the infamous Gratiot Street Prison in St. Louis.

The first recorded channel work on the White was in 1842 when a commercial boater, John Campbell of Springfield, cleared Buffalo Shoals of obstacles at his own expense. In 1851 the Missouri Legislature appropriated eight thousand dollars to help clear channels in other shoal areas. By 1852 steamboats ascended the river as far as Forsyth, though crews sometimes had to work them over the shoals using a donkey engine on the boat to winch lines ferried forward by rowboats and secured to trees or rocks. By 1858 paddlewheelers were sometimes able to go as far north as the mouth of the James, directly south of Springfield.

Over the years of struggle, the river claimed its share of victories. Wrecked hulks of steamboats and flatboats marked the watercourse. In addition to the physical danger to the steamers, there was always the risk of being stranded upriver by the capricious river. One such unfortunate was the *Mary M. Patterson*, stranded at Forsyth by low water from April 1860 to February 1861. A local historian has reported that when this happened, the captain and his crew might rent a field, plant a potato crop, harvest it before the fall rains came, then return downriver with their harvest.

Farmers along the river shipped bacon, live hogs, corn, cotton, and other products of their riverbottom farms and imported such necessities as salt, gunpowder, coffee, calico, numerous articles of hardware (including pots, pans, and knives), drugs, saddles, mill machinery, and other articles more difficult or impossible to supply for themselves. Sometimes the locals bartered for these manufactured goods with hides, lumber, or garden produce. Many earned extra income by cutting wood and stacking it near the landing to fire the steamboat's boilers. When the boat whistled its approach, the farmer dropped what he was doing and hurried to the landing to help load the wood.

Other boats traveling on the White River were the *Mary L. Daugherty*, the *Lady Boone*, the *Woodson*, the *Woodbury*, the *Myrtle*, the *Tycoon*, the *Carrier*, the *Alberta*, the *Quickstep*, and the *Joe Wheeler*. Several boats held mail contracts, including the *Jesse Lazear* and the *Monongahela Belle*. Most could land anywhere a gangplank of two or three boards could be laid down. Since everything had to be loaded and unloaded manually, steep river banks were avoided whenever possible. Every boat had scheduled stops; the trip from Batesville to McBee's Landing, one hundred river miles, took twenty-four hours; the return trip, only twelve.

Steamboat traffic on the White River was virtually halted by the Civil War. But the heyday of steamboats on the river occurred after the war—until a new era of steam was ushered in on the railroad. The last boat to operate regularly on the Upper White River was the *Ozark Queen*. She was 135 feet long, had a thirty-foot beam, and could run on only twelve inches of water "light," or without a load. Her schedule called for two weekly trips from Batesville to Buffalo City and beyond. In April 1903 Capt. Charles B. Woodbury took her as far upriver as Oakland and returned with a cargo of 165 bales of cotton, 135 sacks of wheat and 475 sacks of cotton seed. She made her last trip in June 1903.

The last recorded steamboat on the White River was the *Huff* which came upriver in January 1913 for a load of staves. Her coming created quite a stir, for by then the whistle of a steamboat was only a memory about to fade into history. In 1924 a thirty-gallon keg of whiskey was found in a sandbar several miles above Cotter. Local legend says that just after the Civil War a steamboat captain had taken on a load of several hundred kegs of bootleg liquor. When federal officers got on his trail, he unloaded at Cotter and buried his cargo in the sand. Later he dug it up and took it upriver to Missouri, where it was sold. The keg that was found years later evidently had been overlooked. As late as the 1950s, a long-buried steamboat anchor surfaced near the Wildcat Shoals.

Another reminder of the bygone age of steamboats is moored at Jacksonport State Park near Newport, on the outer fringes of the southeast Ozarks. There an upriver packet sternwheeler, the *Mary Woods No. 2*, is now a riverboat museum, which visitors board by walking a gangplank. The entrance room on the second level of the vessel contains riverboat history in photos, maps, bells, and other artifacts from old steamers. Three small staterooms are furnished as though in use by nineteenth-century travelers. And, up on top, the pilot house is completely original, with its well-worn captain's bench and the massive nine-foot maple pilot's wheel.

(Jacksonport State Park is located just off Arkansas Hwy. 69 three miles north of Newport. Also there is the 1869 Jackson County Museum, with exhibits depicting every historic era, campgrounds, a picnic area, and access to the Lower White River.)

River Parks

For a close-up view of the confluence of the legendary White and North Fork Rivers—and a chance to rub shoulders with the spirits of the past that have surely congregated at the historic spot—turn left (west) for a very short distance on a small unpaved road just north of

Wolf House. The Arkansas Game and Fish Commission (AGFC) has provided a small park there that affords access to both rivers. If the rivers are high, the park may be partially flooded.

An even more pleasant park with river access is River Ridge Fishermen's Park, also an AGFC project. About a mile off Hwy. 5, the small park offers easy access to the North Fork River for handicapped fishermen. To reach the park, turn right (east) soon after crossing the bridge over the North Fork at the town of Norfork. Watch for the sign; it is easy to spot. The access road is paved and winds under a high bluff of the North Fork River.

Fishing the Modern White and North Fork Rivers

Today both the White and North Fork rivers—and their bridles of manmade lakes—are still "delightfully scenic." World famous for their fishing, the lakes figure prominently in all bass records. But newcomers are sometimes surprised to learn that the rivers above and below the dams constitute a world-class trout fishery. And both are equally famous as float fishing streams—and remain two of the world's most beautiful rivers. Thanks to their rocky beds and mostly forested watersheds, the rivers are still as Schoolcraft found them: ". . . Our canoe often seemed as if suspended in the air, such is the remarkable transparency of the water."

The Arkansas Game and Fish Commission says, "Probably more rainbow trout are caught here [in the White] each year than in any other trout stream in America." The Commission stocks hundreds of thousands of rainbows in the river annually, and more than 90 percent of them are caught each year by anglers who come here from the world over. The river boasts the Arkansas state record. The North Fork, in the few miles below its dam, is a record-fish producer too.

While fly fishermen can wade the rivers when generators at the dams are shut down, the water may fluctuate ten feet or more several times in a twenty-four-hour period. As a result, float fishing is preferred, and numerous resorts and docks offer guided johnboat trout floats and rental canoes (see the Practical Matters Charts for Chapters 16 and 17).

The Norfork National Fish Hatchery, said to be larger than any other facility of its kind in the country, is located near the base of Norfork Dam (via Hwys. 5 and 177) and is itself an interesting stop for area visitors. More than 2.2 million trout, of several species, are produced annually for stocking the rivers. The overlook at the dam affords spectacular scenic views of the area, as well as delightful picnicking and camping.

Practical Matters

Chapter 16 — Calico Rock

Checking Out	A Sampling	Phone
Lodging	Wiseman's Motel, Box 546, Calico Rock AR 72519;	(501) 297-3733
	Jenkins Motel, Hwy. 56, Box 303, Calico Rock AR	(501) 297-3715
Bed & Breakfasts	Arkansas Ozarks Bed & Breakfast & Reservation Service, Rt. 1, Box 38, Calico Rock AR 72519: Includes Log Cabins, 1920s Hotel, Riverview Lodges, With Advance Reservations	(501) 297-8211 or (501) 297-8764
Campgrounds	Cedar Ridge R.V. Park, Chesmond Rd., P. O. Box 236, Calico Rock AR 72519	(501) 297-4282
Restaurants	Edna's Steak House, Calico Rock AR 72519;	(501) 287-3999
	The Country Inn, Calico Rock AR	(501) 297-8595
Main Historical Attractions	Calico Rock Hardware and The Landing, Historic Main Street, Calico Rock AR; Entire Downtown Business District, Calico Rock AR	(501) 297-8211 or (501) 297-8764
Outdoor Recreation	Fishing & Floating: Jenkins Fishing Service, Box 303, Calico Rock AR 72519;	(501) 297-8181
	Chesmond Boat Dock, Box 545, Calico Rock AR;	(501) 297-8780
	Calico Rock Boat Dock, P.O. Box 6, Calico Rock AR 72519;	(501) 297-8735
	Gene's Trout Dock, Rt. 3, Box 348, Mountain Home AR 72653	(501) 499-5381
Other Recreational Opportunities	Rodeo, Canoe Races, Riverside Festival: Contact Chamber of Commerce, Calico Rock AR	
Where to Write for More Details	Calico Rock Chamber of Commerce, P. O. Box 245, Calico Rock AR 72519;	(501) 297-8868
	For Information About "A Fisherman's Guide to Public Access Facilities in Arkansas Counties" and a "Floater's Kit," write Arkansas Game & Fish Commission, Information & Education Div., 2 Natural Resources Dr., Little Rock AR 72205;	(501) 223-6341
	Mary Woods No. 2: Newport Area Chamber of Commerce, P. O. Box 518, Newport AR 72112; and Jacksonport State Park, P. O. Box 8, Jacksonport AR 72075	(501) 523-2143

At the site of a former riverport, Buffalo City, Arkansas, and towering Stair Bluff, a boat ramp furnished by the Arkansas Game and Fish Commission draws trout fishermen to the White River below Bull Shoals Dam. Float trip outfitters also use the boat ramp, and occasionally one can be seen serving lunch to his clients here in the shadow of history. About a mile downstream is the confluence of the White and the Buffalo.

CHAPTER 17

Twin Lakes

Although we can no longer—even in a boat—trace the exact routes of the steamboats above the Bull Shoals and Norfork dams, some things have not changed. The crests of bluffs chiseled over the eons by the fast, free-running rivers still look down on blue-crystal waters. The reflections of hilltops that rose four hundred feet or more above the ancient river beds still shimmer on the waters of the lakes.

The lakes do not look "manmade"; a casual observer might easily think that Mother Nature herself poured them among the hills. There is so little development along their shores—and so few crowds —that one can often boat for miles without encountering another human. But it is not unusual to see a bald eagle, some wading cranes, often a few deer, or the Canada geese who make the area their permanent home. Because the shoreline is public land, you can camp, fish, and hunt right from your boat. Besides deer, wild turkeys abound, as do quail, rabbits, and both red and gray squirrels. In the fall, duck blinds are seen on shallow points. And since there is no closed season on fishing—and the lakes rarely freeze—winter fishermen are a common sight. Best of all, surrounding both lakes is Ozarks scenery: oak-and-hickory-forested hills punctuated by dramatic peaks, bald knobs, cedar glades, and canyonlike hollows. Reflecting the Ozarkers' penchant for naming, most areas of the lakes are still known by the charming cognomens bestowed by the pioneers upon the creeks and rivers that feed them—Cow Pen Hollow, Gunnel Fork, Peter Cave Hollow, Promised Land, Music Creek, Buzzard Roost—as keepsakes of the past.

And sometimes, when there is a certain glint of sunlight, or under a full moon, it almost seems as if the lakes are haunted: by a flooded fur outpost dating back to the 1700s . . . by a White River ferry that drowned a boatload of Civil War soldiers and their horses . . . and by a submerged hilltop known as "the Saddle" that seeks revenge by ravaging the boat motors of the unwary.

Lake Norfork

Heading north of the town of Norfork, Hwy. 5 roughly parallels the route of historic Old Salt Road. To visit the Norfork Dam and the Federal Trout Hatchery, turn right (east) on Hwy. 177 at Salesville. John and Peggy Sales, the first settlers at Salesville, came from the Carolinas prior to 1860 in an ox-drawn covered wagon. Freighters on the Old Salt Road camped near the Sales's double log cabin and relished the meals Peggy cooked for them—including her great hoops of tangy, yellow cheese that became famous all over northern Arkansas and southern Missouri.

First and smallest of the "Twin Lakes," Norfork was formed by a dam across the North Fork River about four miles upstream from its confluence with the White at Norfork. Constructed during World War II with old-fashioned methods, the dam cost the lives of seven men.

In contrast to the fate of potential dam projects in the region in recent decades, many area residents welcomed the Norfork Dam with open arms. To the poverty-stricken county still reeling from the Depression, the dam's disadvantages were far outweighed by the desperate need for jobs and the expected much-needed boost to the economy. A month before the contract for the dam was let, the Arkansas State Employment Service opened an office near the site. One thousand people—from a sparsely settled county—applied for work the first week.

Baxter County was changed forever. A local writer recorded, "The building of Norfork Dam was our first mass encounter with the outside world—including the gaudy, bright-light world of dance halls, scantily clad show girls, and gamblers." Not everyone loved the results, but few were willing to give up the new measure of prosperity that had swept over the region.

So enamored were the locals that the construction site became a favorite sightseeing spot. People from all over the area delighted in driving by the dam on Sunday afternoon to see how the work was progressing. A high catwalk allowed spectators to overlook the work being done on the valley floor.

But in January 1942, shortly after the attack on Pearl Harbor, the site was closed to the public due to the fear of sabotage. A high wire fence sealed off the area, while twelve armed guards constantly patrolled the perimeter. The catwalk was closed. Because the dam and its potential for generating hydroelectric power was considered vital to the war effort, work progressed twenty-four hours a day under tight security. Floodlights—borrowed from Hollywood—turned night into day.

On June 2, 1944, the completed dam was opened to the public. By April 1947, *Arkansas Sportsman* magazine declared that Lake Norfork and Mountain Home were "fast becoming nationally famous." In cooperation with the newly formed Lake Norfork Association, the Mountain Home Chamber of Commerce sponsored a booth at the 1948 Chicago Sport Show. And the world began to come to Baxter County. That same year, U.S. Hwy. 62 was finally paved; state roads waited until later, though one or two are still gravel, as are most county roads.

East of Mountain Home the town of Henderson, which once stood on the west bank of the North Fork River, had been inundated by the lake. Henderson was established in the 1880s and named for one of the county's earliest practicing physicians who rode horseback many miles to reach patients' homes.

In 1902 Frank Smith, who had come to the area in 1863, began operating a current-powered ferry across the river at Henderson. He and his five sons provided this service for the next thirty-two years in good weather or bad, day or night. In the 1920s vehicles began to join horses and wagons on the ferry and increasing traffic led to the building of a bridge across the river; it opened, amid local jubilation, on January 1, 1935.

But on February 19, 1944, the new bridge disappeared beneath the rising waters of Norfork Lake. It is said that the old bridge can still be seen under the water when conditions are right.

In its place, in September of 1943, the "Arkansas Navy" instituted a new ferry—and another to serve Hwy. 101 heading north toward Missouri. The ferries served the two highways until finally replaced by bridges in 1983. By that time, the ferries carried heavy traffic around the clock, countless visitors to the area as well as locals. While the visitors, forced to endure the long wait only once, did not seem to mind, able to enjoy the ferries as local color, residents were thoroughly out of patience with the long lines and interminable delays by the time the bridges finally opened.

Now a new community named Henderson is growing on the east side of Lake Norfork. And the old ferries are now excursion boats that tour the lake for the enjoyment of visitors (see the Practical Matters Chart following this chapter).

Overlooking the old ferry landings and both the new bridges is the Panther Bay Corps of Engineers park and campground. The big park offers the lakeshore, a shady picnic area with rest rooms, and spec-

For forty years, these tug boats powered the Hwy. 62 ferry across Norfork Lake at Henderson, Arkansas. With the opening of a new bridge across the lake in 1983, the ferry boat was reincarnated as a lake excursion boat for "Norfork Ferry Tours."

The "Rainbow Bridge," the first highway bridge across the White River at Cotter, Arkansas, was dedicated in November 1930. A toll was charged until April 1938; many who could not afford the change for the toll continued to use the ferry to cross the river. Still in use on the business route (Hwy. 62B) through Cotter, the bridge was listed on the National Register of Historic Places in 1990. (Photo by Jim Reed)

tacular views of the lake. Accessible from either Hwy. 101 or Hwy. 62 East, Panther Bay is one of many such parks on the shores of Norfork Lake.

Mountain Home

Driving into Mountain Home on Hwy. 5 from Salesville, you will cross one of the several branches in the Ozarks of the infamous Trail of Tears. It followed the route of the first white man's trail, dating to about 1800, from east to west across Baxter County. A historical marker recalls the crossing, but the marker itself has apparently been forgotten. It is almost lost amid high weeds and is poorly marked, almost impossible to find.

The town was first called Rapp's Barren (pronounced *Barn*), for 1839 settler "Rapp" Talburt in an area barren of trees. Talburt was the area's first—and probably the largest—landholder. A preacher, and thus no doubt educated, he was certain to be the area's leading citizen. Local legend explains the name change: Another early settler, Col. Orrin L. Dodd, came into the area in the early 1850s and developed a plantation along the White River. Accompanied by his slaves, Dodd traveled back and forth, via steamboats on White River, between his place at Rapp's Barren and his older home near Augusta. Along the way Dodd's slaves boasted to others about their "sweet mountain home." When the post office was established in 1857, its name was officially listed as Mountain Home.

Incorporated in 1888, the town literally grew up around a school— the Male and Female Academy—that was opened in 1853 on land donated by Colonel Dodd. And, like virtually all other Ozarks towns, Mountain Home was leveled during the Civil War. But by 1868 some homes had been rebuilt, businesses resumed, and the academy reopened in a new building to replace the one burned in the war.

Mountain Home began to enjoy electricity in the early 1920s, but the power was on only at night. Operation of the generator was not worthwhile during daylight hours due to insufficient demand. Lights came on at dusk and went off at 11:00 P.M.—because "all the good people of the town were in bed by that time." When area women acquired electric irons and demanded power for them in the daytime, the operator of the "light plant" agreed to run the generator for one afternoon a week so the women could do their ironing.

With a population of only a few hundred prior to the construction of the Norfork and Bull Shoals Dams—and its new position serving the twin lakes—Mountain Home was a pleasant little town dozing in the sun. Most of the streets were dirt or gravel, livestock roamed the town at will (the countryside was still open range), and drought-stricken agriculture and a few struggling mining operations were the extent of industry.

The lakes changed everything. Mountain Home's population has doubled and redoubled and doubled again, until it now stands at almost nine thousand within the city limits alone. The town's trade area is huge, and much of the public it serves is nestled around the shores of the sprawling lakes and lining the rivers. Burgeoning traffic in the early 1980s—especially with the opening of the new bridges at Henderson—required the widening of Hwy. 62 to four lanes. Somehow, however, Mountain Home manages to avoid most of the evils that usually befall rapid development. The town is clean, modern, even progressive. Yet there remains—one suspects because its residents demand it—an air of yesteryear, a certain lingering essence of that sleepy little town dozing in the sun.

Nowadays "I love my Mountain Home" and "I love the whole dam area" bumper stickers adorn almost every car in and around Mountain Home. Well over half of the county's residents have come here from somewhere else, and a great many are retirees, drawn by the area's pleasant climate—especially the milder winters, relatively lower living expenses, the beautiful surroundings, and the unlimited opportunities for outdoors recreation on the lakes and rivers and in the forests. The huge influx of newcomers is gradually taking over government and policy making, at least behind the scenes.

Mountain Home is county seat of Baxter County, organized in March 1873, and named for Elisha Baxter, an Arkansas governor whose election sparked a war. Baxter's campaign had been marked by intensely heated political rivalry. Supporters of his opponent, Rev. Joseph Brooks, insisted the election was rigged and forcibly removed Baxter from the governor's chair in April 1874. Partisans on both sides armed themselves and fought the Brooks-Baxter War; estimates of the dead stand at two hundred. No doubt there would have been more deaths had not President U. S. Grant ordered Brooks's faction to put down their arms. Baxter served out his term, but he was the last Republican governor of Arkansas until Winthrop Rockefeller in 1966.

Highways 5 and 62 pass immediately in front of the Baxter County Courthouse in Mountain Home. In its lobby are memorabilia of the area, including two large murals depicting Bull Shoals and Norfork Lakes and a commemorative placque to the *U.S.S. Maine,* sunk during the Spanish-America War in 1898, made from the ship's metal. Frequently "an avenue of flags" waves in Mountain Home: virtually every light pole and store around the square flies a large American flag—a beautiful and memorable sight.

The Railroad Town of Cotter

With Bull Shoals Lake as the next major destination, the traveler has a choice of two routes. One is to follow Hwy. 5 north to Hwy. 178, turn left (west) to the town of Bull Shoals, site of the dam and a good look at the lake.

A better, more scenic route—and one that will avoid backtracking and afford a glimpse of much more history—is via Cotter, west on Hwy. 62 from Mountain Home, thence to Flippin and north on Hwy. 178 to Bull Shoals.

On the way to Cotter, the little town of Gassville on Hwy. 62 is the home of the Ozark Emporium. An outlet for the crafts of area residents, it features wind chimes, handwoven baskets, wooden toys, blown glass, and woodcarvings—especially those of the famous Ozarks woodcarver, hillman Junior Cobb.

Among Cobb's most favored work are the faces of "woodland spirits" carved in relief on pieces of driftwood. No two are alike, and all have a strange mystical quality, with eyes that seem to follow you. Cobb's carvings are found at several other craft outlets in the Ozarks, and one can even stop by his northern Baxter County home, a ramshackle building in a constant state of reconstruction, on Hwy. 5 just south of the Missouri state line. A hand-lettered sign marks its location.

From Gassville, Hwy. 62 leads on toward Cotter, but be careful to exit the new portion of the highway, which bypasses Cotter and crosses the river on a new bridge, to Hwy. 62B, the "business route" that leads into town.

Two miles downriver from McBee's Landing (on the Marion County side of White river) and a busy river port in steamboat days, Cotter was first settled in 1868 and named Lake's Ferry (or Landing) in 1883. A. C. Lake established the ferry in the early 1880s, and it continued to serve the settlement until 1930, when a bridge was constructed over the White. For many years the community held an annual picnic at a big spring where Indians had once camped. Early industries in Cotter were a cotton gin, a sawmill, a button factory—operated from a flatboat—that cut pearl buttons out of the mussel shells "musselled" from White River, and tie and cedar yards. Most were wiped out during the monstrous flood of 1927 and never rebuilt.

In 1900 the White River steamboats had begun bringing a new cargo upriver: the supplies, equipment, and materials for the building of a railroad. (At first part of the St. Louis, Iron Mountain & Southern, it was later the White River Line of the Missouri Pacific system.) The 240-mile line between Carthage, Missouri, and Batesville, Arkansas, was put into service on January 21, 1906. Ninety-seven of those miles had been blasted, tunneled, and bridged through the rugged mountains between Cotter, Arkansas, and Crane, Missouri, at a cost of a hundred thousand dollars per mile, four times the then-normal railroad-building cost.

When the line first opened, apparently, no one realized the complete extent to which railroads would replace steamboats, for the railroad bridge at Cotter was built so that it could swing to allow the passage of the boats. The turntable was used only once, however, when the steamer *Huff* came upriver after a load of staves in 1913. The trains provided a more economical, more reliable, more efficient, and more expedient service. The exploitation of the minerals and timber, and the timely marketing of farm produce, demanded no less.

Another casualty of the railroad's coming was the Interstate Stage Coach Line from West Plains, Missouri, to Mountain Home and Yellville. The stage line lost to the railroad its contract to carry mail.

On the other hand, the towns and counties served by the railroads often grew and more or less prospered. In addition to improved communication and freight service, the railroads were often instrumental in promoting the towns they served and advertised heavily for passengers. In earlier days, some of the first rail lines to reach the region had even played pivotal roles in recruiting and transporting immigrants to the Ozarks. Those towns bypassed by the tracks often withered and died. Of course, there is a measure of paradox in that many of the Ozarks railroads themselves have long since perished, their tracks taken up and roadbeds put to other uses.

The railroad developed the site of Lake's Landing as a division point—a convenient midway site between Newport, Arkansas, and Carthage, Missouri. Incorporated in 1904, the town was named Cotter for one of the civil engineers on the project.

A division point was the place on the rail line where eight-hour shifts could change and the steam locomotives could be serviced. The railroad brought more than tracks to Cotter; with it came a depot, a railroad bridge over the White, a tunnel through a mountain on the far side of the river, a roundhouse for the steam engines, and hotels and theaters and people. Completed in October 1906, Cotter is said to have resembled a gold rush town of the Old West.

After searching unsuccessfully up and down the White and Buffalo Rivers for a pass through the hills, the railroad engineers concluded that the only way to leave the river was to bridge it, then tunnel through the opposite mountain. A local historian says that, "One wily old-timer took a look at the rails ending abruptly at the river bluff, then at the hole yawning in the mountain across the river and said, 'Well, you might make me believe that with a good running start the train can jump the river, but you'll never make me believe that it'll hit that hole every time.' "

Cotter was the center of other activity, as well. Scaling gangs worked along the bluffs constantly in order to keep falling rocks off the train tracks. Work trains kept the tracks, bridges, and trestles in good repair. The roundhouse, continually besieged by floods, needed constant attention. Enterprising farmers added extra money to the family income by hacking ties to replace the worn ones. Cedar logs—destined for the pencil factory—were cut from the hills and floated down the river in great rafts to the cedar yards at Cotter.

Mary Ann Messick recalls that "a favorite Sunday afternoon pastime was going to Cotter to watch the trains come in. It didn't matter whether you had anybody arriving or not." When the first highway bridge across the river at Cotter was dedicated in November 1930, four thousand people attended. To help defray the cost of the bridge, a toll was charged until April 1938. Many who could not afford the change for the toll continued to use the ferry. Although the span has recently been replaced by a new one just upriver, the beautiful rainbow arches of the old bridge are far more aesthetically pleasing than the modern structure, which is certainly faster and safer. Still in use on the business route through Cotter, the first bridge was designated a National Historic Civil Engineering Landmark in 1986. In 1990 it was listed on the National Register of Historic Places.

With the conversion of the railroad to diesel locomotives, the roundhouse was no longer needed. The passenger trains stopped running in 1960. Cotter seemed destined to die a slow death.

But the White River began to enjoy a new popularity as a trout stream, and the world again began coming to Cotter. Now the little town calls itself "The Trout Capital of the World," and with some justification, since record trout have been caught in the river nearby. Trout docks, river guides, and johnboat outfitters serve a steady stream of visitors. And many are returning to stay. Retirees have found permanent homes in Cotter's picturesque residential areas on the high river bluff.

The downtown area seems little changed from Cotter's heyday; most buildings are of native stone. At City Hall on McClean Street there is a collection of historical pictures and articles highlighting area events.

Top O' The Ozarks

Leave Cotter on Hwy. 62 and drive a couple of more miles west to Flippin. There turn right (north) on Hwy. 178 for a scenic drive over a new highway (which generally follows an old freighters' road) to the town and the lake sharing the name of Bull Shoals, for the shoals on the river at the foot of Bull Mountain.

The town of Bull Shoals was settled prior to the Civil War and known as Newton Flat. In 1945, when he learned that Bull Shoals Lake was planned, land developer C. S. Woods bought the town, advertised it as resort property, paid for paving three miles of Hwy. 178, and established a post office, Bull Shoals, at the base of Bull Mountain.

Thanks to its strategic position near the Bull Shoals dam, the lake, and the White River below the dam, the town of Bull Shoals is very popular with retirees. The pleasant little village is also the site of a huge marina, Bull Shoals Boat Dock, where visitors can rent virtually any kind of water craft, from paddleboats to houseboats.

On top of Bull Mountain, visible for miles, is the Top O' The Ozarks Tower. An elevator lifts visitors to an observation deck well above the treetops for a panoramic view of the dam, the lake, the river, the town of Bull Shoals, and the surrounding hills. If you are squeamish about heights, at least drive to the top of the mountain, where the view from ground level is well worth negotiating the steep, winding road to the summit. The entrance is well marked on Hwy. 178.

Driving on through Bull Shoals on Hwy. 178, you will cross the Bull Shoals Dam, where a visitors' overlook offers photographs of the dam under construction and outstanding views of the lake and the river below it.

Arkansas' sprawling Bull Shoals State Park is laid out on both the lakeshore and the riverbank of the White below the dam, with campsites and a trout dock along the river. The park also offers hiking trails, picnic areas, and an amphitheater where exceptionally worthwhile interpretive programs are presented during the camping season.

Downriver from the state park (watch for the sign) is Gaston's, a famous trout resort on the White. The restaurant at Gaston's is built on stilts over the river, and offers a unique vantage point from which to enjoy the beauty of the river and watch the fishermen and the hummingbirds outside the glass walls. Inside the stunning building, the walls and ceiling are crowded with antiques and "primitives."

Bull Shoals

Construction of the dam at Bull Shoals began in 1947. A 7.5-mile-long conveyor belt brought rock from a quarry near Flippin to the construction site. When the dam was completed four years later, it was the fifth largest dam in the United States. It consumed enough concrete to build a wall six feet high and one foot thick, running the entire length of the West Coast. It cost the lives of three construction workers. The towns of Lead Hill, Arkansas, and Forsyth, Theodosia, and Pontiac, Missouri, were relocated to higher ground. Free twenty-five-minute tours—said to be handicapped accessible—are given of the dam during the summer tourist season.

Not everyone loved the idea of a dam on the White River. Owners of the rich river bottomland, especially, hated to give up their farms; many had been in the same family since the land was homesteaded. Bitterness born of their defeated struggle still lingers, though the eraser of time is successfully at work.

Partially because most of the shoreline is totally undeveloped and protected by a buffer zone (locally called the "take line") owned by the Corps of Engineers, Bull Shoals is an incredibly beautiful lake. Twenty-one Corps of Engineers parks around the lake offer facilities for camping, picnicking, swimming, boating, and fishing. Additionally, there are numerous private campgrounds and resorts.

On July 2, 1952, President Harry Truman dedicated both the Bull Shoals and Norfork dams. A local legend has it that the road to Bull Shoals dam was paved especially for his visit so that the president would not have to travel on a gravel road. Attending the ceremonies were fifteen thousand people. Truman brought along so many of his cabinet members that newsmen referred to Norfork (where the party spent the night of July 1 on the special presidential train) as the "Little White House." After the dedication the party returned to the president's train awaiting them at Cotter.

Both the Twin Lakes—Norfork and Bull Shoals—can boast of thirty- to sixty-foot underwater visibility. For this reason, many dive shops and clubs do their qualifying here. Several boat docks on both lakes offer air stations and rental gear. Snorkeling, underwater photography, and spearfishing are excellent. (Be sure to check local wildlife regulations.)

In spite of all the development that has accompanied the manmade lakes and their enormous popularity, by far the majority of the region is still wilderness. One can read Henry Schoolcraft's journal of his Ozarks sojourn of 1818-19 and follow the explorer's progress down the rivers, recognize the landmarks described in the narrative, and easily visualize Schoolcraft's current whereabouts as she reads. How many other areas of the country have remained so close to their 1818 geography?

The biggest changes have been wrought by the dams. And fewer and fewer are they who can tell us about the wonders hidden beneath the lakes.

Cross Bull Shoals Dam on Hwy. 178 and continue east to Hwy. 5, which will take you north to Ozark County, Missouri, the only county in the country to bear that name.

Practical Matters

Chapter 17 — The Twin Lakes

Checking Out	A Sampling	Phone
Lodging	Ramada Inn, 1127 Hwy. 62E, Mountain Home AR; Best Western Carriage Inn, 963 Hwy. 62E, Mountain Home AR; Bull Shoals Lake: Chastain's Resort, Box 290, Bull Shoals AR 72619; Gaston's White River Resort, #1 River Rd., Lakeview AR 72642; Norfork Lake: Lake Norfork Resort, Rt. 1, Box CC, Henderson AR 72544; Mockingbird Bay Resort, Box 183, Mountain Home AR 72653	(501) 425-9191 (501) 425-6001 (800) 423-LAKE or (501) 445-4242 (501) 431-5202 (501) 488-5144 (501) 491-5151
Bed & Breakfasts Dude Ranch	Mountain Home Country Inn; Scott Valley Dude Ranch, Rt. 2, Box 270, Mountain Home AR 72653	(501) 425-7557 (501) 425-5136
Campgrounds	Dozens of Corps of Engineers Parks on Norfork and Bull Shoals Lakes: Resident Engineer, P.O. Box 369, Mtn. Home AR 72653; Wilderness Point Camping Resort (Lake Norfork) P.O. Drawer 09, Henderson AR 72544; Bull Shoals State Park, Box 205, Bull Shoals AR 72619	(501) 425-2700 (501) 488-5340 (501) 431-5521
Restaurants	Nettie's, College Plaza, Hwy. 62E, Mountain Home AR 72653; Gaston's, #1 River Rd., Lakeview AR 72642; Brass Door, Hwy. 62, Gassville AR	(501) 425-8373 (501) 431-5203 (501) 435-2288
Attractions	Norfork Ferry Tours, Box 867, Mountain Home AR; Ozark Emporium, U.S. Hwy. 62, Gassville AR; Top O' The Ozarks Tower, Hwy. 178, Box 151, Bull Shoals AR 72619; Norfork National Fish Hatchery, Rt. 3, Box 349, Mountain Home AR 72653; Bull Shoals Dam & Powerhouse, Bull Shoals AR	(501) 425-1111 (501) 435-6070 (501) 445-4302 (501) 499-5255 (501) 431-5391
Outdoor Recreation	Fishing, Floating, Boating: Cotter Trout Dock, Box 96, Cotter AR 72626; Bull Shoals Lake Boat Dock, P.O. Box 748, Bull Shoals AR 72619; Hiking: Bull Shoals State Park (See Above)	(501) 435-6525 (800) 447-7538 (501) 445-4424 (501) 445-4166

Checking Out	A Sampling	Phone
Where to Write for More Details	Bull Shoals/White River Chamber of Commerce, Box 354, Bull Shoals AR 72619;	(501) 445-4443
	Mountain Home Chamber of Commerce, Box 488, Mountain Home AR 72653;	(501) 425-5111
	For Information About "A Fisherman's Guide to Public Access Facilities in Arkansas Counties" and a "Floater's Kit," write Arkansas Game & Fish Commission, Information & Education Div., 2 Natural Resources Dr., Little Rock AR 72205	(501) 223-6351

CHAPTER 18

The Old Mill Run

Folks in Ozark County call their home "the *real* Ozarks." Begun as a slogan to attract tourists, the term caught on—possibly because of the ring of truth and certainty. Ozark County is a natural: no theme parks or water slides, no traffic jams, no waiting in lines—and no franchise food. And, although it was seen as a disadvantage until recent years, much of the county's history is still visible.

Gainesville, the county seat and largest town, musters a population of barely seven hundred. Hwy. 160 is the main east-west artery in Ozark County, while Hwy. 5 cuts southward through the seventeen named knobs, hills, and ridges known as the Gainesville Monadnocks, which cover a seven-mile long, five-mile wide area of unparalleled beauty. Geologists say these knobs are "one of the largest groups of monadnocks [isolated rocky hills or mountains] anywhere on the Ozark surface."

A prominent and popular feature of western Ozark County is an arm of sprawling Bull Shoals Lake. A portion of Lake Norfork is east on Hwy. 160 to the other side of the county. Marinas offering rental boats, stalls for private boats, fishing bait, scuba supplies, and all the accoutrements of lake enjoyment are available at both.

What's more, the county is famous for its unspoiled float streams and rivers. Since most of them originate in protected national forest land, they are relatively clean and wonderfully clear. Public access points and rental canoes are numerous in Ozark County (see the Practical Matters Chart at the end of the next chapter).

If your interest is hiking forest trails or backpacking, Ozark County has something for you, too. Parts of the Mark Twain National Forest

343

are here, as well as thousands of acres of official wilderness, named for the long narrow ridge known since early settlement as Devil's Backbone. A network of unmarked trails winds through rugged hills and hollows separated by long, steep slopes or bluffs.

As for scenic drives, almost every road in Ozark County is a breath-catcher. But a couple are real standouts: Hwy. 181 north from Gainesville to Dora, and south off Hwy. 160 on Rte. P to the Arkansas state line. There is also famous Glade Top Trail, part of the Forest Service's new Scenic Byway program, that winds along ridges in the national forest after leaving Hwy. 95 at Longrun (see Chapter 19).

Remote and Isolated

By 1840 there were only about two hundred families in the county, and no local government. The year 1842 saw the county's first post office established at Rockbridge, but because of the rugged hills and the lack of roads and bridges, there were many isolated settlements connected only by foot trails. In the 1930s the sheriff still went about his business on horseback. He could negotiate the hills and hollows and ford the unbridged streams more quickly and easily on a horse, he claimed, than he could in an automobile. As late as 1947, the only place to buy fresh meat in Gainesville, the county seat, was in the drugstore on the square. In 1960, the county still had twenty-nine post offices, more than any other county in the state. Population peaked in 1900 with 12,145 inhabitants, then dropped to 6,744 in 1960. About nine thousand people are now scattered around the 732-square-mile area.

At the turn of the century, the mail hack required twelve hours to journey to West Plains, about forty miles to the east. A ferry carried traffic across the North Fork (of the White) River near the present site of the highway bridge at Tecumseh. A member of the banker's family, a young mother who "always had a new baby" carried deposits to the affiliate bank in West Plains, hiding the money in diapers under the seat of the buggy.

By the early 1900s the virgin pine forests of Ozark County were mostly all timbered off. Tillage farming on the thin soils of these ancient mountains was proving inefficient, and livestock production gradually replaced it. Lead and zinc were mined intermittently, but no great mining boom brought the tide of history here. The railroads bypassed the county, the population steadily declined, and it remained almost completely isolated for lack of good roads. But thanks in part to this very course of events, Ozark County's day would yet come.

The remnant of a bank vault still stands at Hammond Mill on the Little North Fork in west-central Ozark County, Missouri, not far from Glade Top Trail. Built in 1907, the mill had three stories and a basement, and was built of wood and stone with a rock floor. The vault is all that remains of the bank of Hammond. The mill ceased operations in 1940, but is currently being restored. (Photo by Darvin Taylor)

The Old Mill Run

Perhaps the most tangible—and eloquent—echo of Ozarks-past is an old water mill. Looming out of the river's morning mists a shadowy, multistoried millhouse seems almost haunted, a fading reflection of a vanished way of life. It fosters the feeling that through narrowed eyes we might glimpse the teeming activity that once attended it.

Nowhere is that more apparent than at the surviving water mills in Ozark County. Milling was important in the county by the mid-1830s. For more than a century these old mills embraced the pace of the olden times—and to a large extent they still do. Nowadays the mills are within easy driving distance of each other and make for a splendid self-guided tour.

In ways unmatched by other remnants of the past, the remaining mills speak to us of the old Ozarks. Their numbers tell us of their importance, of the vital role they played in the lives of the settlers struggling for enforced self-sufficiency in an isolated and rugged land. Though roads were poor, often impassable, and travel tedious, rivers and streams were everywhere. Where one was just big enough, without being so big as to create an insurmountable engineering problem, there was a potential mill site.

Beside the mill was usually a general store, often run by the miller or his family, supplying coffee, tea, yard goods, and simple clothes. Sometimes the miller branched out into livestock feeds, as well. A blacksmith shop and a post office were nearly always part of the mill scene. Gasoline pumps were usually added after the advent of automobiles. With the mill to grind their corn and wheat, and the miller's sidelines to fill their other needs, the hill folk were supplied with all the necessities of their time that the household did not create for itself.

Because of his importance to the community, the miller—his face, hair and clothes usually white with dust from the meal—was always a prominent and well-regarded citizen. His charge, about one and one-half cents per pound of grain, was usually paid by barter for a "toll," or share, of the meal he ground. (If, however, the miller judged that his patron's family was "on starvation," he might grind their meal for free.) The miller sold his toll, generally one-eighth of the ground grain or eight pounds of meal per bushel, to customers who did not raise their own. In keeping with the Ozarkers' "waste-not, want-not" philosophy, some were said to "fatten out" their pigs on sweepings from the mill floors.

The mill, like the general store, was the neighborhood meeting place. Folks gathered under shade trees in the summer, around a pot-bellied stove in cold weather.

"Goin' to Mill"

"Goin' to mill" was a treat for the backwoods family, for the mill also supplied that other ingredient necessary to a lonely life: the opportunity to socialize and exchange news. Old-timers, when recollecting their childhoods, invariably mention vivid memories surrounding the local mill and their first trips there with Pa. Late in the fall, in the evening when all the kids were home, the family would shell enough corn for a hundred pounds of meal. If they grew wheat, they would take enough for three hundred pounds of flour, which would see them through the winter. Because early Ozarkers preferred corn-bread to light bread or biscuits (the "soft wheat" they could grow did not make good bread) and because their crop ground was better suited to it, more corn was grown than wheat. Mostly white corn was raised and ground in the Ozarks, where yellow corn was often considered fit only for animal feed. Flour was milled more frequently in the flatter, open areas more conducive to growing wheat—prairie regions and riverbottom farms, for example.

Most families took extra bags for the ground meal, refusing to allow the corn to be returned to the sacks in which it was brought. They washed and cared for their own white woven sacks through many uses. And many folks were particular about getting back the meal from their own grain rather than that traded to them by the miller from his holding bin, minus his "toll."

As a result, long waiting lines formed and sometimes customers spent the night. Particularly in the fall, wagons formed encampments near the mill where residents of the area might spend a few days and catch up with visiting while waiting their turns. A miller often provided his customers with feed for their mules, horses, or oxen while camped at his mill.

While they waited, men aired their views on politics and religion. Others stood about, gossiping, inspecting the machinery, or watching the movement of the water wheel. The gathering was an ideal forum for storytellers, and many a myth was no doubt created by the loungers waiting for their corn to be ground and for the watermelon to chill in the icy water of the mill race. A game of horseshoes might also help to pass the time. Others had a horse shoed or a harness mended.

Women exchanged recipes and quilt patterns and the latest neighborhood news, or perhaps traded for some piece goods at the store. Some mills were official polling places; voters still gather at Zanoni Mill in Ozark County.

Since the mill required about two hours to grind a hundred pounds of corn, it often ran twenty-four hours a day to accommodate its business. And the miller knew that if a fellow came in with eight

First headquarters of Caney Mountain Refuge, Ozark County, Missouri, and home to its first two area managers, the log portion of this structure still stands near the entrance and is more than a hundred years old. A native-stone residence was built in 1947 and is still in use. (Photo Courtesy of A. B. Morrison)

hundred pounds of corn to grind, he was not going to use all of it for making cornbread. More than likely, it was to be grist for the whiskey still. Legend has it that the revenuers went looking for stills in the "hollers" that were known to contain springs. But the distillers simply set up shop in the next hollow over—and piped cold water underground to cool their condensers.

Nonpolluting Nonconsumptive Water-Powered Industry

The first settlers into a region quickly pinpointed potential mill sites. Any stream with a swift current or a fall of water was prime property—particularly since some mills boasted indoor privies that took advantage of the fast-running water below.

Powerful springs were also often pressed into service because they usually flowed steadily, even in dry spells, and predictably even in periods of high water elsewhere.

While a river offered a wider choice of location for the new mill, it also posed greater difficulties to be overcome. Unless the river had a steep enough gradient, it did not flow fast enough to provide the necessary power. And in times of flooding, the river could—and did—damage the millhouse or wash it away. Dry spells, on the other hand, might reduce the flow of water and, therefore, power to operate the mill.

Because the first mills ground with just two buhrstones, they were one-story sheds. Since the stones provided no way of separating the bran and wheat germ, the flour they produced was whole wheat. In later years, in response to the demand for white flour, an elaborate setup called a roller mill was installed, the first fully mechanized industry to develop in this country.

The millhouse was constructed of hand-hewn posts and beams, the trunks of single, tall trees, usually pine or oak. The first mills in deep wilderness were usually built entirely of logs, while later buildings were frame. In the eastern Ozarks, in the early-settled Mississippi River area, some mills were brick or stone. To accommodate the extensive system of belts and pulleys that powered the flour-milling machinery, millhouses became three or four stories high.

Another advantage of mill building in the Ozarks was the ready supply of limestone and other rock. To help anchor the millhouse against floods, and to combat the constant problems of damp rot on exposed timbers, many mills were underpinned with massive stone foundations. Such a sturdy base also protected the structure from the constant shaking and vibration accompanying the milling process.

Rock was also used when it was necessary to construct a dam across the chosen stream in order to harness its potential power by damming the flow and creating a millpond. In addition to rock dams, some were constructed of weighted logs, earth, or a combination of the three.

Once dammed, the pent-up water could be directed to the mill by means of a raceway, or millrace. When the mill was not grinding, the flow of water through the millrace or flume could be controlled by gates. The miller could thereby reduce or increase the speed of the wheel and control the mill's rate of operation. Sometimes, particularly when a hillside spring was the source of water, a flume was constructed to carry water down to the mill wheel. In that case, gravity and the power of falling water supplied sufficient power.

Because of the constant danger of explosion and fire presented by the highly explosive grain dust, the tall millhouses were never heated. Dangerous enough was the heat generated by the machinery and the coal oil lamps or candles used as light sources. A great many mills were destroyed by fire. The grain was also susceptible to damage by mice, rats, and birds. Not surprisingly, every mill had a cat, usually named "Dusty."

The Water Wheel

The water wheel itself is rarely seen today. The very heart of the gristmill, the original wooden wheel was usually the long-ago victim of rot and abandonment. The two major types of Ozarks water wheels were the undershot and the overshot. The siting peculiarities of each mill, as well as the local miller's preferences, determined which wheel was used.

Most wooden wheels were eventually replaced by the more modern turbine wheel. Many new mills built after the Civil War were powered either by steam or water turbine. Whereas both types of wooden water wheels turned on a horizontal axis, the metal turbine was on its side with a vertical axis. The turbine was highly efficient because it turned underwater, with water striking all the buckets at once. Occasionally the present-day operators of the old turbine-powered mills install wooden waterwheels "just for looks," strictly to satisfy the demands of tourists.

Besides furnishing the power to turn the grinding stones, the extra power harnessed by the mill was not wasted. Lumber mills and woodworking equipment were also driven by the water wheel and its system of belts and pulleys, as were rock crushers, cotton gins, and wool-carding machines. Water diverted from the mill was sometimes used for irrigation on a neighboring farm, perhaps the miller's own.

Another important industry sometimes on the grounds, especially in very early days of settlement, was a bark mill. This machine ground tree bark, usually oak or hemlock, for use in making tannic acid for tanning leather, now virtually a lost craft in the Ozarks. The gristmills themselves needed leather for belts on the machinery, and nearly every household used it for hinges, boots, saddlery, and harnesses. The tanner, like the miller, took a toll of the finished product, usually one hide for each hide processed.

In later years, most mills also had adjacent overall factories, tomato canneries, garages, and gasoline pumps. Prior to rural electrification, many of the larger mills generated electricity for their neighbors and all the millsite enterprises.

Changing Times

In the early twentieth century many of the mills' customers began to turn to store-bought meal. In an effort to keep pace with the changing times, some millers converted to steam and gasoline engines, but the cheaper and "more desirable" hard wheat imported from the western plains was in demand. By the 1930s and, in a few of the more remote places, the early '40s and '50s, the automobile and its easy access to city markets meant that even the self-sufficient farmers of the Ozarks no longer looked to their own harvest for sustenance.

A few of the old mills continued to grind grain for the miller's family and a few friends and neighbors. Some found a market milling stock feeds. And, for those who hung on long enough and were not dismantled or were easily re-activated, there was a new wave of interest from the tourists who discovered them after World War II. But the war effort had cost many of the old mills their machinery, prized for the high quality of its metal.

Because of Ozark County's relative isolation, its gristmills continued to serve their neighborhoods until almost the middle of this century. As a result, many of them are still standing—and now welcome visitors. In every case the mills are either the centerpiece of another attraction, or have found new uses; none is highly commercialized. They remain almost as they were, in lovely surroundings. You can see them all in as little as half a day—time that will be as well invested as any you spend in the entire Ozarks.

Old Dawt Mill

Begin at Old Dawt Mill, on a back road just upstream from Tecumseh. Look for the Old Dawt Mill sign at the intersection of County Rd. PP, eleven miles east of Gainesville on Hwy. 160. Turn left onto PP for a mile and watch for the small sign indicating a left turn to Dawt. After leaving Rte. PP, less than a mile of gravel road (the only unpaved road on the tour) leads to Dawt.

Dawt's tall millhouse perches on a high bank of the North Fork River. It is said there was a mill on the property as early as 1866. In 1874 President U. S. Grant conveyed the "patent" for the land. The first documented mill on the site was built by 1892. In 1893 a man drowned in the millpond. The v-shaped dam was handmade in 1897 and held until a spring flood in 1969; the dam has also undergone repairs after several storms since then.

Though the tin roof is rusted and the wood siding scoured by wind and time, the present building looks much as it has since its construction in the 1900s by Alva Hodgson, master millwright. The front porch is worn smooth and sags under the passing feet and river floods of nearly a hundred years. A tired wagon leans against the wall where the miller might have parked it many yesterdays ago. You almost expect to round a corner and encounter a woman in a calico sunbonnet. Listen intently enough and you may hear the echo of the blacksmith's hammer or the excited laughter of children swimming in the river below.

And the North Fork is still as much a part of the mill scene as the venerable millhouse itself. Thanks to its protected origins in the Mark Twain National Forest, the spring-fed river flows as crystal clear and cold as in days of yore. A hydrologist for the United States Forest Service calls the river "the jewel of the Ozarks," and trout fishermen from all over the country revere it. The river also affords some of the best whitewater action for modern canoers in the Missouri Ozarks, and the milldam at Dawt is part of the challenge. Since it is known as a "canoe buster," most nonexperts slide their canoes through a shallow chute or portage around the dam.

A bakery in the Dawt mill lures customers by filling the air with the delicious aroma of stone-ground breads and rolls. You may camp on the grounds beside the river, fish for trout (with a Missouri license) and enjoy the rustic and scenic neighborhood.

Hodgson Mill

Next on the tour is Hodgson Water Mill, only a few minutes away through the famous Ozark County scenery. From Dawt, return to Rte. PP and turn left on PP for 4.2 miles to Rte. H. Turn left on H and go north 5.8 miles to Hwy. 181. Turn left again on 181 for 3.8 miles to Hodgson Mill. Watch on your left for an old round gas pump, its glass top now clouded and stained. The first mill on this site was built in 1861 to harness the power of a massive spring flowing into Bryant Creek. Evidence suggests that the mill was forced to close during the Civil War.

The present millhouse was constructed in 1897 by Alva Hodgson,

Now the centerpiece of a long-term restoration project of the Living History Foundation of Ozark County, Missouri, Hodgson Mill—on Hwy. 181 north of Gainesville—still houses original milling machinery. The barn red, three-story frame building nestles against a bluff of Bryant Creek, and inside the mill an opening to a cave in the face of the bluff provides natural air-conditioning. (Photo by Darvin Taylor)

Rockbridge Mill is the centerpiece of a private resort, Rainbow Trout Ranch. Guests pay by the pound for the trout they catch, and the resort will clean and ice—or cook—the fish for you. The restaurant on the grounds is famous throughout the Ozarks, and the setting is one of the most beautiful anywhere in the region. Rockbridge is on Rte. N about two miles north of its junction with Hwy. 95 in Ozark County, Missouri. (Photo by Darvin Taylor)

who bought the property in 1884. Much of the building is built of hand-hewn pine and utilizes mortise joints. Huge support beams were locked into place with wooden pins. A grocery store built about the same time stands near the mill.

The spring still spews millions of gallons of cold water a day. Issuing from the bluff under the millhouse, it nourishes native ferns and mosses clinging to crevices in the sheer rock bluff. Some of the water is diverted to the mill pond, where watercress and other marine plants thrive. In pre-REA days, the power of the water also generated electricity for all the millsite enterprises: a cotton gin, a lumber mill, and a clothing factory. Thanks to the constant fifty-eight-degree temperature of the spring, the mill was a popular site for neighborhood dances.

Although known as Bryant Creek, the spring-fed waterway at Hodgson Mill is river-sized and it, too, provides opportunities for canoeing and swimming. As at Dawt, there are rental canoes and campsites, and both mills are popular sites for outdoors vacations, family reunions, and group picnics.

Zanoni Mill

Continue south on Hwy. 181 for about five scenic miles and watch for Zanoni Mill on your right near a dazzling white mansion, site of the Zanoni Mill Inn, a bed-and-breakfast establishment.

Milling first began at Zanoni, located on spring-fed Pine Creek, in a mill built of logs during the Civil War. In 1900 the property sold and new owners replaced the mill and added a sawmill. When that mill burned shortly before 1905, Aaron Preston "Doc" Morrison built the third mill at Zanoni, which is the two-story building still standing. Morrison equipped his mill with a new set of eighteen-inch flint buhrstones from France. The second story of the mill hosted neighborhood dances for several years.

In addition to the mill itself, in 1906 Morrison established a cotton gin, also powered by the millwheel, and an overall factory in 1920. The sewing machines were run by water power. As well as serving as postmaster for many years, he also operated a blacksmith shop at the site, and his general store building is still standing.

Zanoni sports a rare overshot wheel designed by Morrison and built in 1940 to replace the 1900 wheel. Powered by water carried to the wheel by a flume from a spring—twenty feet above the valley floor— in the face of the rock bluff behind it, the mill generated electricity in the 1940s. Because the spring is a relatively small one, the mill's capacity was limited to about twenty bushels of corn a day. Milling ceased at Zanoni in 1951, but the spring still flows, and the wheel still turns.

Now owned by "Doc" Morrison's grandson and his wife, the mill and the old store building are the centerpieces of a 1,750-acre working ranch that is also a bed-and-breakfast inn. Accommodations are in a new mansion patterned after the house at South Fork Ranch near Dallas, Texas.

Rockbridge Mill

Last on the tour is Rockbridge Mill. Two miles beyond Zanoni, turn right on Rte. N for 5.7 miles. Another two miles after crossing Hwy. 95, watch for the sign to Rainbow Trout Ranch, the site of old Rockbridge, one of the earliest towns in the region and the county seat of the original Ozark County after 1841. When the town was burned during a Civil War battle, a new village grew up around the mill built in 1865.

In 1888 B. V. Morris bought out his partner and either enlarged the mill building or built a new one. The third story of the building, still standing, was added about 1900. Its power also operated a sawmill, a planing mill, and a cotton gin. The mill pond, formed by damming the flow of four springs, was originally impounded by a log and stone dam, which partially washed away in 1887. In 1895 the present stone dam was built. As the last stone was laid, the town band performed on the dam and a dance celebrated the occasion. At its peak, the mill produced fifty barrels of flour per day.

In 1894 Morris built a two-story general store from pine lumber cut from the virgin forest. The store was considered one of the largest and finest in the Ozarks and once offered everything from food to hardware—including coffins. A bank building was added in 1904, founded by Morris and John Edwards, the last surviving Civil War veteran in Ozark County.

After witnessing the stirrings of growth and change in the Ozarks, the general store and the bank closed in 1933; the mill in the late '40s. But in 1954 the tiny mountain hamlet of Rockbridge saw the establishment of a private trout hatchery and fishing resort. Housed in the 1890s store building, until its destruction by fire in early 1986, were a restaurant and the headquarters for the resort and hatchery.

A new "general store," designed to resemble the original with large glass windows and wide front porch, was erected on the site of the old. Once again it is a world-famous restaurant where the trout catches of resort guests are cleaned, cooked, and served to them. And visitors can dine while watching hundreds of ruby-throated hummingbirds at feeders outside the large windows overlooking the mill, its rock dam, and the crystalline creek.

The millhouse itself, like the bank and other original buildings, was spared by the fire. However, it had suffered heavy flood damage a

Established in 1904, the Bank of Rockbridge was closed by moratorium in 1933 during the Great Depression. The bank saw two robberies in its history—in 1927 and 1930. Some of the stolen money from the last robbery was found in a tree stump where the thieves had hidden it as they fled. The old building still enriches the scene at Rainbow Trout Ranch near Rockbridge Mill. (Photo by Darvin Taylor)

few weeks earlier. In the process of saving it, it was semi-restored by adding some new concrete underpinnings and aluminum siding which does not detract from its beauty. A rocking chair in its shelter, almost directly above the falls at the dam, allows an opportunity to experience Ozarks serenity first-hand. The century-old milldam is viewable from close enough to feel the cool spray of the water cascading over it. Nestled into the lovely valley, overlooking the trout stream and the mill and the 1904 bank building are modern guest accommodations.

When you are able to leave Rockbridge, consider a left turn to follow Rte. N back to major Hwy. 5. For fifteen more miles you can wander through a cool green gauntlet of pines and split-rail landscape befitting a tour of the past.

The Barrier Between Past and Present

The water mill demonstrates the best of humankind's interaction with the land: a natural union of the power of nature and the needs of man. The Ozarks water mill is historical proof that man's industry need not destroy, but can become one with, his environment. The evidence speaks for itself. When an old millsite is abandoned, it soon vanishes without a trace—leaving, at most, a rusting turbine, a millstone, and a rock dam. But as long as these old mills still stand, we will go on straddling that barrier between past and present that is so much the essence of the Ozarks.

Now move a few miles west and look at the scenery from Glade Top Trail. Return to Hwy. 5 and turn north toward Ava; watch for the sign marking the turnoff, about five miles south of Ava.

As part of the deer restoration efforts in the early 1940s on Caney Mountain Refuge in Ozark County, Missouri, deer were trapped and tagged to aid in tracking their movements on and off the refuge. (Photo Courtesy of A. B. Morrison)

The Glade Top Trail Scenic Byway through Mark Twain National Forest in Ozark and Douglas counties, Missouri, is enjoyable any time of the year, but particularly in the spring and in the fall. The Trail offers one of the best opportunities anywhere in the Ozarks for viewing dogwood blossoms close-up at a speed that allows them to be safely savored. In the long fall season of riotous color, the viewing is good from late September through October.

CHAPTER 19

Glade Top Trail

To the traveler unfamiliar with the history of the Ozarks, a drive through the Mark Twain National Forest is a pleasant escape from highway hassle and urban sprawl. The road curves and dips through seemingly unending miles of trees, crosses cellophane-clear streams and affords one breathtaking view after another. To one who knows how and why the National Forest came to be, however, the scenery is no less beautiful—but can be seen as nothing short of miraculous.

By the time of the Great Depression, vast tracts of this Ozarks forest land had been laid to waste. Lead miners and loggers had stripped the hills of the pine forests and most of the best hardwoods. In their wake, the exposed rocky topsoil sluiced off the steep hillsides and choked the streams and rivers with gravel bars. Dirt-poor farmers overburned and overfarmed what was left. Those who could, escaped to greener pastures, or to the cities.

But in 1931 the University of Missouri and a group of influential citizens, unwilling to allow the region to become a permanent wasteland devoid of wildlife, requested that national forests be established in the state in an effort to restore the land's health and productivity. The state of Missouri passed legislation in 1933 authorizing the Forest Service to begin buying the abused land. On September 11, 1939, President Franklin Roosevelt signed the proclamation establishing the Clark National Forest and the Mark Twain National Forest in Missouri. By 1945 well over a million acres—much of it denuded and eroded—had been approved for inclusion in the new national forests. (In 1976, the two forests were combined into one, the Mark Twain National Forest.) In the meantime, the Civilian Conservation Corps

(CCC) went to work planting trees, controlling erosion, and constructing buildings and roads. Fires were suppressed, grazing by domestic stock discouraged, wildlife re-introduced and protected. Time passed and the land began to recover.

By the time of the forest's fiftieth anniversary, the mostly reforested land again offered scenic drives, secluded campgrounds, remote picnic areas, Wild and Scenic rivers, habitat for over three hundred species of wildlife, more than sixty-three thousand acres of congressionally designated wilderness, and a sustainable timber harvest. A dozen ranger districts oversee 1.5 million acres; all but fifteen thousand acres are in the Ozarks. And it is beautiful again.

Just driving through the national forest is an enjoyable experience. On a misty morning the sun's rays filter through the pines and cast their shadows on the winding road leading you ever deeper into the beauty. Occasionally a more open area affords a long-range vista of closely folded, heavily forested hills rolling away into blue distance, their once-ugly nakedness now only a half-forgotten nightmare.

Sometimes such pockets of exceptional beauty are quite close to superhighways. Unpublicized, they are easily overlooked by unsuspecting travelers unaware of their existence. To avoid that mistake, send for the informational pamphlets of the National Forest (see the Practical Matters Chart at the end of this chapter). For example, near the junction of Hwy. 181 and CC in Ozark County is the North Fork Recreation Area on the banks of the North Fork River. This location offers hiking trails, access to the Devil's Backbone Wilderness Area, Blue Spring, and secluded camping. A few miles farther north is the Children's Forest and more hiking and scenic views. Beyond that, still on Hwy. 181, is Noblett Lake, a remote campground and picnic area that also offers scenic hiking on the Ridge Runner Trail (see the chart).

Glade Top Trail

You know you have found an Ozarks attraction truly worth your time when you have found one that is a favorite of the locals. The trouble is, in the case of the Glade Top Trail, no one in this Missouri neighborhood—where Douglas, Ozark, and Taney counties come together—can seem to agree when is the best time for driving the trail. If you were to inquire, chances are you would get at least as many answers as there are seasons.

Although recently included as one of the Forest Service's newly designated Scenic Byways, the Glade Top Trail has been a favorite in this area for years—a road for all seasons in every sense. Not only is the all-weather gravel road through Mark Twain National Forest well-maintained all year, but the views from the trail change with the seasons, each spectacular in its own way.

Built by the CCC in the 1930s, the trail is accessible either from the north (south of Ava on Hwy. 5) or from the south, near Longrun (on Hwy. 95) in Ozark County, a pleasant mountain hamlet (but with no services for travelers). In either case, watch for the brown, trapezoidal Forest Service signs.

Ava, "Host of the Trail"

For a third of a century the county-seat town of Ava has hosted a chicken barbecue on an October weekend at a picnic area along the Glade Top Trail. Ava has limited services for travelers, a couple of small motels and restaurants, but plenty of gas stations. A Trappist monastery is located nearby.

One version of a local legend recalls that after fierce rivalry between Vera Cruz and Ava (then known as Militia Springs) to become the Douglas County seat, Ava was successful when the three commissioners appointed to lay out the town in 1871 physically stole the county records from Vera Cruz and brought them to Ava by force. Then the rivalry really heated up; first one courthouse and then another was burned by proponents of the "legal" county seat. Lasting until well into the 1900s, this "feud" over location of the county seat reportedly caused lasting bitterness between the two sides of the county.

But in 1940 fame of another sort flickered briefly for the town when an anonymous benefactor, the "Angel of Ava," began sending residents money through the mail. Although the donor apparently knew of events and personalities in Ava as all the checks—ranging from a few dollars to a hundred—were sent to deserving recipients, the envelopes were all postmarked in Kansas City. Typewritten notes accompanied some of the checks, eventually thought to total about three thousand dollars, but gave no clue to the "angel's" identity. After a few months the "money shower" ended and has not, so far, resumed.

The town is world headquarters of the breed registry for the Missouri Fox Trotting Horse Breed Association, and their world championship horse show is held there annually in September during Labor Day week. The fox trotter is a "hillbilly horse" developed in the Ozarks. The hills demanded a sturdy, sure-footed, even-tempered horse, so the early settlers crossed their high-spirited five-gaited horses with the calmer Tennessee Walkers to slow—and calm—them down. Later they used mustang mares to add endurance and cut down on size. And, since most Ozarkers could not afford both a riding horse and a work team, fox trotters were bred to be all-purpose horses. They plowed fields all day and then furnished transportation to social gatherings at night and to church on Sunday. The gentle breed soon gained favor far and wide. Easy to ride because of its graceful, rhythmic gait, the horse "fox trots"; that is, he walks with his front feet and trots with his hind feet. The name comes from the fox, which leaves only two tracks. Its hind foot steps in the track left by the front one. A fox trotter is said to "cap his tracks." Today the "hillbilly horse" is at home the world over, but he comes home to Ava in the fall.

Glades and Forests

True to its name, the self-guided and well-marked Glade Top Trail primarily follows the ridgetops, offering grand vistas of glades intermingled with the oak-and-hickory forest. You may well see some deer and other smaller wildlife, including wild turkeys.

A glade is an open area characterized by shallow soil, rocky outcrops, and prairie vegetation. Wildflowers are abundant among the prairie grasses, and the species in bloom change constantly throughout the growing season. Red cedar is the most common woody plant in the glades, so you will sometimes hear them referred to as "cedar glades." The glades are also home to the smoke tree, sometimes called *yellowwood* locally. During Civil War times the wood was used to make a yellow dye. The smoke tree is found only in these three counties in Missouri. Named for the feathery blooms that cover the tree in late spring and resemble bluish smoke from a distance, this small tree also burns with the brilliant red-orange colors of flame in the autumn. It and the scarlet sumac (pronounced SHOE-make locally) and crimson dogwood lend intensity to an Ozarks fall.

Since the smoke tree is one of the best reasons to drive the Glade Top Trail, a special vista called the Smoke Tree Scene is maintained by the Forest Service. There large numbers of the tree can be viewed and admired. Several more of these "vistas" are provided along the trail, where you can park your car and get closer to nature on foot. At most of these turnouts you will find informative placards to enhance your knowledge, and therefore your enjoyment, of what you are seeing around you.

Another special feature of the glades is the influence of the arid Southwest. Many plants and animals more commonly associated with the desert reach their northeastern limits here. Watch for the collared lizard and, in the fall, you may see a tarantula on the move. Scorpions also live in the glades, but you probably will not see one unless you pick up a large rock. Where a glade exists on top of a hill, it gives the knob a "bald" look. It was in just such openings that the Bald Knobbers, the infamous vigilante group, once held their meetings.

The mixture of habitat—forest and glade—makes for excellent birding along the Glade Top Trail. The best time to see birds is during the breeding season in May and June. Turkey vultures are almost constantly overhead, and you may spot a black vulture. The adjacent forest is slow growing and provides good habitat for many of the cavity nesters, including the pileated woodpecker.

The forest is so dense near the "Arkansas View" that in 1965 a light plane that crashed not far from there in early May was not found until November, when falling leaves at last rendered it visible through the trees. During the spring and summer months, a dozen Civil Air Patrol planes and more than a hundred ground searchers had hunted in vain for the missing craft. The wreckage was finally spotted through the trees in a deep draw.

Beyond the Arkansas View is the Caney Lookout Tower. Now abandoned, the fire tower was originally built near McClurg, some three miles north. In 1937, however, it was discovered that the tower had been built on private land. The CCC dismantled the tower and reassembled it on the present site. Once more, thanks to faulty land records, the Forest Service was informed that the tower was squarely in the middle of a privately owned 120-acre tract of land. Since by this time a house and garage for the towerman and his family had already been built nearby, the Forest Service simply purchased the land. A forest technician who was working at the tower summed up the situation as "all kinds of confusion from start to finish."

Dogwood Trail

Just beyond the Caney Lookout Tower is the picnic area, the highlight of the Glade Top Trail. There you will find picnic tables, a fire pit, primitive rest rooms—and some of the finest views along the trail. Watch also for a faint path from the parking area that leads to a small but interesting cave in the hillside. The picnic ground is the site of Ava's annual chicken dinner. Another offering on that one weekend in October is free Ozarks-style entertainment: music and singing provided by local musicians and groups on an open-air stage.

But many locals favor the springtime panoramas from Glade Top Trail. A particular favorite in the spring is the section of the trail known as Skyline Drive. Since the trees are yet leafless, the long-range viewing is much better than in the fall when the leaves, however colorful, still block most views from the trail through the forest.

Of all the scenic drives in the Ozarks, the Glade Top Trail offers one of the best opportunities to see blossoming dogwoods close-up. A humble understory tree, the dogwood stars briefly in April, usually for the last half of the month, though sometimes earlier. Widespread

On a clear day you can see forty miles into Arkansas from this mountaintop on the Glade Top Trail in Mark Twain National Forest. Although visitors have been enjoying Glade Top Trail for years without much fanfare, the Trail was recently named an official Scenic Byway by the U.S. Forest Service as part of their national scenic byways program.

throughout Missouri, where it is the state tree, the dogwood seems especially spectacular in the Ozarks.

The Skyline Drive (Forest Road 149) portion of the Glade Top Trail exits in Taney County near the Hercules Glades Wilderness and affords continued viewing of the National Forest scenery in either direction along paved-but-curvy Hwy. 125.

Glade Top Trail itself supports two-way traffic in most places and is more than adequate for passenger cars, campers, or even motorhomes. It is also negotiable by a vehicle pulling a trailer, though this is not recommended during the weekend of Ava's barbecue.

Watch for Hayden Bald, a State Natural Area; Watershed Divide, the divide between Beaver Creek Watershed and the Little North Fork Watershed; the abandoned schoolhouse at the Skyline Drive junction where more than forty children attended school in the 1930s.

Last stop on the trail is the Pinnacle, where local hill folk once gathered for an all-day church service on the first Sunday of every May. A crowd of five hundred people was commonplace. If you are really curious, search out Mother Murray's gold mine nearby. According to the legend, Mrs. Murray had a vision in which she was instructed to search for gold on the Pinnacle. Though she hired help and dug for years, she never found gold.

Allow a minimum of half a day to drive the trail in either direction. Although the distance is only twenty to thirty miles one way, depending upon your choice of alternate routes, you will be driving slowly and stopping often, savoring all that you see and experience.

At the end of Glade Top Trail travel east on Hwy. 160 to Hwy. 63 at West Plains. Turn south on Hwy. 63 to the once-bustling peach capital of Koshkonong and thence to Grand Gulf State Park, Missouri's "Grand Canyon," near Thayer.

Practical Matters

Chapters 18 & 19 — Ozark County

Checking Out	A Sampling	Phone
Lodging	Rainbow Trout Ranch, Rockbridge MO 65741; Ft. Cook, Theodosia MO 65761; Pontiac Lodge, Pontiac MO 65729; Twin Forks Resort, Rt. 1, Isabella MO 65676; Lakepoint Resort, Isabella MO 65676	(417) 679-3619 (417) 273-4444 (417) 679-4169 (417) 273-4344 (417) 273-4343
Bed & Breakfasts	Zanoni Mill Inn, Zanoni MO 65784	(417) 679-4050
Campgrounds	Pontiac Cove Marina, Pontiac MO 65729; Ft. Cook, Theodosia MO 65761; Dawt Mill, Tecumseh MO 65760; Hi-Lo Campgrounds, Sycamore MO 65758; Both primitive and developed camping in Mark Twain National Forest, District Ranger, P.O. Box 99, Willow Springs MO 65793	(417) 679-3676 (417) 273-4444 (417) 284-3540 (417) 261-2590 (417) 469-3155
Restaurants	Rainbow Trout Ranch, Rockbridge MO 65741; Gig's Restaurant, Hwy. 160, Isabella MO; Lakeview Restaurant, at the Theodosia Marina	(417) 679-3619 (417) 273-4235 (417) 273-4401
Main Historical Attractions	The Old Mill Tour (see text) Glade Top Trail, U.S. Forest Service, Ava Ranger Station, Ava MO 65608	(417) 683-4428 (417) 683-3410
Outdoor Recreation	Trout Fishing: North Fork River (Missouri Wildlife Codes Apply); Rainbow Trout Ranch, Rockbridge MO 65741; Canoe rentals: Dawt Mill, Tecumseh MO 65760; Hi-Lo Campgrounds, Sycamore MO 65758; Roy's Store, Hwy. 181 at CC, Dora MO 65637; Guided River Fishing: Taylormade River Treks, Box 183, Tecumseh MO 65760; Guided Lake Fishing: Inquire at marinas: Pontiac Cove Marina, HCR 1, Pontiac MO; Ft. Cook Marina, Theodosia MO 65761; Mule packing: Devil's Backbone Wilderness Outfitters, Rt. 1, Dora MO 65637; Hiking: The Ridge Runner Trail, U.S. Forest Service, Ranger District, P. O. Box 99, Willow Springs MO 65793; Devil's Backbone Wilderness; Bull Shoals and Norfork Lakes: Corps of Engineers Resident Engineer, Mtn. Home AR	(417) 679-3619 (417) 284-3540 (417) 261-2590 (417) 261-2259 (417) 284-3055 (417) 679-3676 (417) 273-4444 (417) 261-2474 (501) 425-2700

Checking Out	A Sampling	Phone
Where to Write for More Details	Ozark Co. Chamber of Commerce, P.O. Box 605, Gainesville MO 65655; Missouri Bull Shoals Lake Assoc., Box 324, Isabella MO 65676; Theodosia Area Chamber of Commerce, P. O. Box 11, Theodosia MO 65761; Ava Ch. of Commerce, Box 83, Ava MO 65608; Devil's Backbone Wilderness, Hercules Glades Wilderness: District Ranger, Mark Twain National Forest, Box 99, Willow Springs MO 65793; Booklets: "Missouri Ozark Waterways," "Missouri Hiking Trails," from Missouri Dept. of Conservation, P. O. Box 180, Jefferson City, MO	(417) 683-4594

SECTION 6

Big Spring Region

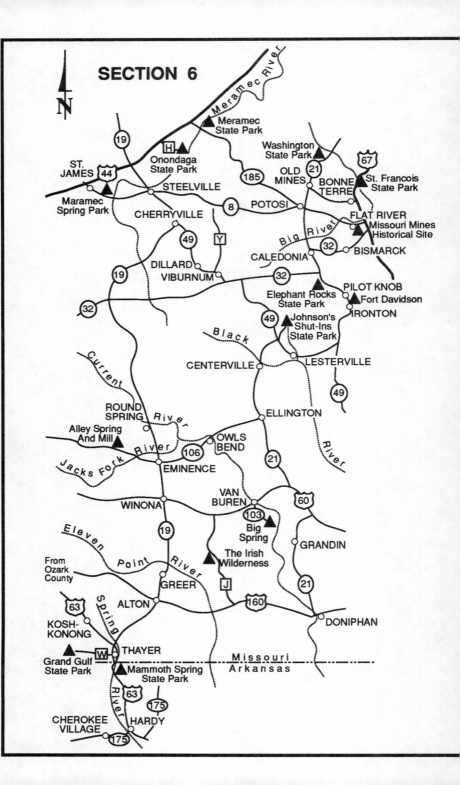

SECTION 6

N

19

ST. JAMES
44
Maramec
Spring Park

Meramec River

Meramec
State Park

H Onondaga
State Park

STEELVILLE

CHERRYVILLE

8 POTOSI

Washington
State Park

185 OLD
MINES

21 BONNE
TERRE

67 St. Francois
State Park

FLAT RIVER
Missouri Mines
Historical Site

Big River

32 BISMARCK

49

Y

DILLARD
VIBURNUM

19

CALEDONIA

32

Elephant Rocks
State Park

PILOT KNOB
Fort Davidson
IRONTON

32

49 Johnson's
Shut-Ins
State Park

Black

CENTERVILLE

LESTERVILLE

49

Current

River

ROUND
SPRING

River

ELLINGTON

Alley Spring
And Mill

River

Jacks Fork River

106 OWLS
BEND

EMINENCE

21

River

WINONA

VAN
BUREN

60

19

103
Big
Spring

GRANDIN

Eleven

Point River

The Irish
Wilderness

From
Ozark
County

GREER

J

21

63

ALTON

160

DONIPHAN

KOSH-
KONONG

Spring

THAYER

W

Missouri
Arkansas

Grand Gulf
State Park

Mammoth Spring
State Park

River

63

175

CHEROKEE
VILLAGE

HARDY

175

CHAPTER 20

Overview:
Tall Pines and Lead

Although it runs counter to most folks' vision of the Ozarks, the region is one of the most intensely mined in the nation. The eastern Ozarks has been heavily exploited—if not more so than other areas, certainly for longer.

The French—the first white settlers in the Ozarks—were mining lead on the Meramec River in the early 1700s. The small mines yielded no great riches, but they did attract the first settlers and the first investors to the Ozarks. When they continued to hear of huge caches of silver and gold seized by the Spaniards in Mexico and Peru, the French ventured into the interior of the Ozarks.

Unlike later settlers, they lived in villages and were not interested in farming for a living; they raised only what they needed to survive. The town of Old Mines was laid out as any fifteenth- or sixteenth-century Normandy village, with houses facing the road with farms behind them. ". . . that way they could live together . . . [and indulge] their social nature." Interestingly, the French understood the Indians, respected their claim to the land, and were not troubled by them. French families had been in the area for several generations when the "Americans" arrived.

In 1723 Mine La Motte was established a few miles north of present Farmington and mining began in the Old Mines area north of Potosi about 1725. At first lead mining was a part-time occupation. Digging and smelting began in late summer after harvest and lasted until bad weather set in, usually just before the Christmas feasting and holiday.

With only a pick axe and a wooden shovel, the workmen dug on the surface of the ground. When they encountered bedrock, or got to such depth that it was no longer convenient to throw the dirt out of the hole, they began a new digging a few feet away. Under such primitive mining methods, the "diggings"—merely shallow holes with earth piled up about their edges—were said to resemble prairie dog colonies. Prospecting amounted to digging test holes three or four feet deep and judging by the quantity of ore in each hole which would be most productive.

The ore was heaped on piles of burning logs to be melted down. As was so often the case in the Ozarks, the great distance to a market or shipping point proved a serious detriment to development. At first the lead was molded into the shape of a collar and draped across a horse's neck for transportation to the Mississippi. Later ox-drawn carts hauled the ore to the wharf at Ste. Genevieve, settled from about 1735, and thence by raft or boat to New Orleans, where it was sold. In 1851 a forty-two-mile plank road, the longest ever constructed in this country, was built between Iron Mountain and Ste. Genevieve and used primarily for hauling ore.

Since they were here first, an important legacy of the French in the Ozarks is the names they bestowed upon the land and its features. Often we still use the original nomenclature—or rather, local corruptions of it—but sometimes we have adopted the English translations of the French terms.

The French culture and language, localized in this remote area, persisted for a long time. As late as 1937 a local historian exclaimed that ninety percent of the people at Old Mines still spoke both French and English. He described their language as "sort of a Creole French." Many French customs and folktales persist to this day in the area.

Ultimately Americans were attracted to the lead district. Moses Austin, entrepreneur and metallurgist, secured a Spanish land grant at Mine a Breton (later Potosi) in 1798, and a year later a settlement was established. The families who accompanied Austin settled near the mines and on fertile farmlands in the Belleview Valley. By 1804 there were twenty-six families living there. In 1819 the geologist and explorer Henry Rowe Schoolcraft listed forty-five mines in Washington County, twenty-five of them in the vicinity of Potosi.

The "Old" Leadbelt

Washington County was organized in 1813, one of Missouri's earliest. A historian reports that "because the miners were an unruly class, county governments were organized in Washington and St. Francois counties at an early date to provide for sheriffs, courts, and jails."

During the Civil War the Union forces closed down most of the mines to keep the Confederacy from gaining control of them. What lead was produced was used to make gunshot. After the war the mining area attracted outside capital. Organized in 1864, the St. Joseph Lead Company (now the St. Joe Mineral Corporation) hired a number of experienced Cornish hard-rock miners. The invention of the diamond drill, first used by the St. Joseph Lead Company in 1869, led to the discovery and exploitation of deep lead deposits. In time the company became the largest individual producer of lead in the world and gradually absorbed many smaller or less successful companies.

From 1869 on, underground mining was possible. Enormous cathedral-like tunnels were dug with dynamite and picks and shovels, and mule-drawn carts on tracks transported ore to hoisting shafts. Steam engines powered the hoists and mill machinery. And because the company depended on wood for fuel, it owned vast timberlands.

But transportation of products continued to be a big problem. The companies built their own railroads and encouraged others, but supplies and pig lead had to be hauled to and from the rail lines. During the spring and fall, roads became impassible because of heavy, sticky mud. In fact, the shipping stations were changed from time to time in the hope of finding routes with shallower ruts.

Within thirty years, the Leadbelt progressed from shallow and widely timbered shafts, from which ores were hoisted by bucket and windlass, to modern steam cable hoists that brought ore to the surface from depths of four to five hundred feet. As deeper mines and larger mills were developed, the imprint of mining on the landscape was obvious. Shaft houses, concentrators, furnaces, sediment basins, rail lines, and huge chat piles were visible everywhere. The heart of the old Leadbelt centers around an urbanized area that is actually a cluster of towns, among them Bonne Terre, Flat River, Leadville, Elvins, and Desloge.

By the turn of the century, the St. Joseph Lead Company employed approximately eight hundred workers, operated twelve farms and owned about thirteen thousand acres of land. In 1960 the company controlled 90 percent of the area's lead production. But in September of 1961 the huge Bonne Terre mine closed, and in 1973 the last of the old mines in the Leadbelt shut down.

"Scrapping Tiff"

The Tiff Belt covers about seventy-five square miles in northeast Washington County. Many descendants of the early French settlers remain here today. Until the 1850s, the area produced lead. Then in 1857 began the buying and selling of tiff (barite). *Tiff* is a relatively

In the huge Bonne Terre lead mine at Bonne Terre, Missouri, miners used carbide lamps on their hardhats before the days of batteries. They dynamited in the mine twice a day, once on each shift. The blasts could be heard all over town, and those who can remember hearing them say "you could set your watch by them." (Courtesy of State Historical Society of Missouri)

soft, white-to-gray mineral. Most is used in oil drilling to hold gas pressure. Other uses are as a filler in paint, ink, paper, textiles, and asbestos products.

Many of the French who lived in the vicinity of Old Mines eked out a living digging tiff after the lead mines closed. The tiff miner dug with a pick, tossing the material out until the hole became too deep. Then a homemade windlass let down a bucket, which was filled with dirt, tiff, and rocks, and drawn up by a helper. A tiff hatchet, a short-handled tool with a sharpened flange on each end of a curved head, was used to break unwanted rock off the ore that was piled on scraps of tin to be sorted. Different colors of barite brought different prices and the entire family could help sort. Often the ore was placed in a "rattle-box"; the worker rocked the box back and forth to jar off the dirt and adhering rock. Haulers later collected the ore.

Mine holes seldom reached more than twenty-five feet deep, but miners were sometimes overcome with a case of the "damps" when they broke into an old lead mine tunnel and encountered polluted air. To help feed the family, women and children assisted at "scrapping tiff." They gleaned the piles of debris and picked up the scraps of tiff overlooked by the digger. A great many children scrapped tiff instead of attending school, so that they and their siblings could eat. For their efforts the families were paid thirty-five cents per hundred pounds for average tiff and eighty-five cents per hundred pounds for white. But by 1934 the price of tiff had dropped and demand lessened.

Living by their old traditions and with their old language and religion, the French Creoles remained culturally isolated. In the 1930s a visiting professor wrote, "Scattered all along the countryside I found six hundred French-speaking families living in this community." Living under semi-feudal conditions, they mined tiff and sold it to the landowners, who kept the royalties for themselves. The impoverished Creoles lived rent free on the land, but earned barely enough to purchase necessities from the landowners' stores.

The Tiff Belt is a pockmark on the face of the Ozarks. With its shallow pits (most of the older ones scabbed by scrubby growth and often used as dumps) and hillocks of waste, it appears as bleak and desolate as the moon. Even the miners who dug tiff for a living had a saying: "The land was so exhausted a crow had to bring his own food in order to fly over it."

Although lead mining has brought in money and a few jobs, it has historically been costly to the Ozarks environment. Still of particular concern are the vast tailings ponds, which many fear will lead to pollution of the vulnerable groundwater. The lead companies, however, insist that modern mining methods are safe.

This photo was probably staged by the Missouri Lumber and Mining Company about 1900, since men would not be working where a tree was about to fall! Usually after the trees were felled, trimmers prepared the logs for transport and the wagons moved in to carry them to the tramline. (Courtesy of State Historical Society of Missouri)

After the fallers and trimmers had readied logs for transport to the lumber company's tramlines, they were hauled out of the forest on horse- and mule-drawn wagons. Many men and mules were needed. Usually ten or eleven wagons were in each group, and each group had approximately a hundred mules in its string. (Courtesy of Bittersweet, Inc.)

The Primordial Forest

From earliest settlement, the trees of Ozarks forests were cut to fuel the boilers of blast furnaces and lead smelters, to build and heat the homes of settlers, to construct plank roads, and for railroad ties, fencing, and many other uses. Even today the traveler will notice many small sawmills dotting the countryside and encounter log-hauling trucks on the highways.

But both the early and recent timbering are mere echoes of the intense lumbering once done in the area by mammoth companies making huge profits. The presence and influence of these enormous companies and their selfish endeavors drastically altered the Ozarks and its history. They exploited the natural resources and took the resulting profits elsewhere, leaving in their wake only desolation and destitution.

In the primordial forests of the Ozarks were ancient hardwoods—oak, hard maple, ash, walnut, hickory and sycamore—and immense groves of virgin yellow pine, often three feet or more thick, towering above an open understory and the grass-covered forest floor, much different from the brushy undergrowth of today's second- and third-growth forests.

The rich riverbottom was settled before 1820 by farmers who altered the land very little, "taking what was offered and asking little more." Away from the rivers, however, the soil was rocky and unproductive. Timber was the only other resource worth anything, but the owners of the timberlands were unable to realize profits from the asset because they did not have the necessary capital—the old paradox of "it takes money to make money." Even if, working alone or in twos and threes, they had been able to cut a few trees, they were hundreds of miles from either transportation for the gargantuan product or a market.

Huge lumber companies, on the other hand, saw great potential in the magnificent forests of the Ozarks. Encouraged by a booming market brought on by the country's rapid western expansion and homesteading—vast numbers of new houses, barns, stores—and the need for oak railroad ties and barrel staves, the stockholders decided to invest in the future need for the reserves in the Ozarks. When eventually the hard-pressed settlers' land sold for back taxes, the lumber companies snapped it up like buzzards on a road kill.

In one purchase, the Missouri Lumber and Mining Company paid as little as $6.90 a half-section. In 1871 principals of the company visited Reynolds, Shannon, and Wayne Counties and bought thirty thousand acres of timberland in Carter County at an average of a dollar an acre; this acreage became the nucleus of the company's holdings.

Eventually some of the company's land was purchased at higher prices, but they picked up a great deal of acreage at tax sales for an average price of twenty-five cents per acre. In 1879 and 1880 they managed to buy, at a sheriff's sale in Carter County, two sections of land for twelve and a half cents per acre. And not only was the cost of the timber negligible; there were other advantages for the companies in the Ozarks that permitted colossal profit margins: mild winters allowing year-round cutting and the availability of cheap labor.

Due to the Ozarks' old nemesis—the lack of transportation—the companies sometimes held the land for years before they cut the timber. But with the coming of the railroad to the area, the fate of the forest was sealed. At their new town of Grandin, the Missouri Lumber and Mining Company erected the then-largest sawmill in the world.

"Working in the Timber"

Because it was most in demand, the companies first timbered the virgin pine that often towered to eighty or ninety feet and grew to five feet in diameter. All trees with a diameter at the base of at least twelve inches were cut. Logs forty-five inches thick at the base and forty-two inches thick at the top on a sixteen-foot cut were not uncommon.

Supplying the huge mills in Grandin with timber for sawing was the job of the men who worked in the trees. Logging camps could be moved from one site to another, set up, and be back in operation in only two days. Portable houses and buildings, including a company store, a church, and a doctor's office, moved from camp to camp on flatcars. Sawyers and support crews stayed in the woods in lumber camps for up to ninety days at a time, camping in tents.

Cutting wood with crosscut saws at all seasons, "fallers" worked in pairs. A pair was expected to cut ten thousand feet per day; failure to meet that goal resulted in the worker's pay being docked. Next, logging crews moved into areas where cutters had felled trees. They carried tents, food, and supplies, a portable barn, and hay and grain for their mules. Trunks were limbed, cut in sixteen- to eighteen-foot lengths, skidded by mule (oxen were first used, but they proved too slow) to the nearest logging road, loaded onto mule-drawn wagons, and finally transferred to flatcars on one of the tramlines. Connecting the lumber camps with the mills, the tram railroads ran the mountain ridges on narrow-gauge track laid by specialized crews. When all the trees in an area served by a tramline had been cut, the track was taken up and moved to a new cutting site.

Ninety carloads of logs a day were required to supply the two ten-hour shifts in the two mills at Grandin, which turned out 220,000

At the peak of the company's productivity, the sawmills of the Missouri Lumber and Mining Company in Grandin sawed ninety train car loads of logs a day. Seven locomotives and three hundred log cars transported logs to the mill over 108 miles of railroad operated by the company itself, employing 235 men as train operators, shop repairmen, line repairmen, and construction crews. Even then some of the work was contracted. (Missouri Department of Conservation photo)

The former office building of the Missouri Lumber and Mining Company in Grandin, Missouri, is now the Masonic Lodge. Built as a showplace when grades of lumber used today were considered scrap and not worth milling, the old building contains flooring, wall paneling, trim, and ceiling "made of the best virgin Missouri yellow pine when the very best was available to choose from."

board feet of lumber per day. Seven locomotives and three hundred log cars transported logs to the mill over 108 miles of railroad operated by the company itself, employing 235 men as train operators, shop repairmen, line repairmen, and construction crews. Even then some of the work was contracted.

At really remote locations, a portable mill capable of cutting ten thousand feet per day was set up. Sometimes logs were skidded to the riverbank, accumulated there, then set loose in downstream log drives. Eight to ten men usually accompanied a drive, which could take as long as a week or more on the water. Jams occurred frequently on the twisting trip downriver; "sinkers" had to be rescued and spiked to more buoyant wood to keep them from being lost.

The irresistible force of running water, logs weighing several tons, headstrong mules inclined to bolt, and steam trains on steep grades combined to make the timber jobs difficult and often dangerous; injuries were commonplace.

Death of a Forest

Voracious and powerful though it was, the Missouri Lumber and Mining Company was only one of the giant firms that eventually cut almost 1.5 billion board feet of lumber from nearly half a million acres of Ozarks hillside. At the peak of lumbering in the area in 1899, it is reported that 723,754,000 board feet of timber were cut.

From then on, production dropped steadily; in 1931 it totaled only seventy-five thousand board feet. Had the cutting been selective, the industry could have survived for years, but young trees were destroyed in getting out the older ones, and the hills were stripped of their cover. No effort was made to replant. The resultant erosion— plus the abuses of destitute former lumber workers desperate to make a living—destroyed what little was left. When they could no longer buy timberland cheaply enough to ensure gargantuan profits, the companies took the money they had made in the Ozarks and left the region. The results of their "cut-and-get-out" policy were nothing less than catastrophic for both the land and the people.

In the aftermath of the deforestation the water table dropped drastically. The thin top soil quickly washed away; virtually nothing grew in the remaining rocky barrens. Choked by the silt and gravel washed from the denuded hillsides, the once deep and clear rivers and streams dried up. Many of the profusion of springs, once found in every hollow, disappeared and never flowed again. But, due to the accelerated runoff from the naked hills, floods became more severe than ever. Wildlife vanished. The few new trees that sprouted spontaneously were not allowed to grow because of the custom of "burning off" the woods each spring so that cattle could find forage.

After years of living on the cash economy under the watchful eye of "the company," the destitute populace found it impossible to return to its former barter system. There were no other jobs to be had. A very few of the timber workers followed the companies to new cutting areas. Others who could leave the devastated area for jobs elsewhere did so, but the rest of the nation was soon plunged into the Great Depression and had problems of its own.

Many of those who remained in the environment thus totally ruined for even subsistence farming, land that would no longer support wildlife, much less domestic stock, practiced timber cutting on a much smaller scale for years in an effort to make a living. So desperate were some that they cut timber wherever they could find it, particularly on the holdings of absentee landowners. If questioned about where he had cut the logs he had for sale, the woodcutter often replied, "From Grandma's land." The practice became known as "grandma-ing." Others turned to moonshining bootleg whiskey.

Most of the abused land left behind by the lumber companies was unsalable. The Missouri Lumber and Mining Company made a few abortive efforts to mine the land, but profits proved so skimpy that prospecting was soon abandoned. Likewise the company's attempts to establish orchards and stock farms to convince potential buyers of the land's productivity also failed miserably. Eventually most of the land was sold for back taxes, with the federal government the major buyer. On this devastated land the government established Mark Twain National Forest.

By 1938, Grandin's population had shrunk to three hundred. The railroad was taken out in the 1950s when Hwy. 21 was blacktopped and improved. In 1980 some thirty buildings in Grandin, all built by the Missouri Lumber and Mining Company were listed on the National Register of Historic Places. Most remain in private hands and serve as family dwellings. Many residents of today's Grandin are descendants of the employees of the Missouri Lumber and Mining Company. Some still live in houses more than a hundred years old, built of knot-free yellow pine.

Rebirth and Modern Lumbering

In the half-century of nurturing care since it was replanted by the Civilian Conservation Corps during the Depression, the beauty and most of the health of the environment have been restored. And during much of the time that the forest was recovering, it was also producing timber. Today the Mark Twain National Forest supplies wood that is used to make flooring, pallets, railroad ties, charcoal, and other products. Scientific principles have been applied to make harvesting timber more environmentally acceptable. Harvest areas are generally limited to no more than forty acres, and guidelines have been established to protect soils, endangered species, wildlife habitat, and scenic beauty. Areas that are harvested are reforested. According to the Forest Service, harvests are managed so that the rate of harvest is currently about half the rate of growth.

And now the former cut-over timber tracts provide scenic trails, secluded campgrounds, remote picnic areas, the Eleven Point Wild and Scenic River, habitat for over three hundred species of wildlife, more than sixty-three thousand acres of congressionally designated wilderness, and a sustainable timber harvest.

CHAPTER 21

Grand Gulf, Mammoth Spring, and the Irish Wilderness

Two geological features in close proximity, Grand Gulf and Mammoth Spring, serve as dramatic illustrations of the "spongeworks" of the Ozarks.

Grand Gulf is a National Natural Landmark operated by the Missouri Department of Natural Resources as a state park. Located on Hwy. W, six miles west of the village of Thayer, a railroad division point established in 1881 in Oregon County, the park features the collapsed remains of a major cave system, with a sinkhole, cave, natural bridge, and the Gulf itself—perfect examples of the karst features so prevalent in the Ozarks region.

Formed by the "recent" collapse of a cave system's roof (within the past ten thousand years) Grand Gulf is not beautiful, though it can legitimately claim to be educational or even spectacular. Around its perimeter are lovely pockets of forest quietude, striking views, and abundant peace and quiet.

Today the Gulf is a canyon three-fourths of a mile long with sheer dolomite walls as high as 120 feet. A portion of the cave roof that did not collapse remains as a natural bridge that spans two hundred feet and has an opening seventy-five feet high, making it one of the largest in the state. Sinkholes have collapsed along the floor of the Gulf, indicating additional cave levels below. Bussell Branch, which once flowed above the cave system while it was still intact, now flows through the

Besides providing a place for the community band to serenade, the town bandstand also made a handy place to have a town meeting. This one is at Cabool, in Texas County, Missouri, ca. 1900. (Courtesy of The Ozarks Mountaineer)

Although Mammoth Spring, at Mammoth Spring, Arkansas, surfaces silently, the state has constructed two large "pour-offs" so that visitors can properly appreciate the beauty and drama of nine million gallons of water per hour welling out of the ground. The water flows into a ten-acre lake and then over a handmade rock dam to form the Spring River.

canyon and into a part of the cave system still underground. The water that flows into the cave eventually reappears at Mammoth Spring in Arkansas, nine miles away. Pioneers learned the connection to their satisfaction by dumping cornstalks and straw into Grand Gulf and watching it emerge later at Mammoth Spring.

The most complete look at Grand Gulf is available from the quarter-mile loop trail around the chasm and a primitive trail that crosses the natural bridge and winds through the oak-hickory forest along the western edge of the Gulf. But for those unable to make the hike, four overlooks—one of which is handicapped-accessible—provide visitors with spectacular views of the Gulf from observation platforms. From these perspectives, it is easy to visualize the passageways of the ancient cave. Several picnic tables are provided, and the area is spangled with dogwood trees. The park also has an interpretive shelter with exhibits that explain how the Gulf was formed and how the water it collects makes its way to Mammoth Spring.

Via Hwy. 63 to Mammoth Spring you pass through once-thriving orchard land and the home ground of "Ma" Barker and her boys, notorious criminals of the 1920s and '30s.

A Mammoth Spring

Although the orifice of Mammoth Spring is just over the state line in Arkansas, nearly all of the water collected by the spring originates in Missouri. And, as with most springs in the Ozarks, there is a Native-American legend to explain its origin. Long ago, a group of Indians camped in this area along Main Fork River when a long and terrible drought occurred and the river was nearly dry. The chief of the people sent his son and others to seek water. During the search, the chief's son died. When the Indians dug a hole to bury him, a large stream of water shot from the grave site. The chief vowed that this new spring would flow forever since his son had died searching for water and it had been found while burying him.

Mammoth Spring flows at the rate of nine million gallons per hour, swelling Spring River from an insignificant stream to a sizable river. With a constant temperature of fifty-eight degrees and stocked with trout from a hatchery on the grounds, Spring River is one of the most popular fisheries in the Ozarks. In addition to the rainbow trout found in its upper stretches and the walleye and bass in its lower reaches, the Spring River is also rated one of the state's best float streams. Whitewater shoals and rushing falls challenge the canoeist for thirty-one miles downstream from Mammoth. And thanks to the constant water flow from the spring, it is floatable year-round.

The actual spring cannot be seen at Mammoth because it emerges more than seventy feet below the water level of the spring pool. The great force of the spring can be easily observed, however, by watching the "pour-offs" along a trail that circles the lake and includes two footbridges over the spring branch. The overlook above the old mill-dam is another spot to see the awesome flow of water.

Once a popular watering hole for wild animals drawn to the clear, cold water, the spring pond has likewise always attracted ducks, geese, and other aquatic birds. Shown on early nineteenth-century maps as Great Spring, the huge natural fountain was also called "Big Spring" in the 1820s by area settlers who established a village there known as "Head of the River." Thanks to a gristmill powered by the water, the town prospered.

During the Civil War, soldiers burned the mills along the river and the trading post at the spring. It was the mid-1870s before the area began to grow again. In 1886, the Frisco Railroad built lines into the area and constructed a depot in the town, now called Mammoth Spring. In the 1890s Mammoth Spring boasted a large flour mill, a cotton factory (later a shoe factory), new churches, a bustling business district, an opera house, fine Victorian homes, two newspapers, the depot, several hotels, and summer resorts.

Each stone for the dam, which forms a ten-acre lake between the spring and its river, was hand-quartered and fit into place without the aid of mechanical equipment. A stone structure on the far side of the dam was once the milling company's vault. The safe and time clock are on display at the visitors' center. The Arkansas-Missouri Power Company bought rights to the dam in 1925 and constructed a hydroelectric plant which provided electricity to the area until 1972.

The spring is now the centerpiece of an Arkansas state park. The visitor center features exhibits, brochures, rest rooms, and souvenirs. A pleasant walking trail circles the lake formed between the dam and the spring. Waterfowl—ducks, geese, and swans—in and around the lake add to the pathway's charm. The easy-walking trail leads to the 1886 depot-museum (or one can drive to the museum, where there is a small parking lot.)

The depot was restored in 1971 and houses exhibits of railroad memorabilia including a Frisco caboose and historical objects from the area. Adjoining the depot is a baggage room containing local historical exhibits. No admission is charged. Built in 1904, the Federal Fish Hatchery adjacent to the park may be toured, and an aquarium there offers a look at native fish.

Huge oak trees shade a picnic area at the park, and a playground overlooks Spring Lake. A covered pavilion may be reserved. Overnight lodging and camping are not provided, but along the Spring River nearby resorts and towns offer a variety of facilities (see chart).

Unlike the relatively undisturbed settings of many of the other huge springs in the Ozarks, Mammoth Spring—because humankind has so long taken advantage of its copious flow—seems almost overly domesticated and tame. But surrounded as it is by the park and the town of Mammoth Spring, both extremely pleasant, it is nonetheless a natural wonder. And nine million gallons of water an hour pouring over a handmade dam is a sight to behold.

Fishing for Pearls

For several generations families living along the Spring River, as well as the Black and the White rivers, supplemented their meager farming incomes by "pearling" and "musseling" in the rivers. The pioneers knew from the beginning that the Indians had eaten the meat of mussels—freshwater clams—that inhabited the rivers in great numbers. But the whites considered the meat tough and tasteless and passed it by for the plenitude of fish and frogs and the meat of fur- and feather-bearers from the forest.

Then in 1857, according to Vance Randolph, a fisherman found a big pearl in one of the mussels he had gathered for bait. The news that a St. Louis jeweler had paid fifteen hundred dollars for the pearl "rippled up and down the rivers and back into the deepest hollows." The industry of *pearling* had been born. The hunt for pearls occupied many Ozarkers from the time the crops were in the ground until fall weather made it too cold to wade in the rivers. For those lucky enough to have jobs, wages for a long day's hard work were no more than fifty cents. It is easy to understand why pearl fever swept over the river basins when pearl buyers began to converge in the area, paying from five to fifty dollars—and occasionally more—for a single pearl.

Although they started out opening every mussel they found in their quest for pearls, folks soon learned to discriminate. They discovered that some types of mussels (out of the dozens of different species in the rivers) did not produce pearls at all; that pearls were more common in sandy streams than in gravelly ones; that it takes several years for a sizeable pearl to develop and, therefore, the larger and older mussels were the only ones worth opening. "The old-timers claim that one good pearl is found in every 12 tons of shell examined, but even that estimate errs on the optimistic side," Randolph said.

A pearl forms in the mussel when an irritant—such as a grain of sand—lodges in the delicate flesh inside the shell. The mussel covers the foreign substance with nacre (mother-of-pearl), the substance that coats the inside of its shell, until the intruder is completely encased. If the resulting shape happens to be round, it is called a pearl; otherwise, it is known as a *slug*. The largest pearl known from Arkansas waters was about five-sixths of an inch in diameter and sold for about three thousand dollars. A White River pearl has been set into a crown of England.

By the turn of the century, 1910 or 1912 at the latest, the pearl-fishing boom had run its course, simply because most of the pearl-bearing mussels had been harvested. But a few years after pearling had begun, it was discovered that the mussel *shells* were also market-able at Northern button factories. Soon, however, the button factories came to the Ozarks. Forty carloads of shells were required to make one carload of buttons, so it made good economic sense to move the factories closer to the source.

In fact, many buttonmakers set up on flatboats and made blank buttons from the raw material they bought from the locals. These blanks were then shipped to actual factories for drilling and finishing. With the establishment of a market for shells, the shellers needed a way to harvest more mussels in less time. When pearling, they had merely opened mussels with a sharp knife. Now that they were pri-marily interested in the shells themselves, a faster way was needed.

They were taught the technique of "boiling out" the shells. Mussels were thrown into barrels or tubs of scalding water to make them open easily. The meat was scraped out and used for hog feed or fish bait, while the shells—sorted by species and quality—were then sold by the pound to shell buyers who established buying points along the rivers.

Various methods of obtaining the mussels were worked out, rang-ing from forking them up from sandy bottoms, clasping them in long-handled tongs, or grubbing them out by hand. In some cases divers went into the deeper water, often rigging homemade diving helmets and living on the brink of danger. Especially during cold weather, crowsfoot dredges or "brails" were dragged along the bottom, and open mussels clamped down on the hooks. But in the 1940s, new plastic buttons from Japan destroyed the pearl button industry.

Today, however, mussel shells are still important moneymakers for some Arkansans, who harvest with brails or by diving. Used primarily in the cultured pearl industry centered in Japan, Arkansas shells are shipped overseas and processed into pearl nuclei by stripping the outer layer and punching appropriate-sized blanks into round pellets. These round, mother-of-pearl nuclei are then inserted into pearl oys-ters suspended in cages in a suitable estuary or ocean bay. Oysters are allowed to create their own mother-of-pearl around the nucleus for six months to three years, depending on the quality of pearl desired. Pearls are then harvested, graded, and sold.

For a look at relics from turn-of-the-century pearl hunting, and other rich archives housed in an 1888 Victorian building, consider a side trip to the Old State House Museum in Powhatan, southeast of

Hardy on Hwy. 63. Nearby is Old Davidsonville State Park, the site of the first post office in what is now Arkansas. At Maynard is the Living Farm Museum and Pioneer Museum. (And a few miles to the south at Jacksonport State Park is the *Mary Woods No. 2*, the restored steamboat mentioned in Chapter 16. Nearby is another museum housed in the restored Civil War era Jacksonport Courthouse.)

A Door to the Past in Oregon County, Missouri

Northeast of Mammoth Spring on Hwy. 19 back into Missouri, through lush green Oregon County, the traveler finds a door to the past in Alton, established in 1859 as a central location for the new county seat. Built to replace the building burned in 1863 during the Civil War, the courthouse is made of Missouri red granite. An old pitcher pump still adorns its lawn, and many old buildings crowd around the square. A big John Deere dealership and a chapter of the Future Farmers of America bespeak an agricultural community.

Oregon County suffered greatly during the Civil War. Though its courthouse was burned, the county's vital records survived the war— concealed in a cave on Piney Creek. There they remained from 1862 to 1865. Even when the war was finally over, an outlaw band preyed on the people until finally routed by the "county militia" in 1868.

The Irish Wilderness

MacKinlay Kantor once said that the Ozarks are "spooky." In fact, the Irish Wilderness is widely believed to be haunted. And, according to a local legend, chiggers completely devoured a twenty-mule-team caravan in the Irish Wilderness some years ago, harness and all. Part of the area so rapaciously lumbered at the turn of the twentieth century, the indefinite region long widely known in Ozarks legend as "the Irish Wilderness" was in 1984 officially designated a 16,500-acre wilderness by that name.

The true story of how the area acquired its colorful name, however, is one of tragedy. It begins with the Irish potato famine of 1848 that drove a large portion of Ireland's people to "the new world." Some thirty thousand came to St. Louis, Missouri, where they eventually made up one-third of the city's population.

Unfortunately, the Irish were not much better off in Missouri than they had been in Ireland. Impoverished and oppressed by their German- and Anglo-American neighbors, the men could find only the most menial of work, often in competition with slaves and free blacks or by following the new rail lines away from home and family. Their wives and daughters served others as domestic servants.

Filled with compassion for his parishioners and their social dilemma, a conscientious and idealistic young priest, Fr. John Joseph Hogan, conceived of a settlement in the Missouri Ozarks where the Irish could, ". . . using the same thrift and energy in southern Missouri, successfully cultivate land, and establish on it for themselves and their posterity a permanent homestead."

With the perfect vision of hindsight, it is highly doubtful that Father Hogan fully realized what he was asking of his flock. Ill-prepared and poorly equipped to found a community in what was then a true wilderness in every sense of the name, setting out in 1859 on the eve of armed conflict, their problems were monumental.

When the Civil War burst upon the star-crossed settlement, the Irish, their situation already precarious, were at the mercy of the wilderness—a desolate, ravaged no-man's land. The deep forests became a refuge where bands of bushwhackers hid after their murderous raids. Periodically detachments of Union cavalry on retaliatory sorties combed the area, killing any man they found and burning or confiscating whatever scraps might have been left behind by the guerrillas. Father Hogan (who ultimately became Bishop of Kansas City) later reported in his autobiography that the wilderness had been picked so clean that soldiers venturing through it were obliged to carry feed for their horses with them. Only the hardiest, most resourceful, most *experienced* of hill folk could have survived in the resulting wasteland.

History records that in October 1863, a Union major dispatched a detachment to Pilot Knob with some prisoners and a train of refugees from Oregon County. "If none of the Irish were in that sad column, it was only because they could not hold out that long," wrote a later historian. Defeated by the irony of time and place, the experimental society had tragically failed. The forty families left few archeological remains in their sphere of influence—outlined by the Current River on the east, the Eleven Point River and Hwy. 19 on the west, Hwy. 60 to the north, and Hwy. 160 to the south.

For a quarter of a century after the Civil War, "the Irish Wilderness" healed itself, but already it seemed haunted by its bloody past. It became known as a hunting ground and remained virtually unsettled, "not because the Wee Folk had cursed it, but because men did not know how to live with it."

Then, in the 1890s, the timber boom began. The Ozark Land and Lumber Company, operating out of Winona, scalped the Irish Wilderness of its great stands of virgin pine and hardwoods, leaving behind nothing worth taking—only place names like Bear Pen, Hungry Horse, Devil's Horn, Fool's Catch Holler, and isolated pockets of timber to supply tie rafts that swirled down the Current and the Eleven Point.

Again the Irish Wilderness was ignored. By the end of World War I, it had reverted to a dense tangle of thickets and scrub timber, to a terrain of forgotten hollows lurking in perpetual gloom. Only the moonshiners and a few trail-wise locals dared to venture into it.

Between 1935 and 1940, the Irish Wilderness came under the protection of the U.S. Forest Service. The Civilian Conservation Corps went to work re-establishing pines, building ponds and roads, and erecting fire lookout towers. Through the 1950s, the Forest Service and the Missouri Conservation Commission nurtured wildlife there, particularly deer and turkey that had been nearly wiped out in southern Missouri. And mostly because nobody could figure out how to exploit it any further for profit, the wilderness continued to heal.

In the late 1940s the battle began to establish official wilderness status for "the Irish." Special interest groups (pro-development locals, lead miners, loggers, and others) fought hard to defeat the wilderness designation, as did many of the area residents and their elected representatives, who were willing to accept even lead mining and its dangers in return for jobs.

More recently, some of the latter would have welcomed an Anheuser-Busch plant because it promised forty jobs. Said one young woman, "I wouldn't care if it had turned out to be Six Flags. . . . All we got down here is our beautiful land, and we can't eat that."

So desperate were the locals for economic development, in fact, that many would have welcomed even a facility to build nuclear bombs. In August 1950, the Eminence (Mo.) *Current Wave* reported that "public spirited citizens throughout this section are making a strong campaign to have the plant established in the Irish Wilderness. . . ." But others continued to defend "the Irish," and H-bombs did not come. Later it defeated the best efforts of uranium prospectors.

Then the U.S. Army Corps of Engineers set their sights on the Current and Eleven Point rivers, threatening to flood the entire region. An unusually outraged public response delayed that project until more permanent protection became available for the Current and Jacks Fork rivers with the establishment of the Ozark National Scenic Riverways. A few years later, the Eleven Point was given the protection of designation as a National Wild and Scenic River. And finally, in 1984, "the Irish" was given official wilderness status and protected from further exploitation.

Although the "wilderness" in this case is hardly pristine, it has demonstrated an amazing resiliency. Now, although you will find no primeval landscapes or towering virgin forests, there is plenty of second-growth, mixed hardwood forest: a "restored" wilderness, and the "authentic sense of vastness" that all proper wilderness is expected to exhibit. Many people were here, intermittently, over the past two centuries; but if wilderness is "an uncultivated and uninhabited region," then "the Irish" has a legitimate claim to that definition.

Dan Saults, a beloved conservation writer who loved the Irish Wilderness, probably exulted as he wrote:

> Blue-gray haze still softens stark ridges, like time blurring ancient paint; and morning mists still lift gently out of Fool's Catch. . . . Away from the edges you must find your own trail and imagine your own imaginings. . . . The Irish Wilderness is neither hostile space nor a friendly land; it is indifferent. The ghosts that haunt it are not menacing spectres nor friendly phantoms, but Pan-hooved spirits of deep-cut valleys and steep divides. So it does not matter to the land what classifications are drawn upon maps by Act of Congress, nor does it matter to the earth spirits whether they be called leprechauns, haunts, or hillbilly fantasies. But such labeling *may* matter to human happiness, including those who will never visit the region but want to know it's there. . . .

The Irish Wilderness is located on the Doniphan Ranger District of Mark Twain National Forest. It is accessible from Doniphan via Hwy. 160 to Hwy. J, then north seven miles to the White's Creek Trailhead at Camp Five Pond. This same trailhead may also be reached from Hwy. 60 to the north by turning south on Hwy. J for sixteen miles to Camp Five Pond.

A Wild and Scenic River

The Eleven Point River was supposedly named by French fur traders for eleven points, or bends, in the river. More than half of the flow of the Eleven Point is contributed by the torrent of water from Greer Spring. (As of this writing, it seems likely that the legendary Greer Spring will soon be included in the protected corridor of the Eleven Point River.)

Since the 1930s much of the watershed of the river has been in the Mark Twain National Forest created in the wake of logging devastation. Beleaguered by many of the same dangers that have confronted the Irish Wilderness, the river was successfully defended against damming in the 1950s.

Originally the Eleven Point was included in the legislation that eventually led to the establishment of the Ozark National Scenic Riverways, but it was eliminated from the final version of the plan. Nevertheless, the successful struggle to protect the Current and the Jacks Fork paved the way for other rivers to be protected. Just a year after signing the Ozark Riverways bill, President L. B. Johnson announced, "The time has come to identify and preserve free-flowing stretches of our greatest scenic rivers before growth and development

After the Civil War, although Samuel Greer's mill on Greer Spring was still in the deep hollow of the spring branch, a quarter of a mile down a steep hill from the road, the miller enjoyed a brisk business—so much so that he had to enlarge the mill he had built to replace the one burned during the war. Ultimately even this remodeled mill would prove inadequate and Greer would decide to build again, a decision that would cost him his son. (Courtesy of State Historical Society of Missouri)

One of the most picturesque and peaceful spots in the Mark Twain National Forest is Falling Spring Mill, near the Irish Wilderness and the Eleven Point River south of Winona, Missouri. Built in the 1920s, the mill was powered by a spring issuing from the bluff behind and above it. The falling spring water, carried to the wheel by a flume, generated electricity and ground grain. The flume has collapsed and the millpond is filling in. It is to be hoped that the mill will be stabilized and restored before its condition deteriorates past the point of no return.

make the beauty of the unspoiled waterway a memory. . . ." That promise was fulfilled by the National Wild and Scenic Rivers Act of 1968, protector of eight rivers initially, including the Eleven Point.

The Eleven Point Wild and Scenic River is administered by the Forest Service. The river and its surrounding scenery is similar to the Current River, except that there are fewer gravel bars. The precipitous hills along the river are forested with pines and afford beautiful views. Because it is spring-fed, the Eleven Point is a good year-round float stream, but access points are limited. Since motorized traffic is considered detrimental to the unusual qualities of the river and its territory, access is mostly limited to walk-in traffic except at specified access points. One of those accesses is at Greer Crossing on Hwy. 19 north of Alton.

The river is a deep jewel green at Greer Crossing. Trees overhang the bank and the scene is pastoral and quiet. The limited development there includes a boat launching ramp, primitive campsites, shady picnic areas, and a trailhead for a 3.7-mile hiking trail.

For the most explicit directions on how to access floatable rivers in Missouri, including extraordinarily detailed maps, the little book, *Missouri Ozark Waterways*, is highly recommended and absolutely invaluable, particularly for rivers affording limited access, such as the Eleven Point. Probably the biggest bargain in the state, this comprehensive guide to Missouri rivers is available at some book stores, some ranger stations, and by mail; the current edition sells for two dollars. For more information about the book and other useful titles, or to order by mail, write: Outdoor Library, Missouri Department of Conservation, Box 180, Jefferson City MO 65102.

Falling Spring Mill

About seven miles beyond Greer Crossing on Hwy. 19, watch for a tiny sign reading simply, "Falling Spring Mill." A right turn onto a gravel road (Forest Road 3170) and a two- or three-mile odyssey into the forest will lead you to one of the most picturesque sites in the entire region. When the road forks, bear left (Forest Road 3164). Numerous dogwoods line the road, so that in both spring and fall the route offers an especially lovely drive. The dirt road is narrow and susceptible to the vagaries of the weather.

At the end of the trail, on your right, set back some distance from the road at the foot of a tall bluff, is Falling Spring Mill. Dating to the early 1920s, the mill once generated electricity for its neighborhood and, according to the Society for the Preservation of Old Mills, it was a feed mill.

The small one-story frame building cozies up to the bluff to take advantage of a spring issuing from the face of the cliff somewhat above the roof of the building. Once a flume carried water to an overshot waterwheel, but the structure supporting the flume has collapsed. Now, once again, the spring water falls into a pool at the base of the cliff. The Forest Service says Falling Spring flows 125,000 gallons a day on the average.

A footbridge across the spring branch and mill pond carries the path from the small parking lot to the open door of the mill. One can step inside to inspect the old machinery still there and be transported in imagination to the days when the wheel hurried around and was accompanied by the laughter and conversation of the miller and his customers. The overshot wheel appears to be the original and would probably still turn if the flume were intact to supply it with water power.

On the parking lot side of the footbridge there is a log cabin, said to be a hundred years old. In full view of the mill are two picnic tables and a fire pit. A more perfect place for a picnic would be difficult to imagine.

Heading east on Hwy. 60, one quickly re-enters rolling pine-clad hills for the short journey to the corridor of the Ozark National Scenic Riverways.

Practical Matters

Chapter 21 — Grand Gulf, Mammoth
Spring, The Irish Wilderness

Checking Out	A Sampling	Phone
Lodging	Riverview Motel, Hwy. 63 South, P.O. Box 281, Mammoth Spring AR 72554; Village Vacations, P.O. Box 448, Cherokee Village AR 72525; Tally Ho Motel, Hwy. 19, Thayer MO; Best Western Village Inn, Rt. 6, Box 115, Hardy AR 72542; The Rusty Nail, Hwy. 19 South, Winona MO	(501) 625-3218 (800) 331-5896 or (501) 257-3258 (417) 264-2127 (501) 856-2176
Bed & Breakfasts	River Country Bed & Breakfast (Reservation Service), 1900 Wyoming, St. Louis MO 63118	(314) 965-4328 or (314) 771-1993
Campgrounds	Mark Twain National Forest, Winona MO: Greer Crossing, McCormack Lake; Many Islands Camp, Rt. 2, Mammoth Spring AR; Hardy Camper Park, Box 5, Hardy AR 72542	(314) 325-4233 (501) 856-3451 (501) 856-2356
Restaurants	Christianos, Rt. 2, Box 157, Hardy AR (Hwy. 167); Kitchen Cupboard, Box 456, Hardy AR 72542 (Downtown); The Rusty Nail, Hwy. 19 South, Winona MO	(501) 856-2550 (501) 856-2615
Main Historical Attractions	Grand Gulf State Park, Thayer MO 65791; Mammoth Spring State Park, P.O. Box 36, Mammoth Spring AR 72554 (Hwy. 63); Hardy Old Town, Main Street, Hardy AR 72542; Indian Culture Center, P.O. Box 8, Cherokee Village AR 72525	(314) 548-2525 (501) 625-7364 (501) 257-2442
Other Attractions	Arkansas Traveller Folk & Dinner Theatre, P.O. Box 536, Hardy AR 72542	(501) 856-2256
Outdoor Recreation	Irish Wilderness: Doniphan Ranger District, 1104 Walnut, Doniphan MO 63935; Mark Twain National Forest: Biking; Fishing, Floating Eleven Point River; Wood's Float & Canoe Rental, Rt. 2, Box 2549, Alton MO 65606; Spring River, Lower Current River: Fishing, Floating (For more information on both, see Where to Write); Golf: Thayer Country Club, Thayer MO; Hiking: Ozark Trail and others, Big Spring, Ozark National Scenic Riverways	(314) 996-2153 (417) 778-6497 or (417) 778-6144 (417) 264-7854

Checking Out	A Sampling	Phone
Where to Write for More Details	Mammoth Spring Chamber of Commerce, Box 1, Mammoth Spring AR 72554;	(501) 625-3959
	Hardy/Ash Flat Chamber of Commerce, Box 300, Hardy AR 72542;	(501) 856-3210
	Ozark Gateway Tourist Council, 409 Vine St., Batesville AR 72501;	
	Newport Area Chamber of Commerce, Box 518, Newport AR 72112;	(501) 523-3618
	For Information About "A Fisherman's Guide to Public Access Facilities in Arkansas Counties" and a "Floater's Kit," write Arkansas Game & Fish Commission, Information & Education Div., 2 Natural Resources Dr., Little Rock AR 72205;	(501) 223-6351
	Mark Twain National Forest Ranger District, Rt. 1, Box 182, Winona MO 65588;	(314) 325-4233
	For Information about "Missouri Ozark Waterways" and other titles, write Outdoor Library, Missouri Dept. of Conservation, Box 180, Jefferson City MO 65102	

CHAPTER 22

Ozark National Scenic Riverways

The Jacks Fork and the Current: ". . . rivers so priceless they made a park of them and let the world know that Missouri is more than mules and hillbillies."

Within a comfortable day's drive for more than twenty million people, the Ozark National Scenic Riverways includes 80,788 acres of land (61,374 of them federally owned) and 134 miles of managed river. Its annual budget approaches three million dollars, mostly for employee salaries. The Riverways celebrated its twenty-fifth anniversary in 1989.

But the rivers themselves are so old they are, on human terms, almost infinite. Scattered along their courses are knobs of igneous rock 1.5 billion years old and the impervious-to-weathering chert of gravel bars. Little wonder that the timeless rhythm of the Current and the wild canyon of the Jacks Fork stir something primeval in us.

Venture no farther than the water's edge and become aware of a river's wondrous continuity, of its link with eternity. Float on the current like any other of nature's children and be overwhelmed by the sense of kinship—a oneness with the universe you may never have previously experienced. Your ride downstream in a canoe or a johnboat may well change your view of the universe; and when you leave the river, you take it all with you: the morning's mist, the beaver that scurried up the bank, the bluejays that flew overhead screaming alarms, the tiny violets and umbrellaed mayapples under a canopy of dogwood, the dusk-blessing of an unseen whippoorwill, and even the solid bluffs that yield so slowly to the wear of time.

Backward in Time

Time seems to be reversing in the Riverways. Like a video run backward, buildings are disappearing instead of being built, forests are reclaiming roads and fields. Here is an old railroad grade, but the tracks were taken up two or three generations ago. The remainder—a one-room schoolhouse here, a pile of sawdust there, over yonder a family cemetery with weathered monuments or field stones—speak eloquently of the past. Little remains of human activity, and it is slowly fading.

During the summer "season," the Park Service offers demonstrations of corn milling, blacksmithing, and sorghum making, as well as cave tours, campfire programs, interpretive hikes, and the like. But the Riverways is not a museum. And some of man's changes are irreversible: Channels were blasted in the riverbed to allow for the transportation of logs. The gravel bars that seem so much the essence of today's Ozarks are, for the most part, undesirable results of human intervention. Comprised of gravel washed from the lumbered, unprotected slopes, they clog the streambeds.

The National Park

But even as the damage was being done, the conservation movement began. In October 1909, Missouri governor Herbert S. Hadley went johnboating on the Current River. Though not a single fish was caught on the expedition (the governor was accompanied by a large entourage, including reporters), the early "media event" drew attention to the river and the still-beautiful land remaining along its banks.

The controversy over what should be done with the Current River country began. Some wanted to preserve it in its "natural" state, others wanted it developed as a recreation playground, and still others wanted it further exploited—and dams to provide hydroelectric power.

Tourists began coming into the area to see for themselves. Between 1920 and 1930, Missouri developed state parks at Big Spring, Round Spring, Alley Spring, and Montauk Springs. There was little money to spend on developing the parks, but at least the land was set aside. And while it waited, it began to heal.

While the Missouri Department of Conservation worked to bring back the wildlife, the Forest Service (established under Teddy Roosevelt in 1905) began in 1934 to acquire land around the rivers. Civilian Conservation Corps workers planted millions of shortleaf yellow pines. The CCC operated in the region until 1941: planting, building trails, and trapping wildlife for transportation to areas better suited to

"From the horse and buggy days until the jet age," longer than most, the Powder Mill Ferry carried people across Current River at Owl's Bend, between Eminence and Ellington, Missouri. Pictured here in 1940, the ferry was called the Powder Mill Ferry for the high bluff on the east side of the river where Civil War soldiers had mined saltpeter from a cave to make gunpowder. (Courtesy of Bittersweet, Inc.)

Built in 1851, this log cabin was moved and reconstructed on the courthouse lawn at Van Buren, Missouri, in 1959 to commemorate the county's first hundred years. The twenty-four-foot logs were hand-hewn and interlocked with half-dovetail corners. Some are secured with still-visible wooden pegs. The cabin is furnished just as it might have been left by its builders.

support it. By their toil, the state parks of the region gained buildings, bridges, and spring branch channels.

In the mid-1930s the Corps of Engineers proposed damming the Current River. The success of other nearby manmade lakes sweetened the proposal for many, but area residents were bitterly opposed, as were many others who had grown to love the splendid free-flowing streams. In the midst of controversy, the first attempt to pass legislation establishing an Ozark Rivers National Monument failed. In the meantime, the waterways and their neighborhoods suffered increasing abuse. Leonard Hall, then a columnist for the St. Louis *Post-Dispatch*, warned that the area was in danger of becoming a permanent "rural slum."

The Missouri Conservation Commission and the Department of Conservation opposed the dam, and the then-governor Forrest Smith announced there would be no dam built on Current River as long as he was in office. The *Kansas City Star* and the St. Louis *Post-Dispatch* opposed the dam editorially, and numerous writers published against it. In the river valley itself almost everybody was against the dam, but they were also against a national park.

For many it was an emotional battle. Years later Dan Saults said, "The Current was a sacred stream to Missourians. There were probably 500,000 Missourians who knew, and crossed themselves at the [mention of] the name of the Current River, who never saw it. . . ."

Finally, on August 27, 1964, President Lyndon Johnson signed the act establishing the Ozark National Scenic Riverways. By mid-1966 the first tract of land had been purchased. Missouri signed over the state parks at Alley, Round, and Big springs in 1969. Formal dedication of the river park came on June 10, 1972, when Tricia Nixon Cox "christened" the Ozark National Scenic Riverways by tossing a bouquet of flowers into the waters of Big Spring.

Running the Rivers

The canoe is a relative johnny-come-lately on the rivers, popularized along with the concept of the national park. Prior to the late 1950s and early '60s, the wooden johnboat—powered and controlled by a long wooden pole—was king of the river-road. Only the river guides and the boat ride concessionaire at Big Spring Park used outboard motors; most people did not know how to maneuver a powerboat through the shallow places. Boaters might see only five or six other people on the river.

Now a floater on a summer weekend may encounter a hundred or more canoes, numerous motorboats, and hordes of people on innertubes. As a result, many experienced floaters prefer being on the river in the spring and the fall, when one is much more likely to have it almost to himself. Some even float the river in winter; they are often rewarded by the presence of bald eagles.

The visitor can easily share the experience of "running the river." A number of canoe outfitters along the rivers rent canoes by the day or by the trip, and usually included in the fee is shuttle service between put-in and take-out points. Many also offer campgrounds and over-night cabins and other amenities (see the Practical Matters Chart following this chapter).

Two Rivers and Two Towns

A certain amount of backtracking is inevitable in Riverways country —and essential if you hope to give it more than a cursory glance. Highways 60, 19, and 106 serve most places you will want to see. Two rivers—the Current and its major tributary, the Jacks Fork—comprise the Ozark National Scenic Riverways, along with numerous springs that feed them both. Two towns are the major centers of activity on the rivers: Van Buren, on Hwy. 60, and Eminence, on Hwy. 19.

The main areas of interest on the Current River are at Akers Ferry, Pulltite Spring, Round Spring, Big Spring, and Owl's Bend. On the Jacks Fork, visitors must see Alley Spring and Mill. Lists of scheduled events at the various locations are posted at the park headquarters in Van Buren and at each of the other sites.

Remarkably, the little town of Van Buren has been little changed by its encounter with world fame. Since the offices of the administrating National Park Service are located there, it is the "capital" of Ozark National Scenic Riverways. Settled as the seat of Ripley County, organized in 1833, Van Buren became instead the seat of Carter County when it was organized from parts of Ripley and Shannon Counties in 1859. Artifacts from thirty-six villages and camps of early Indians have been found near the rivers. During the Civil War, the Union Army of Southeast Missouri wintered here, 1862-63.

The unimposing courthouse building in Van Buren was built of native stones. Behind it is a log cabin, built in 1851. The cabin was moved and reconstructed on the courthouse lawn in 1959 to com-memorate the county's first hundred years. The hand-hewn twenty-four-foot logs are interlocked with half-dovetail corners; some are secured by wooden pegs. The fireplace was built in 1853 of hand-hewn rocks originally joined with mortar homemade of salt and ashes. Inside are authentic antique furnishings, including a spinning wheel and a loom.

For a good look at Current River in a lovely setting accessible even to the handicapped (such places are somewhat rare in this land of

At Watercress Spring Recreation Area on the Current River near Van Buren, Missouri, visitors can lounge in the shade with the river virtually at their feet. This is a campground in the Mark Twain National Forest near the site of the Chinese Wall—the boom that stopped railroad ties and logs being floated down the river to the railhead.

Log drives were not popular with the folks who lived along the river. Log jams often blocked the channel for days, causing flooded property and barring passage across the river. Ferry service was disrupted and people crossing the river on horseback or in wagons were endangered. In response to government hearings, regulations were formulated that restricted the floating of ties and logs on the Current River after March 1, 1915. The last recorded log drive on the Current was in 1935. (Courtesy of Bittersweet, Inc.)

steep hills and rocky ground), turn north off of Hwy. 60 in Van Buren at the National Forest garage, top the hill and follow the signs to the Watercress Spring Recreation Area. There are picnic tables under enormous old shade trees near the river—a lovely spot close to town. A hiking trail begins here, and there are campsites equipped with kitchen shelters and pine trees and lots of shade, but no hookups.

Big Spring

On your way to or from Big Spring, do not miss Skyline Drive, entered off Hwy. 103—the "scenic route" to the spring.

Big Spring is awe-inspiring the year around, but it is probably at its best in early May, when the bluff above the spring is draped in flowering Columbine and other wildflowers bloom from every rocky nook and cranny. Of all the dramatic springs in the Ozarks, none other is so accessible and easy to see. You would not even have to leave your car—but you will want to. (You may also wish to be forearmed with a can of insect repellent; for some reason, bugs love Big Spring as much as humans do. No visitor to the Ozarks should be without such protection anyway.)

Aptly named, Big Spring is the largest of the huge springs in the Ozarks, and—with an average daily flow of 276,000,000 gallons—one of the world's largest. The massive outpouring rises through a jumble of giant boulders, which causes the dramatic "boil" at the orifice, emerges as a river, and flows about a thousand feet to enlarge the Current River. During World War I, Big Spring was contaminated by chemical wastes discharged into the dry valley of Davis Creek from the Midcontinent Iron Company at Midco, a few miles north of Fremont and about ten miles from Big Spring. But when the iron furnace and chemical plant ceased operation in 1921, the spring soon cleansed itself.

Site of an early state park with more than five thousand acres, there was little development at Big Spring until 1933. Then the CCC undertook the construction of trails and bridges and the building of dikes to contain the spring branch. Many of their structures remain, including the dining lodge.

Near the lodge is a boat concession offering rides on Current River. If you do not have your own boat or do not plan to rent a canoe, this trip is highly recommended. It is well nigh impossible to fully appreciate the worth of Ozark National Scenic Riverways other than from the river itself.

The park is also a trailhead for the Ozark Trail. The peaceful hollows and narrow ridges in the Big Spring area invite you for an hour, an afternoon, or a day to explore the solitude of the forest and perhaps recapture a bit of what the pioneers in this area experienced. One can hike cross-country on the Ozark Trail, through a variety of habitats and terrain, or take one of the cut-off trails down a hollow or across a ridge for a shorter walk. Request a map at the headquarters in Van Buren or at the ranger station at Big Spring.

Eminence

By returning to Van Buren and backtracking on Hwy. 160 to Hwy. 19 and turning north, one takes the shortest and best approach to Eminence, one of the most charming of Ozarks towns. As you near Eminence on Hwy. 19 from the south, the highway becomes ever more winding, the hills longer and harder to climb. At last there is a glimpse of an old-fashioned water tower with its jaunty red cap peeking up through the trees.

Eminence was founded as the seat of Shannon County, organized in 1841 and named for George "Pegleg" Shannon, youngest member of the Lewis and Clark Expedition (by most accounts, only seventeen at the time; he later lost a leg to an infection following a skirmish with Indians). First located on the Current River, the town was burned in the Civil War by guerrillas who overran the area. After the war Eminence was laid out on the Jacks Fork of the Current.

The area was first settled in the 1820s by pioneers from Kentucky and Tennessee. Missouri's first copper mine was opened near here by Joseph Slater in 1837. Others were established, but mining was done only intermittently after Michigan's mines were opened in 1846. Iron was also mined for a time, and in World War II Missouri's only manganese mine was opened nearby.

In 1909 the Missouri Lumber and Mining Company bought forty thousand acres of timberland in Shannon County. By late 1907 they were cutting this tract exclusively and had gone to four days a week at the mill in Grandin. When the Frisco Railroad offered the company a lower freight rate if it would mill the lumber in Shannon County and ship the finished products over the Frisco lines, the decision was made to move the mill to Shannon County. Farmer Shade Orchard had sold his two-hundred-acre farm to Missouri Lumber and Mining Company in December 1906; it became the site of the company town of West Eminence, built with pieces of Grandin.

Prior to the coming of the lumber company, the settlers of the Eminence area were mostly farmers; there were a few tie hackers. Just as elsewhere in the Ozarks, people made their own soap, grew their own vegetables, hunted and trapped for their meat and fish. They depended on "store-boughten" only for what they could not raise or forage for themselves.

West Eminence, like the Missouri Lumber and Mining Company town of Grandin, consisted of the mill and its outbuildings—and about three or four hundred company-built and owned houses. Most of them had three rooms, running water, and bathrooms. The town had fire hydrants and street lights, rarities in that time and place. For a time the nation's only hub mill was located here, producing wagon-wheel hubs of the finest oak. Eight to ten men turned out seventy-two thousand sets of hubs a year, four in a set.

A newspaper editorial of the time proclaimed:

> Shannon County is "on the improve . . ." nearly every man drives a spanking (and kicking) team of mules; new wagons are now the rule; the men wear better clothes and drink more whiskey; a new baby can be found in almost every hollow stump, and the girls—bless their dear hearts—are able to wear red stockings, long dresses and bustles as big as the Shannon County debt used to be. Oh, we're getting in fine shape.

But West Eminence endured smallpox epidemics in 1900 and 1901. The 1918 flu epidemic hit hard, sometimes killing as many as five or six people a day. Whole families were wiped out.

During the tenure of the Missouri Lumber and Mining Company, railroads were expanding at a rapid pace; tie cutting became big business. Doniphan, just fifteen miles south of Grandin, was a shipping point for a large area and became the "Crosstie Capital of the World." Regularly floated on the Current River, the ties were made in the woods during the winter and early spring, then hauled to the river and stacked to dry, out of reach of high water. They were run down the river in the fall when the threat of flash floods was minimal. Near Van Buren, a boom across the river stopped the rafts of ties or logs. Known as the Chinese Wall, the boom was built of fourteen-inch pine beams strung from bank to bank. On at least one occasion, the Chinese Wall yielded to the force of moving logs and five thousand of them were lost downstream.

The river drives were the controversy of their time. Jams often blocked the river for days, causing flooded property and barring passage across the river. They disrupted ferry service and endangered people crossing the river on horseback or in wagons. Public resentment against the drives surfaced in 1913 when the Corps of Engineers held hearings at Van Buren. Regulations were formulated that governed the floating of ties and logs on the Current River after March 1, 1915. The year 1935 saw the last recorded log drive on the river.

At the corner of Main and Missouri Streets in Eminence are the "new" courthouse (1941) and an old log cabin. Diagonally across the street to the south is a Rexall Drug Store that features an old-time soda fountain. The store is also outfitted with antique display cases and other fixtures; for those old enough to remember when such things were "modern," stepping into the drug store is truly nostalgic.

Eminence is famous for its Cross Country Trail Rides. For a week at a time in May, June, August, and October, thousands of "horsey people" converge on the area with their mounts to ride through the hollows and over the ridges of Shannon County and across Current River. Many have been returning for years; for them, it is like a reunion where they visit with friends made on the ride. "I always tell people it's like riding through *National Geographic* magazine," said one woman. "It's a beautiful place to ride. As many times as we've ridden through this country we're still in awe." Riders come from nearly every state and several foreign countries (see the Practical Matters Chart).

Alley Spring and Mill

West of Eminence on Hwy. 106 is Alley Spring and Mill, another "mandatory" stop for every visitor to Ozark National Scenic Riverways. A separate parking lot is available for the handicapped; to reach it, go west a little farther on Hwy. 106 and watch for the turnoff just beyond the ranger station.

The spring is named for John Alley, one of the region's first prominent farmers, and an early postmaster at a nearby location. With an average flow of eighty-one million gallons daily, the spring wells up from beneath a hundred-foot bluff, mounds slightly into a one-acre pool before spilling over a dam made of river rock and concrete, and then surges down a half-mile branch to the Jacks Fork River. The dam channels a portion of the spring water through a headrace that drives a turbine wheel at the mill.

Once, sometime before 1930, the spring ceased to flow. After about twelve hours, the flow resumed; but the spring was muddy for several days. Later it was learned that at about the same time, a large sink formed in the upland about fifteen miles northwest of the spring. Geologists now believe that the spring's supply channel was temporarily blocked by the collapse of the sinkhole.

Alley Spring Mill was once better known as "Red Mill." In 1858 a land deed for eighty acres, including the spring, was granted to James McCormac, who apparently did not develop it. In 1869 his heirs sold the land to Ike Barksdale, a blacksmith, and his partner, John Dougherty, who built a smithy and a small store at the spring. They also built a dam to furnish power for turning a water wheel to grind corn.

In 1881 the eighty acres and "Barksdale Spring," the mill, and store sold to Charles Klepzig. When Klepzig died, his family allowed the dam and the mill to deteriorate. In 1893 George McCaskill bought the site, restored the dam, and built the present mill building. He installed a steel turbine waterwheel and roller mill machinery. McCaskill milled both flour and meal and ran the store and smithy. The spring, however, was still referred to as Barksdale Spring.

When McCaskill's mill was successful, he invited John Alley to move his post office upriver to the mill site to better serve the neighborhood. The mill became the center of a community that included the post office, a general store, a blacksmith shop, a sawmill, and a school. Four of the original milling machines remain of what was then one of the most up-to-date mills in the Ozarks. The machinery could grind fifty barrels of flour a day; in addition to flour and cornmeal, the mill turned out cattle feed, powered a sawmill, and furnished electricity for nearby homes.

People began to speak of going to Alley instead of to Barksdale Spring. The post office survived for almost half a century. The site became the fourth Missouri state park in 1924 and is now included in Ozark National Scenic Riverways. A small museum in the millhouse is open to visitors during the summer. A one-room school building is also on the grounds near the mill.

Near Alley Mill a footbridge across the Jacks Fork affords an excellent view of that river—and one of the most popular swimming holes in the Ozarks. The Jacks Fork was named for "Captain" John Jacks, a Shawnee Indian who settled near the headwaters of the river. He acquired the title of "captain" when he was taken to see a steamboat on the Mississippi. Jacks was so excited by the boat that the steamer's skipper gave him his cap. And the legends began to grow around the Indian who lived up a wild fork of the Current. With long black hair and the dark blue river captain's cap, he was no doubt a memorable figure as he poled his boat on the river.

North of Eminence, near the Shannondale Community Church, is the Shannondale Craft Center. By long tradition, classes in the old cabin crafts are taught there in the summer.

More Big Springs

Although springs are common in the Ozarks, they are revered. Most of the largest or most beautiful springs are now protected by state or national forests or by national parks. For most of the region's history, springs have supplied the water of life. Many were thought to be medicinal and capable of restoring health and vigor to the afflicted. Mineralized springs were a source of salt for the earliest pioneers. With its constant cool temperature, spring water provided the best means of refrigeration known to most Ozarkers until well into this century. The log cabin homes of settlers were built as close as possible to springs. Like veritable fountains of life, they were the sites of religious services, picnics, and—as suppliers of power for mills to grind meal and saw logs—often the center of community life. Even the first electricity experienced in many areas was generated from the power of a spring.

More than fifty springs contribute their waters to the Current and the Jacks Fork rivers; the Current is approximately 70 percent spring water. Many of the springs and other scenic sites can be viewed only from the rivers themselves, but some of the more spectacular sights are reachable on foot, and even by automobile. To see them, it is necessary to do some driving and backtracking, but since the scenery is so pleasant, even the drives are enjoyable. You can not be said to have truly seen Ozark National Scenic Riverways unless you have seen the major springs.

Round Spring

On Hwy. 19 north of Eminence is quietly intriguing Round Spring. Though it does not gush or roar as do many other Ozarks springs, Round Spring is one of the most beautiful. The spring forms a pool of water of a shade of blue that seems almost unearthly, a deep aquamarine blue tinted slightly green by the profusion of moss growing in and around it, and reflecting the colors of wildflowers blooming on the bluff encircling it.

The water rises quietly—deceptively so—in a nearly circular basin —about eighty feet across and thirty feet high—formed by the collapse of a cavern roof. Part of the roof remains intact as a natural bridge beneath which the spring water hurries toward nearby Current River. Curiously, the pool seems to rise and fall somewhat in correlation to the rise or drop in barometric pressure. The average daily flow is twenty-six million gallons.

Osage Indian lore says that an Indian brave became so angered by insults from his companions that he struck the ground with his war club, using such force that the tremors he produced caused the cave-in.

The spring is some distance from the oversized parking lot, and there are no signs to direct the visitor. Follow the path across the spring branch and climb the hill beyond, almost to the top.

Pulltite Spring is not accessible by car; but at the junction of Hwy. 19 and Road EE, the turnoff to the Pulltite river access, there is a picnic ground known as Shannondale Inspiration Point where you can look out over the surrounding hillsides to the south. The riverside campground at Pulltite is delightful, as are the shady picnic grounds there.

The place names in this neighborhood are as colorful as any in the Ozarks. *Pulltite,* for example, is said to have resulted when horses and mules, pulling a heavily loaded wagon up the hill from a mill near Pulltite Spring, stretched their harnesses to the snapping point; it was a "tight pull."

Jerktail Landing in Clow State Forest was named in a similar manner when muleskinners, hauling heavy loads of copper and iron ore across the river and up the slick riverbanks, would yell, "*Jerk tails!*" at just the right moment to encourage the mules to strain extra hard.

Owl's Bend and Blue Spring

The visitor center at Owl's Bend, on Hwy. 106 east of Eminence, is the site of demonstrations staged by the Park Service. (From Round Spring or Pulltite, backtrack south to Eminence on Hwy. 19 and turn left [east] onto Hwy. 106 at Eminence.) There are no campsites at Owl's Bend, but the river access is beautiful; several shaded picnic tables are nearby. Pit toilets are available if the visitor center is closed.

This locale on Current River was home to several Indian encampments and, later, one of the most prosperous early farms. One of the last water-powered ferries in the state ran at nearby Powder Mill Creek. The canoe landing at Owl's Bend affords the visitor an especially fine look at Current River.

The main attraction on this side of the Riverways is Blue Spring. The Indians called it "the Spring of the Summer Sky." There are several "Blue Springs" in the Ozarks, but this one is undoubtedly the biggest, the bluest, and the most beautiful. Experiencing it requires some work, but it is worth the effort.

Blue Spring is in Shannon County not far west of the Reynolds County line. From Owl's Bend continue east on Hwy. 106 and watch for a small sign indicating the right turn to Blue Spring. The gravel road is narrow and often steep, winding down the side of a forested mountain for about three miles. At the end of the trail, deep in the forest, are a couple of picnic tables and a sign directing visitors to the trail to Blue Spring.

Still almost a half mile from the tiny parking area, the spring is protected by its isolation. Most of the shady trail through the woods is fairly flat, either bare earth or gravel, and it parallels the Current River for some distance, adding to the charm of the walk. The river is wide and beautiful here, and a number of gnarled old trees lean over its bank to greet canoeists at a small, steep landing.

You hear the spring branch before you see it, as it rushes toward you and hurries to join the Current. The air becomes appreciably cooler as you near the spring. At the end of the trail an observation platform extends slightly over the surface of the spring pool so that you can stand above the water and look down into its blue depths. The deepest known spring in the Ozarks, with an explored depth of 256 feet (divers could go no farther), Blue Spring averages ninety million gallons per day. The water rises quietly, but flows swiftly toward the Current. The spring pool is about seventy-five feet across, and you can see some forty feet down and clearly make out the huge chute from which the water wells and the bowl-shaped basin that contains it. The pool is deeply shaded by a semi-circle of bluff overhead. The tubular orifice of the spring plunges beneath the towering bluff at a steep angle; it is this steep angle and extremely deep water that heightens the deep blue color of the spring.

Occasional air bubbles break on the surface of the pool like the ripples from rain drops. Although the spring emerges from the chute absolutely silently, the slight current keeps in motion the profusion of green mosses and watercress growing along the bottom and sides of the rock bowl and ripples the ribbon grass. Cool air occasionally wafts from the surface of the crystalline water.

The intense blue color is said to be caused by quantities of minute particles of mineral or organic matter leached out of the ground and held in suspension in the pool. The particles diffuse the blue wavelengths of light in the visible spectrum. But scientific explanations notwithstanding, the spring appears to be a deep lapis lazuli that intensifies to near-inkiness in its depths. At the same time, it is absolutely clear—a phenomenon one must witness for himself to comprehend.

Once the site of an early trading post on the river, the spring is steeped in hill legend. One story remembers a woodcutter who, with his mule, worked on the steep hillside near the sheer-walled bluff above the spring pool. The pair skidded logs from a cutting site above the bluff to a nearby ridge road. Suddenly the mule stepped on a nest of yellow jackets. When the wasps attacked him, the frenzied mule bolted over the edge of the bluff and plummeted into the depths of the pool with a horrendous splash. When the poor woodsman ran to peer over the edge of the cliff, he saw nothing but bubbles rising from the deep pool below. He figured his mule was drowning. The bubbles continued to come up for a long time, and eventually so did the mule, swimming hard but free of yellow jackets.

After your trip into the forest to see Blue Spring, you can easily imagine settlers "bowin' and spikin' in the jillikins."

"Bowin' and Spikin' in the Jillikins"

"If someone told you he was 'goin' bowin' an' spikin' in th' braintch' you would have no idea what he was going to do unless you are an

Early Ozarkers did not fish for sport. They fished to put food on the family table—"meat fishing," an old-timer called it. But strings of fish like this one brought men from the cities to fish the Ozarks rivers in very early times. (Courtesy of Bittersweet, Inc.)

older native of the southeastern Missouri Ozarks," says Dr. James Price, who directs the University of Missouri's Southeast Missouri Archaeological Research Center. "Translated, it means he is going to shoot fish with a bow and arrows in a small stream or spring branch. The word 'jillikins' means rugged, uninhabited country."

Possibly as early as the 1830s, natives of the Current, Jacks Fork, Eleven Point, Black, and St. Francis valleys used bows and arrows to kill fish and game. The practice lasted into the 1950s, prolonged by the privations of the Great Depression. For people so poor they could not afford a firearm or who had to save their severely limited ammunition for large game only, this kind of hunting was undertaken to provide survival rations for the family. Since the practice seems to be found only in the southeastern Missouri Ozarks, and because he has found similar projectiles in an excavated Shawnee site, Dr. Price believes the early pioneers may have learned the practice from the Shawnee or Delaware Indians who briefly occupied the Current and Jacks Fork valleys in the 1820s. "Dogs usually accompanied the hunter to keep the game moving," says Dr. Price, "and it was said of a good dog that one had to stop up one of his nostrils to keep him from chasing two rabbits at the same time."

The Ozarker fashioned small arrowheads from large horseshoe nails, a project typical of the ingenuity of his "make-do" philosophy. Other projectile points were made from scrap iron, ranging from bits of wagon or buggy rims to bolts. Forging was done in a small blacksmith shop, or often in the cabin yard using a charcoal fire to heat the metal. The frugal hunters made the arrowshafts used in fishing from straight-grained pine so they would float in the water with the point downward, making them easier to recover. Bows were handmade, preferably of red cedar, and strung with heavy twine—or with baling wire.

Another way men put food on the table was by *gigging* fish. Without thought of sport, fish were taken for food in the most expedient and efficient manner. "Gigging is meat fishing," said an old-timer recently. Still done by natives, gigging is now limited by law to "rough" fish, mostly suckers. Like "bowin' and spikin'," gigging requires great skill in knowing how to compensate for light refraction in the water and in judging the depth of the deceptive, crystal-clear water. Newcomers to the art rarely master the skill of simultaneously balancing in the bow of the boat—standing erect, gauging the flow of the current and the direction and speed of the moving boat, the depth of the water, the movement of the target fish.

Once made by hand from yellow native pine, today the gig pole is available at a lumberyard. In the southwest corner of Missouri during the heyday of the lead mines, a popular gig pole was the powder stick used in tamping explosives in the mine.

Nowadays gigging is usually done at night. Before gas lanterns, the old-timers used burning pine knots to provide primitive illumination, then graduated to carbide lights. With the advent of gas lanterns, they nailed a board across the gunwales of the boat to project about a foot on each side and lashed a lantern on either side to light the deep holes in the river. These days quartz halogen lamps powered by a portable generator illuminate the night. And where a homemade wooden johnboat poled by hand was once the craft of choice, now it is an aluminum johnboat and outboard motor equipped with a jet unit for shallow running.

Noodling is another form of fishing in the Ozarks, now illegal. Taking advantage of the fact that catfish are virtually immobile while spawning or when protecting their nests, the fisherman had only to locate a nest, block the fish's exit, and then reach into the cavity and grab the fish with his bare hands. Some used a hand-held hook about six inches long in order to avoid injury to hand and arm from the catfish's formidable defenses.

Also sometimes known as *hogging* or *bulldogging*, noodling was likewise not done for sport, but to feed hungry families. "I don't like to fish with a pole," one man explained. "You might sit there and starve to death." Because the fish were so important to his family's livelihood, the fisherman might even construct nest cavities to attract the fish. This also gave him the advantage of knowing where the fish would be. Since noodling was so devastating to catfish populations, it was banned. Occasionally a noodling poacher is still apprehended.

From Owl's Bend or Blue Spring, continue east on Hwy. 106 to Hwy. 21 and turn left (north) on Hwy. 21 for the remarkable journey from Ozark National Scenic Riverways to the Old Leadbelt.

Practical Matters

Chapter 22 — The Riverways

Checking Out	A Sampling	Phone
Lodging	River's Edge Resort, HCR 1, Box 11, Eminence MO 65466;	(314) 226-3233
	Montauk State Park (cabins and motel), Rt. 5, Box 278, Salem MO 65560;	(314) 548-2434 (800) 334-6946
	Skyline Lodge, Skyline Drive, Van Buren MO 63965;	(314) 323-4144
	Smalley's Budget Host Motel, Hwy. 60 East, Box 358, Van Buren MO 63965	(314) 323-4263 or (800) 727-4263
Bed & Breakfasts	Hawkins House, Box 27, Main St., Eminence MO	(314) 226-3793
Campgrounds	Riverways: Alley Spring, Rt. 106, 5 miles west Eminence MO;	(314) 323-4236
	Big Spring, Rt. 103 south 4 miles, Van Buren MO;	(314) 323-4236
	Montauk State Park, Rt. 5, Box 278, Salem MO	(314) 548-2434
Restaurants	Skyline Supper Club, Skyline Drive, Van Buren MO 63965;	(314) 323-4144
	Jacks Fork & Spoon, Hwy. 106 West, Box 118, Eminence MO 65466;	(314) 226-5529
	Float Stream Restaurant, East of Bridge on Hwy. 60, Van Buren MO	(314) 323-9606
Main Historical Attractions	Alley Spring Mill and Story's Creek Schoolhouse, Hwy. 106, 5 miles west Eminence; Round Spring Cave, Hwy. 19 north of Eminence; Devil's Well near Salem; Blacksmith Shop and Sorghum Mill at Owl's Bend Visitors Center, Owl's Bend, Hwy. 106 east of Eminence MO; Historic CCC Buildings, Big Spring south of Van Buren MO; Akers Ferry (all Ozark National Scenic Riverways); Log Cabins at Van Buren MO and Eminence MO Courthouses; Rexall Soda Fountain, Main Street, Eminence MO; Mill at Montauk State Park near Salem MO	(314) 323-4236

Checking Out	A Sampling	Phone
Outdoor Recreation	Deer Run Golf Course, Hwy. M, 2 mi. north of Hwy 60, Van Buren MO 63965;	(314) 323-8475
	Jetboat Tours, Eminence Excursion Tours;	(314) 226-3642
	Hiking: Ozark Trail;	(314) 323-4236
	Cross Country Trail Rides, Box 15, Eminence MO;	(314) 226-3492
	Fishing, Floating, Canoeing: Akers Ferry Canoe Rental, HCR 81, Box 90, Salem MO 65560;	(314) 858-3224 or (314) 858-3228
	Jacks Fork Canoe Rental & Campground, Box 188, Eminence MO 65466;	(314) 226-3434
	Boat Rides on Current River, Big Spring south of Van Buren MO	
Where to Write for More Details	Ozark National Scenic Riverways, Box 490, Van Buren MO 63965;	(314) 323-4236
	Eminence Chamber of Commerce, Box 415, Eminence MO 65466;	
	Van Buren Chamber of Commerce, Box 356, Van Buren MO 63965;	
	Montauk State Park, Rt. 5, Box 278, Salem MO 65560;	(314) 548-2434
	Mark Twain National Forest, 1221 South Main, Salem MO 65560	(314) 729-6656

CHAPTER 23

The Leadbelt

The "Leadbelt" was one of the earliest-settled areas of the entire Midwest—certainly by the early 1700s. The region includes Washington, St. Francois, Madison, and Iron counties. Within that broad area, "Tiff Belt" was applied to the Washington County barite mines, while the iron mines of northeast Iron County were sometimes referred to as the "Iron Mountain District." To confuse the matter even further, the entire area began to be called the "Old Leadbelt" after discoveries in the 1960s of lead deposits in western Iron and Reynolds counties, which then became the "New Leadbelt." *Leadbelt* appears as a place name throughout the entire region on everything from banks to beauty shops.

But sometimes the neighborhood is referred to as the Courtois Hills (pronounced CODE-away locally), as well as loosely termed "the eastern Ozarks." Frequent reference is also made to the St. Francois Mountains (pronounced St. Francis). And, paradoxically, a common sight seen in the leadbelt is a large truck loaded with logs.

In the 1880s the beautiful Belleview and Arcadia valleys were discovered by wealthy families from St. Louis, and the St. Francois Mountains were popular with vacationers from soon after the Civil War. Despite its long history of human habitation and exploitation, this area of the Ozarks has retained its rural character as well as its scenic beauty. But there also seems to be an unspoken awareness of the proximity of the "big city." The St. Louis metroplex casts a long shadow—and a certain faint flavor of sophistication largely lacking in other more rural locations in the Ozarks.

The hills in this area—knobs of igneous rocks such as granite—

419

were originally volcanic mountain-islands in a sea of sedimentary rock, much of which has already been eroded away. Deep gorges called shut-ins are being water-carved into the resistant igneous rocks, a geological happenstance that produces scenery of stunning beauty and diversity. A refreshing visual treat is the frequent juxtaposition of pink granite and green pines, varied occasionally by a splash of blue water.

By the time the traveler reaches Ellington on Hwy. 21 via Hwy. 106 eastward from Eminence, he is increasingly aware of the vast pine forests. South of Centerville on Hwy. 21 is a highway cut where the exposed granite is almost a perfect pastel pink.

Reynolds County

Lovely Reynolds County is very sparsely settled—and wild. Its seat, Centerville, is one of the smallest county seats in the Ozarks, and one of the most picturesque. The present courthouse was built in 1872 from handmade bricks at a cost of eight thousand dollars. On its lawn are numerous old maple trees. Fur trappers were the county's first white settlers, dating to 1812. Slowly the banks of the numerous small streams became dotted with log cabins.

Almost alpine in its piney profusion, the drive east toward Lesterville offers pleasant pastoral scenery of valleys with the hills as a backdrop. Before you reach Lesterville, a popular outfitting point for float trips on the Black River, you will want to visit one of the most accessible and dramatic of the fifty-five shut-ins in Missouri, most in the St. Francois Mountains.

About a mile east of the junction of Hwys. 21 and 49, watch for Road N leading to Johnson's Shut-Ins State Park.

Johnson's Shut-Ins

The area surrounding the Johnson's Shut-Ins State Park retains the wilderness qualities of presettlement times. In the park the swift waters of the East Fork of the Black River flow through a canyonlike gorge, called a "shut-in." The blue-gray, steel-hard rocks that are exposed in the shut-ins are nearly 1.5 billion years old, formed when towering volcanoes erupted, spewing avalanches of magma, clouds of ash, debris, and turbulent gases. The molten material spread out layer upon layer, and cooled to form the igneous rocks. Subsequently, about five hundred million years ago, a shallow inland sea surrounded the already ancient and eroded volcanic mountains. Hundreds of feet of sediment in the sea hardened into rock—such as dolomite, limestone, sandstone, and shale—that buried the older volcanic rock.

When the sea retreated about 250 million years ago, rain and wind eroded away great volumes of the sedimentary rock. Streams sliced down through the soft sedimentary rock layers and encountered the buried igneous rock below. Some sections were caught in igneous rock saddles, or low places between buried igneous hills. Now trapped between these hills, the water churned over the resistant rock, and erosion occurred most rapidly along the rock's weaker fracture zones. Swirling over and between the rocks, the river scoured and carved the potholes, chutes, and spectacular canyonlike gorges locally called shut-ins.

Shut-in is a term commonly used in the southern Appalachian region to describe a gorge. People from that area who moved into the Ozarks extended the meaning to refer to "a gorge cut by a stream whose valley is locally restricted as it cuts through or between resistant igneous rocks." Above and below the shut-in, the stream flows through a wide or open valley, and it has cut a canyon through an isolated mass of rock instead of flowing around it. Topographically, there is only one shut-in, but because of two distinct areas of rapids, the plural form of the word commonly has been used in the state park.

The shut-ins are viewable at the end of a level quarter-mile asphalt-and-wood path. The overlook is accessible by motorized wheelchair with care. Beyond the platform is a more strenuous hiking trail that affords spectacular views. An unusual water playground, the shut-ins are popular with swimmers and those just wishing to cool off in the clear, cold water. Under normal conditions, the area is a safe and attractive place to swim, but it must be avoided in high water because of the tricky currents and swirling potholes. Under no circumstances should one dive.

The park offers fifty-two campsites, half of which have electrical hookups; many are reserveable two weeks in advance. A gate at the entrance to the campground helps ensure that only registered campers enter.

The Ozark Trail

In addition to the hiking trails in the state park, there are a number of trails in this neighborhood that have been developed by the Mark Twain National Forest (see the Practical Matters Chart). Taum Sauk Mountain, about six miles southwest of Ironton on Hwy. 21, offers a trailhead for a portion of the Ozark Trail. Accessible on Road CC off of Hwy. 21, the mountain is the highest point in Missouri. At the summit there is a shady picnic area and pit toilets, but no view from ground level because of a dense forest blanketing the hilltop.

Spectacular in wet weather, Mina Sauk Falls on Taum Sauk Mountain is accessible only from the Ozark Trail, a trans-Ozarks hiking trail that offers walkers a chance to challenge the geography. In this part of the Ozarks, sections of the trail traverse official wildernesses, cross Taum Sauk Mountain, slice through Johnson's Shut-Ins State Park and across the Ozark National Scenic Riverways. The combined trails provide a path through Ozarks history, leading from a St. Louis older than the United States into Arkansas, where it becomes the Ozark Highland Trail.

The trails are marked as lightly as possible; take a map and compass with you. No wheels are allowed, but some sections are open to horse-backing. Trailheads in this neighborhood are at Johnson's Shut-Ins State Park, Taum Sauk Lookout Tower on Hwy. CC, and Hwy. 21 north of the Royal Gorge Natural Area.

Royal Gorge is a dazzling pink-granite shut-in virtually in the shadow of Hwy. 21. The creek runs only in wet weather, and because of its proximity to the highway on an almost blind curve, it is not a good place to loiter. But there is a turnout at the base of the sheer granite bluff on the west side of the highway across from the shut-in, as well as a foot-path into the gorge.

Arcadia Valley

The first settler arrived in the Arcadia valley about 1807. Missouri's first working iron furnace, Ashbrand's, was built about 1815. Before the Iron Mountain Railroad reached here in 1858 and the town of Pilot Knob was founded, iron ore was hauled over the 1843 Ste. Genevieve-Iron Mountain-Pilot Knob plank road.

Since the railroad had been completed to nearby Pilot Knob before the Civil War, this area was important during the war. In order to defend the railroad, Union troops were garrisoned at Ironton. For a short time in 1861, U. S. Grant, a brigadier general in the 21st Illinois Regiment, served as commander.

Ironton, at the base of Shepherd Mountain in pastoral Arcadia Valley, is the seat of Iron County. To reach the town, turn off Hwy. 21 onto Road M and follow the signs to the business district. Ironton was laid out as the seat of Iron County in 1857 and the courthouse—two-story brick with Greek Revival-style cornice and entrance—was built 1858-60. Occupied intermittently by both sides during the Battle of Pilot Knob, September 1864, the building still bears the scars of Con-federate gunfire. As in a great many other Ozarks county seats, a century-old gazebo graces one corner of the courthouse lawn and a memorial to the county's war dead stands on another.

In 1867, near the site in Ironton where U. S. Grant had been commissioned brigadier general, a twelve-room brick mansion was built. Judge J. W. Emerson of St. Louis landscaped the six-acre site

This statue of Ulysses S. Grant was erected in the 1880s by his former troops to commemorate the time and place that he received his commission as general in 1861 and "parting from this place entered on his career of victory." Only a few miles from this spot in Ironton, Missouri, is Fort Davidson, a Civil War battlefield, at Pilot Knob, Missouri.

with shrubs and flowers, preserving several great oak trees. A lake was built below a small spring and became home to ducks, geese, and other fowl. At some point a graceful gazebo was added to the peaceful scene. The estate became known as Emerson Park. In 1899 the survivors of General Grant's 21st Illinois Volunteer Regiment erected a monument in Grant's honor at Emerson Park. Eventually the mansion—which had served for a time as a hospital—was demolished and a Catholic church built on the site. The statue of Grant (and the lake, the ducks, and the gazebo) were allowed to remain in place amidst the towering shade trees. But a few years ago the statue of General Grant disappeared without a trace.

Then, after an absence of about two years, the statue just as mysteriously reappeared—minus one broken-off arm. Now restored and back in place on its Missouri red granite pedestal, General Grant's statue again looks serenely across the lovely little lake and the peaceful setting of "Emerson Park." To reach the churchyard, turn left at the four-way stop at the Ironton square after leaving Hwy. 21 on Hwy. M. Go one block and watch for a stone retaining wall on your right. Near the end of the wall is a small entrance and a narrow drive leading to the statue; go slowly and watch out for the ducks.

The Battle of Pilot Knob

Back on Hwy. 21, just a couple of miles north of Ironton, lies Pilot Knob. And looming over the town is Pilot Knob Mountain, presumably so named because it was used as a landmark by the Indians and early pioneers. In the iron mining boom of the 1840s and '50s, Pilot Knob and Iron Mountain in nearby St. Francois County were thought to be of solid iron. Smelting was expanded when the railroad reached Pilot Knob in 1858. The mines have been worked intermittently since then.

Pilot Knob was the site of a dramatic Civil War battle in September 1864. At nearby Fort Davidson Historical Site, the battlefield is preserved. Here Missouri has recently opened an excellent interpretative center and museum featuring an audio-visual program accompanied by an eye-witness account of the battle, artifacts, photographs, and more. To reach the site, turn right off of Hwy. 21 onto Hwy. V in Pilot Knob. The fort is almost immediately on your right.

Built in 1863 by Union forces to guard the ore deposits and the railhead on the St. Louis and Iron Mountain Railroad, Fort Davidson is an "earthen redoubt"—surrounded by a dry moat—in the gap between Pilot Knob Mountain and Shepherd Mountain. The fort was situated so the enemy would have to cross hundreds of yards in the open to reach it, but it was vulnerable to artillery on top of the encircling hills.

In September 1864 Gen. Sterling Price led a Confederate force, estimated at about twelve thousand men, into Missouri with the objective of capturing St. Louis. Union general William Rosecrans, when he heard that Price had crossed into Missouri, sent St. Louis district commandant Gen. Thomas Ewing and a detachment of about a thousand men to Pilot Knob by train. By noon of September 26, Ewing had reached the earthworks known as Fort Davidson. That afternoon he sent two companies of infantry through Ironton to patrol the Fredericktown road. They ran head-on into the advance brigades of the Confederates. Quickly driven back into Ironton, the Union patrol sought refuge in the courthouse. Nightfall and a heavy rainstorm brought the battle to an end. At dawn, as a misty rain fell on the Arcadia Valley, the Union patrol fought its way from the courthouse to the fort.

And then the Federals found themselves completely bottled up in the fort with no avenue of escape. At 2:00 P.M. Confederate cannons opened on the earthen fort from the top of Shepherd Mountain. Troops—formed in long columns three ranks deep—slowly moved toward the fort. Inside the walled enclosure, the Union soldiers waited while their artillery fired upon the advancing Confederate lines. At short range across the flat, the big guns could not miss. But the Confederates came on. When they were five hundred yards from the walls, the Union troops were ordered to fire. Since there was not room for all the riflemen around the walls of the fort, they worked in details to reload the guns. With empty muskets being passed down and loaded ones handed up, the three hundred rifles along the walls spewed forth lead without pause. Dense clouds of smoke blanketed the fort and rose in a column hundreds of feet high, adding to the confusion.

At two hundred yards the Southern brigades broke into a crazed running charge. Met with the barrage of fire from the fort, the Confederate line hesitated, surged again, hesitated, and then stormed ahead. Some of the determined Rebels plunged into the dry moat surrounding the fort, which they had not expected. The Union gunners leaned over the walls and tossed grenades on the huddled Confederates. The rest of Price's soldiers finally turned and ran, only to be shot in the back as they attempted to flee.

When finally the smoke cleared, the terrible carnage was revealed. For five hundred yards on three sides of the fort the ground was covered with dead and wounded men. In a short few minutes one of the bloodiest clashes of the Civil War had taken place. The Con-

The courthouse lawn in Ironton, Missouri, is perhaps the loveliest in the Ozarks. Dating to 1858, the courthouse, although occupied by both sides during the Battle of Pilot Knob, September 1864, is one of the few courthouses in the region to escape destruction during the Civil War. However, the building does still bear the scars of Confederate gunfire. A century-old gazebo graces one corner of the lawn.

Pink elephants rest at Elephant Rocks State Park just off Hwy. 21 on Hwy. RA near Graniteville, Missouri. The huge "elephant" rocks are on top of the hill beyond the picnic area. The gray rocks on the side of the hill—still imprisoned in its grasp—are more strongly reminiscent of half-submerged humpback whales. Found only in this location, the gigantic granite menagerie is extraordinary.

federacy had lost nearly fifteen hundred men. That night Price's entire command lay in a state of confusion. Most companies were scattered, and only a few of them posted sentries or maintained any military discipline. Many searched for friends and relatives among the fallen.

Inside the fort, Ewing knew that with the dawn Confederate artillery—perched on top of Shepherd Mountain—would render the fort untenable. His intelligence told him that the enemy were building three hundred scaling ladders with which to breach the walls of the fort at daybreak. His own stock of ammunition would be insufficient to carry his troops through another attack.

Ewing summoned his officers for a council. They had three options: remain and fight; surrender; evacuate. By a majority of one, the officers elected to evacuate the fort. At midnight they muffled the horses' hooves and the wheels of the six field guns, blanketed the drawbridge with a layer of straw topped by a few tents, and marched the column silently out of the fort. They moved north along the road to Potosi and marched unchallenged right through the loose Confederate lines. In a few hours, Ewing and his men were miles away from the fort.

At 2:00 A.M., a demolition squad left behind in the fort prepared to destroy the powder magazine in the center of the earthen enclosure. After forming a pile of gunpowder in the middle of the magazine—and unable to find a fuse—they trailed gunpowder across the drawbridge. Then they mounted their horses while the sergeant applied a match to the powder. As the sparks flew, he leaped onto his horse and rode off with the others. They had ridden only about seventy-five yards before the magazine erupted in a tremendous explosion, but the squad made it safely through the Rebel lines.

The blast was heard twenty miles away. Windows shattered in Pilot Knob, trees fell and dirt was thrown in every direction. From his headquarters in nearby Ironton, Price saw the flash and heard the explosion, but believed it to be an accident. The survivors, he reportedly thought, would surrender in the morning. At dawn his dwindling army awakened to find the fort empty, with a giant smoking hole in the center (today the crater is a wet-weather pond).

With his best assault troops lost and two of his divisions in disarray, Price was unable to mount an attack on the now-reinforced city of St. Louis.

Pink Elephant Walk

Just three miles north of Pilot Knob on Hwy. 21, Graniteville was the site of a granite quarry dating to 1869. This stone was used for the

Surrounding Fort Davidson, the "earthen redoubt" defended by Union troops during the Battle of Pilot Knob in September 1864, is this remainder of the "moat," or trench, that surrounded the fort. In was in this trench that hundreds of Confederate soldiers died. Though this picture is thought to date to the 1920s, the moat looks much the same today. The fort is now a Missouri Historic Site at Pilot Knob, Missouri. (Courtesy of State Historical Society of Missouri)

piers on historic Eads Bridge and many buildings in early St. Louis, as well as for cobbles in the city's streets.

Near Graniteville are the gargantuan pink Elephant Rocks: Elephant Rocks State Park is just off Hwy. 21 on Road RA. Near the park's entrance is a shady picnic area where tables are situated under and between gigantic boulders of different colors of pink, ranging from a pinkish brown to almost magenta. The huge "elephant" rocks are on top of the hill beyond the picnic area, but the entire park is covered by monstrous granite rocks that have eroded into bizarre shapes. The gray ones on the side of the hill—still imprisoned in its grasp—are strongly reminiscent of half-submerged humpback whales.

An elliptical walking trail to the area of pink elephants and back to the starting point is about a mile in length. It is blacktopped for easy walking and is accessible to motorized wheelchairs. The grade is moderately steep in places. The path itself is enjoyable; much of it winds through a leafy copse. Near the crest of the hill an abandoned quarry has filled with water to produce a breathtaking sight: jumbled walls of pastel pink stone cradling an emerald pool that mirrors trees and clouds. Who would have believed an old industrial site could be so stunningly beautiful? An overlook is provided for prolonged enjoyment.

A unique feature of this state park is the "Braille Trail." Descriptive placards set on posts along the trail are written both in regular text and in braille. This is the first self-guiding trail for the visually handicapped in a Missouri state park. It has gained national recognition and was designated a National Recreation Trail by the U.S. Dept. of Interior's Bureau of Outdoor Recreation.

The exact number of "elephants" in the park is uncertain. Predictably, the largest one has been named Dumbo. This pink granite "patriarch of the herd" is twenty-seven feet tall, thirty-five feet long, seventeen feet wide, and weighs 680 tons.

The same geological forces that yielded the local mountains left us this expanse of 1.5-billion-year old pink granite. Under extreme pressure, hot granite magma forced its way upward and slowly cooled to eventually crystallize into deeply buried masses of granite. As it cooled, nearly vertical cracks, called "joints," developed. The joints were accentuated as they were stressed in the uplifting of the Ozarks dome.

Over millions of years the overlying layers of softer rock were eroded away, exposing huge, oblong blocks of granite. Continuous freezing and thawing and wearing by wind and rain smoothed and rounded the edges until the elephant rocks evolved. Although the rocks are continually decomposing as time goes by, more stone elephants are in the making between the rocks and joints of the granite hillside in the park. There are other locations in the St. Francois Mountains where ancient granite has been exposed, but Elephant Rocks is the only place where the huge, pinkish brown granite boulders can be found.

Flat River

Still on Hwy. 21 across a corner of Washington County through yet another lovely valley, the Belleview, charming old Caledonia was founded in 1819. American settlers had been in the valley since 1798 on land granted by the Spanish government. Several antebellum houses are in Caledonia, and a seventeen-acre historic district along Main and Central streets is on the National Register of Historic Places.

At Caledonia turn east on Hwy. 32, which undulates through peaceful countryside. Watch for the picturesque old depot at Bismarck, backed by downtown buildings that face the railroad tracks. Near the depot is a World War II memorial. Bismarck was founded by the Missouri Pacific Railroad and named after a German prince in a successful effort to lure immigrant German farmers to the area. Just after World War I, to make sure people did not question their loyalty, residents voted to change the town's name to Loyal. The railroad and the post office vetoed the change.

Beyond Bismarck on Hwy. 32 are the town of Flat River and St. Joe State Park. Flat River lies in the heart of the now defunct Old Leadbelt. The first mine shaft here was sunk in the fall of 1870, but it was not until 1890 that the boom began. The mine at Flat River was the last to shut down in the Old Leadbelt when it ceased operations in 1973, leaving the earth beneath the town honeycombed by flooded mine tunnels. At the city park, just a block off the highway and visible from there, is a World War II Sherman tank and an anti-tank gun; various other pieces of military equipment are scattered throughout the park.

Missouri Mines State Historic Site

At Flat River is Missouri Mines Historic Site on the northern edge of St. Joe State Park. Drive through Flat River on Hwy. 32 and watch for the sign indicating a right turn.

The Missouri Mines State Historic Site centers on sixteen structures remaining from a twenty-five-building complex—Federal Mill No. 3—once used by the St. Joe Mineral Corporation. From the outside, the site is a good example of how ugly a lead mine can be. But these buildings reflect the important role of the Leadbelt in the region's history.

The Belleview Christian Church in Caledonia, Missouri, was built in 1870 by a congregation founded and organized in August of 1816. The beautiful red-brick building has blue-gray shutters, chimneys on both sides, and pigeons on the roof. The church stands high on a hill on College Street; watch for the steeple from Hwy. 21 south of Caledonia.

Missouri Mines Historic Site at St. Joe State Park in Flat River, Missouri, offers visitors a chance to see and understand lead mining in "The Old Leadbelt." The complex was begun in 1906-07 by the Federal Lead Company; the old powerhouse has been converted into a museum of mining history and geology, including mineral specimens, historic films, machinery, and much more. The knowledgeable guides are retired miners.

The complex was begun in 1906-07 by the Federal Lead Company, then purchased in 1923 by St. Joe and further developed. The power-house has been converted into a museum of mining history and geology. One gallery contains a large collection of minerals, rocks, ores, crystals, semi-precious stones, fossils, and petrified wood. A highlight of this gallery is a room where fluorescent minerals can be viewed under ultraviolet light.

A second gallery contains a collection of mining machinery and equipment, including the famous St. Joe shovel—an innovation that revolutionized hard-rock mining—and a fifteen-ton mainline loco-motive used for hauling ore underground. The museum also includes a small theater that screens films on mining history.

When the St. Joe Mineral Corporation relocated to the Viburnum Trend—the "New Leadbelt"—the corporation donated more than eighty-five hundred acres to the state. Most of the land is now St. Joe State Park. The rest of the park is a blend of second-growth oak-hickory forests (and opportunities for hiking, picnicking, and camping) and the wasteland created by the mining operation. During the mining process, the pulverized limestone, after being separated from the lead, was deposited behind a dam built across a branch of the Flat River. These sandlike tailings have all but filled the valley behind the dam. There are approximately eight hundred acres of these sandflats, in some places nearly a hundred feet deep.

After the mining ceased, the company planted prairie grasses and trees on the sandflats to stabilize the area. They are now part of a special section in the park set aside for off-road vehicles, including motorcycles, all-terrain vehicles, dune buggies, and four-wheel drives. The wasteland can also be used for snowmobiling in the winter.

Bonne Terre

North on Hwy. 67 from Flat River is Bonne Terre, the oldest town in the former leadmining district and for more than a hundred years the mining and shipping center for innumerable small mines. Just driving the streets of Bonne Terre is a trip into the past; at every turn are old houses and churches. The restored Bonne Terre Depot, dated 1909, is a real beauty, and is now a bed-and-breakfast inn. A couple of old railroad cars on a nearby siding lend appropriate ambiance.

Open to visitors is the cavernous Bonne Terre Mine that was closed in the 1960s. Here a knowledgeable guide leads tours through the mine, now a national historic site. Be aware that its first impression is of the worst kind of cheap tourist trap, but do not be deceived by that outward appearance. Remarkable sights are to be seen in the wet, dark world far underground, including the place where the mine's mules lived out their lives in darkness, and the tools and scaffolding left where they were last used by miners on their final day of work in the mine.

Since the water table has invaded the mine, a pontoon boat tours the flooded portions of the cathedral-like tunnels. Powered by a silent electric motor, the boat ventures onto a huge underworld lake, dimly lit and eerie. The water is crystal clear; you can see into its depths, a mirrorlike image of what you see all about you. Scuba divers can also arrange to explore the billion-gallon underground lake.

Not far from Bonne Terre, via Hwy. 67 north, is St. Francois State Park. The wild, forested terrain of the Pike Run Hills was a refuge for desperate Civil War outlaws. Local residents still speak of Sam Hildebrand, a guerrilla fighter who fought for the Confederacy to revenge the death of his brother at the hands of the Union's Missouri Militia. Hildebrand and many other such outlaws took refuge in a cave in these rugged hills.

Place names in the area give an idea of another part of the local cultural heritage. Many residents still remember the moonshine stills that flourished in Mooner's Hollow. Several miles of hiking and equestrian trails wind through the park, including Mooner's Hollow. The Old Logger's Trail, which makes use of old logging roads, is a ten-mile equestrian and hiking trail that loops through the eastern half of the park and provides access to the Coonville Creek Wild Area.

Big River, which forms the southern boundary of the park, is a slow-moving stream ideal for families and novice canoeists. Many put in at St. Francois State Park and float to Washington State Park, a distance of twenty-four miles.

Old Mines

Returning to Bonne Terre on Hwy. 67, turn west on Hwy. 47 through the Tiff Belt to the junction with Hwy. 21 and the town of Old Mines, one of the oldest communities in the Ozarks and the Middle West and site of lead mining for more than two centuries. When new mines were opened a few miles west, this place became "old mines." By far the most imposing feature of the village straggling along Hwy. 21 is St. Joachim Catholic Church, said to be the second oldest parish in Missouri. Constructed of hand-molded brick, the present church was built about 1830. A log church, built about 1802, preceded St. Joachim's. The church was enlarged, 1852-1868, and restored in 1945.

In the Old Mines vicinity are still many indications of the surviving French language and culture of the settlers, including the signs on local businesses—"la barbière," for example. Outside a bar along the highway is a sign offering to trade "tin for ale." But with the departure of the lead mines, many old buildings in the area are dilapidated and boarded up.

Indian Rock Carvings

North of Old Mines on Hwy. 21, the terrain becomes more rugged and rolling. Here a civilization flowered and died before Europeans came to these shores. Its people left a record carved in some rocks now part of Washington State Park, which is known for its petroglyphs: Indian rock carvings.

The Middle Mississippi people, prehistoric Indians related to the builders of the Cahokia Mounds in Illinois, as well as the mound builders who inhabited the area around what today is St. Louis, participated in a religious cult that used numerous symbols. The symbols included crosses, maces or batons, arrows, hands, weeping eyes, sunbursts, snakes, and birds and were placed on sacred objects and at venerated places. An outstanding example of these carvings—a petroglyph site—has been preserved here.

Archaeologists believe that the Washington State Park petroglyph site was probably the junction of game trails and war trails, and was possibly a consecrated spot where young men were initiated into secret society rites and taught the mythology associated with the initiation. The rock carvings may have been memory aids for songs and rites that were part of the ceremony. The symbols probably had magical as well as religious meaning, and participation in the ceremonies at the sacred spot may have been the means of receiving the powers of the symbols.

The petroglyph site is easily reached at the end of a short path that is wheelchair accessible. A roof has been built over the carvings to protect them from further weathering. The shelter is visible from the highway, and it is a strange sensation to stand in the presence of the ancient rock carvings—apparently made between 1000 and 1400 A.D.—while within sight and sound of a modern highway. Even today, as you view the petroglyphs, you are aware of something like magic hovering about them. A shiver may go up your spine as you struggle to discern the faint weathered markings in the stone. Some are difficult to make out, but an interpretive sign by each is helpful.

An interpretive center, located in a rustic cabin built by the CCC, houses artifacts and other exhibits about the Indians' lives. Several other smaller petroglyphs are nearby.

There are three marked hiking trails in the park, including the Thousand Steps Trail, which was constructed by the CCC in the 1930s. The lookout shelter on the trail is typical of the stone structures built by the corps. Along the Opossum Track Trail, depressions

Examples of petroglyphs—Indian rock carvings—are preserved and interpreted at Washington State Park north of Old Mines, Missouri, on Hwy. 21. The park also offers examples of CCC buildings, hiking trails, wildflowers, lovely scenery, and exhibits of Indian artifacts and history.

In a cemetery in Potosi, Missouri, lies Moses Austin, the first Austin to dream of an American colony in Texas. The dream was later fulfilled by his son, Stephen Austin, "Father of Texas." In April 1938, Texas attempted to remove the elder Austin's remains to the state cemetery in Austin where Stephen is buried, but Potosi refused. The building was a very early church and is now the historical society museum. Many old graves are in the cemetery.

in the ground are remnants of the tiff mining that occurred in the area before it became a state park. Park visitors canoe, swim, and "tube" in Big River in the park.

The Father of the "Father of Texas"

South on Hwy. 21 from Washington State Park is Potosi, the seat of Washington County, a former leadmining and smelting town, and the chief trading center of the Tiff Belt. It was once an important shipping point for railroad ties, and one of the big sawmills of the era was located near here.

One of the very first Ozarks settlements, the Potosi area is layered in history: Indian, early French, Daniel Boone and the settlers that came through the Cumberland Gap, the Civil War, lumbering, and leadmining. Lead deposits were discovered at Mine Au Breton (later Potosi) about 1773. The settlement grew into a healthy village of two hundred which defended itself against Indian attacks in 1799 and in 1804.

In this area Moses Austin built the first reverberatory furnace west of the Alleghenies, a shot tower, a plant for making sheet lead, a sawmill, a flour mill, a store, and an imposing home he called Durham Hall. When Washington County was organized in 1813, Austin donated forty acres and Potosi was laid out and named for the Mexican silver mining city of San Luis Potosi. Austin was bankrupted, however, by the depression following the Napoleonic Wars and the collapse of the Bank of St. Louis in 1818. The following year he conceived the dream of forming a colony in Texas, which he imparted to his son Stephen Fuller Austin—who later became "the Father of Texas."

Moses Austin secured permission to settle three hundred American colonists in Texas, but the rigors of his round trip on horseback to San Antonio destroyed his health. He died near Potosi on June 10, 1821. He is buried at a cemetery in Potosi a block northwest of the courthouse, at 212 W. Breton Street, in the churchyard of what was, until 1908, the Potosi Presbyterian Church, built about 1833. The steeple has been removed, but a slave balcony remains. The brick building is now the Mine Au Breton Historical Society Museum.

Now, leap forward another hundred years and head for Dillard Mill, a postcard-perfect restored mill on Huzzah Creek. Drive west of Potosi on Hwy. 8 to Road Y. Turn left on Y, which meanders through the Mark Twain National Forest to Viburnum, capital of the New Leadbelt.

Practical Matters

Chapter 23 — The Leadbelt

Checking Out	A Sampling	Phone
Lodging	Bonneville Motel & Restaurant, Hwys 67 & K, Bonne Terre MO 63628;	(314) 358-3328
	Scenic Rivers Motel, Box 151, Ellington MO 63638;	(314) 663-7722
	Roseners Budget Hotel, Hwy. 67 N., Flat River MO 63601;	(314) 431-4241
	Mimosa Motel, Hwy. 21 N. Box 295, Ironton MO 63650;	(314) 546-7418
	Black River Lodge, Rt. 1, Box 14, Lesterville MO 63654;	(314) 637-2550
	Cabins at Washington State Park, DeSoto MO 63020	(314) 586-6696
Bed & Breakfasts	River Country Bed & Breakfast (Reservation Service), 1900 Wyoming, St. Louis MO 63118; 1909 Depot B&B and Mansion Hill Inn, Bonne Terre MO;	(314) 965-4328 or (314) 771-1993 (314) 358-5311
Campgrounds	Parks Bluff Campground & Canoe Rental, Box 24, Lesterville MO 63654;	(314) 637-2290
	Twin Rivers Landing & Canoe Rental, Box 150, Lesterville MO 63654 (800) 331-4820 in MO	(314) 637-2274 or (800) 331-6439
Outdoor Recreation	Hiking, backpacking: Mark Twain National Forest, Box 188, Potosi MO 63664; Hiking, Bicycling, Horseback Riding, or Swimming: Elephant Rocks, Johnson's Shut-Ins, St. Joe, and Washington State Parks (addresses above);	(314) 438-5427
	Golf: Arcadia Valley Country Club, Ironton MO;	(314) 546-9508
	Fishing, Canoeing: See Canoe Rentals under "Campgrounds," above; Scuba Diving: Bonne Terre Mine, Bonne Terre MO	

Checking Out	A Sampling	Phone
Main Historical Attractions	Indian Petroglyphs, Washington State Park, 14 mi. northeast Potosi MO on Hwy. 21; St. Joachim Catholic Church, at Old Mines MO on Hwy. 21; Potosi Presbyterian Church (1833), Breton Street and Tomb of Moses Austin in Churchyard, Potosi MO, All Washington County;	(314) 586-2995
	Missouri Mines Historic Site, Northern Edge of St. Joe State Park Near Flat River MO on Hwy. 32; Bonne Terre Mine, Bonne Terre MO; Both in St. Francois County;	(314) 431-6226
	Johnson's Shut-Ins, 8 mi. North of Lesterville MO on Hwy. N, Reynolds County;	(314) 546-2450
	Elephant Rocks, Just off Hwy. 21 at Graniteville MO; Ft. Davidson State Historic Site, on Hwy. V Just off Hwy. 21, Pilot Knob MO; Courthouse in Ironton MO, Hwy. M Just Off Hwy. 21; St. Paul's Episcopal Church, N.W. Corner Knob & Reynolds Streets; Grant Statue, All in Ironton MO, Iron County;	(314) 697-5395
	Dillard Mill State Historic Site, 1 Mile South of Dillard MO off Hwy. 49, Crawford County	(314) 244-3120

CHAPTER 24

Caverns and Ironworks

The new town of Viburnum was built by the St. Joe Mineral Company (formerly St. Joseph Lead Company) on the site of a former crossroads settlement served by a logging railroad taken out in the 1920s. The town now has a new railroad, this time a heavy gauge system built by the Frisco to haul lead concentrates.

Viburnum is the heart of the "New Leadbelt" in western Iron and Reynolds counties. The ore, primarily lead with some zinc, copper, and silver, lies in flat beds about nine hundred to eleven hundred feet beneath the surface. In some areas the ore bodies are 140 feet thick and three thousand feet wide. The mines use diesel-powered, rubber-tired trucks to haul to underground crushers. Repair and maintenance shops are also located beneath the surface.

At Viburnum turn northwest on Hwy. 49 and then watch for the sign for Dillard. The old post office is near the junction of Hwy. 49 and the road to the mill, about a mile off Hwy. 49.

Dillard Mill

The red dirt road to Dillard Mill, a Missouri Historic Site, is narrow. The branches of trees on either side of the road meet overhead to form a pleasant, green tunnel. Near the parking lot at the mill are picnic tables and rest rooms. The millhouse is near the end of a fourteen-hundred-foot walk, but it can be viewed from the path just an easy distance from the parking lot. Inviting benches overlooking the millpond allow for resting along the way. The natural rock dam is spectacular; the falls are a rush of sound and sparkling spray.

439

At Dillard Mill, the dam is formed of solid rock; space for the turbine was blasted out. Now a Missouri Historic Site, the mill has been restored. Tours are conducted and grain is ground for visitors. In 1915 a St. Louis magazine reported that the fishing hole at Dillard Mill was one of the best in the state—if you did not mind the journey, which amounted to 115 miles by rail, six miles by stagecoach, twelve miles by log train, and a mile and a quarter on foot. Now Dillard Mill is easily accessible from Interstate 44.

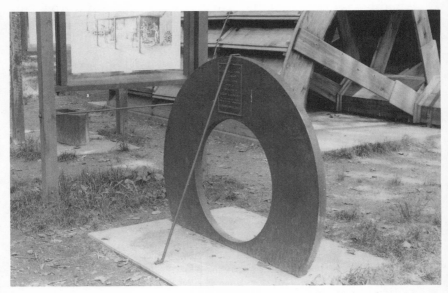

This wagonwheel rim-shaper formed one of Maramec Ironworks' chief products. Many wagons rolled westward on rims made of iron from the Missouri Ozarks. But during the Civil War, other Maramec products—sheathing for gunboats and cannon balls—made the ironworks a target for Confederate raiders.

"In the 1890s there were more than 650 gristmills in Missouri," says Tony Czeck, former site administrator at Dillard Mill. "By the 1920s, this number had dropped to 250. And by 1948, there were only a hundred water-powered mills operating in Missouri." Dillard ceased milling for farmers in the 1950s, but it operates now for visitors. A guided tour through the restored interior includes an explanation of the milling procedure. A small fee is charged for the tour to help offset the expense of maintaining the building.

The first mill on this site was built in 1853. It had several owners, including Joseph Dillard Cottrell, for whom the town of Dillard was named. The original town grew up around the mill, but after the millhouse burned in 1895, the village moved a mile north to be near the railroad.

On December 12, 1900, Emil Mishke, a Polish immigrant, bought the property and by 1904 began building the present mill, for which he salvaged some of the hand-hewn timbers of the earlier building. The exterior walls were of wood sheathing covered with metal siding painted a bright red. In order to use a modern underwater turbine, Mishke blasted out part of the bluff on which the mill is built and installed a log dam, which was replaced by a rock and concrete dam in the mid-1920s. He also blasted out a millrace. Mishke's Mill was completed in 1908, and still houses almost all of its original equipment. When World War I broke out, Mishke made a mixture of flour and cornmeal that was not covered by the rationing laws; by the end of the war the mill was prosperous. In 1927 when he was sixty-six years old, Mishke decided to get married; he sent for a mail-order bride. The woman who answered his request came from California. She never felt welcomed by her Ozarks neighbors, and by 1930 she had convinced Emil to sell the mill and move to the West Coast.

Lester Klemme became the new owner on April 11, 1930. He added on to the mill and began producing cattle feed. He also took advantage of the natural beauty of the area and began Klemme's Old Mill Lodge. For seven dollars a day, a guest could enjoy a small log cabin, swimming and fishing in the millpond, and meals at Klemme's house. Even after he closed the mill in 1956, Klemme remained very protective of the property. He kept the mill and its equipment intact until he sold it to the L-A-D Foundation in 1974. In 1975 the Foundation leased the mill and property to the state of Missouri, who developed the state historic site.

Returning to Hwy. 49 from Dillard, turn left (north). At Cherryville, at the junction of Hwy. 49 and Hwy. 19, watch for a large rock-veneered building flying the flag. The establishment, complete with creaky wooden floors, is the Cherryville post office, filling station, cafe, and the gathering place for the local whittlers and spitters.

Continue north on Hwy. 19 to Steelville, a pleasant outfitting post for float trips on the Meramec River and Huzzah Creek. Turn west on Hwy. 8 for the short trip to Maramec Spring Park, where there is an unusual peephole to the past.

Maramec Spring Park

An industrial outpost in the Ozarks when Missouri was still being settled, Maramec Iron Works established a network of wagon trails through the wilderness that have become modern highways. Bars and blooms were hauled seventy-five miles north along the Iron Road (now, in part, Highway 19) to Hermann, a steamboat port on the Missouri River. Kettles, plows, and bar iron were sold at the plant or hauled by oxen-drawn wagons to St. Louis or Springfield and other western points. In the Gold Rush of 1849, Maramec iron rolled to California on the wheels of covered wagons. When the Civil War began, most of the ironworks' output went into cannon balls and plate for gunboats built at St. Louis.

For a visit to this pioneer manufactory, drive west of Steelville on Hwy. 8. After a few miles, watch closely for a sign heralding Maramec Spring Park, a right turn. A two-dollar-per-car admission fee is collected at a gate near the entrance.

The well-founded tradition about the origin of Maramec Iron Works says that a band of Shawnee Indians, on their way to see the Great White Father in Washington, D.C., camped on the grounds of Thomas James, near Chillicothe, Ohio. James, experienced in iron production, recognized their decorative peace-paint as hematite, a red, earthy iron-ore producing mineral, "of highest grade and quality." The Indians told James of an enormous free-flowing spring, abundant forests, and red earth near their homeland. James sent his brother-in-law and business partner, Samuel Massey, to accompany the Indians back to Missouri to inspect the site.

But knowledge of the vast deposits of iron ore in the impossibly difficult northeastern Ozark hills was already a given by the early 1800s. Smelting and refining that ore, however—in the midst of formidable wilderness—seemed insurmountably expensive despite the presence of plenty of raw materials. Getting any ultimate product to market over nonexistent or crude roads or capricious rivers seemed virtually impossible. But, in the face of obvious potential wealth, the entrepreneurial spirit rose to the challenge.

Massey's Iron Works

In 1826 Massey and James bought the land around Maramec Spring from the U.S. Government and built Massey's Iron Works, as the business was first known. As feared, construction in the wilderness was slow. It was April 9, 1829, before the production book of the furnace reflected the modest entry, "Two pipes molded." But eventually the venture flourished, and about a hundred men were employed, including woodcutters and charcoal burners. A small village called Stringtown, occupied mainly by the ore miners, foundry workers, and their families, grew up around it and along the road to the iron mine. The name was descriptive of the string of homes bordering the winding mine road overlooking the Meramec River. This road was the first between Ste. Genevieve and Springfield. All lands, buildings, and equipment belonged to the "Company," somewhat like a feudal manor. Some of the foundry workers were slaves leased from their owners for a hundred dollars a year and keep.

In addition to the village gristmill, Maramec Spring supplied the swift-running stream to turn seven wooden undershot water wheels to power the ironworks. Since the plant made its own charcoal, and to supply their need for wood, James acquired ten thousand acres of land surrounding the ironworks. This acreage also supported cattle and crops to feed the village.

"Modernization" of the Iron Works

In 1843 James's son William came West to assume management of the business. The new ironmaster modernized the works and changed its name. Henceforth it would be known as the Maramec Iron Works. (Historians believe that the variance in spelling between Meramec River and Maramec Spring resulted from the uncertain frontier spelling. Older sources call both the spring and the river Meramec while respecting James's Maramec spelling for his ironworks. In the park, however, the spring is also Maramec.) Still standing is the cold-blast furnace built in 1847 as part of William's modernization. The furnace was flanked by five refinery forges powered by the undershot water wheels. Remains of the forges also still stand.

Always hopeful that an easier and cheaper method of freighting their products could be found, Massey and James turned to the nearby Meramec River. But except in times of high water, the Meramec was too shallow and had too many fallen trees in the channel to permit even a keelboat to make it upriver the full 172 miles from the Mississippi to the ironworks—not worth the effort except for items almost impossible to transport overland, such as large forge hammers and anvils.

As early as 1835 and 1836, Massey and James petitioned the Missouri legislature for help in opening the Gasconade River to steamboats. In return for a charter to collect tolls based on tonnage, Massey

For almost half of the nineteenth century, Maramec Ironworks was an industrial outpost in the Ozarks wilderness. This furnace achieved, for its day, "quantity production." According to a contemporary account in the Rolla Express, the iron ". . . is very elastic and of rather waxy character, which will bend and cleave rather than break. . . ."

and James proposed to clear the Gasconade of all logs and snags obstructing navigation, to construct wing dams to channel the water, and to keep the river clear for two years.

Although the state turned them down, Massey and James cleared the river anyway. Steamboats did try to ascend the river, but were turned back by low water. In 1849, however, flatboats successfully transported iron blooms from Paydown to the Missouri River, where they were loaded on steamboats.

Bankruptcy and a New Life

Although the Civil War and its demand for iron extended the life of Maramec Iron Works, by the early 1870s, competition from more modern "hot blast" furnaces and the discovery of rich iron deposits around Lake Superior sounded its death knell. These and other financial setbacks forced William James into bankruptcy in 1876, and the huge furnace was "blown out" for the last time. Most of the residents of Stringtown turned to lumbering and agriculture and moved to nearby Saint James, where James had built his own mansion. Saint James was platted in 1859 by John Wood in anticipation of the westward extension of the St. Louis-San Francisco Railway. Completed in the early 1860s, the railroad was a shipping point for the Maramec Iron Works and replaced its wagon trains.

Upon the death of William James in 1912, Lucy Wortham James, great-granddaughter of founder Thomas James, bought the interests of the remaining heirs and reacquired much of her ancestors' holdings around the ironworks and Maramec Spring. A well-traveled, widely known hostess in Washington, D.C., Lucy James loved this region of Missouri and was interested in ecology and recreation. She established a trust fund which, after her death in 1938, became the James Foundation, administrators of two-thousand-acre Maramec Spring Park.

Remnants of the Past

Scattered amid the wooded area are artifacts from the ironworks; a placard identifies each and explains its use in the manufacturing process. Inviting benches are placed strategically under the trees. For those who want to know more about the ironworks and the geology of the area, the Maramec Museum, accredited by the American Association of Museums, was created to "display a page from the history of the region and to show the impact the production of iron had on these people and their surroundings." The museum's exhibits, dioramas, and working models trace the origin of the ironworks, iron manufacture, and life of the Shawnee Indians. Other exhibits include geology, archeology, transportation—and mementos of the James family. The museum is open daily from March through October; group tours can be arranged. Visitors can also tour the community's old cemetery and view the ruins of Stringtown.

Also on the grounds is an eight-thousand-square-foot Ozark Agriculture Museum that houses a large collection of rare artifacts and is entertaining as well as educational, thanks to the arrangement of the exhibits into logical units. For example, there is a "back porch," displaying a variety of tools that might have been used there daily, a Victorian kitchen, and a blacksmith shop. The displays also emphasize how agriculture was different in the Ozarks and, in some ways, unique. Many of the exhibits are "hands on"—you can see for yourself how the equipment worked. There are several old buggies, a horse-drawn sleigh, a twelve-ton steam engine hooked up to a huge threshing machine, a hundred-year-old wooden beam plow, and equally old tools of timbering along the Meramec River.

Two hiking trails are near the Maramec Nature Center, with exhibits portraying the plants and wildlife of the area and the interrelationships between them. Slide-tape presentations and films are also offered.

Maramec Spring

More than a century and a half after the Shawnees were shoved out, Maramec Spring is little changed. Varying from a delicate blue to a deep aquamarine, the spring rises almost vertically and "cold boils" into a pool at the base of an overhanging dolomite bluff. (The water appears to boil because of its egress through a narrow constriction in the exit.) Maramec Spring is a totally water-filled tube, a "working model" of how Ozarks caves are born. The water, at the rate of some ninety million gallons a day, spills over the rock dam, built during development of the ironworks, and races away to double the flow of the Meramec River, about a mile away. Majestic trees still shade the branch and a mossy path—lined with wildflowers and cooled by the spring—that accompanies it to the river, which it crosses via suspension bridge. Visitors will little wonder why Maramec Spring has been designated a National Natural Landmark.

Fishing for Trout and Scenery

Though not part of the Missouri state park system, the cool waters of the spring are now home to a trout hatchery. The Missouri Department of Conservation and The James Foundation cooperate to provide nearly two hundred thousand trout annually. From a footbridge over crystal-clear pools, visitors can feed and watch the trout. For anglers, trout season is from March 1 to October 31; a daily trout tag is required in addition to a Missouri fishing license. During the winter months, no-take fishing is allowed on Friday, Saturday, and Sunday.

The park is also a Missouri State Cooperative Wildlife Refuge, and scenic drives wander throughout. An observation tower overlooks it all: the spring, the river, the lovely park, and miles of Ozarks scenery. Riverside camping is permitted in Maramec Spring Park, and there are picnic areas and shelter houses, tennis courts, a basketball court, a softball diamond, and playground equipment.

Continue west on Hwy. 8 to the charming town of Saint James. At the junction there of Hwy. 8 and Interstate 44, turn east (right) on I-44 to Exit 214: Onondaga Cave State Park, where tours of the cave are offered as a park concession.

Awesome Caverns

More than three hundred springs and four hundred caves have been discovered in the upper Meramec River basin, many of them spectacular. Some are located in Missouri state parks, along with campgrounds, access to the Meramec River, and canoe rentals.

Onondaga Cave has been famous the world over since the beginning of the twentieth century, and now it is protected as a Missouri state park. Onondaga is extensively decorated by stalactites, stalagmites, rimstone dams, cave coral, draperies, flowstone, and soda straws. Many of the formations are actively growing with the continued deposition of calcium carbonate. Massive draperies are intricately deposited and deeply folded, while simply formed soda straws hang by the thousands from the ceiling. A stream meanders through the cave in its entrenched canyon. At one time visitors—carrying lanterns—entered the cave in johnboats that followed the winding channel of the underground river for about nine hundred feet. Because of the tremendous quantity, quality, and diversity of its formations, Onondaga Cave has been designated a National Natural Landmark by the National Park Service. Its history is almost as colorful as its formations.

Daniel Boone gets the credit for being the first white discoverer of Onondaga Cave in 1798. Use of its springs for water power to run numerous gristmills led to the damming of the river that flows from the cavern, inundating the entrance so that no exploration of the cavern could take place until 1886. Then two explorers sank an Ozarks johnboat and refloated it inside the cave. They emerged thirty-six hours later with tales of wonder and the great treasures within the cavern.

In 1900 a mining group purchased the cave, intending to mine onyx from its great rooms. One formation alone, the "Queen's Canopy," was estimated to be worth more than a million dollars in polished onyx for the ornate Victorian buildings of the period. Fortunately the mining threat was never carried out. The 1904 St. Louis World's Fair encouraged the owners to open Onondaga Cave to the public. Visitors from St. Louis were brought to Leasburg by the Frisco Railroad and then transported by surrey and spring buggy to the cave itself.

Onondaga's popularity as a tourist attraction reached its peak in the 1950s and '60s under the masterful touch of Lester Dill, "America's No. 1 Caveman." Dill carefully preserved the natural integrity of the cave and promoted it into one of the country's most famous natural attractions. Far and wide, billboards and barn sides proclaimed "Visit Onondaga Cave!" Before his death in 1979, Dill expressed the wish that the cave be preserved as a Missouri state park.

In 1980 The Nature Conservancy, a private national conservation organization dedicated to the preservation of ecologically and environmentally significant land, purchased the cave and surrounding acreage. Subsequently the Conservancy transferred administration of the cave and park to the Missouri Department of Natural Resources.

Also at this park are canoe rentals and a campground. The visitor center at Onondaga State Park is exceptionally worthwhile. There, in addition to the many other interesting and educational exhibits, is the recording mechanism for a seismograph located in the depths of Onondaga Cave. The needle is always moving.

Meramec State Park, established in 1926, is near Sullivan and is also easily accessible from Interstate-44; continue east on I-44 from Onondaga.

Indian Hunting Grounds

The 6,734 acres at Meramec State Park once provided rich hunting grounds for Indian tribes who first made the valley their home. Spear points, arrowheads, pieces of pottery, ax heads, and other artifacts discovered in the park are evidence of the area's long usage by prehistoric Indian hunters and possibly groups of the Osage, Delaware, and Shawnee tribes. Now you will find hiking trails, a campground, and shady picnic areas on the banks of the Meramec, rental canoes, cabins and lodge, and a general store.

Twenty-two caves are known to exist within Meramec State Park, and some of them provide all-important shelter for bobcats and bats. Both the beneficial Gray and Indiana bats are now endangered. A naturalist leads tours of Fisher Cave. Legend has it that in 1865 a Missouri governor attempted to hold his inaugural ball in what is now called the "ballroom" of this cave, but smoke and crowded conditions drove most of the guests away.

In the Meramec Upland Forest Natural Area, you may see wonders of another kind: a lady slipper orchid tucked away on a moist hillside, a rare red-shouldered hawk known to nest in undisturbed bottomlands along the Meramec River, or a desertlike glade opening on a south-facing slope. You can witness for yourself where different plants and animals make their homes, each filling a specific niche as the environment changes from valley floor to ridgetop.

A highlight of Meramec State Park is the new interpretive center. There you will find exhibits demonstrating how the Ozarks aquifer functions, aquariums full of river wildlife, a "please touch" display for children, and extremely attractive and informative displays of area history and geology.

Widely advertised Meramec Caverns is a commercial cave, first opened to the public in 1935, near Stanton. Since this establishment calls itself a "natural park," it is often confused with Meramec State Park. It is not, however, affiliated with the state park system—and is not nearly as attractive. It also offers a motel, campground, and canoe rental. Public meetings are held in a vast "ballroom" inside the cave, and there are also a restaurant and other facilities in the cavern.

Although it is often difficult to separate historical fact from folk legends or even advertising hype, it is easy to imagine that Meramec Caverns has been known and used by humankind for a long time. Escaping slaves are thought to have sheltered there as part of their trip north on the "Underground Railroad." An important source of the saltpeter used for making gunpowder, the cave was the site of a Federal powder mill during the Civil War. The facility was raided by Confederate guerrillas under William Quantrill, whose band included Jesse James.

According to folklore, James and his gang later valued the depths of the vast cavern as a hideout because it would shelter their horses as well. Most scholars doubt the story, however, convinced that James's far-flung network of friends and admirers provided sanctuary for the outlaw wherever he needed it—without having to resort to hiding in caves.

The Once and Future River

The Meramec River is a contradiction. It flows through some of the most rugged terrain in the region, but it is the most heavily used Ozarks river. Since the first trappers came down the Mississippi, the Meramec has been used—and abused. The spring-fed river flows for some 240 miles, joined by sizable tributaries that are also part of

Ozarks lore: the Bourbeuse, the Big, and river-sized creeks Huzzah (HOO-zaw) and Courtois (CODE-away). Stocked with trout below Maramec Spring and floatable year-round for almost two hundred miles of its length, the Meramec and its equally floatable feeder streams form a recreational network webbing the northeastern Ozarks. Although it glances off the St. Louis metroplex and is available to hordes of day-trippers as well as visitors from elsewhere, the Meramec drains some of the wildest territory in the eastern Ozarks. Around 1800 Daniel Boone led groups of hunters and prospectors through the typically Ozarkian river hills: towering limestone bluffs, huge springs, deep sinkholes, natural bridges, and caverns so vast and beautiful they have inspired humankind—and spawned myths and legends—for hundreds of years.

For all that time the Meramec has been an integral part of life along its length. It has been a highway, a playground, a canal for tie rafters, an irrigation ditch for farmers, a dumping ground—and a sewer. And it has been the center of controversy for almost as long as humans have been aware of it.

They first began to talk of damming the Meramec in the mid-1800s, when frontier manufacturers needed a quicker, more dependable access to the Mississippi River freighters. St. Louisans have had a love-hate relationship with the river for most of their history—playing in it and drowning in it for generations. Periodically the river flooded, as rivers are wont to do. And early on in the twentieth century the Army Corps of Engineers decided that the Meramec should be dammed.

Gradually enlarged and expanded over the years of Depression and World War II, the Corps' Meramec Basin Plan was finally authorized by Congress in 1966. Preparations for the construction of the dam began immediately, and the Corps began buying—and condemning —land along the river in 1968. In spite of some disorganized public opposition to the dam, the much-loved and much-maligned Meramec appeared doomed.

But three years after the Corps starting acquiring land, environmentalists decided to challenge the inadequate and flawed eight-page Environmental Impact Statement. In 1972 they were joined by rural opponents of the dam, mostly farmers who were about to lose their land by the power of eminent domain. Forming an organization they called the Citizens Committee to Save the Meramec, they struggled cooperatively to bring the issue, belatedly, to public attention. But while the battle raged, work on the dam continued. Even as opponents made speeches, distributed bumper stickers, and sent huge petitions to the governor, the Corps of Engineers built a $1.4 million visitor center that opened to the public in 1975, a new blacktop road, and a sizable parking lot. Construction began on the dam itself.

Then President Carter, trying to halt pork-barrel federal projects, included the Meramec Dam on his "hit list." Gradually Missouri politicians on all levels were reluctantly drawn into the fray. In response to pressure from their opposition, the Corps commissioned belated studies to determine the dam's impact on wildlife in the Meramec basin, including the endangered and newly valued Indiana bat. The natural flooding along the river had created many wildlife habitats: log jams, gravel bars, sloughs, and aquatic homes from shallow riffles to deep pools. There a variety of plants and animals thrived. If the river was dammed, there was no place else for most of these animals and plants to live; they would simply disappear. Also at stake were numerous archaeological sites and more than a hundred caves, including the most beautiful of them all, Onondaga. Smaller caves were discovered to undermine the dam site and threatened, at the least, to cause huge cost overruns; at the worst, they were potentially dangerous to the dam itself.

As the controversy raged, newspapers and magazines polled their readership, both within the immediate area and throughout the rest of the state. Most of Missouri at large got into the debate, as did many out-of-staters who also loved the Ozarks and its most abused river. The informal polls indicated that the majority opposed the dam. When at last public opinion could no longer be ignored by cautious politicians, the issue was put to a vote of the people. The public decided that the advantages of a free-flowing river outweighed whatever benefits might have been gained by impoundment of the river. Sixty-four percent of those voting said *no* to a dam on the Meramec. Construction halted, but the debate then turned to the disposition of the land already acquired. The project was not officially deactivated until December 1981. Ownership of some of the land was transferred to the state of Missouri; some of it was sold back to its former owners with the inclusion of restrictive covenants to halt further development and protect the river corridor.

The saving of the Meramec, the third major Ozarks river to be rescued from damming (following the Current and the Buffalo), appears to have cemented in the public consciousness a new appreciation for free-flowing streams and all they represent. Canoeing the Ozarks has become an industry and has introduced thousands to the outdoors and fostered a new appreciation of—and reverence for—nature and its preservation.

Located in such proximity to Interstate-44 and a huge metropolis, the Meramec is the most heavily canoed and fished river in the Ozarks.

But as a result of its close brush with oblivion, it has gained millions of new supporters. And on the threshold of the twenty-first century, a river can not have too many friends.

The juxtaposition of the incomprehensibly aged caverns and the ruins of once state-of-the-art manufactories so close to the Interstate highway and the high-speed comings and goings of modern humankind serves as a dramatic reminder of how *temporary* we and our "busy strivings" can be.

And the fate of the once and future river still hangs in the balance—as does the rest of the wild and lonely Ozarks.

Practical Matters

Chapter 24 — Caverns & Ironworks

Checking Out	A Sampling	Phone
Lodging	Best Western I-44, 307 N. Service Rd., Sullivan MO 63080; many others there; Rustic Cabins at Meramec State Park	(314) 468-3136 (314) 468-6519
Bed & Breakfasts	River Country Bed & Breakfast (Reservations for the area), 1900 Wyoming, St. Louis MO	(314) 965-4328 or 771-1993
Campgrounds	Meramec State Park, Sullivan MO 63080; Onondaga Cave State Park, Leasburg MO; Meramec Caverns, Stanton MO 63079; Primitive camping at Huzzah State Forest, District Forester Box 248 Sullivan MO 63080; Garrison Canoe-Raft Rentals, Steelville MO; Indian Springs Lodge, Box T, Steelville MO	(314) 468-3166 (800) 367-8945 (800) 392-1110
Restaurants	Meramec State Park & Lodge, Rt. 4, Sullivan; Numerous, in Sullivan and Steelville MO	(314) 468-6072
Main Historical Attractions	Meramec Caverns, Stanton, MO 63079; Onondaga Cave, Onondaga Cave State Park just off I-44 near Leasburg MO; Fisher Cave, Meramec State Park just off I-44 near Sullivan MO; Scotia Furnace & Ironworks, Huzzah State Forest, near Sullivan MO; Daniel Boone Home, Defiance MO; Antique Toy Museum, Stanton MO; Iron Mine, Nature Center, Mining Museum, Ozarks Agricultural Museum: Maramec Spring Park, Hwy. 8, St. James MO 65559	(314) 468-3166 (314) 987-2221 (314) 927-5555 (314) 265-7387
Outdoor Recreation	Trout Fishing: Maramec Spring Park, Hwy. 8, St. James MO (Mo. Wildlife Codes Apply); Hiking Trails and Canoeing: Huzzah State Forest, Dist. Forester, Box 248, Sullivan MO 63080; Meramec State Park Rt. 4, Sullivan; Golf: St. James Golf Club, St. James MO	(314) 265-7387 (314) 265-8688
Where to Write for More Details	Sullivan Chamber of Commerce, P.O. Box 536, Sullivan MO 63080; Steelville Chamber of Commerce, P.O. Box 1002, Steelville MO 65565; For Information about "Missouri Ozark Waterways" and other titles, write Outdoor Library, Missouri Dept. of Conservation, Box 180, Jefferson City MO 65102	(314) 468-3314 (314) 325-4233

The giant redwood water wheel at War Eagle Mill: long may it keep on turning!

Epilogue

For all its rugged appearance, the Ozarks is not as lonely as it once was, nor as wild. And friends and neighbors sometimes chide me for writing about the region. "Why do you have to go and tell everybody how great it is?" they wonder. "Maybe if you didn't write about it so much, there wouldn't be so many people coming." Obviously, these people are not connected with the tourism industry. If they were, they would no doubt agree with many of us that *tourism* is a far more benign industry for the Ozarks than lead mining and lumbering.

But even if I did not favor tourism in the Ozarks, it would be impossible to keep secret what I know of the region. For the same reasons that cave dwellers painted pictures on their stone walls, I am compelled to record my place and time. I am driven by the same pride of belonging, and the same desire to transmit, that caused scientists to install the golden plaque on the Voyager space ship to carry pictures and "murmurs of Earth" even unto the stars.

Further, the Ozarks is not a vast museum or a gigantic time capsule; it is not a specimen to be frozen for the amazement of future generations. The Ozarks is a dynamic, imperfect place that needs to be understood, loved, and protected.

And loving the Ozarks as I do and convinced of my obligation to communicate, perhaps I understand something that my friends and neighbors do not: I understand that visitors come to the Ozarks just to touch the way we live—to belong, even for a little while, to our way of life. What's more, whether they realize it or not, our visitors also long to share our *history*.

All the time America was growing up and people were leaving the farms and small towns for the cities, we consoled ourselves with the thought: When things get too rough, I can always go *home*. If I get too homesick, I'll go back for a while.

But all too soon the farms were foreclosed or swallowed by corporations. The little towns died, abandoned by the farmers and by the small industries that had kept them alive. There came a year when *home* was no longer there—and no one remembered where it was. America lost sight of an organic component of human life: its history. We faced the loss of our *community memory*. A very wise man, a Kentucky hillside farmer and essayist named Wendell Berry, has written that "everywhere in our country the local succession of the generations has been broken." It has been replaced, Berry says, by a "vast amnesia."

When people are drawn to the Ozarks, I believe it is because they are searching for—and can find here—that lost community memory. Perhaps without recognizing it, without even "remembering" it, they know they have come home. When I first moved back to the Ozarks almost a decade ago, I had an overwhelming sense of having come home. I thought it was because I *had* come home, back to where I started from. But others I know here—those who were born in Kansas, Tennessee, Michigan, New York—speak of the same sensation of homecoming. Now I believe it is because the Ozarks region is still blessed with many places that are reminiscent of remembered hometowns, of "boyhood and girlhood places knowable only through memory."

But what of younger people, those who never knew the small towns and the old ways? Often they have deliberately severed their ties with the past, broken free of the "old ideas." Now they are adrift, cut loose from their roots, consumed with longing—for what, they do not know; they can not remember. They have no frame of reference, no knowledge of our rural past, our community memory.

As they age, if they are lucky, they come to realize that they yearn for *connectedness*. They go in search of a history. And if they are *very* lucky, they discover the Ozarks—and adopt it as their own "home," their own place to come back to when things get rough.

And so I write of the Ozarks to serve as a beacon to all those who are struggling to remember it. I write of the Ozarks to safeguard its history, its culture, its community memory, to keep it from being replaced by the *alternate histories* that regions sometimes erect for themselves when the real history is forgotten, or not perceived as exciting enough, or glamorous enough, or attractive enough for tourists and economic development.

But even if I did not help illuminate the way to the Ozarks, people would find it anyway. Many of the region's deepest thinkers believe, as did Dan Saults, that "there's something here that pulls people in. . . . Almost everywhere you go in the Ozarks you find that somebody has come in here long ago seeking something—I don't know what. It's almost as though there were some sort of an emanation coming up from the ground."

In fact, many of the world's great thinkers believe that there are "sacred" places on our planet that have the power to move us into a greater spiritual awareness of the world. They suggest that the earth itself somehow seeks our friendship and our help in its current struggle for survival.

If this idea has merit, I am convinced that the Ozarks must be one of those locations. It is almost impossible to experience a misty morning on a wild river or the quietude of dusk in a deep, wooded valley without sensing that all around you there is some force larger than yourself, some benevolence of nature that convinces you nothing— not profits, not comfort, and certainly not convenience—is as important as its preservation.

But thereupon hinges the dilemma. So why, my friends and neighbors argue, keep on telling everyone about it and just bring in more and more people? Why indeed, when the Ozarks is already experiencing a population explosion in some areas? There's no denying that the region has changed more in the past fifty years than it had in the previous fifty centuries.

The reason is: The more people there are who love the Ozarks, the more champions of the region there will be. In the last decade alone I have seen many more join the ranks of those who actively safeguard, not only the environment, but also the culture. Indeed, many Ozarkers realize that the very retirement and recreation industries that are bringing so many long-overdue blessings to the region depend on the preservation of the Ozarks environment and its regional culture.

Perhaps for the first time in their history, Ozarkers are realizing the value of their unique heritage. Often led by newcomers, many are working to preserve their folkways and folk music, to gather oral histories and recipes. They are forming historical societies, tracing their genealogies, and depositing family records and photographs in historical archives. They are working to save and restore old buildings, to have entire towns named to the National Register of Historic Places. They are finding and caring for the threadbare quilts, the discarded spinning wheels, the time-worn farm implements. They are working to protect scenic rivers from pollution, to find better ways to dispose of trash and sewage.

In fact, says Dr. Robert Gilmore, "Knowledgeable and concerned writers, artists, educators, historians, conservationists, planners, photographers, and, yes, businessmen and developers, are dedicated to this enterprise and actively seeking knowledge about how to deal with the responsibilities of living in the presence of the past."

So come and fall in love with the Ozarks, as visitors have been doing for at least a couple of centuries. And while you are traveling around the region and learning to love it, take the time to feel that indefinable something that emanates from the ground, that can draw you into its spell and make you one of us.

PHYLLIS ROSSITER
Ozark County, Missouri

Appendices

Suggested Reading List

Periodicals:

The Ozarks Mountaineer, bimonthly, HCR 3 Box 868, Kirbyville MO 65679

OzarksWatch, quarterly, Southwest Missouri State University, 901 S. National, P.O. Box 134, Springfield MO 65804

Books:

Bittersweet Country, edited by Ellen Gray Massey, University of Oklahoma Press, Norman, Oklahoma, 1986

Bittersweet Earth, edited by Ellen Gray Massey, University of Oklahoma Press, 1985

The Ozarks, by Richard Rhodes, Time-Life Books Inc., Alexandria, Virginia, 1974

Ozark Baptizings, Hangings, and Other Diversions, by Robert K. Gilmore, University of Oklahoma Press, 1984

Ozarks, photography by David Fitzgerald, text by Clay Anderson, Graphic Arts Center Publishing Company, Portland, Oregon, 1985

Bald Knobbers, by Lucile Morris Upton, The Caxton Printers, Ltd., Caldwell, Idaho, 1939

Bald Knobbers: Vigilantes on the Ozarks Frontier, by Mary Hartman and Elmo Ingenthron, Pelican Publishing Company, Gretna, Louisiana, 1988

Ozark Magic and Folklore, by Vance Randolph, Dover Publications, Inc., New York, 1964

Down in the Holler, A Gallery of Ozark Folk Speech, by Vance Randolph and George P. Wilson, University of Oklahoma Press, 1953

The Land of Taney, by Elmo Ingenthron, *The Ozarks Mountaineer*, Branson, Missouri, 1983

Borderland Rebellion, A History of the Civil War on the Missouri-Arkansas Border, by Elmo Ingenthron, *The Ozarks Mountaineer*, 1980

Indians of the Ozark Plateau, by Elmo Ingenthron, *The Ozarks Mountaineer*, 1983

Water Mills of the Missouri Ozarks, by George G. Suggs, Jr., University of Oklahoma Press, 1990

The Ozarks: Land and Life, by Milton D. Rafferty, University of Oklahoma Press, 1980

Two Ozark Rivers, the Current and the Jacks Fork, text by Steve Kohler, photographs by Oliver Schuchard, University of Missouri Press, Columbia, Missouri, 1984

The Buffalo River Country, by Kenneth L. Smith, The Ozark Society Foundation, Little Rock, Arkansas, 1978

Passages of a Stream, A Chronicle of the Meramec, by James P. Jackson, University of Missouri Press, 1984

Grandin, Hunter, West Eminence and the Missouri Lumber and Mining Company, by Jerry Ponder, Ponder Books, Doniphan, Missouri, 1989

Wilderness Bonanza: the Tri-State District of Missouri, Kansas, and Oklahoma, by Arrell M. Gibson, University of Oklahoma Press, 1972

The WPA Guide to 1930s Arkansas, compiled by workers of the Writers' Program of the Work Projects Administration, University Press of Kansas, Lawrence, Kansas, 1987; originally published in 1941 by Hastings House

The WPA Guide to 1930s Oklahoma, compiled by workers of the Writers' Program of the Work Projects Administration, University Press of Kansas, 1986; originally published in 1941 by University of Oklahoma Press

The WPA Guide to 1930s Missouri, compiled by workers of the Writers' Program of the Work Projects Administration; originally published in 1941 by Hastings House

Ozark Log Cabin Folks: The Way They Were, by Paul Faris, Rose Publishing Company, 1983

Ozark Mountain Humor, by W. K. McNeil, August House, Little Rock, Arkansas, 1989

Li'l Charley, by Lois Mounce, Bittersweet, Inc., and White Oak Press, Reeds Spring, Missouri, 1990

Hill and Holler Stories, by Douglas Mahnkey, *The Ozarks Mountaineer*

Life in the Leatherwoods, by John Quincy Wolf, Memphis State University, Memphis, Tennessee, 1974

Museums and Historical Displays

Missouri:

Miller County Historical Society Museum, Hwys. 52 & 17, Tuscumbia MO, (314) 369-2317

Morgan County Historical Museum, 210 N. Monroe, Versailles MO, (314) 378-5556

Camden County Museum, Hwys. 54 and V, Linn Creek MO, (314) 346-7191

Kelsey's Antique Car Museum, Hwy. 54, one mile east of Camdenton Square, Camdenton MO, (314) 346-2506

Stone Jail, Courthouse Lawn, Hermitage MO

Greenfield Museum and Opera House, Greenfield MO

Old Jail Museum, 214 S. Main, Bolivar MO, (417) 326-6850

North Ward Museum, Main and Locust, Bolivar MO, (417) 326-6850

Old Jail Museum and Richard Bland Statue, 262 N. Adams, Lebanon MO

Laura Ingalls Wilder Home and Museum, Rt. A, one mile east of Mansfield MO, (417) 924-3626

Museum of Ozarks History, 603 E. Calhoun, Springfield MO 65802, (417) 869-1976

Powers Museum, 1617 Oak Street, Carthage MO, (417) 358-2667

Jasper County Courthouse, Carthage MO

Tri-State Mineral Museum, 7th Street and Schifferdecker Avenue, Joplin MO, (417) 623-2341

Dorothea B. Hoover Museum, Schifferdecker Park, Joplin MO, (417) 623-1180

Harold Bell Wright Museum and Theater, P.O. Box 1420A, Branson MO 65616, (417) 334-0065

Ralph Foster Museum, College of the Ozarks, Point Lookout MO, (417) 334-6411 Ext. 407 or 408

Antique Toy Museum, Stanton MO, (314) 927-5555

Missouri Mines Historic Site, on Hwy. 32, northern edge of St. Joe State Park near Flat River MO, (314) 431-6226

Mining Museum, Ozarks Agricultural Museum: Maramec Spring Park, Hwy. 8, St. James MO 65559, (314) 265-7387

Arkansas:

Arkansas Air Museum, 4290 S. School, Drake Field, Hwy 71 S., Fayetteville AR 72701, (501) 521-4947

Headquarters House and Grounds, 118 E. Dickson St., Fayetteville AR 72701, (501) 521-2970

The University Museum, University of Arkansas, Garland Avenue, Fayetteville AR 72701, (501) 575-3555

Rogers Historical Museum, 322 S. Second, Rogers AR 72746, (501) 621-1154

Shiloh Museum, 118 W. Johnson, Springdale AR, (501) 751-8411

Wal-Mart Visitors Center, 105 N. Main, Bentonville AR 72712, (501) 273-1329

Saunders Memorial Museum, Berryville AR, (501) 423-2563

ES & NA Railway, P.O. Box 310, Eureka Springs AR 72632, (501) 253-9623 or (501) 253-9677

The Castle and Museum, 5.5 miles west of Eureka Springs AR on Hwy. 62 (Rt 2 Box 375), (501) 253-9462

Abundant Memories Heritage Village, Rt. 5 Box 759, Eureka Springs AR 72632, (501) 253-6764

Carroll County Heritage Center, 1880 Courthouse on the Square, Berryville AR, (501) 423-6312

Robinson's Museum of the Ozarks, twelve miles southeast of Harrison off Hwy. 65, Rt. 1, Box 324, Everton AR 72633, (501) 429-5855

Dogwood Hollow Primitive Museum, one-half mile north of Folk Center Road on Hwy. 5, Mountain View AR

Old Railroad Depot, Mammoth Spring State Park, P.O. Box 36, Mammoth Spring AR 72554 (Hwy. 63), (501) 625-7364

Indian Culture Center, P.O. Box 8, Cherokee Village AR 72525, (501) 257-2442

Oklahoma:

Har-Ber Village, Grove; Cherokee Heritage Center; Davis Gun Museum; Will Rogers Museum, and many more. Write Oklahoma Museums Association, P. O. Box 1321, Guthrie, OK 73044, (405) 282-5052

Gristmills

Wommack Mill, Fair Grove MO (community park near Hwy. 125)

War Eagle Mill, Rt. 5, Box 411, Rogers AR 72756, (501) 789-5343

Johnson Mill, 1835 Greathouse Springs Road, Johnson AR 72741, (501) 443-1830

Edwards Mill, College of the Ozarks, Point Lookout MO, (417) 334-6411 Ext. 407 or 408

The Old Mill, one block west of square, Mountain View AR, (501) 269-3354

Zanoni Mill, Zanoni MO 65784, (417) 679-4050

Dawt Mill, Tecumseh MO 65760, (417) 284-3540

Rockbridge Mill, Rainbow Trout Ranch, Rockbridge MO 65741, (417) 679-3619

Hodgson Mill, Sycamore MO 65758

Falling Spring Mill, seven miles north of Greer MO on Hwy. 19, then 2.2 miles right on Forest Service Road #3170 (bear left when the road forks; one-eighth mile past the cemetery)

Alley Spring Mill, Hwy. 106, five miles west of Eminence MO, (314) 323-4236

Montauk Mill, Montauk State Park near Salem MO

Dillard Mill State Historic Site, one mile south of Dillard MO off Hwy. 49, Crawford County

Ferries and Bridges

Interesting Bridges:

Hurricane Deck Bridge over Lake of the Ozarks, Hurricane Deck, MO (Chapter 2)

Stone-Arch Bridge built by CCC at Bennett Spring State Park, Lebanon, MO (Chapter 3)

War Eagle Bridge over War Eagle Creek at War Eagle Mill, AR (Chapter 7)

Y-Bridge over James River at Galena, MO (Chapter 9)

Rainbow Bridge over White River at Cotter, AR (Chapter 17)

Little Golden Gate Bridge over White River at Beaver, Arkansas, not far from Eureka Springs. A 528-foot steel cable suspension bridge built in 1947 to replace an earlier cement bridge washed out by a flood, its twin towers and glistening cables are seen to best advantage when approaching from the south on state Hwy. 187.

Remaining Ferries:

The *Lady Marion*, the "Peel Ferry" across Bull Shoals Lake (Chapter 10)

Akers Ferry across Current River in the Ozark National Scenic Riverways (Chapter 22)

The *Roy J.* across Gasconade River on Hwy. J between Osage and Gasconade Counties, Missouri

Civil War Battlefields and Monuments

Wilson's Creek National Battlefield, Rt. 2, Box 75 (Postal Drawer C) Republic MO 65738, (417) 732-2662

Pea Ridge National Military Park, ten miles northeast of Rogers AR on Hwy. 62, (417) 451-8122

Prairie Grove Battlefield State Park, P. O. Box 306, Prairie Grove AR 72753, (501) 846-2990

Headquarters House and Grounds, 118 E. Dickson Street, Fayetteville AR 72701, (501) 521-2970

Ft. Davidson State Historic Site, on Hwy. V just off Hwy. 21, Pilot Knob MO

Native Americans

Indian Burial Cave, Osage Beach MO, (314) 348-2207

Bluff Dwellers' Cave, Rt. 2, Box 229, Noel MO 64854, (417) 475-3666

Indian Culture Center, P.O. Box 8, Cherokee Village AR 72525, (501) 257-2442

Indian Petroglyphs, Washington State Park, fourteen miles northeast of Potosi MO on Hwy. 21, (314) 586-2995

Thong Trees (see Chapter 1)

Cherokee Heritage Center, Cherokee National Museum and Tsa-La-Gi Ancient Village, P.O. Box 515, Tahlequah OK 74465, (918) 456-6195; three miles south of Tahlequah on Willis Rd. off Hwy. 62

Caves and Caverns

Blanchard Springs Caverns, Ozark National Forest, P.O. Box 1, Mountain View AR 72560, (501) 757-2213

Bluff Dwellers' Cave, Rt. 2, Box 229, Noel MO 64854, (417) 475-3666

Bonne Terre Mine Tours, Bonne Terre MO

Bridal Cave Thunder Mountain Park, Hwy. 5 North, Lake Road 5-88, Camdenton MO 65020, (314) 346-2676

Civil War Cave, Rt. 3, Box 28, Bentonville AR, (501) 795-2406

Cosmic Cavern, Rt. 4, Box 168, Berryville AR, (501) 749-2298

Crystal Cave, five miles north of I-44 on Hwy. H, Springfield MO Exit 80B

Crystal Caverns, Cassville MO, (417) 847-4238

Devil's Well, Ozark National Scenic Riverways, near Salem MO, (314) 323-4236

Fantastic Caverns, Hwy. 13 North, Springfield MO 65803, (417) 833-2010

Fantasy World Caverns, Hwy. 54, one-fourth mile west of Jct. Hwy. 52, seven miles east of Bagnell Dam, Lake Ozark, MO

Fisher Cave, Meramec State Park, Sullivan MO 63080, (314) 468-6072

Indian Burial Cave, Osage Beach MO, (314) 348-2207 or -2270

Jacob's Cave, Rt. 2, Box 129, Versailles MO 65084, (314) 378-4374

Marvel Cave, Silver Dollar City, Marvel Cave Park MO 65616, (417) 338-2611

Meramec Caverns, Stanton MO 63079, (314) 468-3166

Onondaga Cave, Onondaga State Park, Leasburg MO 65535, (314) 245-6600

Onyx Cave Park, three miles east of Eureka Springs AR on U.S. 62, three miles north on Onyx Cave Road

Ozark Caverns, Lake of the Ozarks State Park, Linn Creek MO 65052, (314) 346-2500

Ozark Wonder Cave, Rt. 2, four miles north of Noel MO 64854, (417) 475-3579

Round Spring Caverns, Ozark National Scenic Riverways, P.O. Box 490, Van Buren MO 63965, (314) 323-4236

Talking Rocks Cavern, two miles south of Lakeview MO on Hwy. 13, (417) 338-8220 or 272-3366

War Eagle Cavern, one-half mile off Hwy. 12, Rt. 5, Box 748, Rogers AR 72756, (501) 789-2909, (501) 756-0913

Heritage Crafts

The products of Ozarks craftsmen and women are offered everywhere in the Ozarks at all times. Some of the best are available at the many fairs and festivals held throughout the region (for an up-to-date listing, write to the tourist organizations in the area you plan to visit or see any issue of *The Ozarks Mountaineer*, HCR 3, Box 868, Kirbyville MO 65679). Here are some favorite outlets:

Ozark Arts and Crafts Fair Association, Inc., War Eagle Mills Farm, Rt. 1, Hindsville AR 72738, (501) 789-5398 (Spring and Fall Fairs)

Arkansas Craft Gallery, 33 Spring Street, Eureka Springs AR

Mutton Hollow Craft Village, West Hwy. 76, Branson MO 65616, (417) 334-4947

Silver Dollar City, West Hwy. 76, Marvel Cave Park MO 65616, (417) 338-8100

Engler Block, 1335 West Hwy. 76, Branson MO 65616, (417) 335-2200

Pendergraft Ozarks Crafts, Hwy. 7, six miles south of Jasper AR, Top of the Mountain, HCR 31, Box 110A, Jasper AR 72641, (501) 446-5267

Ozark Folk Center, Mountain View AR, (501) 269-3851

Arkansas Craft Guild, two miles north of Mountain View AR

Ozark Emporium, U.S. Hwy. 62, Gassville AR, (501) 435-6070

The Ozarks Outdoors

The states of Arkansas, Missouri, and Oklahoma offer very helpful information in colorful brochures about camping and other outdoor activities in their sections of the Ozarks. With these in your car or camper, you'll see the region as never before.

Request "Arkansas State Parks" and "Arkansas Camper's Guide" (which also includes the Buffalo National River and U.S. Forest Service, Corps of Engineers, and private campgrounds in Arkansas) from Arkansas Dept. of Parks and Tourism, One Capitol Mall, Little Rock AR 72201. These two booklets offer complete information about camping in Arkansas, including golfing, hiking, and equestrian trails, access to rivers, etc. If you like to hike, also write to "Trails" at the same address.

For details on hunting and fishing in Arkansas, write: Arkansas Game and Fish Commission, Two Natural Resources Drive, Little Rock AR 72205.

For inexpensive canoeing guides to the Buffalo, Mulberry, and Illinois rivers, write for a price list from Ozark Society Books, Box 3503, Little Rock AR 72203.

You'll want "Missouri's State Parks and Historic Sites" from Missouri Dept. of Natural Resources, Division of Parks and Historic Preservation, P.O. Box 176, Jefferson City MO 65102. A comprehensive chart lists facilities (including those for the handicapped) available at each, plus hiking, backpacking, horseback riding, and bicycling.

Also request "The Outdoor Map of Missouri," which includes hiking trails and hunting and fishing areas, from Missouri Dept. of Conservation, P.O. Box 180, Jefferson City MO 65101. This agency also provides specifics about hunting and fishing in Missouri. You might also want to ask for a list of their other fine publications, including "Missouri Ozark Waterways," and "Missouri Hiking Trails."

For a complete list of campgrounds, float fishing outfitters—and everything else to see and do in Missouri, get the amazingly complete and beautiful "Missouri Travel Guide" from Missouri Division of Tourism, P.O. Box 1055, Jefferson City MO 65102. Or pick it up at one of the tourism centers scattered around the state.

For an overview of Oklahoma's piece of the Ozarks, write for "Discover Oklahoma's Grand Lake o' the Cherokees" from Grand Lake Association, Rt. 2, Box 40, Grove OK 74344. And don't miss the "Green Country" brochure from Green Country, Inc., P.O. Box 946, Muskogee OK 74402 (or from the tourism department, below). "Oklahoma's Camping Guide" is available from Oklahoma Tourism and Recreation Dept., 500 Will Rogers Building, Oklahoma City OK 73105. The same address offers other helpful brochures, such as "Oklahoma Equestrian Trails," "Canoe Trails," and "Motorcycle-ORV Areas."

Lake maps make it easier to move around on the surface of the lakes and to find the campgrounds handiest to where you want to be. They also pinpoint the locations of marinas where you'll find stalls for your own boat, as well as water craft for rent, fishing guides, licenses, bait and tackle, and, often, improved swimming beaches. For free copies of maps of the Corps of Engineers lakes—including the locations of Corps of Engineers campgrounds—write to U.S. Army Corps of Engineers, Resident Engineer, for the appropriate lake (see "Lakes" in this appendix).

Detailed county maps of Arkansas, which include lake and river access points, are included in "A Fisherman's Guide to Public Access Facilities in Arkansas Counties," a book published by Arkansas Game and Fish Commission, Information and Education Division, Two Natural Resources Drive, Little Rock AR 72205. The same office also offers a "Floater's Kit," a collection of maps detailing the floatable rivers in the state.

Another kind of map you'll find helpful, especially if you want to hike and/or backpack, is the topographic map. In conjunction with a compass, a topographic map of the area you're visiting is good insurance against getting lost. "Topos" are also fascinating for reference since they list every feature—natural (including contours of the ground) and manmade (including roads, cemeteries, fence lines, homes)—on the surface of the land. Fishermen use topos that predate the artificial lakes to determine the approximate depth of the water and features on the bottom. Many camping-hunting-fishing supply stores sell topos of their surrounding territory. Or you can write:

Missouri: Wallace B. Howe, Missouri Geological Survey, P.O. Box 250, Rolla MO 65401.

Arkansas: Arkansas Geological Commission, 3815 W. Roosevelt Road, Little Rock AR 72204.

Besides the state and private facilities, the federal government also offers outdoor opportunities in the Ozarks. The National Forests, under the U.S. Forest Service, afford some of the best chances to "get back to nature," often primitive or nearly so. According to the forest service, some of the trails through the national forests are the very same Indian travelways that the pioneers used to settle this country. Included in the public lands in the Ozarks are several official wilderness areas. Visitor maps showing the location of equestrian or hiking trails, campgrounds, etc., are available for a small fee. Other brochures are available at no charge.

If you prefer to see the scenery from the air-conditioned comfort of your car, you'll enjoy the Scenic Byways designated especially for leisure driving. Request a brochure and map from the supervisor of the forest you'll be visiting.

The Forest Supervisor of the Mark Twain National Forest, in Missouri, is at P.O. Box 937, Rolla MO 65401.

The Forest Supervisor of the Ozark National Forest, in Arkansas, is at Box 1008, Russellville AR 72801.

National Forests and National Parks

Ozark National Forest, P. O. Box 1, Mountain View AR 72560

Mark Twain National Forest, Headquarters, 401 Fairgrounds Road, Rolla MO 65401, (314) 364-4621

Ozark National Scenic Riverways, Box 490, Van Buren MO 63965, (314) 323-4236

Wilson's Creek National Battlefield, Rt. 2, Box 75 (Postal Drawer C) Republic MO 65738, (417) 732-2662

George Washington Carver National Monument, Alt. US 71 to Hwy. V, Diamond MO, (417) 325-4151

Pea Ridge National Military Park, ten miles northeast of Rogers AR on Hwy. 62, (501) 451-8122

Buffalo National River, P.O. Box 1173, Harrison AR 72602

Floatable Rivers

Missouri:

Big Piney, Little Piney, Gasconade Rivers, near Licking MO

Niangua River near Lebanon MO

Elk River and Big Sugar River near Noel MO

Huzzah Creek, Bourbeuse River, Meramec River near Steelville, MO

Bryant Creek, Norfork River near Gainesville MO

Eleven Point River near Alton MO

Current and Jacks Fork Rivers, Ozark National Scenic Riverways, near Eminence and Salem MO

Black River near Lesterville MO

Big River near Bonne Terre MO

St. Francis River near Patterson MO

Request information on booklet, "Missouri Ozark Waterways," from Missouri Dept. of Conservation, P. O. Box 180, Jefferson City, MO

Also see Practical Matters Charts for Outfitters

Arkansas:

War Eagle River near Rogers AR 72756

Mulberry and Illinois rivers in Ozark National Forest

Buffalo National River near Yellville and Harrison AR

White River near Cotter and Calico Rock AR

Spring River near Mammoth Spring and Hardy AR

Numerous small rivers and streams in Ozark National Forest

Ask for "Floater's Kit," from Arkansas Game and Fish Commission, Information and Education Division, Two Natural Resources Drive, Little Rock AR 72205

Also see Practical Matters Charts for Outfitters

Oklahoma:

There are several canoeable rivers in the Oklahoma portion of the Ozarks. Write: Oklahoma Scenic Rivers Commission, P.O. Box 292, Tahlequah, OK 74465, (918) 456-3251

Also write for "Green Country" brochure: Green Country, Inc., P.O. Box 946, Muskogee, OK 74402, (800) 922-2118

Hiking Trails

Both Missouri and Arkansas have hundreds of hiking trails in their state parks and forests, the national forests within their boundaries, and on Buffalo National River and Ozark National Scenic Riverways land.

Request information on the inexpensive booklet, "Missouri Hiking Trails," from Missouri Dept. of Conservation, P.O. Box 180, Jefferson City, MO. For information on Arkansas offerings, write Arkansas Trail Council, Arkansas Parks and Tourism, One Capitol Mall, Little Rock AR 72201.

Of special interest is the Ozark Trail, now under development. A long-distance trail that traverses the Missouri portion of the Ozarks, crosses over into the mountains of northwest Arkansas and becomes the Ozark Highlands Trail. Portions of the trail are now completed and hikeable. Ultimately it will provide a seven-hundred-mile hike through some of the most scenic country in the United States. For more information on this trail, write:

Ozark Trail Coordinator, P.O. Box 176, Jefferson City MO 65102, (314) 751-3443 and

Ozark Highlands Trail, Arkansas Trails Council, One Capitol Mall, Little Rock AR 72201.

Lakes

Missouri:

Lake of the Ozarks: Lake Area Chamber of Commerce, P.O. Box 193, Osage Beach MO 65065, (314) 348-2730; Camdenton Area Chamber of Commerce, P.O. Box 1375, Ryland Center, Camdenton MO 65020, (314) 346-2227; Greater Lake of the Ozarks Visitors Bureau, P.O. Box 98, Lake Ozark MO 65049, (314) 365-3371 or (800) 325-0213

Lake Pomme de Terre: Corps of Engineers, Hermitage MO 65668, (417) 745-6411; Pomme de Terre Lake League, P.O. Box 36, Hermitage MO 65668, (417) 645-6432

Stockton Lake: Corps of Engineers, P.O. Box 610, Stockton MO 65785, (417) 276-3113; Stockton Lake Association, P.O. Box 345, Stockton MO 65785; Stockton Area Chamber of Commerce, P.O. Box 410, Stockton MO 65785, (417) 276-5213

Table Rock Lake: Table Rock: Shell Knob Chamber of Commerce, P.O. Box 193, Shell Knob MO 65747, (417) 858-3300; Corps of Engineers Resident Engineer, P.O. Box 1109, Branson MO 65616, (417) 334-4101

Lake Taneycomo: Branson Lakes Area Chamber of Commerce, Box 220, Hwy. 65N, Branson MO 65616, (417) 334-4136

Bull Shoals Lake (Missouri Portion): Corps of Engineers Resident Engineer, Mountain Home AR, (501) 425-2700; Missouri Bull Shoals Lake Association, Box 324, Isabella MO 65676

Arkansas:

Beaver Lake: Corps of Engineers, Beaver Resident Office, P.O. Drawer H, Rogers AR 72756, (501) 636-1210; Scenic Hwy. 12 East Assoc., 2018 Hwy. 12 East, Rogers AR 72756, (501) 925-2222

Greers Ferry Lake: Corps of Engineers, P.O. Box 310, Heber Springs AR 72543, (501) 362-2416; Greers Ferry Lake and Little Red River Association, P.O. Box 1170, Fairfield Bay AR, (501) 723-8332; Greers Ferry Area Chamber of Commerce, P.O. Box 354, Greers Ferry Lake AR 72067, (501) 825-7188; Heber Springs Chamber of Commerce, 1001 W. Main, Heber Springs AR 72543, (501) 362-2444

Bull Shoals Lake (Arkansas Portion): Corps of Engineers Resident Engineer, Mountain Home AR, (501) 425-2700; Bull Shoals/White River Chamber of Commerce, Box 354, Bull Shoals AR 72619, (501) 445-4443; Mountain Home Chamber of Commerce, Box 488, Mountain Home AR 72653, (501) 425-5111

Norfork Lake: Corps of Engineers Resident Engineer, Mountain Home AR, (501) 425-2700

Oklahoma:

Grand Lake o' the Cherokees: Grand Lake Association, Rt. 2, Box 40, Grove OK 74344, (918) 786-2289; Grove Area Chamber of Commerce, 104 W. 3rd, Grove OK 74344, (918) 786-9079

State Parks

Missouri:

Lake Stockton State Park, Stockton MO, (417) 276-4259

Lake of the Ozarks State Park, P.O. Box C, Kaiser MO 65047, (314) 348-2694

Lake Pomme de Terre State Park, Hermitage MO, (417) 745-6909

Ha Ha Tonka State Park, Rt. 1 Box 658, Camdenton MO 65020, (314) 346-2986

Bennett Spring State Park, Lebanon MO, (417) 532-4338

Roaring River State Park, P. O. Box D, seven miles south of Cassville on Hwy. 112, Cassville MO, (417) 847-2539

Table Rock State Park, Branson MO 65616, (417) 334-4704

Grand Gulf State Park, Thayer MO 65791, (314) 548-2525

Montauk State Park, Rt. 5, Box 278, Salem MO, (314) 548-2201

Washington State Park (fourteen miles northeast of Potosi MO on Hwy. 21) DeSoto MO 63020, (314) 586-2995

St. Joe State Park on Hwy. 32, Flat River MO

Johnson's Shut-Ins State Park, eight miles north of Lesterville MO on Hwy. N, Reynolds County, (314) 546-2450

Elephant Rocks State Park, just off Hwy. 21 at Graniteville MO, (314) 697-5395

St. Francois State Park, on Hwy. 67 in St. Francois County (314) 358-2173

Sam A. Baker State Park, three miles north of Patterson on Hwy. 143, (314) 856-4411

Meramec State Park, just off I-44 near Sullivan MO 63080, (314) 468-6519

Onondaga Cave State Park, just off I-44 near Leasburg MO, (314) 245-6417

Arkansas:

Withrow Springs State Park, Rt. 3, Huntsville AR 72740, (501) 559-2593

Devil's Den State Park, West Fork AR 72774

Prairie Grove Battlefield State Park, P.O. Box 306, Prairie Grove AR 72753, (501) 846-2990

Bull Shoals State Park, Box 205, Bull Shoals AR 72619, (501) 431-5521

Mammoth Spring State Park, P.O. Box 36, Mammoth Spring AR 72554 (Hwy. 63), (501) 625-7364

Ozark Folk Center, P.O. Box 500, Mountain View AR 72560 (501) 269-3871

Oklahoma:

For details on state parks, a camping guide and much more, write: Oklahoma Tourism and Recreation Dept., Division of Marketing Services, 500 Will Rogers Building, Oklahoma City, OK 73105

Index

478 A LIVING HISTORY OF THE OZARKS